Los Angeles County Historical Directory

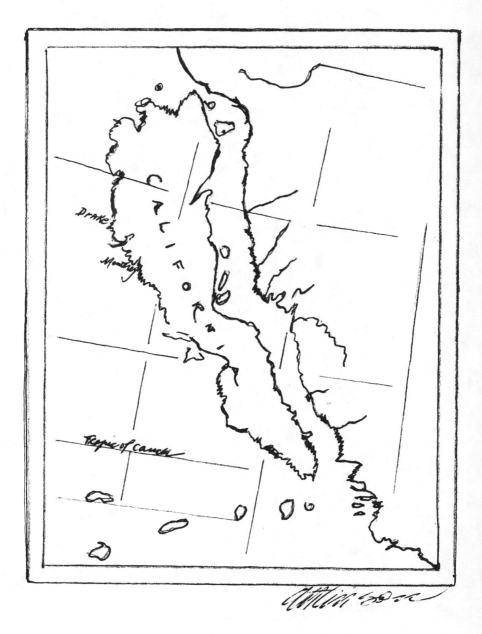

Los Angeles County Historical Directory

by

Janet I. Atkinson

McFarland & Company, Inc., Publishers
Jefferson, North Carolina, and London

*Frontispiece from an early 16th century map
showing California as an island.*

Library of Congress Cataloguing-in-Publication Data

Atkinson, Janet I., 1933–
  Los Angeles County historical directory.

  Bibliography: p. 197.
  Includes index.
  1. Los Angeles County (Calif.)—Directories. 2. Los
Angeles County (Calif.)—History—Societies, etc.—
Directories. 3. Historic sites—California—Los Angeles
County—Directories. 4. Historical museums—California—
Los Angeles County—Directories. I. Title.
F868.L8A85   1988   979.4'930025   88-42523

  ISBN 0-89950-301-2 (lib. bdg.)

Printed in the United States of America (50# acid-free natural paper) ∞

McFarland   Box 611   Jefferson NC 28640

To Sari and Tari,
whose love and encouragement
make all things sweet

Acknowledgments

One person cannot put together such a sweeping project as the *Historical Directory* without misgivings. That I have tried to do so is a little like convincing others one can walk on water. Not only do telephone numbers change overnight, but people move in the Southland with great regularity. In the field of history and preservation longevity is the exception, change typical. One year the city runs an historic site, the next year they turn it over to a private group, or vice versa. It is hard to keep up. Another impediment is that sources are difficult to locate. My method for research usually began with the local chamber of commerce. They in turn gave me the names and addresses of the local historical society if one exists. That's when all goes well. When there is no chamber and, alas, no historical society, I tried to find a homeowner's group. There is almost always the local library. But when all of this fails, there is the city hall and a department of parks and recreation. Usually someone there knows an "old-timer" who is familiar with the town. Realtors, especially those who have been around for a while, are invaluable. They know where the historic homes are, who has owned them, and who lives in them now. Some, like Jim Dunham, specialize in historic properties (see Historic Realtors). Others, like Jeff Hyland (Alvarez, Hyland & Young) of Beverly Hills and Jerry Berns in the San Fernando Valley, have either written books and/or articles on their local communities. In addition to all of these, there are local congressmen, retired postmasters, and even mayors who are often willing to part with excellent information on their towns.

In a city where the new seems to have priority over the old, sadly, historical information is discarded, scattered, or not even written down. When I recently asked to see masters' theses in history at a well-known university, I was told they are rarely written but are usually oral! (What that does to research is catastrophic, and there should be a law.) When I asked another history professor what his students were doing in local history, he replied, "nothing that I know of." Where compilation of significant material is so haphazard, accuracy is hard to ascertain.

If all of this is not enough, there are the confusing boundaries of towns cut into townsites from the original Spanish and Mexican land grants.

Many of the historic landmarks contained therein were located in older towns and still bear the name of that town, but are today within the boundaries of newer cities. Then there are the soaring land costs that have forced landmarks to be relocated to other communities (e.g., the Hollywood Palmer House now in Calabasas). To add to the confusion, we are currently designating historic neighborhoods and districts, areas that blend and are hard to distinguish from each other (West Adams and North University Park). Your diligence here would be appreciated. Please inform me when and where you find that changes or inaccuracies have occurred.

I am very grateful to the many local historians who spent much time answering my questions. These are unsung heroes and heroines who collect vital information simply because they enjoy doing it. They are in effect the "keepers of the flame." My thanks to the many librarians who took time away from their busy schedules to assist me. My thanks to dozens of businessmen who told me stories about their families "way back when." My sincere gratitude to the many local chambers of commerce who sent me directories about their city's history. And last, but by no means least, my everlasting thanks to the Los Angeles Conservancy. It is the one single group in Los Angeles to which everyone should belong! It has done much to coalesce preservation into a strong single-mindedness whose purpose is to not only preserve our signficant sites, but to work alongside developers and others in making alternative choices to demolition. It is the one glowing light in a sometimes dark tunnel.

Janet I. Atkinson
352 Inwood Road
Simi Valley, CA 93065

Contents

Preface

Why an *Historical Directory?* Because we too often lose the battle to save our historic past. Anyone living in Los Angeles quickly learns that the new is forever "in," the old, out. It seems easier to get a 1950 home designated an historic landmark as an early example of our future than it is a pre–1900 home. We rush to acknowledge how quickly L.A. welcomes its prophets of tomorrow, less ready to admit we have a past. Demolition and development are the name of the game, and a way of life. It often seems that concerned people and even powerful groups can do little to halt the process. My desire was to document as many of these sites, structures and landmarks as possible before they were not only out of sight, but out of mind.

Generally, people have some knowledge of the Southland's major historic sites. Seldom, however, do they have any idea of the rich abundance of lesser-known landmarks in the local communities. For this reason, I tended to concentrate on the smaller towns in order to enhance their resources.

My foremost desire was to make these significant landmarks more accessible. One cannot comfortably sort through the dozens of telephone directories necessary to "plug-into" our colorful past. Also, many of the activities around which our history revolves are available only through membership in private groups. One must belong to a great number of separate historical societies to cover the field adequately. In addition, one cannot always depend on the local newspapers to list events of interest to preservationists. That depends on who is handling the events; and press releases, if any, may never get beyond the local neighborhood. Also, the range of activities covered in the burgeoning field of preservation is so varied it is next to impossible to zero in on any one of them. Broadly, they are concerned with preservation in some overall way, but to know where to begin to look is difficult. All of this at a time when interest in our unique past is growing. Ironically, there are few books to help us. Aside from the movie star guides and hypertourist pabulum, there is Gebhard and Winter's excellent *A Guide to Architecture in Southern California.* It concentrates however, on contemporary architecture — hence my focus on properties from the earliest times to about 1925. Another excellent book is Grenier's *A Guide to Historic Places in Los Angeles County.* It is brief and barely skims the surface of current information. Another problem is the fact that these books may not be available in the local bookstores. Many people may not yet realize we have specialized bookstores like Dawson's, or Hennessey and Ingalls, or Jim Dunham's bookstore.*

Of course the basic reason for these difficulties is Southern California itself. The city never grew outward from a central urban "navel" like other normal cities. Its growth depended on land developers and Henry Huntington's little "Red Cars." The motto "live in the country, work in the city" created a maze of small suburbs connected now by glue-like freeways. In a city so heavily reliant upon the automobile, one must return to the local neighborhood to find the information they seek.

The categories I chose were not always applicable to each and every city. For example, in older communities like Pasadena it is easier to list businesses that are 50 years or older. But in areas such as Long Beach, where the earthquake of '33 leveled much of the city, or in Malibu, not even accessible until the 40s, the oldest business may be quite young in comparison. I tried to maintain a cutoff of 1945 for these businesses. There is also a growing "nostalgia" phenomenon especially in 50s diners. There are brand-new businesses in old buildings. There are old businesses in new structures. There are new buildings being constructed in historical themes such as Victoriana. I have tried to include as many of these as possible when their importance is obvious to the community. All of this is symptomatic of an area that sets the pace in many ways for the rest of the country. Constant change is more important than the traditional; beginning something new more significant than conformity to a long and continuous historic heritage.

I have also included Los Angeles's Cultural Heritage Monument designation, using the letters "CHM" beside the landmarks so designated. There are to date 321 such structures listed in the city of Los Angeles.

Dawson's, at 535 N. Larchmont, L.A.; Hennessey and Ingalls, at 1254 Santa Monica Mall, Santa Monica; and Jim Dunham's, 1314 West 25th St., L.A.

Communities

———— AGOURA ————

History: Originally the area was part of the old Spanish *Rancho El Conejo,* which comprised about 48,000 acres. It was granted to two Spanish soldiers in 1803. The Russells were the first American family to come into the area in the 1880s (Westlake). They farmed for over 90 years. In 1924 the area now known as Agoura was called *Independence.* Then Paramount Studios bought approximately 335 acres on the northwest corner of Cornell Road and Mulholland Highway. It was known as *Picture City.* In 1928 the newly formed Picture City Chamber of Commerce petitioned for a permanent post office. The Postal Department requested a list of names to be submitted for consideration. Last on the list was Pierre Agoure, a basque settler. He was born in the Pyrennes and came to California when he was 17. He herded sheep on the Rancho Conejo. In 1875 he began his own ranch, rising to prominence as a rancher. His name was chosen for the new community. The "e" was dropped, and an "a" added—hence Agoura.

Books: *The History of Agoura Hills,* published by the City of Agoura, 1985. Available in county library or Agoura City Hall.
Patricia Russell Miller's *Tales of Triunfo,* 1985. Available Stagecoach Inn, Newberry Park.
J.H. Russell's *Heads and Tails, Odds and Ends,* Thomas Litho Printing,

1963. Also available at Stagecoach Inn.
Historians: Mr. Robert Boyd, old-time resident (818-889-2039). Mr. Sy Rimer, Librarian (818-889-2278). Diane Venable (818-991-7389). City Historian: Marilyn Draper at City Hall (818-889-9114). A.J. "Sandy" Sandoval, President, Las Virgenes Historical Society, 30473-50 Mulholland Highway, Agoura, CA 91301. Can be reached at 818-889-0836.

Historical Society: *Las Virgenes Historical Society,* P.O. Box 124, Agoura, CA 91301. Sandy Sandoval, President. 818-889-0836.

Other Groups: Several strong homeowner groups. Organized to protect environment. There is also a design committee which has been formed to make recommendations on maintaining historical buildings. The homeowner group is *Las Virgenes Homeowners Federation,* Dave Brown, President, P.O. Box 353, Agoura Hills, CA 91301. 818-889-0356.

Indians: Apparently a great deal of recent archeological work has been conducted in the area revealing 5 or 6 Indian villages in the Agoura Hills, *Chumash sites.* Both California State University at Northridge and Pierce College (Dr. Robert Pence) have worked on sites in the area. There is also a private group, Archeological Associates of Sun City, that has conducted digs here.

1

Historic Landmarks: The beautiful *Reyes Adobe,* built between 1797 and 1820 is the most exciting structure in the area. Exciting because it will soon be listed on the National Register of Historic Places, and is undergoing restoration in order for it to take its place alongside other outstanding historic structures. It was one of the first Spanish rancheros-haciendas on one of the smallest Spanish land grants (El Rancho Las Virgenes) given to Miguel Ortgea by King Philip of Spain. The Ranchero covered 17,760 acres. The house has been documented by the Historic American Building Survey in the Library of Congress Washington, D.C., and the California Inventory of Historic Resources. The City of Agoura Hills has obtained a grant to restore the adobe, and architect Melvin Greene's plans have been approved. Plans include a museum as well. Adobe is owned by the L.A. County Parks and Recreation Dept. Located off of Reyes Adobe Road and Rainbow Crest Drive, Agoura Hills.

Chief White Eagle, 1940. Count Jean de Strelecki, a Polish artist, settled in Agoura in the 1930s. He was so impressed by the remaining Chumash Indians in the area that he designed and built a 14-foot statue of a Seminole Indian chief. He had heard about Seminole Hot Springs in the nearby Santa Monica Mountains, so he based his design on the Seminole Indians. The statue was placed atop Mount Strella and was unveiled on May 5th, 1940. Ten Chumash Indians were there, and today, the statue is a local landmark which overlooks the old town of Agoura. Located above intersection of Lewis Road and Agoura Road.

Oak Tree. Near Indian statue. One of the largest in the area. Known as Neil's Oak, because it is located on the old Neil's Ranch.

Lady Face Mountain, 2,034 feet.

Agoura Sign, 1925–6. Corner of Agoura Road and Lewis Road.

The German Schloss of Agoura. A castle-like private residence. Built in

1940 by Theodore Sparkuhl. Located in the hills of Triunfo Canyon.

Site of *Morrison Ranch House.* An old turn-of-the-century cattle ranch. Located at or around Kanan Road, Agoura.

Site of *Lewis Ranch,* 1901. A 5,711 acre ranch near Dorothy Drive and Lewis Road.

Paramount Ranch and *Peter Strauss Ranch see* Santa Monica Mountains.

Courtesy Renaissance Pleasure Faire.

Renaissance Faire (Renaissance Pleasure Faire). It dates from 1962, but its historical theme, 16th century Elizabethan England qualifies it for the Directory. Faire is held each April–May for six weekends. Ventura Freeway West to Kanan Road exit to Faire. Those interested may write: P.O. Box 341, Santa Monica, CA 90401 or call 213-202-8854.

Historic Restaurants: *California Fettuccini Bar.* In 1930s this was a bus stop originally owned by Oscar and known as Paramount Inn. Lots of movie extras enjoyed place. In the 1940s it was known as *The Seminole Hot Springs Inn,* later, *A Matter of Taste.* Delightful place to dine. Located at 29008 West Agoura Road, Agoura. 818-991-3000.

The Old Place Restaurant, 29983 Mulholland Highway, Agoura, CA (Cornell). 818-706-9001. Tom and Barbara. This is a very unusual place, to say the least. I thought it had been closed, and it was for awhile, but is going strong again. Opposite the Peter Strauss Ranch. The area is special as well.

Businesses: *Stage Door Theatre,* 28311 West Agoura Road, Agoura, CA. 818-889-5209. Was originally a service station known as Gilmore's in the 1920s. Then the Old Carlson's Trading Post in 1925–26. Later, Homer Sprague bought it and transported many of the buildings to Hoover Dam to be used as temporary housing for men working on the dam. Finally an electrician came in and in 1942 put up permanent buildings. Also used at one time as the Agoura Post Office.

Amazing Kate's. Building dates from 1926. 28317 West Agoura Road, Agoura, CA. 818-991-5148.

Special Events: *Pony Express Days.* Held in October each year. Originally held as the Fall Festival Days in 1948 in order to get far-flung ranches and merchants together. There were picnics, barbecues, rodeos, dances and parades. Then in 1968, when the Post Office issued a stamp commemorating the ending of the Pony Express, it was decided to change the name to Pony Express Days.

Chamber of Commerce: Agoura-Las Virgenes Chamber of Commerce, 30101 Agoura Rd., Agoura. 818-889-3150.

———— ALHAMBRA ————

History: Once part of the enormous *Rancho San Antonio,* a Spanish land grant acquired by Antonio Maria Lugo in 1810, it was Benjamin Wilson who would take the first steps toward developing it. Coming overland in 1841 with the very first English-speaking group of settlers to arrive in Los Angeles, *Benjamin Wilson* was among them. His destination was China. Fortunately for Angeleno's he settled instead in Southern California. He married Ramona Yorba, beautiful heir to the Yorba holdings. In 1854 he purchased a 128 acre ranch in San Gabriel Valley called Huerta de Custe. He renamed it Lake Vineyard. It covered what is now Alhambra, San Marino, South Pasadena and parts of Pasadena. By 1873, a Mr. J.C. Wallace had built the first residence within the city limits of Alhambra's 1200 block on Granada Ave. Why the name Alhambra? Wilson's two daughters, Ruth and Maria had been reading a popular novel of the day: Washington Irving's romantic "Tales of the Alhambra." Since the novel's setting was Moorish Spain, Benjamin Wilson decided to call his new subdivision The Alhambra Tract. All the streets also took the names of characters in the novel. There were Granada, Boabdil, Vega, and Almansor. Alhambra was off and running and agriculture was its main business. In 1885 H.W. Stanton built a store and post office at Main and Garfield, the first commercial stores in the tract. The boom of the 1880's brought the Alhambra Hotel, a three-story Moorish structure that opened in 1887. In 1903 the Pacific Electric came. The city was incorporated that year.

Books: *The History of Alhambra,* by William M. Northrup. Published by A.H. Cawsto, 1936.
Alhambra, San Gabriel Monterey Park Community Book, by William M. Northrup. Same publisher, 1944.

Historians: *Mr. Winston Smoyer,* 709 E. Norwood Place, Alhambra, CA 91801. 213-283-5473.
Mrs. Ruth Barry, 613 N. Hidalgo, Alhambra, CA 91801. 213-283-3886.

Historical Society: *The Alhambra Historical Society,* Founded in 1966. Housed in the Alhambra public library. 410 W. Main St., Alhambra,

CA 91801. 818-570-5008. Mrs. Kinman, President (818-284-7294).

Courtesy Alhambra Historical Society

Other Groups: The Historical Society has been very active in working with Alhambra's city officials to preserve, locate, restore and mark historic structures. Ruth Barry has met with city manager and other city officials to try to get an Historic Preservation ordinance for city. In 1984–85 the Alhambra Historic and Cultural Resources Survey was published, prepared by Johnson-Heumann Research Associates. It listed over 450 extant homes built between 1910 and 1920. It also recommended over 100 sites for local or national registry landmark status. This survey available at the Alhambra City Hall.

Historic Landmarks: Probably the most unique, if not the most outstanding landmark is the *Pyrenees Castle,* built in 1926. The Mansion was modeled after a castle in Northern Spain and was the brainchild of Sylvester Dupuy, an immigrant who made a fortune in agriculture. The castle was built at a cost of $250,000 atop a hill in unlikely Alhambra. In 1986 it was purchased by Cris C.Y. Yip and restored by Bruce Wei of St. John Construction Co. Located at 1700 Grand View Ave. Alhambra, CA 91801.

Ramona Convent. Established 1880s by James de Barth Shorb. Benjamin Wilson's daughter Maria married de Shorb and was given as a wedding gift 1,000 acres of land adjoining Lake Vineyard. Mr. Shorb named the estate "San Marino." He also subdivided a town called Ramona, at Shorb Station,

(now the Alhambra Southern Pacific Station). This 15 acre site became home of the Ramona Covent. The first building was dedicated on January 29, 1890. The main building was lost in the 1987 earthquake and will be replaced with a modern structure. Located at 1700 Marengo Ave., Alhambra, CA 91801. 818-282-4151.

Historic Sites: Town of *Dolgeville,* west of Marengo. It was annexed to the city in 1908. The brick and iron buildings still extant exemplify the beginnings of industry in the city. Some date from the 19th century.

The *Captain Gray Home* 1887. Large, magnificent Victorian home which the Historical Society tried to save. It was demolished in 1970. Corner of 2nd Street and Commonwealth.

Historic Homes: *Kajal Home,* or Cajal. Presently the Ratkowski Home. Built in 1906 it is an unusual blend of California craftsmen, and Japanese influence. Located at 1350 S. Fremont, Alhambra.

Halstead Home, 1878. Located at 11 Halstead Circle, Alhambra. The oldest residence in Alhambra. It was built by the Halstead family shortly after their arrival in 1877. Mr. Halstead died in 1879. His wife operated the "orienta Ranch" for many years.

Oldest Residences in Alhambra: 200 Beacon St., 1890. 204 Beacon St., 1899. 208 Beacon St., 1888. 217 South First St., 1890. 403 South Garfield, 1895. 300 North Granada, 1880's. 111 North Stoneman, 1888. 117 North Stoneman, 1887. Note: 111 North Stoneman was moved in 1986 to Marengo Ave., Pasadena after a successful Victorian Lawn Party was launched to try to save the home. Other residences include that of F.Q. Story, one of the founders of Alhambra's citrus industry. His home, located at 502 North Story, was built in 1883–84.

Historic Schools: *Garfield School,* established 1886. Corner of Garfield and Alhambra Road, Alhambra.

Alhambra High School. Established 1898. Located at 200 South First Street,

Alhambra.

Granada Elementary School. Established since 1900. Located at 6th and Norwood, Alhambra.

Historic Churches: *First United Methodist Church.* Established 1887. Present location at 9 East Almasor is second location.

Presbyterian Church. Established 1880's. Moved to present site at Commonwealth and First Street.

Holy Trinity Church. Established 1908. Located at 9 East Grand Ave.

Carmel of St. Theresa. Built in 1923. Designed by noted Southern California architect, John C. Austin. Located at 215 E. Alhambra Road.

Historic Theatres: *Alhambra Theatre.* Located at the corner of Atlantic and Main.

El Rey Theatre. Located at 4th and Main St.

Garfield Theatre. Since 1925–26. Is now the Valley Grand Building. Located at 1240–1314 East Garfield.

Historic Parks: *Alhambra Park.* Since 1900. Corner of Palm St.

Granada Park. Since 1900. 2233 Whitney Dr.

Story Park. Since early 1900's. 210 North Chapel.

Other Buildings: *Alhambra Women's Club.* Or the Wednesday Afternoon Club. Organization founded in 1893 by Mrs. George Rice. Craftsman clubhouse was originally located at the corner of Main Street. Moved to present location around 1913. 204 South 2nd Street, Alhambra.

Businesses: *Van's Jewelers.* Since 1934. Located at 21 West Main St., Alhambra. 818-282-3542.

Alhambra Shade & Linoleum Co. Established since 1925. Located at 411 North Main St., Alhambra. 818-282-6713.

Alhambra Camera Inc. Since 1937. Located at 127 West Main St., Alhambra. 818-282-6365.

Crown Brass Manufacturing Co. Since 1908. Located at 400 South Palm Ave., Alhambra. 818-289-5397.

Turner and Stevens Funeral Directors. Since 1895. Located at 550 East Main St., Alhambra. 818-282-4131.

Potts Plumbing, 1939. 2130 W. Valley Blvd., Alhambra. 213-283-8959.

Emmett's Restaurant. Since 1940. Located at 29 South Garfield, Alhambra. 818-289-5747.

Lieburg's Dept. Store. Since 1930s. Located at 421 East Main St., Alhambra. 818-282-8454.

Hamm's Plumbing. Since 1905. Located at 425 West Main St., Alhambra. 818-282-2151.

Fosselman's Ice Cream. Since 1941. Located at 1824 West Main St., Alhambra. 818-282-6533.

P.&W. Parts Store. Since 1925. Located at 515 West Main St., Alhambra. 818-282-2148.

Alhambra Upholstery. Since 1932. Antiques Restored, caning. Located at 904 East Main St., Alhambra. 818-282-1586.

Prober's Shoes. Since 1936. Located at 215 East Main St., Alhambra. 818-289-5363.

Special Note: *Standard Felt Co.* Established prior to 1900. Just closed its doors in 1986. Located at 115 South Palm. Alhambra. Was the oldest industrial site in Alhambra.

Historic Streets: Vintage street lights on Commonwealth, Bushnell, Electric and Marguerita Avenue. Also on South 7th, 8th, and 9th Streets. Also those on Valley Blvds. Also historic neon signs.

Special Individuals: Mr. Warren Doty. Member of the Alhambra Historical Society. Resident of the San Gabriel Valley and Alhambra for over 70 years. Postal employee and member of many civic organizations. Knowledgeable on many facets of Alhambra.

Historical Museum: The Alhambra Historical Museum is planning to select for their future home, a 1930 residence at 310 S. Garfield Ave. Contact Historical Society for more on this.

——— ALTADENA ———

History: Rancho San Pasqual — probably named for Saint Paschal, a Franciscan of the 16th century canonized in 1690. The rancho began with the seculariation of 1834 opening up the former mission lands for private ownership. Spanish ex-artilleryman, Juan Marine, resident of the Mission San Gabriel, became the first individual to own it. The rancho then passed to Manuel Garfias who received a formal grant for it in 1843. Later, came Benjamin Wilson whose descendants would include a famous grandson, General George Patton of World War II fame. "Don Benito" as he was called came west with the Workman-Rowland party of 1841. In 1858 he purchased the 700 acre rancho. A year later he sold a half interest in it to Dr. John S. Griffin. The latter came West with none other than the pathfinder himself, John C. Fremont in 1846. After California became a state, Dr. Griffin decided to settle in the southwest. He and Benjamin Wilson became close friends and through purchase and exchange owned what later became known as Pasadena. Both men sold their land to a group of Indiana residents who had formed a colony called The San Gabriel Orange Grove Association. Later it became Pasadena. Because the land lying to the northeast of that portion was unwatered and was too high to benefit from the natural flow of the Arroyo Seco, Dr. Griffin simply "threw" it into the deal, so to speak. What Dr. Griffin and others perhaps overlooked, was that in spite of that 1400 acre parcel being covered with heavy chapparal and too far from known sources of water, the colonists would find water elsewhere and turn it into a prosperous community known today as Altadena.

The name "Altadena" was first coined in 1886 by Byron O. Clark to designate his 40 acre nursery and home placed on upper Lincoln Avenue flat.

Books: *Altadena's Golden Years,* by Robert H. Peterson. Self-published in 1976. Recently re-printed.

Altadena, by Miss Sarah Ives Noble. Published by Altadena Historical and Beautification Society, 1938.

Both books available at the Altadena Library, 600 East Mariposa, Altadena, CA 91001. 818-798-0833.

Historical Society: *Altadena Historical Society.* P.O. Box 144, Altadena, CA 91001. Mary Jean Crunk, President. 818-791-3903.

Other Groups: *Preservation group* headed by Dorothy Bridal. 818-798-8328.

Heritage Committee 1986, headed by Tim Gregory. 818-798-1268.

Chamber of Commerce: Altadena Chamber of Commerce. Located at 2526 El Molino Avenue, Altadena, CA 91001. 818-794-3988.

Historic Landmarks: *Christmas Tree Lane.* Mile-long avenue of 150 Deodars planted by Colonel Woodbury in 1885, who imported seeds from China. They were lighted for the first time in 1920. Located between Woodbury and Altadena Drive on Santa Rosa. For more information, contact Christmas Tree Lane Assn., Chamber of Commerce, Altadena, 818-794-3988, or Ed Turley, Pres., Christmas Tree Lane, 468 W. Pentagon, Altadena.

Mt. Wilson Observatory. In 1889, Harvard University astronomers brought a 13″ telescope to the summit and operated it for over 40 years. The Mt. Wilson Observatory dates to 1903 when astronomer George Ellery Hale of the Yerkes Observatory worked here. The Mt. Wilson Observatory began its operation of the 60″ telescope in 1909 and the 100″ Hooker telescope in 1917. Both the Carnegie Institution of Washington D.C. and the California Institute of Technology operated the Mt. Wilson telescopes. But as of 1976 the park was closed, and the access road to the observatory closed as well. Located in the Los Angeles Angeles Crest Highway, south of Red Box ranger station.

Souvenir of MOUNT LOWE CALIFORNIA

MOUNT

LOWE

MUSEUM

Located in the restored
1906 Pacific Electric Railway
Substation No. 8
2245 North Lake Avenue, Altadena
Offices of JIM DICKSON Realtors

Courtesy Astrid Ellersieck and artist Jim Manning.

Mt. Lowe Museum, Restored 1906 Pacific Electric Railway Substation No. 8. Located at 2245 North Lake Avenue, Altadena. Formerly home of Jim Dickson Realty.

Historic Sites: *Mt. Lowe Railway.* On July 4th, 1893, the Mt. Lowe Railway opened to the public. It ran up Lake Avenue to a point just below Alta Vista Street. The electric trolleys climbed into Rubio Canyon via Mt.

Lowe Drive or today's MacPherson Parkway, across the top of what is now Rubio Highlands and into the canyon. Henry Huntington continued the railway when Lowe went into bankruptcy. Huntington made the Mt. Lowe Railway and its resorts the jewel of his railway system. Then came fires, winds floods and the great depression. In 1937 the spectacular railway came to an end.

Chalet Hotel, later Echo Mountain House, 1893–94. Contained an observatory and a menagerie. Also contained Lowe's original generators. Located at top of the incline.

Mt. Lowe Springs and Hotel, formerly Oak Mountain Hotel.

Rubio Hotel. Contained a magnificent dining pavilion and adjacent bridges, walkways and waterfalls. 1894. There was a zoo, a museum, an observatory and searchlight. Located at the base of a 3,000 foot incline.

Historic Homes: *Private Residence,* 1915. N.E. corner Mar Vista and Sonoma Drive, Altadena.

Scripps Hall, 1907. Built by Mr. Scripps as his home. 209 E. Mariposa, Altadena.

Elena Scripps Studio, 1914. 2760 Scripps Place, Altadena.

Gillette Hunting Lodge, 1890. 1391 E. Palm Street, Altadena.

Benziger Victorian home, 1890s. 466 E. Mariposa, Altadena.

Vanderbilt Home. 2016 Mar Vista, Altadena.

Parson's Home, 1909. 1605 E. Altadena Drive, Altadena. Designed by Arthur Heineman, moved from Pasadena, 1979.

Keyes Airplane Bungalow, 1911. 1337 E. Boston Street, Altadena. On the National Register.

Scripps Home, turn-of-the-century. Established now as a retirement home. Located as 2212 North El Molino, Altedena.

Colonel Woodbury Home, 1880s. Home purchased by the Story family in 1892, then the Goddards in 1922. By 1950s most of the remaining five acres were subdivided. It is the oldest existing residence in Altadena. Located at 2606 Madison Street, Altadena.

Zane Grey Home, 1907. Originally the home was built for Arthur H. Woodward, president of the International Register Company in Chicago. It was purchased by Zane Grey, popular western writer in 1918, and lived in by the Grey family until 1970. Located at 396 East Mariposa Street, Altadena.

J. Crank Home, 1862. "Fair Oaks." Built for the widow of General Albert Johnston, killed at the battle of Shiloh. When her brother, Judge Benjamin Eaton invited her to come West, she came here, to Fair Oaks. Unfortunately more tragedy was to come. Her son died in the steamship "Hancock" when it blew up in the harbor of San Pedro. She left California never to return. Today the home is owned by Dr. and Mrs. Judson, who have lavishly restored it. Many television dramas filmed here. 2186 Crary Street, Altadena. Private Residence!

McNally Home, 1887. Located at the southeast corner of Marengo and Mariposa, Altadena.

Historic Schools: *Jackson Elementary School,* established in 1910 as a one-room school house. Located at that time at 593 Atlanta Street, Altadena. Present school dates from 1926. Located at 593 West Woodbury, Altadena. 818-798-6773.

SaHag-Mesrob Armenian Christian School. Established since 1920. Located at 1045 East Mariposa, Altadena. 818-798-5020.

For additional information on schools contact The Board of Education, 818-795-6981. Also see *81 Years of Public Education in Pasadena.* 20 page booklet.

Businesses: *Webster's Pharmacy,* established over 60 years. 2450 North Lake, or P.O. Box 308, Altadena, CA 91001. 818-797-1163.

Altadena Hardware. Since 1927. 849 East Mariposa Avenue, Altadena, CA 91001. 818-794-4393.

Realtors: *Jim Dickson Realtors.* Mr. Dickson is one of those rare breed of men who does not just sell real estate. He worked hard to restore the historic Pacific Electric Railway Substation. It is now on the National Register of Historic Places, and is a Museum that houses the sights and sounds of the past, especially those of the old Mt. Lowe Railway. Located at 2245 North Lake Avenue, Altadena. Dickson Realty has since moved to 1471 E. Altadena Drive, Pasadena. 818-791-1000. The historic Substation will have new tenants. For more historic reading on Mt. Lowe, there is Charles Simms, *Railroad in the Sky.*

------ # ARCADIA ------

History: The area was once a Gabrielino Indian village. In 1839 Scotch trader Hugo Reid was granted the 13,319 acre rancho. In 1875 the very flamboyant "Lucky" Baldwin purchased the remaining 8500 acres of the *Santa Anita Rancho.* He built the beautiful Queen Anne Cottage in 1882, the Coach Barn in 1892 and planted thousands of magnificent trees, crops and lush vegetation. Today the rancho is home to 127 acres of trees, shrubs, vines and groundcover for research and science. Generally well known as the *Los Angeles State and County Arboretum,* it is probably even better known as the setting for television's *Fantasy Island.*

Books: *Arcadia, Where Ranch and City Meet,* by Pat McAdam and Sandy Snider. Published by the Friends of Arcadia Library, 1981.

Historians: *Sandy Snider.* Can be reached at the Los Angeles County Arboretum, 818-446-8251, ext. 63.

Historical Society: *Arcadia Historical Society*. Thomas Miles, President, 623 Duarte Road, Arcadia, CA 91006-6241. 818-445-1595.

Historic Landmarks: *Los Angeles State & County Arboretum*. 301 North Baldwin Avenue, Arcadia, CA 91006. 818-446-8251. An absolutely wonderful place to visit. It's all here—California history at its best. No one had a livelier personality than Elias Jackson Baldwin. His life, his times, the legacy he left behind is written all over Arcadia. The Arboretum has the charming Queen Anne Cottage built for his fourth wife, 16-year-old Lillie Bennett. But she left when it was discovered that Baldwin had a child and mistress.

Courtesy Los Angeles County Arboretum.

There are the Cottage, the Santa Anita Depot of 1887 (moved to the area) and a lush tropical forest. Perhaps even more significant than all of this is the meticulously restored Hugo Reid Adobe and Indian hut. Hugo Reid may be slightly overlooked in contrast to the more flamboyant Baldwin, but historically he cannot be forgotten. His marriage to an Indian woman; his documentation of Indian languages, customs and traditions was rare for his time. His efforts to preserve and honor the Indians of Southern California are praiseworthy. The Arboretum is open to the public 7 days a week. 9-4:30. Not all the buildings are open to the public. Call 818-446-8251.

Santa Anita Race Track and Arcadia County Park. Opening day in 1907 saw over 20,000 spectators attend the festivities. Closed in 1909 when the state banned horse racing. In 1918 the former race track property became *Ross Field* or *The Balloon School,* as it was also known. Soldiers were trained to drop bombs from observation balloons. A huge hangar was built on the southwest corner of the field. Today, this is the site of the Arcadia County Park. In 1934 the horses ran again. During World War II the tract served as an assembly center for the Japanese. During the war the area was used as a training center for over 20,000 men. It also served as a facility for prisoners of war. Located at 289 West Huntingon Drive, Arcadia, CA. 818-574-7223.

Historic Homes: *Anoakia*. Originally part of the Santa Anita Rancho. Baldwin's daughter Anita organized the Anoakie Breeding Farm, and in 1913 oversaw the construction of a three-story 50 room home at the corner of Baldwin Avenue and Foothill Blvd. In 1936 she sold 1300 acres of the Baldwin ranch to Harry Chandler of the Los Angeles Times. In 1939 Flintridge School of Pasadena purchased the property, and in 1941 Mr. McCaslin bought the school. Today, it is a co-educational school from nursery to 6th grade. Directors are: Mrs. Thornton and Mrs. Carlson. Located at 701 West Foothill Blvd., Arcadia. 818-355-7259.

Clara Baldwin Home 1907. 290 Foothill Blvd., Arcadia. Private Residence.

Historic Sites: *First School in Ar-*

cadia 1903. Located at the corner of Santa Anita and Wheeler Street, Arcadia.

The Oakwood Hotel 1887–1911. Now the Huntington Bank. There are exhibits of the hotel on display in the bank. Located at 125 North First Avenue, Arcadia. 818-445-7350.

Museums: Arcadia's first historical museum is scheduled to open soon. Location: Corner of Campus Drive and Huntington in the Rose Garden.

Other Notes: First *Eucalyptus* tree planted on Santa Anita Rancho prior to 1873 when William Wolfskill planted a seed from Australia brought by a friend.

Arcadia Public Library: My thanks to *Janet Sporleder,* reference librarian, who gave me so much information. Library located at 20 West Duarte Road, Arcadia, CA 91006. 818-446-7112.

Historic Churches: *Arcadia Presbyterian Church,* established 1914. 121 Alice Street, Arcadia, CA 91006. 818-445-7470.

Businesses: *Arcadia Lumber Co.* Since 1949. 214 North Santa Anita, Arcadia. 818-446-3181.

Arcadia Welfare Thrift Shop. Since 1943. 323 North First Street, Arcadia. 818-447-2881.

Glasser & Johns Chapel and Mortuary (Glasser-Miller Lamb, Ar-

cadia Mortuary). 500 South First Street, Arcadia. 818-447-8148.

Arcadia Nursery. Since 1924. 404 South Santa Anita Avenue, Arcadia. 818-447-2411.

Historic Restaurants: *The Derby.* Since 1922. 233 East Huntington Drive, Arcadia. 818-447-8173.

Business involved with history: *The William Barton Family* Horse Drawn Old Carriages for Hire. 518 Fairview Avenue, Arcadia. 818-447-6693.

Craftspeople: *Mr. Mike Thomas,* Kalnoski-Thomas Construction Company Historical Restoration, 251 East Newman Avenue, Arcadia. 818-793-2805.

Old Newspapers: *The Arcadia Journal,* 1918. Holdings of this paper can be seen at the Arcadia Public Library, 20 West Duarte Road, Arcadia. 818-446-7112.

Chamber of Commerce: *Arcadia Chamber of Commerce.* 388 West Huntington Drive, Arcadia. 818-447-2159.

Other Books on Arcadia: *A Scotch Paisano: Hugo Reid's Life in California, 1832–1853,* by Susanna Bryant Dakin.

Lucky Baldwin, The Story of an Unconventional Success, by C.B. Glasscock.

Arcadia, City of the Santa Anita, by Gordon Eberly.

ARTESIA

History: In existence as a community since 1875, Artesia was the business center of a thriving agricultural and dairy district. Mr. Daniel Gridly was its original founder in 1869. In 1874 Artesia was subdivided by a group of farmers known as the Los Angeles Immigration and Land Cooperative Association. The group published *The New Italy,* a monthly newspaper. In 1875 Artesia was born after a three day auction. By late 1875, 3,500 acres had

been sold and about 50 farms established. In 1959 the area was incorporated. Land which cost $15 an acre was then sold for $50,000 an acre. The dairy farmers moved north or to Chino. Today Artesia consists of about 1,000 acres.

Historians: *Mr. Al Little* is currently writing a history of Artesia. He lives at 11864 East 187th Street, Artesia, CA 90701. 213-860-6712.

Other Sources: The Artesia Library

has the Historical Volume and Reference Works which cover Artesia. Vol. IV 1965. Library is located at 18722 Clarkdale Avenue, Artesia, CA 90701. Librarian Martha Mandel is very helpful.

Historic Homes: *Al Little Home,* built 1912. 11864 East 187th Street, Artesia, 90701. Private residence.

Dr. Carlisle Ahrens Home 183rd Street, Artesia. Private residence.

Historic Sites: *Judge Gamble's Victorian Home,* 1880s. Torn down.

Methodist Church, founded 1876. Corner 186th and Pioneer Blvd. Torn down.

Bank Building 1923. 186th and 187th and Pioneer Blvd. Was the First National Bank of Artesia. Now vacant.

Other: *Water Tower* Clarkdale Avenue between 183rd and 186th Street, Artesia.

Business: *Artesia Ice Co.* Since 1929. 17119 South Clarkdale Avenue, Artesia, CA 90701. 213-860-1391.

Artesia Milling Co. Since 1940. 18005 South Studebaker Road, Cerritos, CA 90815. 213-865-1632; 213-865-7613.

Old Family: *Mr. Bill Frampton.* Owner of Artesia Ice Co. His family has been in Artesia area since 1850s.

———— ATWATER ————

History: The little community takes its name from *Harriet Atwater* Paramor. Mr. Paramor subdivided the area, purchasing land from the Verdugo heirs for $1 an acre. The land was subdivided in 1912. Glendale Blvd. was not paved until 1920.

Articles: The Los Angeles Times Glendale Section, see October 18, 1984, on Atwater Library and October 24, 1985, on Atwater businesses. Also contact Joanne Avery, Branch Librarian at 213-664-1353.

Studios: The area was formerly the home to *Walt Disney Studios* once located at Griffith Park Blvd. and Hyperion.

The *Tom Mix Studios* and stables were located where the old Mixville Market once stood.

Mack Sennett's Studios on Glendale Blvd., as were the Marshall Neilan

Studios.

Former Sites: *King's Roller Palace* once served an enthusiastic clientele on Glendale Blvd.

Also, the *Riverside Riding Stables* were located at 3145 Riverside Drive, Atwater.

Theodore Payne Nursery was once located at 2969 Los Feliz Blvd. Since 1922. Now only the Payne Foundation exists. 818-768-1802.

Historic Churches: *Holy Trinity Church,* since 1928. 3722 Boyce Avenue, Atwater. 213-664-4723.

Oldtimers: *John Crosetti.* Once Owned *Piedmont Dairy* which he opened in 1913. He is at 3116 Riverside Drive, Atwater.

Businesses 40 Years or Older: *Beach Market and Grocery,* since 1930. 3104 Glendale Blvd., Atwater, CA 90039. 213-661-2589.

———— AZUSA ————

History: The first recorded reference to Azusa is found in the dairy of Father

Juan Crespi in his journal of 1769. Father Crespi noted that the Shoshonean Indians had a large village near the mouth of the canyons.

The first land grant was given to Luis Arenas in 1841, an area that comprised about three square miles. He called it *El Susa Rancho*. In 1844 Arenas sold his holdings to Henry Dalton, an Englishman who had acquired his wealth in buying and shipping goods from Peru to Wilmington. Mr. Dalton paid $7,000 for El Susa Rancho, renaming it *Rancho de Dalton.*

Here, Dalton planted vineyards, a winery, distillery, a vinegar house, a meat smokehouse and a flour mill. During 1854 gold was discovered in the San Gabriel Canyon and a town named *Eldoradoville* was built at the fork of the San Gabriel to handle the thousands of miners who had staked claims along the east fork of the canyon. During the next 20 years some $12,000,000 in gold was mined and shipped throughout the United States.

In the 1860s land grants were questioned, surveyed and often boundaries changed. When the United States land office surveyed Dalton's rancho they decided that three miles from both his southern and eastern boundary should be removed and opened for homesteading settlers. Dalton went to court, and for the next 24 years, he fought to get his land returned. By the time it was over, he had lost just about everything. All that was left was a 45 acre parcel near Azusa Avenue and Sierra Madre Avenue. Having borrowed heavily from Mr. Slauson to pay his court costs, eventually everything wound up in Slauson's hands. In 1887 Mr. Slauson laid out the new town of Azusa and in 1898 it was incorporated.

Henry Dalton was responsible in 1874 for importing from Italy 15 stands of Italian honey bees, considered to be the first honey bees imported into the United States.

Books: *A British Ranchero in Old California, the Life and Times of Henry Dalton,* by Sheldon Jackson. Arthur Clark Co. 1977.

Historians: *Mr. Jack E. Williams.*

1020 North Soldano, Azusa, CA 91702. 818-334-4512.

Historical Society: *Azusa Historical Society.* Mr. Jack Williams, President. P.O. Box 1131, Azusa, CA 91702. 818-334-4512.

Other Groups: *Cultural Heritage Landmark Commission* appointed by the mayor and city council, 1982. Purpose: to research, catalogue significant buildings and sites.

Indians: Near the mouth of the San Gabriel Canyon, southerly from the Duarte Ditch, are to be found stones in a long rambling line which had some important significance to the Indian. Also at the forks there is an old Indian burial ground. Seven bodies were uncovered many years ago. Each body had a cairne of stones placed over the abdomen and at the top near the head was placed a stone mortar. Also in the West Fork of the San Gabriel Canyon near Camp Rincon, are several huge rocks, weighing 75–80 tons. These are covered with Indian markings. A site marker has been placed by the historical society. Private property.

Historic Landmarks: *Dalton Hill.* Formerly Rancho de Dalton. Located at 6th Street and Cerritos. Azusa Historical Society will be placing marker.

Monrovia Nursery 18331 E. Foothill, Azusa. 818-282-8481.

Historic Homes: *Slauson Home,* after 1900. Is now the *Manresa Retreat* of the Jesuit Fathers. It originally belonged to Mrs. McNeil, the daughter of Mr. Slauson. Located at 18337 East Foothill Blvd., Azusa. 818-969-1848.

Vosberg Home, built prior to 1900. Now home to Monrovia Nursery Co.

Was originally home of Jonathan Slauson's daughter, Mrs. Vosberg. Located at 18331 East Foothill Blvd., Azusa. 818-334-9321.

Lindley Scott Home, 1912. Home is a private residence, however, wedding receptions are held there. Located at 720 East Foothill Blvd., Azusa. 818-334-5215. See Mr. George Pipper.

The Gladstone Home, 1887. Intersection of Citrus and Gladstone, Azusa. Private residence.

The Bowers Home, 1907. 1007 North Angeleno, Azusa. Private residence.

Museum: Home to the *Azusa Historical Society.* (Museum did not materialize in 1986. See Historical Society.)

Historic Buildings: *Azusa Women's Club,* since 1928. 1003 North Azusa, Azusa.

Well's Fargo Bank. Formerly Azusa Valley Savings. Before that was First National Bank. Oldest bank in town. Dates from the 1890s.

Commercial Building, 1870. Now a pawn shop. Located at the corner of Dalton and Foothill, southwest corner. Azusa.

Masonic Temple, since 1907. 510 North San Gabriel Avenue, Azusa. 818-334-9111.

Historic Site: *Azusa Library.* Originally a Carnegie Library. Torn down, but historical society was able to save bricks and they plan to build a monument. Also extensive collection of the original library remains.

Parks: *Slauson Park.* A memorial park, unusual because it was built in one day. Located at 320 North Orange Place, Azusa.

Schools: *Citrus College* Founded 1915. 18824 E. Foothill Blvd., Azusa.

Historic Churches: *Good Shephard Presbyterian Church,* 1892. 611 North Alameda Avenue, Azusa. 818-334-7414.

Parish Hall, early 1900s. Fourth and Dalton, Azusa.

The Presbyterian Church, since 1913. 639 Soldano, Azusa.

Historic Theatres: *Azusa Theatre,* built prior to 1920. (Now a florist shop). 719 North Azusa Avenue, Azusa.

Historic Depots: *Sante Fe Railroad Station,* 1882. 100 block East Sante Fe Avenue, between Azusa Street and Alameda Avenue on Sante Fe. Azusa.

Historic Restaurants: *El Encanto.* Location dates from 1887, old home on property. Original structure was known as *Camp One* in San Gabriel Canyon. Home dates from 1921, turned into a restaurant in the 1930s. Owners are Mr. and Mrs. Hinkley. Located 100 East Old San Gabriel Road, Azusa. 818-969-8877.

Pancho Villa, located in an old building. 239 West Foothill Blvd., Azusa. 818-334-0512.

Businesses: *Arrow Jet Electro Systems,* since 1930s. 1100 West Hollyvale Street, Azusa, CA 91702. 818-334-6211.

Leo Nasser Men's Shop, since 1930. 706 North Azusa Avenue, Azusa, CA. 818-334-1511.

Foothill Drug Store. Oldest drug store in Azusa. 190 West Ninth Street, Azusa. 818-969-4267.

Azusa Transit Mix Concrete, for over 50 years. 1201 Gladstone, Azusa. 818-969-4311.

Chamber of Commerce: *Azusa Chamber of Commerce,* 568 East Foothill Blvd., Azusa. 818-334-1507.

———— BALDWIN PARK ————

History: When the Franciscan Padres established the San Gabriel Mission in 1771, those lands included area of Baldwin Park. William

Workman and John Rowland were granted the Rancho de la Puente in 1845 owning the land south of what is today Ramona Boulevard. Henry Dalton, an Englishman owned the land north of Ramona. When California became the 31st state in 1850, all the ranchos were caught up in the frenzy of documenting legally who owned what. In spite of the United States Government giving a patent to Workman and Rowland in 1867, they lost their holdings to "Lucky Baldwin" in a tragic financial arrangement. Henry Dalton lost his holdings through contested surveys.

Austin Brown built the community's first house and sunk the first well on a site that would now be the southwest corner of Hornbrook Avenue and Los Angeles Street. The area was called "Pleasant View." Then in 1880 it became Vineland as a small business began around a general store where Los Angeles Street and La Rica intersect today. The Butterfield Stage Coach went through the area. In 1890 the Vineland School was formed in a two-story schoolhouse which also served as a community center. In 1906, "Lucky" Baldwin gave his permission to call one of his buildings the Baldwin Park Store, and by 1912, the name was applied to the entire community. Baldwin Park was incorporated in 1956.

Historical Society: *Baldwin Park Historical Society,* P.O. Box 1, Baldwin Park, CA 91706. 818-337-3163. Mr. Henry Littlejohn, President. Note: Present location, at 13009 Ramona Blvd., was formerly the site of the chamber of commerce. The Historical Society was given $10,000 by the city to restore the building.

Historians: *Mrs. Aileen Pinheiro,* 13009 Amar Road, Baldwin Park, CA 90706. 818-337-3285.

Historic Landmarks: *In and Out Drive Through Restaurant,* established 1947. Very first drive-through restaurant established in Southern California. 13502 East Virginia Avenue, Baldwin Park, CA 91706. 818-338-5587.

Historic   Buildings: *Civic Auditorium.* A W.P.A. project of 1935. East Pacific and Baldwin Park, Baldwin Park.

City Hall of Baldwin Park, 1914. 14403 Pacific Avenue, Baldwin Park.

Baldwin Park Women's Club. Established 1906, located in a 1921 building. 3817 Baldwin Park Blvd., Baldwin Park. 818-337-9105.

Historic Theatres: *Baldwin Park Theatre.* Established 1920s. Main Street, Baldwin Park.

Depots: *Pacific Electric Power Station,* 1906 (now vacant). Badillo and San Bernardino Roads, Baldwin Park.

Historic Parks: *Morgan Park,* established 1928–31. 14100 Ramona Blvd., Baldwin Park. Call Mr. Lucas, a storehouse of information on Baldwin Park at 818-960-4011, ext. 208.

Businesses 40 Years or Older: *Cole's Market,* since 1926. 14503 Pacific Avenue, Baldwin Park, CA 91706. 818-337-2712.

Knoll's Pharmacy, since 1920. 14300 Ramona Blvd., Baldwin Park, CA 91706. 818-337-1550.

Books: *History of Baldwin Park.* Unpublished Master's Thesis by Donald Hatchcock, Whittier College, 1954.

Heritage of Baldwin Park, published by the Baldwin Park Historical Society, 1981.

——— BEL-AIR ———

History: This elegant residential area was once part of two Spanish and Mexican land grants. One was the Rancho San Jose de Buenos Ayres; the other, the Rancho San Vicente y Santa Monica. The former passed through many hands since first being granted in 1843. Owners included Dr. Wilson Jones, one of the first doctors in Los Angeles; Mr. Sanford, an early postmaster of Los Angeles. Benito Wilson bought it for $.35 an acre. John Wolfskill paid $40,000 for it in 1884. Mr. Wolfskill sold the rancho in 1887 for $438,700 — an indication of how real estate prices had soared. The Danzingers were the first to develop it. Jake Danzinger was a Los Angeles attorney married to Daisy Canfield (the daughter of Charles Canfield, partner of E.L. Doheny and developer of Beverly Hills). In 1923, Alphonzo Bell purchased 1,760 acres from the Danzingers. What is now the West Gate near Beverly Glen Drive was the original palm-tree lined entrance to the Danzinger Ranch and the only road into the estate. Bell later added another 22,000 acres which include parts of Pacific Palisades, Westwood, Brentwood and Castlemare.

The original unit of Bel-Air was laid out by engineer Wilkie Woodard; the landscape designed by Aurele Vermuleon (1923). In 1931 Bel-Air Woodland opened. In 1937 Bel-Air was extended westward to Sepulveda Blvd. The multitude of curves along Sunset was not intentional but was due to the difficulty of obtaining the right of way. It was one of Los Angeles' first subdivisions to use underground utilities, and the first to have a patrolled security gate. An interesting note — only 400 lots had been sold at the time of Bell's death in 1947. The depression was one reason. Also, Bell prohibited Sunday sales. He did not want to allow motion picture people to buy in the area.

For additional information on Alphonzo Bell, see Bell and Santa Fe Springs.

Historical Society: None. There is, however, a *Bel-Air Association*. The Association is located at: 100 Bel-Air Road, Los Angeles, CA 90077. Elaine Gerdau.

Historic Landmarks: *Bel-Air Sunset Gates* 1920s. West gate, entrance to the old Danzinger Estate near Beverly Glen and Sunset.

Bel-Air Hotel 1923–1946. 701 Stone Canyon Road, Bel-Air. 213-472-1211. Originally this was the Bel-Air office administration building adjacent to stables. Joe Drown converted this into a hotel. He purchased 18½ acres from the Bell interest in 1945. The conversion took place in 1946. The architect was Burton Schutt. The administration building once housed an antique shop and a tea room. Drown had the restaurant, kitchens, garden room and pavilion room constructed. Later he built a pool and bungalows where the riding ring had been. Some of the hotel's well-known guests have been Princess Grace, David Niven, Dean Martin, Deborah Kerr, Sir Laurence Olivier and many, many more.

Bel-Air Country Club, 1924. 10768 Bellagio Road, Bel-Air.

Bel-Air Bay Club, 1931. See Pacific Palisades.

Historic Homes: *Gordon Kaufman Home,* 1929. 245 Carolwood, Bel-Air.

Lion's Gate, 1938. A Paul Williams home. Bel-Air.

Colbert House, 1935. 615 N. Faring, Bel-Air.

Norcross House, 1930. 673 Sienna, Bel-Air.

The Atkinson-Kirkeby Estate, 1930s. Bel-Air Road, Bel-Air.

The Weber/Conrad Hilton Estate, 1930s. Chalon Road, Bel-Air.

Victor Fleming Home, 1930s. Moraga Drive. This was to have been

Clark Gable's home. While he was filming in a remote place, Mr. Fleming built a home here.

Howard Hawkes Ranch, 1930s. Moraga Drive, Bel-Air.

Historic Schools: *Westlake School for Girls,* 1904. 700 N. Faring Road (1928).

Historic Sites: *Capo-di-Monte,* 1913–1952. The Danzinger/Bell/Kent Home, Bel-Air Road, Bel-Air. This magnificent home was built by the Danzingers in 1913. Alphonzo purchased the land and moved into the 40 room mansion. He terraced the land wanting to build a truly spectacular hanging-gardens to rival that of Babylon. No longer there.

Old Rock House, lakes, Bear Cage, back roads. In a conversation with Mr. Bell, Jr. (June '87) he described in great detail the wonderful old road, the pet baby bear kept in a cage and how the Bell children loved to play with it. There was only one entrance or road to the home and a back road that gave the children great fun.

Books: *A Brief History of Bel-Air,* Joseph K. Horton. Published by the Bel-Air Association, 1982.

Pohlmann, John, "Alphonzo E. Bell: A Biography" *The Southern California Historic Quarterly,* Vol. 46, parts 1 and 2.

Old Families: Mr. Alphonzo Bell, Jr., 727 West 7th Street, Suite 753, Los Angeles, CA 90017.

Note: According to demolition permits filed in Los Angeles City Hall since January, 1986, 29 residences have been demolished in Bel-Air and Holmby Hills. This "tear-down" phenomenon is devasting to significant homes that could be designated as historic structures. One bright spot is interior designer-decorator Kathleen Spigelman who is in demand because she knows how to restore these gems! Contact her at 623 N. Almont Drive, Los Angeles, CA. 213-273-2255.

BELL

History: James George Bell laid the foundation stones of progress that later became the City of Bell. From the day in 1875 that he came to California at the suggestion of his old friend, J.E. Hollenbeck, Bell was closely associated with the growth of much of Southern California. Born in Kentucky in 1831 he first invested in California land in what would become Bell. Erecting a home known as the Bell Ranch he raised cattle, farmed, developed water resources and encouraged others to get involved. In the fall of 1902 the first tract of 5 acre parcels was put on the market. Bell became the little town's first postmaster, got the railroad to come through, started schools, churches and more. He assisted in the founding of Occidental College. Bell's son, Alphonzo E. Bell

JAMES GEORGE BELL
...founder of the City of Bell

Courtesy, City of Bell

became the founding father of Bel Air, not to mention the many other real estate projects throughout the southland. Cityhood — 1927.

Historical Society: None. Bell's 60th Anniversary was 1987. Mayor Jay Price asked local residents for historical information.

Historical Homes: *Bell Ranch,* 1880s. (Home) 6500 Lucille Avenue, Bell. The home was erected on Gage Avenue near Salt Lake Avenue, and has been moved to this address. Con- tact City Hall 213-588-6211, parks and recreation. Mayor Jay Price also very helpful.

Time Capsule: buried 1977. Corner Gage and Pine, Bell.

Historian: Bill Vasquez. Works with Parks and Recreation Dept. Also, Dr. Arena did an oral history on the old- timers for the anniversary.

——— BELLFLOWER ———

History: The beginning of Bellflower as a community was marked by the first run of the Pacific Electric "Red Car" on November 5, 1905. The community did not even have a name at that time. Prior to that, the Bixby family grazed cattle on their Sommerset Ranch, to- day the central part of Bellflower. A settlement sprang up almost im- mediately after the advent of the Red Cars. At first it was called "Firth" in honor of the first subdivider in the area. Around 1908 the community was called Somerset. The U.S. Postal Dept. refused the name because of its similarity with Somerset, Colorado. The name Bellflower, coming from Bellfleur apple orchard, was decided upon and in 1910 became the official name. The population? Around 100.

Historical Societies: *Bellflower Heritage Society,* formed 1975. 16600 Civic Center Drive, Bellflower, CA 90706. 213-804-1424, ext. 221.

City Curator: *Muriel MacGregor.* Also located at 16600 Civic Center Drive, Bellflower. 213-804-1424, ext. 221.

Heritage Square: Original plans for a *Heritage Square* consisted of conver- ting the old Pacific Electric ticket sta- tion into a Heritage Square which in- cluded the old powerhouse and a much larger area. Lack of funds made this impossible. Instead the ticket station is a center for the nurturing of respect and concern for the nation, community and each other. Southern Pacific Sta- tion, 1908. Located on Bellflower Blvd., Bellflower, 90706.

Museums: *Carpenter's House,* 1928. 10500 East Flora Vista, Bellflower, CA 90706. 213-867-2212. Former home of the Fred B. Carpenter family, a pioneer dairyman. The home was originally on Carpintero Avenue two miles south of Caruthers Park. Also at that site were a garage, water tower and dairy barn. The home was moved to the present location and houses a museum of Bellflower. Open Saturday, 10:30 to 2:30. Sunday, 12:30 to 3:00.

Historic Churches: *Presbyterian Church,* since 1913. Located at 9630 Mayne Street, Bellflower, CA 90706. 213-866-1787.

Historic Theatres: *Holiday Theatre,* 1930. (now Hosanna Church). 16605 Bellflower Blvd., Bellflower.

Historic Homes: *Gerald House,* 1929, 10106 Walnut, Bellflower. Built on three acres by R.H. Bess in 1929 and later sold to the Gerald family. This home included a Spanish style guest house in the rear. Private Residence.

Historic Restaurants: *Cherokee Cafe,* established 1949. 16639 Bellflower Blvd., Bellflower. 213-867- 6415.

Books: *Bellflower: A Pictorial*

Essay, by Darlene Miller. Issued by the Bellflower Heritage Committee, 1982.

A Historical Study of the Early Development of Bellflower, by John C. Groeling.

Available at the *Brakensiek Library.*

9945 E. Flower, Bellflower, CA 90706. 213-925-5543.

Businesses: *Thompson's,* 1910. 16411 Bellflower Blvd., Bellflower, CA 90706. 213-866-8211.

——— BELL GARDENS ———

History: From its beginnings the history of Bell Gardens has been linked to the Rancho San Antonio. The 29,500 acre Spanish land grant was awarded to Antonio Maria Lugo, a Spanish soldier. Lugo established his ranch in the Rio Hondo area located within the fork of the Los Angeles and San Gabriel Rivers. Bell Gardens changed with the depression. A novel proposition by developer O.C. Beck offered land for $20 down and $10 a month. As the old Rancho San Antonio was broken up by small farms and ranch homes, the last remaining vestiges of the Lugo properties changed as well. Incorporated in 1961.

Historical Societies: *Bell Gardens Historical Society* (El Rancho San An-

Don Antonio Maria Lugo. Courtesy Helen Atkins.

tonio Historical Society). Located in the Woodworth House Museum. 6821 Fosterbridge Blvd., Bell Gardens, CA. Open 2nd and 4th Wednesday; 2:00 to 4:00 p.m. Open 1st and 3rd Sunday; 2:00 to 4:00 p.m. 213-927-5055.

Historian: *Margaret Human,* Bell Gardens Cultural Heritage Commission, 5629 Fostoria, Bell Gardens. 213-927-1031.

Historic Landmarks, Homes: *Barberina Home,* 1913. Corner of Priory Northeast of Jaboneri, Bell Gardens. Private Residence.

Peterson Home, 1906. 7535 S. Perry Road, Bell Gardens. Also boasts of having the only surviving windmill around. Private Residence.

Clara Street Water Company, established in 1920. Now the Southern California Water Co. Located on Priory Street. The office of the original business still there. Bell Gardens.

The Henry Gage Home, 1840. 7000 East Gage Avenue, Bell Gardens. Belonged originally to the Lugo family. Henry Gage became a Governor of California, marrying one of the Lugo descendants. (1899–1903) Home still intact.

Museums: *The Woodworth Home Museum,* built 1924. 6821 Fosterbridge Blvd., Bell Gardens. Woodworth married one of the famous Lugos and was given this home as a wedding gift. The magnificent furniture which came via clipper ship to the original Lugo home on San Pedro Street, was brought here. It is totally intact. Owned by the City of Bel Gardens. Home is utilized by the Bell Gardens Historical Society.

Historic Sites: *Site of the famous Lugo Adobe.* 1850. 6360 East Gage

Avenue, Bell Gardens. This magnificent Monterey Style wood and adobe Hacienda was once part of the Rancho San Antonio, a 29,413 acre grant given to Antonio Maria Lugo in 1810. Long the scene of a bitter preservation controversy, it fell prey to vandalism and finally fire. A replica of the adobe has been built in the Lugo Plaza and contains material from the original. See Huntington Park.

Site of the Old Laguna School. Corner of Garfield Blvd. and Gage Blvd., Bell Gardens. Now owned by the Edison Co. An historic marker on the site.

Historic Churches: *Saint Gertrudes Catholic Church, 1937–38.* Eastern Avenue, Bell Gardens. First church in the area.

Books: *Lugo: A Chronicle of Early California,* by Dr. Roy Elmer Whitehead, M.D., 1978. Mimeographed material at the Woodworth Home on the history of area compiled by Mrs. Barbarini.

Early Residents: *The Dimmett family.* 5629 Clara Street, Bell Gardens. They began the first water company in the area.

Businesses 40 Years or Older: *Gano Culwell Paint Co.,* since 1925. P.O. Box 351, Bell Gardens, CA 90201. 213-587-8195.

Bell Gardens Rexall, since 1937. 7501 South Eastern Avenue, Bell Gardens, CA 90201. 213-773-3800.

Eastern Hardware, since 1937. 7601 S. Eastern Avenue, Bell Gardens, CA 90201. 213-773-2764.

Mills Fencing Co., since 1936. 5545 East Gage Avenue, Bell Gardens, CA 90201. 213-773-3844.

Morrison Electric, 1927. 6430 Clara Street, Bell Gardens, CA 90201. 213-869-2897. Craftsman as well.

Library: *Bell Gardens Public Library.* 213-927-1309.

BEVERLY HILLS

History: Even Gaspar de Portolá liked the area. On August 3, 1769, he and a small group of Spanish soldiers camped at a spring surrounded by a large grove of Sycamores. They called it The Spring of the Sycamores of St. Stephen. The approximate site has been marked on La Cienega Blvd., between Olympic Blvd. and Gregory Way in Beverly Hills.

In 1822 Mexican settlers Maria Rita Valdez and her husband Vicente Valdez were granted the *Rancho Rodeo de las Aguas,* the Gathering of the waters. Vicente died in 1828, leaving the 4500 acre rancho in the hands of his widow and seven children. Maria was plagued by the rival claims of a relative, Luciano Valdez. He drove her cattle away and built a house right in front of her own. Eventually she won a judgment against him in 1844. Luciano was ordered to leave his home and the rancho and about $17.50 in recompense. The beautiful Rancho Rodeo de las Aguas was hers at last. Her small adobe home was located around Alpine Drive and the northwest corner of Sunset Boulevard.

There was an Indian raid here. Too bad Hollywood couldn't film it. One of the young members of Dona Maria's family escaped and went for help. A posse was sent out from the little town of Sherman (West Hollywood) and chased Chief Walker and his Utah Band to walnut groves near today's Chevy Chase and Benedict Canyon. Dona Maria sold her beautiful ranch in 1854. By 1860 there were almost 2,000 acres planted in wheat. By the 1880s the ranch was acquired by Charles Denker and Henry Hammel.

In 1906 Charles Canfield, Burton Green and Max Whittier, Los Angeles businessmen and oil millionaires, signed a contract to buy the 3,055 acre ranch of Hammel and Denker for $400 an acre. Boundaries were Wilshire Blvd. on the south, Whittier Drive on the west, the foothills above Sunset Blvd. on the north, and Doheny Drive on the east. They called themselves the Rodeo Land and Water Company. Burton Green named the new subdivision Beverly after Beverly Farms in Massachusetts.

Historic Estates: *Green Acres,* 1928. On the National Register of Historic Places. #279 C.H.M. Harold Lloyd Estate, 1225 Benedict Canyon Road, Beverly Hills. Harold Lloyd was one of Hollywood's great comics. The home was lived in by Selznick when he filmed *Gone With the Wind.* The Solomons once owned the home. Now it is owned by Ted Field, Chicago Dept. Store magnate of Marshall Field fame.

Pickfair, 1920. Douglas Fairbanks and Mary Pickford. 1143 Summit Drive, Beverly Hills.

Grayhall, 1909–1919. Douglas Fairbanks Hunting Lodge, Carolyn Way, Beverly Hills. Fairbanks bought 14 acres from the 56 acre Spalding Estate (Mayor of Beverly Hills). Apparently Carole Lombard's uncle built it as a hunting lodge on the estate. Fairbanks then built Pickfair on his remaining land.

Greystone Estate, 1927. 905 Loma Vista Drive, Beverly Hills. George Kaufman, architect. Part of the original 429 acre Doheny Ranch. (See sites). Lawrence Doheny, Sr., built this for his son, Ned and his wife Lucy and their five children.

The Knoll, 1955. The Battson Estate, Schuyler Road, Beverly Hills. Lucy Doheny later married Mr. Battson and had this smaller home built.

Historic Realtors: Alvarez, Hyland & Young, 210 N. Canon, Beverly Hills. 213-278-0300.

Historical Society: *Beverly Hills Historical Society,* Ms. Phyllis Lerner, President. 213-475-9802. It took a long time, but at last the area that has tried hard to keep people out (Douglas Fairbanks said a fence should be built around the city) is now opening itself up to the rest of Los Angeles for some of the most spectacular home tours

ever held in our city. The last one had champagne on the balcony of the Greystone Estate, fruit, hors d'oeuvres and chocolate coated strawberries!

Historic Landmarks: *Marker.* Portolá Trail Campsite, No. 2. Expedition of Don Gaspar de Portolá and his men on August 3, 1769. La Cienega Boulevard between Olympic and Gregory, Beverly Hills. Marker no. 665.

Right of Way Sunset Boulevard. When the Beverly Hills Hotel opened in 1912, a right of way provided by the Pacific Electric brought customers right to the door of the hotel. When the company discontinued service in 1923, the question of what to do with the obvious eyesore in an area already very cognizant of such things, had to be decided. *A Bridal Path Association* was formed, plants brought in, the tracks removed, and soon a steady stream of horse-back riders became commonplace.

Monument. When water became a problem as it does in the Southland, and small cities right and left were annexing to the City of Los Angeles to solve their water problems, Beverly Hills had a heated debate over the question. Movie stars campaigned for a no vote, and the no's carried the day. In 1923 the residents built this monument as a tribute to independence, and their right to stay as separate from that "ghastly" city to the east as possible. Located at the intersection of Beverly Drive and Olympic.

Fountain. 1930. Corner of Santa Monica Blvd. and Wilshire Blvd., Beverly Hills. Ralph Flewelling architect. Mrs. Elizabeth Frazer Lloyd, Harold Lloyd's mother, president of the Women's Garden Club at the time, was the person who inspired the building of the fountain. It was the first electric fountain with colored lights. Merrell Gage did the mural which depicts early California history. Figure: Symbol of an Indian in prayer.

Marker. 1700 Chevy Chase, Beverly Hills. To commemorate Indian raid of 1852. Located in front of the Beverly

Hills Women's Club. Placed by the Daughters of the American Revolution. 213-276-5804.

Milton Goetz Estate/Marion Davies, William R. Hearst, 1925–27. 1017 North Beverly Drive, Beverly Hills. Gordon Kaufman, architect.

Frances V. deBottiller Estate, 1927. Sunset Blvd. near Hillcrest Drive, Beverly Hills.

George Lewis Estate, 1920s. Benedict Canyon, Beverly Hills. A ten acre estate.

Carrie Guggenheim Estate, 1927–28. Copley, Beverly Hills.

Conrad Veidt Home, 1920s. Foothill Drive south of Sunset Blvd., Beverly Hills.

Burton Green Estate, 1913–1914. Lexington Road (1601), Beverly Hills. One of the founders of Beverly Hills.

Charles and Al Christie, 1925 (Waverly), Sunset Blvd., Beverly Hills.

Jay Paley Estate, 1936. Brooklawn Drive, Beverly Hills.

Kirk B. Johnson Estate, 1912. Alpine Drive, Beverly Hills.

J.W. Robinson Estate, 1910. 1008 Elden Way, Beverly Hills. On the National Register of Historic Places. Now owned by the L.A. County Arboretum. Architects, Sumner Hunt and Silas Burns. Also credit is given to Nathaniel Dryden, who built El Miradero in Glendale. Open to the public. Call 213-276-5367.

Historic Homes: *David O. Selznick Home,* 1934. 1050 Summit Drive, Beverly Hills.

Henry C. Clark Home, 1907. Crescent Drive near Lomitas, Beverly Hills. One of the first homes in Beverly Hills.

"Breakaway House," *Charlie Chaplin's Home,* 1923. 1085 Summit Drive, Beverly Hills. Designed by Clinton Kolyar.

Samuel Goldwyn Home. 1200 Laurel Way, Beverly Hills.

Anthony Home, 1909. 910 Bedford at Benedict Canyon, Beverly Hills. Greene and Greene Architects.

Harry Cohn Home, 1927. Designed by Robert Farquhar. North Crescent Drive near Lexington, Beverly Hills.

Jack Warner Home, 1926. Angelo Drive, Beverly Hills.

George Cukor Home. 9166 Cordell Drive, Beverly Hills.

Rudolph Valentino's Home, "Falcon's Lair," 1920s. 1436 Bella Drive, Beverly Hills.

Spadena House, 1921. 516 Walden Drive, Beverly Hills. This is the Hansel and Gretel Home, designed by Henry Oliver as a movie set.

Lupe Velez Home. 732 North Rodeo Drive, Beverly Hills.

Clara Bow Home. 512 North Bedford, Beverly Hills.

Buster Keaton Home, 1920s. 1018 Pamela Drive, Beverly Hills.

King Gillette Home. Later Gloria Swanson's home. Northeast corner Sunset Blvd. and Crescent Drive, Beverly Hills.

Fred Astaire Home, 1935. Summit Drive, Beverly Hills. A Roland Coate design.

Howard Hawkes Home, 1932. Benedict Canyon, Beverly Hills.

Joan Bennett Home, 1938. Mapleton Drive, Beverly Hills. Also owned by Hal and Martha Wallis.

John Gilbert Home, 1400 Tower Grove Road, Beverly Hills.

Thomas Ince Home. 1051 Benedict Canyon Drive, Beverly Hills.

Theda Bara Home. 632 North Alpine Drive, Beverly Hills.

Ronald Coleman Home. 1002 Summit Drive, Beverly Hills.

John Barrymore Home. (Bella Vista). 1400 Seabright Place, Beverly Hills.

Marion Davies Home. 1700 Lexington Road, Beverly Hills.

Corrinne Griffith Home. 1033 Summit Drive, Beverly Hills.

Mr. & Mrs. Edmind D. Locke, 1913. 801 North Rodeo Drive, Beverly Hills. A Greene and Greene design.

Winston Millet Home, 1915. 905 North Camden Drive, Beverly Hills. Former President of the Historical Society.

Jeanette and Clark Parker Home, 1916. 901 North Camden Drive, Beverly Hills. Built for an unknown resident. In 1918 silent film star Charles Ray bought home.

Private Residence, 1923. 910 N. Bedford Drive, Beverly Hills. Moved from Los Angeles. A Greene and Greene design.

Very First Homes, 1908. (1) 601 N. Canon Drive; (2) 619 N. Canon Drive; (3) 703 N. Canon Drive; (4) 718 N. Crescent Drive. One of first "model" homes — 515 N. Canon Drive, Beverly Hills.

King Vidor Home, 1939. A Wallace Neff design. Summit Ridge, Beverly Hills.

Frank Niblo Home. "Misty Mountain," 1330 Angelo Drive, Beverly Hills. A Wallace Neff design.

Historic Churches: *Church of the Good Shepherd,* 1923–25 (First church in area). Santa Monica Blvd. and Bedford Drive, Beverly Hills.

All Saints Episcopal Church, 1925. Roland E. Coate design. Northeast corner Santa Monica & Camden, Beverly Hills.

Historic Hotels: *Beverly Hills Hotel,* 1912. 9641 West Sunset Blvd., Beverly Hills. 213-276-2251. Elmer Grey, Architect.

Beverly Wilshire Hotel, 1926. (Walker and Eisen Design). 9500 Wilshire Blvd., Beverly Hills.

Historic Theatres: *Beverly Theatre,* 1925. 206 North Beverly, Beverly Hills. L.A. Smith, architect. The center of a recent controversy to demolish historic theatre. The owner of this 57 year old theatre has agreed to delay demolition until preservationists can find a way to save it.

Fox Wilshire, 1929. 8440 Wilshire Blvd., Beverly Hills. A Charles Lee design.

Warner Theatre, 1930 (Beverly). 9404 Wilshire, Beverly Hills. Marcus Priteca, Architect.

Historic Schools: *Berkeley Hall School,* 1911. North Swall Drive, Beverly Hills.

Beverly Hills High School, 1927. 241 Moreno Drive, Beverly Hills.

Other Buildings: *Beverly Hills Women's Club,* 1916. 1700 Chevy Chase, Beverly Hills.

Beverly Hills Post Office, 1933, Ralph C. Flewelling, architect. Southeast corner Canon & Santa Monica, 469 N. Crescent Dr., Beverly Hills.

Beverly Hills City Hall, 1931. William Gage, architect. East side Crescent between Santa Monica and Little S.M., 450 N. Crescent Dr., Beverly Hills.

Famous Street: *Rodeo Drive,* Tres Chic. From name of original rancho, Rodeo de Las Aguas and later, the Rodeo Land and Water Co.

Historic Sites: *Maria Rita Valdez Adobe Home,* 1840s. Approximately intersection of Sunset Blvd. and Alpine Drive, Beverly Hills.

Dias Dorados. Thomas Ince Home. 1922. A portion of this land was sold to Harold Lloyd which became Green Acres.

Speedway, 1920 –24. Located between Beverly Drive and Spaulding.

Peck Building, 1907-1929. Beverly Drive and Santa Monica. Community's first "landmark."

Max H. Whittier Home. One of founders of Beverly Hills. Saudi Arabian Sheikh Mohammed Al-Fassi restored home. Burned, later demolished. Sunset Blvd., Beverly Hills.

Hobart Bosworth Estate. (James Dolena design). Starred in the first film made in Los Angeles. Sold his estate to William Powell in 1935. Demolished. Hillcrest Drive, Beverly Hills.

Cord Estate. Hillcrest Drive, Beverly Hills.

Doheny Ranch, 1912 –1954. 409 Hillcrest Drive, Beverly Hills. This 429 acre estate once lined the entire road along Hillcrest Drive, around curve and Greystone Estate to Sunset Blvd. on south, north to top of mountains. It was the private retreat of the Dohenys. Chester Place was residence of family from 1901 to Mrs. Doheny's death in 1957. Several homes on ranch, in addi-

tion to smaller homes of families who worked on the ranch.

Tree — for years cattle round ups used this famous eucalyptus. When it became endangered, everyone from Cecil B. deMille on tried to save it. Unfortuantely their efforts failed. Located on Pico Blvd. off Preuss Road (Robinson Blvd.)

Morocco. Imaginary town that was short-lived.

1890 Coldwater School District formed, but the first school was opened in 1877. It was located at the entrance to coldwater canyon.

Brown Derby, 1931. Located at the corner of Wilshire Blvd. and Rodeo Drive, Beverly Hills. The other Derbys were Los Angeles (1926), Hollywood (1929), Los Feliz and Beverly Hills.

Museum: *Fowler's Museum.* 9215 Wilshire Blvd., Beverly Hills. 213-278-8010.

Parks: *Virginia Robinson Gardens,* 1910. Three blocks north of Sunset on Elden Way. By appointment only. 213-446-8251.

William O. Douglas Outdoor Classroom. Significant because this was the "rear" of the Doheny Ranch. The old gate house is still there, as is the home of the ranch's superintendent Mr. Fred Mailey. Also home of the ranch's reservoirs. Located at 1936 Lakedrive, Beverly Hills. 213-858-3834.

Other: The city of Beverly Hills has completed an architectural survey of the city by the firm of Johnson, Human. 8 vols. Available at city library. Also, Windsor Publications

will be publishing a book on the History of Beverly Hills. In addition to this, the city also recently completed a History of Greystone which includes information on the Doheny Ranch. This report available through Beverly Hills Director of Community Services, 213-550-4815.

Books: *Beverly Hills, Portrait of a Fabled City,* by Fred E. Basten, 1975. *The Estates of Beverly Hills,* by Charles Lockwood.

Murals: *Murals of the City* by Einer Petersen can be seen at the Security First National Bank, Beverly Hills branch.

Murals by Charles Kassler, 1938 depicting "scenes in the development of the mail service and representative views of modern life." At the Beverly Hills Post Office, 469 N. Crescent Dr., Beverly Hills.

Businesses 40 Years or Older: *Beverly Stationers,* since 1932. 422 North Beverly Drive, Beverly Hills, CA 90210. 213-276-4161.

Wilshire Colonial Fireside Shop, since 1924. 8636 Wilshire Blvd., Beverly Hills. 213-657-7176; 213-657-8183.

Max Rouse & Sons, Inc., since 1920. 361 S. Robertson Blvd., Beverly Hills, CA 90211. 213-655-9300.

Edelwiss Chocolates. Handdipped for over 43 years. 444 North Canon Drive, Beverly Hills, CA 90210. 213-275-0341.

Beverly Hills Luggage, since 1897. (Los Angeles). 404 North Beverly Drive, Beverly Hills, CA 90210. 213-273-5885.

Frances Klein Antique Jewelry. 310 North Rodeo Drive, Beverly Hills, CA 90210. 213-273-0155.

Geary's, 1930s. 351 North Beverly Drive, Beverly Hills, CA 90210. 213-273-4741.

Hunter's Book Store, since 1851. (California). 420 North Beverly Drive, Beverly Hills, CA 90210. 213-274-7301.

E.L. Payne, since 1915. Serving Beverly Hills since 1924. Beverly Hills. 213-275-5331.

Hillcrest Motor Company, 1927 (and museum). 9230 Wilshire Blvd., Beverly Hills. 213-274-8411; 213-272-3234.
Newspapers: *Beverly Hills Citizen*

News 1923–1970. Located in its entirety at the Beverly Hills Public Library. 444 North Rexford Drive, Beverly Hills. 213-285-1083.

———— BOYLE HEIGHTS ————

History: Andrew Boyle headed south from San Francisco purchasing the "Old Mission Vineyard" east of the Los Angeles River, the first American to move to that side of the stream. He paid $.25 cents an acre for parts of the land considered worthless, and $3,000 for the vineyard. Mr. Boyle built the first brick house on the east side of the river, fronting Boyle Avenue.

The family history is significant, beginning with *William Workman* who arrived in 1841; his brother William Henry Workman followed in 1854. Andrew Boyle, from the other side of the family, came in 1851. His daughter, Maria, married William Henry Workman. Their eldest son Boyle wrote a fire book on L.A. history. The Workmans and Boyles are still active in city government.

Historic Landmarks: *Andrew A. Boyle Home,* 1858/1910/1975 (Japanese Retirement Home) 325 South Boyle Avenue, Boyle Heights. 213-263-5301. This remarkable home, built by the founder of Boyle Heights, was only recently "rediscovered." Built in 1858 on part of a 22 acre site when the area was still grazing land. After Boyle's death in 1871 his daughter Maria and her husband, William H. Workman, stayed in the home. Mr. Workman became a city councilman and mayor. In the 1880s he subdivided the area naming it in honor of his father-in-law. In 1910 the home was reconstructed by William Workman, Jr. He hired Robert Farquhar to add a second floor and a red tile roof. It eventually became a *Japanese Retirement Home* and only recently has its earlier history been revealed.

Historic Homes: *Paradise House,* 1890. 1411 Pleasant Avenue, Boyle Heights.
Private Residence, 1890s. #102 C.H.M. 1030 Macy Street, Boyle Heights.
Private Residence, 1905. 603 Gillette, Boyle Heights.
Victorian Home, 1890. 1530 Pleasant Avenue, Boyle Heights.
Victorian Home, 1890. 1519 Pleasant Avenue, Boyle Heights.
Collins Residence, 1888. #266 C.H.M. 2930 Whittier Blvd., Boyle Heights.
Cottage, 1885. 914 Michigan, Boyle Heights.
Cottage, 1889. 327 State, Boyle Heights.
Private Home (Neighborhood Music Center), 1890. 358 Boyle, Boyle Heights.
Home, 1882. 2018 East Second Street, Boyle Heights.
Home, 1887. 2123 East Second Street, Boyle Heights.
Residence, 1890. #262 C.H.M. 2700 Eagle Street, Los Angeles.
Home, 1890. South Side Euclid Place, Boyle Heights.
Home, 1886. 3050 East Fourth Street, Boyle Heights.
Home, 1884. 3407 E. Fourth Street, Boyle Heights.
Home, 1890. 2533 E. Michigan, Boyle Heights.
Home, Southside 2nd St. west of Mott, Boyle Heights.
Historic Churches: *St. Mary's Church.* 407 S. Chicago, Boyle Heights. 213-268-7432.
First Hebrew Christian Church, 1905. Northeast corner Michigan & Chicago. Boyle Heights.

Mission Revival Church. 1526 Pleasant Avenue, Boyle Heights.

Iglesia Baptista Unida 1895. 132 N. Chicago, Boyle Heights.

Calvary Baptist Church, 1906. 206 South St. Louis Street, Boyle Heights.

Grace Methodist Episcopal Church, 1906. 200 North St. Louis, Boyle Heights.

Park: *Hollenbeck Park.* St. Louis Street and Fourth, Boyle Heights. Named for John E. Hollenbeck, whose widow, along with William Workman, donated 21 acres of land in 1892.

Hollenbeck Home for the Aged, 1890. 573 South Boyle Avenue, Boyle Heights. State's first such retirement home.

Boyle Hotel, 1887. Boyle Avenue and First Street, Boyle Heights.

Other: *Boyle Heights Murals.* 3000 Block of East Olympic Blvd., Boyle Heights.

Bridge at Fourth & Lorena, 1928. #265 C.H.M.

Macy Street Viaduct, 1926. #224 C.H.M. Cross L.A. River between Mission Street on Vignes St.

Historic District: *Pleasant Avenue.* Now on the National Register of Historic Districts.

Book: Boyle Workman, *The City that Grew,* The Southland Publishing Co., L.A., 1935.

Historic Library: *Malabar Branch Library,* 1927. #304 C.H.M. 2801 East Wabash Avenue.

Businesses: *Mt. Pleasant Bakery,* 1880s. 1418 Pleasant Avenue, Boyle Heights. May be the oldest bakery still standing in L.A.

Cemetery: *Evergreen Cemetery,* 1876. Michigan Avenue, Boyle Heights. Many of the tombstones here are more than 100 years old. Small stone chapel designed by Arthur Benton in 1903.

Historic Sites: *Sixth Street Wooden Bridge,* 1898. Across Hollenbeck Park Lake. L.A. Removed 1968.

Site of *Residence of 1890s.* #97 C.H.M. 1620 Pleasant Avenue. Beautiful high-Victorian home. Demolished 1973.

BRADBURY

History: Lewis Leonard Bradbury was born in 1822 in Maine. He moved to Portland Oregon and established a merchandising business. He became ill from asthma and so he moved to Mazatlan, Mexico. There he discovered large gold and silver mines and became a millionaire. He met and married Senorita Martinez. They had a large family. When his asthma returned, he left Mexico and moved with his family to Oakland, California, then to Southern California in 1883. Lewis Bradbury purchased the old Homestead of the Rancho Azusa de Duarte, about 2,749 acres. Here he built "Oakhurst." The next generation of Bradburys, the Polks, built the "Polk Place" renaming it "The Chateau Bradbury."

Today, much of the old Bradbury acreage is no longer in Bradbury, but Monrovia. The City Hall of Bradbury, if one can so describe it, consists of three city employees. There is a file on the history of Bradbury. The City Hall is in one of the original Bradbury caretakers' homes.

City Hall: Originally a caretaker's home. Located at 600 Winston Avenue, Bradbury, CA 91010. 818-358-3218.

Historic Home: *Chateau Bradbury,* 1912. Note: this home is now in Monrovia. Built for Minerva and Issac Polk, daughter and son-in-law of Colonel Lewis L. Bradbury for whom the city of Bradbury is named. Designed by noted Southern California architect Robert D. Farquhar. The Polk family owned it until 1922. A private residence.

─── BRENT'S JUNCTION ───

History: Today, it is only a name on a map. Upon inquiry however, like so many other places whose names have faded with the years, Brent's Junction has an interesting history. Around what is now the Ventura Freeway and Las Virgenes Road, there was an old store—the Los Angeles Pie Company, built around 1904. It was owned by the Cooper family. In 1920, that store was moved to Calabasas, and later became known as the Cooper-Kramer Store. The name Brent refers to movie mogul, Mr. Brent. Apparently Mr. Brent was involved with the Craig Mountain Resort, now the Malibu Creek State Park. (See Santa Monica Mountains). Prior to Brent's Junction it was called Las Virgenes Junction. Originally a Mr. Dominguez owned the land. In 1914 there was a tile factory in Brent's Junction. Also Billingsley Restaurant and a small hotel and grocery store, known as The Corners. Lots of history in them there hills!

─── BURBANK ───

History: This history goes back just about as far as one can in Southern California. Only three land grants were given to retired Spanish soldiers in 1784. The *Rancho San Raphael* was one of those. It was granted to Jose Maria Verdugo and comprised about 36,000 acres. David Burbank arrived in 1866 and he purchased 4,064 acres of the La Providencia Ranch. In 1887 he transferred his holdings to Providencia Land Water and Ranch Development Company. Burbank was born.

Historical Society: *Burbank Historical Society.* 1015 Olive Ave., Burbank, CA 91506. 818-841-6333. President: *Loraine White* 818-845-2026 (Home).

Historians: *Mr. Ed Olin.* 818-848-7151.
Doris Vick 818-845-5811.

Historic Landmarks: *Mother Cabrini Shrine,* 1917. Mother Cabrini was born in Italy (1850). Came to the United States and opened orphanages for young girls. She eventually settled in Southern California and began the Cabrini School for Girls. located on Glen Oaks Blvd., where the Lutheran School is now. A chapel, or shrine if you will, was built about two miles above her school in the Verdugo Hills. When she died in 1917, the shrine became a chapel. Yearly pilgrimages were made to it by thousands of grateful people in Burbank. When the school was sold, the chapel was moved to St. Francis Xavier Elementary School. It is now located at 3801 Scott Road, Burbank, CA 91504. 818-767-2445. The gentleman who lovingly restored the chapel and moved it is Mr. Orlando Granata. He can be reached at 818-848-9882.

Starlight Theatre, 1950. *Starlight Lane,* 1959. Sunset Canyon Drive to Bowl. Burbank.

Burbank Airport (Burbank-Hollywood Airport). Originally United Airport, later became known as Union Airport as other airlines joined. Main Terminal, altered is still there. Off of Hollywood Way and Empire. 818-840-8847.

Warner Brothers Studios, now the Burbank Studios, from the 1920s. Several original buildings dating from the early 20s. Dressing rooms, offices are still there. Originally this site was Dr. David Burbank's home and ranch.

(1864). It became First National Pictures in 1926, then Warner Bros. Located at 4000 Warner Blvd., Burbank, CA 91522. 818-945-6000.

Pillars and Arch, Old Country Club House, 1921. Formerly entrance to the private clubhouse. There was also at one time a gate. Located at the top of Olive Avenue and Country Club Drive, Burbank.

Historic Homes: *House,* 1913. 323 Providencia, Burbank. Moved here from San Fernando Road and Providencia, Burbank.

Two Sisters' House, 1887. When the Providencia Land and Water Development Co. first laid out Burbank, they built six homes. These two are the only ones left. They are known locally as the Two Sister's houses. Both have been heavily remodeled, or remuddled, as you wish. On Angeleno and Orange Grove, Burbank.

Two Stone Houses, 1920s. Built by O.C. Lane. Located on Olive and 9th Street, Burbank.

The Monseigneur Home, 1920s. Originally built by Allan of Allan Motor Car Co. Located on San Fernando Road and Alameda, Burbank.

Historic Clubs, Hotels: *Old Country Club,* 1925. Burned in 1927. Taken over by the Mormon Church. Church plans to have a grand reopening of their recent restoration and public will be invited. Located on Sunset Canyon, Burbank. Note: Pillars and Arch, see Landmarks.

Women's Club of Burbank, 1924. Originally known as the Lavendar and Lace Club. Located at 705 East Olive Avenue, Burbank, CA 91501. 818-502-2850.

Elk's Club, around 1930. 145 East Palm, Burbank, CA 91501. 818-848-5508.

Addison Hotel, formerly the Elizabeth Hotel, 1922. Located on San Fernando Road and Angeleno, Burbank.

Other: *Commercial Building,* 1887. First bank block built in 1887 and still standing. Has been remodeled. Located at the corner of Olive and San Fernando Blvd.

Books: Jackson Mayers, *Burbank History,* 1975. *Burbank California, an Historical Geography,* 1976.

Museum: *Gordon Howard Museum,* 1920. 1015 W. Olive Avenue, Burbank. Open Sundays and by special arrangements. 818-841-6333. This is also the home of the Historical Society.

Depot: *Southern Pacific Depot,* 1929. Located next to Olive Avenue overpass. Replaced an earlier structure.

Historic Sites: *Burbank Villa Hotel,* 1890 (Burbank's Ranch Home). Built by Dr. David Burbank. Later it was called Santa Rosa Hotel. Lasted until the 1920s. Today, the site is occupied by the Burbank Post Office. 100 Olive Street, Burbank.

Cemeteries: *Valhalla Memorial and Mausoleum Park,* 1923-27. *Portal of the Folded Wings.* Former 63 acre ranch. Takes its name from the Palace of Odin, the Norse mythical god of death. Among monuments here is a memorial to the 241 U.S. Marines killed in Beirut attack of 1983. Memorial plaque for Oliver Hardy and Amelia Earhart. The Memorial is to commemorate the 50th anniversary of powered flight. In 1953 Burbank set up a national shrine for aviation's historical documents. 10621 Victory Blvd., Burbank. 818-763-9121.

Libraries: *Walt Disney Archives,* 500 S. Buena Vista Street, Burbank, CA 91521. 818-845-3141 ext. 2425. The history of Walt Disney Productions from 1923 on. Archives include letters, original art, much more.

Burbank Central Library: The Warner Research Collections. 110 North Glenoaks Blvd., Burbank, CA 91503. 818-953-9737. One of the most unique collections in the world. The Warner Brothers donated these materials. Mostly pictorial. Special arrangements must be made to gain access to the materials.

Historic Churches: *St. Robert Ballarmine Catholic Church,* 1907. 133

North 5th Street, Burbank. 818-846-3443.

Businesses: *The Smoke House,* 1946. 4420 Lakeside Drive, Burbank, CA 91505. 818-845-3731.

J.P. Weaver & Co., 1914. 2310 W. Victory Blvd., Burbank, CA 91506. 818-841-5700.

Menasco Manufacturing Co., 1927 L.A. 1935 Burbank. 805 South San Fernando Blvd., Burbank, CA 91502. 818-843-2272.

Andrew Jergen's Soap Factory, since 1920. Originally located in Cincinnati, 1882. 99 West Verdugo Road, Burbank, CA 91502. 818-846-9822.

Martino Bakery, since 1930. 901 West Alameda, Burbank, CA 91506. 213-849-1253.

Story's Hardware, since 1915. 122 South Golden Mall, Burbank. (As of 1986 Story's closed its doors).

Colorful Character: Dubbed "Crazy Fawkes" by the locals, Joseph Wesley Fawkes was a brilliant but irascible loner who invented and proposed a monorail system way before its time. Born in 1861 in Pennsylvania he came to California. Eventually he had a ranch in Burbank located on Olive Avenue between Victory Boulevard and Flower St. One remarkable feature of Fawkes terrain from 1910 onward, was his ill-fated monorail. The hull of the infamous machine sat unused and rusting until the property was purchased around 1940. He used an air-cooled Franklin engine to power the monorail's front and rear propellers. Fawkes even formed the *Aerial Trolley Car Company* and was trying to sell stock for $100 a share to help finance his public monorail system. He boasted of a sixty-mile-an-hour run via Burbank to Los Angeles. Why his plan failed and the results of years of litigation can be followed more closely in: *Westways,* "The Fawkes and the Swallow," by E.M. Rafn, March 1976.

—— CALABASAS ——

History: Calabasas may mean squash or pumpkin. Having one of the more interesting histories of any community in Southern California, it is also known by some as the "last of the old West."

From Tubac, Mexico in 1775 Bautista De Anza headed north to pioneer a new overland route to Monterey. With 240 men, women and children, the intrepid trail-blazer endured one of the most severe winters ever, crossing today's Anza Borrego Desert, reaching the San Gabriel Mission on January 4, 1776. In February, the group camped in Calabasas, having passed what is now Travel Town in Griffith Park, later descending Calabasas Pass to the Las Virgenes Valley.

In 1834 Secularization of the Missions brought changes throughout California. The name *El Scorpion* or *El Escorpion* began to appear on maps. It was a large ranch which encompassed Calabasas and it was granted to three ex-mission Indians: Urbano, Manuel and Oden. It was, however, around Miguel (or McGill) Leonis that Calabasas as a town originated. Known as the Basque "King of Calabasas," Leonis came to the area in 1858. He acquired the ranch, partly by purchase, partly by marriage to Chief Oden's daughter, Espiritu. He built the beautiful Leonis Adobe in the late 1850s. After his death in 1889 on Caheunga Pass, Espiritu lived in the adobe until her death in 1906. Then Lester Agoure bought the house from Espiritu's son in 1912. Finally the property reverted to a developer who planned to raze it and build a shopping center. Kay Beachy stepped in and dramatically saved the old landmark. It became Cultural Historic Landmark No. 1.

Historical Society: *Calabasas Historical Society,* P.O. Box 8067, Calabasas, CA 91302. Current President: Nancy Lauridsen. 818-340-8786.

Historic Landmarks: *The Hanging Tree.* Today it is west of the Sagebrush Cantina, but was moved there. Originally it stood where the Cantina parking lot is today.

Leonis Adobe. #1 C.H.M.. 23537 Calabasas Road, Calabasas, CA 91302. August 6, 1962. Open 1 to 4 Wed., Sat. and Sun. 818-712-0734. Director: Mr. Glenn Hiatt.

The Cooper-Kramer Store (Hunter's Inn). Corner Calabasas Road and El Canon, Calabasas. Built around the turn of the century near Brent's Junction. Continued as the Cooper-Kramer Store well into the 1960s. Today home to a variety of shops, restaurants.

Sagebrush Cantina, 1900. 23527 Calabasas Road, Calabasas, CA 91302. 818-888-6062. Housed a variety of businesses. Once a butcher shop, flower shop, Miller's boat shop, a bakery, antique shops, restaurants. The Cantina began in one small store and has expanded now to take over the entire building. Where the parking lot for the Cantina now stands, the Calabasas Town Hall stood until it burned.

The Old School House, 1924–48. Today *Pelican's Retreat Restaurant.* 24454 Calabasas Road, Calabasas, CA 91302. 818-710-1550.

Sepulveda Adobe, 1863. Corner of Las Virgenes Road and Mulholland Highway, Calabasas. Pedro and Soledad Sepulveda built this with the help of Chumash Indians. Also site nearby of large Chumash Indian Village. Plans in the making to turn this into *White Oak Farm.* History of farming would be historically displayed for 100 years. Area is still pristine, untouched. Dr. Juliana Gensley worked for years to get this designated as an historic landmark. As of 1988, the adobe caught the attention

of Santa Monica Mountains district superintendent Maurice Getty. Plans are now in the works to restore the adobe. Good news!

King Camp Gillette Ranch, 1920s. Las Virgenes Road and Mulholland Highway. Southeast corner. (26800 W. Mulholland Highway), Calabasas. Built for Gillette, the razor blade inventor, later Clarence Brown, motion picture director owned it, 1932. Became Seminary of the Claretian Order, then the Thomas Aquinas College, then the Church Universal. Now, it has been purchased by Soka University. 818-880-6400.

The Plummer Home, 1878. Currently located on the Leonis Adobe Site. Plummer home does not belong to Calabasas History. Only in Southern California, where land cost is more important than our history, do historic homes "move around." Plummer home originally located in Hollywood. (See Hollywood).

Historic Homes: There are several older Craftsmen homes that once dotted Calabasas Road. Due to the recent construction of Leonis Plaza, many of these have disappeared.

Home of Theresa Thilmony, 1921. Formerly the old Charles Daic Home. 23538 Calabasas Road, Calabasas.

Daic Family home, garage, 1921. 23528 Calabasas Road. Calabasas. Daic family homesteaded in the area in 1888. Garage active from 1921–45. Became known later as Calabasas Junction. This was built on the site of the original Leonis Barn which burned in 1912. West of this was Daic's Electric appliance shop. Now known as Gaetano's Restaurant. 23536 Calabasas Raod. 818-716-6100.

Joseph Daic Family, 1921–1950. 23540 Calabasas Road, Calabasas.

Frank Farmer Home, 1937. 4803 El Canon, Calabasas.

Peter Coig Home, 1922. 23548 Calabasas Road, Calabasas.

Ranch Home, Mr. Whitaker, 1940. 23556 Calabasas Road, Calabasas. This housed various small businesses,

Calabasas Town Center, circa 1972. From an original pen and ink sketch by Michael Tooke. Used with permission of the artist. Courtesy Calabasas Historical Society.

including a popular restaurant operated between 1947 and 1952 by Russell and Eleanor Eckberg before they opened "Eckberg's" with its bells in Woodland Hills. Later building headquartered Las Virgenes Enterprise Newspaper.

Lot West of 23556 Calabasas Road. Vacant lot since 1920s. Once site of blacksmith shop belonging to son of Espiritu Leonis. Joseph Daic bought property in 1915 and built a garage which he managed until the Daic Brothers built the Calabasas Garage in 1921 at 23528 Calabasas Road.

West of vacant lot was *Dan Poyer Home* and Garage at 23564 Calabasas Road, 1927. Calabasas.

Gypsy Wagon. Used to be a regular feature in the Pumpkin Festival held in the 1960s. No one is sure where it came from, but many believe it was once part of the Warner Bros. Movie Set. Leonis Plaza, Calabasas.

Home of Jim & Winn Hope. 2755 Las Virgenes Road, Calabasas. A large barn and farm house, long a beautiful site to see from the road. Jim Hope is Bob Hope's brother. Originally the Collier Home.

Historic Parks: *Malibu Creek State Park.* Craigs Country Club, Calabasas. See Santa Monica Mountains.

Calabasas Creek Park. Corner Mulholland Drive and Calabasas Road, North. A rare glimpse at the natural tangle of native plants which once comprised the entire San Fernando Valley. Valley White Oak, Coastal Live Oak, the Elderberry, Willows, Cactus. Fifty years ago this also was the site of Hutchinson's Nursery.

Park Moderne, 1929. Ventura Freeway to Valley Circle Offramp, southeast on Mulholland to Valmar, south on Valmar to Bluebird in Calabasas. Laid out in 1929 by William Lingenbrink, a believer in modern architecture. Both R.M. Schindler and Jock Peters designed buildings for the community. With the depression, the project faltered.

Other: *The Motion Picture Home.* 1942. 23388 Mulholland Highway, Woodland Hills. 818-347-1591. Technically, located in Woodland Hills, but very much a feature and landmark of Calabasas. Begun as an idea of Gene Hersholt, architect William Pereira.

Charles Mureau Recreation Room. Victorian Design. Next to his 40-year-old home near Ventura Freeway at the overpass of Mureau Road, named for his family.

Saddle Peak Lodge, 1940s. 419 Cold Canyon Rd., Calabasas, CA 91302. 818-340-6029.

Businesses: *The Quilt Emporium,* 4835 El Canon Avenue, Calabasas, CA 91302. 818-704-8238. Located in one of the oldest homes in Calabasas.

Porter Blanchard Silversmiths, since 1788. Established in the San Fernando Valley since 1921. 23951 Craftsman Road. Calabasas, CA 91302. 818-347-1702.

New: *Leonis Plaza.* A new shopping center opposite the Leonis Adobe, designed in the Monterey Style of architecture, in keeping with the adobe.

Books: Laura Gaye, *The Last of the Old West:* A book of sketches about the Calabasas area. 1965.

Catherine Mulholland, *Calabasas Girls: An Intimate History, 1885–1912.* Published 1976.

Kay Beachy Room, Pierce College Library. Kay saved the Leonis Adobe, in addition to many other landmarks in the San Fernando Valley. The Calabasas Historical Society began this excellent small library devoted to information on the Valley. Pierce College Campus. 6201 Winnetka Avenue, Woodland Hills. 818-347-5017. Open by special permission only.

Historians: Calabasas is blessed with some of the most outstanding women who have compiled, organized the area's history. Among these are: *Dr. Juliana Gensley,* 24466 Mulholland Highway, Calabasas, CA 91302. 818-347-3617.

Ruth Loring, 4133 Meadow Lark Drive, Calabasas, CA 91302.

CANOGA PARK

History: Name applied to the station when Southern Pacific branch from Burbank was built in the 1890s. Park was added when the community was developed. Probably named after Canoga, New York which was taken from the name of an Indian Village called *Ganogeh,* meaning "place of the hot-hole." Some think the name Canoga came from the Spanish word for canoe—la canoa. Between 1911 and 1931 the area was called Owensmouth for its proximity to the mouth of the Owens River Valley aqueduct. On March 1, 1931, *Mary Orcutt* succeeded in having the name changed to Canoga Park.

Owensmouth almost became a college town in 1925. It was considered for a University of California campus by the Board of Regents. Westwood won out. Read *The Owensmouth Baby: The Making of a San Fernando Valley Town* by Catherine Mulholland (Santa Susana Press, 1987) for more information.

Historical Society: None. Area falls under the *San Fernando Valley Historical Society.* See Mission Hills. 10940 Sepulveda Blvd., Mission Hills, CA 91345. 818-365-7810.

Indian Sites: *Huwam,* a Valley Chumash village site existed in the low hills of Canoga Park for perhaps as long as 1,500 years. Work was begun in 1970s by archeologists from State University at Northridge. The team uncovered the ancient Indian village site along Bell Creek. Also found was the only cave painting or pictograph to have been discovered in the Valley.

Historic Landmarks: *The Workman House.* #9 C.H.M. *The Shadow Ranch House,* 1869-72. 22633 Vanowen, Canoga Park, CA 91307. 818-703-9126. Once this ranch covered over 60,000 acres. Owned by Isaac Lankershim and I.N. Van Nuys, who used it in conjunc-

junction with wheat farming. Albert Workman obtained 13,000 acres of land and built this ranch. Renamed Shadow Ranch in 1932. Consists of 9 acres. Open to public.

W.W. Orcutt Ranch Home (Rancho Sombra del Roble), 1920. #31 C.H.M. 23555 Justice, Canoga Park, CA 91304. 818-883-6641. Originally 200 acres. Today 24 acres. Native Oaks over 700 years old. Open to the public.

Landmarks: *Canoga Mission Gallery.* 1934–36. #135 C.H.M. 23130 Sherman Way. Canoga Park, CA 91307. 818-883-1085. Once part of the Francis Lederer horse stable. It has now been converted to a cultural arts center. The Gallery is constructed of stones quarried form the nearby hills.

Casa de Lederer, 1934. #204 C.H.M. 23134 Sherman Way, Canoga Park. Once popular movie idol, Francis Lederer purchased 250 acres of land in Canoga Park. Today, only his home that sits high above a knoll close to the Mission Gallery is left of the original property. Home has been declared an historic monument. The Lederers are still active in community affairs.

Large Knoll on corner of Saticoy and Woodlake supports one of the oldest homes still extant in area, circa 1915.

Knapp Family Home, 1920 or the *Owensmouth Castle,* 7511 Owensmouth Avenue, Canoga Park. Frank Knapp came to Owensmouth in the 1920s. Built this home out of limestone. Private residence.

Chapel in the Canyons, 1957. 9012 Topanga Canyon Blvd., Canoga Park. Part of this orginally was wing of the old Lankershim home which was located in Universal City.

Old Canoga Park Fire Station No. 72 (Canoga Park Historical Museum), 1933. (Note: Women's Club under leadership of Mrs. Beth Shirley now has a permanent exhibit on old Canoga Park.) 818-347-7911.

Platt Building, 19725 Sherman Way, Canoga Park, CA 91306. 818-700-1880. Spectacular Victorian Office Complex.

Historic Sites: *Brant Rancho,* 1909. 5545 Canoga Avenue, Canoga Park. Absolutely beautiful rancho and Hacienda surrounded by Lombardy poplars. Mr. Brant was the founder of the Title Insurance & Trust. The Brants farmed over 10,000 acres from Calabasas to what is now Reseda Blvd. The powers that be not only tore it down, but destroyed the beautiful row of trees loved by everyone.

Stone Arches, Remmet to Alabama Avenue on Sherman Way, Canoga Park. The first families in Owensmouth needed shops so the local merchants responded by building a shopping center. Beautiful stone arches remained and were renovated in 1950s. Then burned and torn down when street was widened.

Other: Many motion pictures stars settled in the Valley or had ranches here. Among them were Stan Laurel, whose home was called *Fort Laurel.* It is now a school.

Bob Burns Ranch, Sherman Way, Canoga Park. Once a 200 acre ranch for radio comedian. Now the First Baptist Church of Canoga Park.

Others who lived in the area were Spencer Tracy, silent screen actress Irene Rich, director William Dieterle and comedians Joe E. Brown and Lou Costello. Lou Costello's ranch house apparently still stands in the *Rocketdyne Park,* although the home has undergone extensive remodeling. Movie producer Rowland V. Lee purchased 66 acres and a small spring-fed lake. Mr. Lee's ranch house was relocated to a Hidden Lake housing development.

Homes: *Private Residence,* 6550 Shoup and 6964 Shoup. Both outstanding examples of early craftsman homes, around 1915.

Private residence: 8431 Pinelake, 1939 (West Hills). Built by Craig Movie Company.

Businesses: *Hull Bros. Lumber Co.,* 1922. 21350 Sherman Way, Canoga Park. 818-347-7881.

Plusko's, since 1957. 21013 Sherman Way, Canoga Park. 818-348-2880.

CARSON-COMPTON

History, Carson: Carson lies in the heart of the original Rancho San Pedro, one of the earliest Spanish land grants in California. (1784). Its owners, the Dominguez family, were able to maintain control of the rancho well into the 20th century, unusual for Spanish land grants. The Carson involvement began in 1857 when George Henry Carson married one of Don Manuel Dominguez's daughters. Carson assumed management of the

Rancho after the death of his father-in-law. He developed much of the south bay area of Los Angeles County, including the land encompassng the City of Carson. Carson was incorporated in 1967.

Historic Landmarks: *Dominguez Adobe,* 1827. 18127 S. Alameda Street, Compton, CA 90220. 213-631-5981; 213-636-6030.

The *Dominguez Adobe,* site of the former *Carson Home.* Home of the *Dominguez Memorial Seminary,* site of the *Domiguez Air meet* of 1910. Museum houses artifacts from that air race, as well as artifacts of the DelAmo, Carson and Watson families. Adobe is open for guided tours.

Dominguez Air Meet Site, 1910. 1000 East Victoria Street, Carson, CA 90747. 213-515-3300. Site of the actual air race is on the California State Campus, Dominguez Hills. Plaque.

Heritage House, 1869. City Hall Park, Willowbrook Avenue, Compton. Home was moved in 1959 to the City Hall Park.

Other Landmarks: *Angeles Abbey.* Modeled after the Taj Mahal of India. 1515 E. Compton Blvd., Compton. 213-636-6950.

The Eagle Tree, 2,000 years old. Corner Poppy and Short Streets, Compton. One of the oldest landmarks in state. Marked northern boundary of Rancho San Pedro. Eagles once nested in its branches.

Businesses: *Watson Land Co.,* since 1900. 22100 S. Wilmington Avenue, Carson.

Rodgers and McDonald Graphics, since 1926. 1141 Sandhill Avenue, Carson, CA 90749. 213-604-1012.

Other: *The Goodyear Airship.* Located along San Diego Freeway, Carson. 192 foot airship has been based in Carson since 1969.

History, Compton: Land purchased by the 49ers was originally part of the famous *Rancho San Pedro,* a 75,000 acre tract granted to Don Juan Jose Dominguez in 1784 by King Carlos III of Spain. Two enterprising Yankees,

Francis Temple and Fielding Gibson purchased a 4,600 acre section of the Rancho in 1865 for $.36 an acre. They subdivided it and sold 40 and 80 acre parcels to gold miners for $5 an acre.

In 1867 a ten-family caravan rolled into Compton with belongings piled high in covered wagons. By the end of 1868 the little village of Compton was sufficiently well established to allow the settlers to devote some time and energy to civic planning. One of the first buildings erected was a schoolhouse, which also served as a church. Although the town was named Gibsonville, it soon came to be known as *Comptonville,* named after Griffith Dickenson Compton, leader of the original scouting party. The name was later shortened to Compton in 1869.

Rancho San Pedro in Dominguez Hills. Courtesy Father Patrick, Dominiguez Adobe.

Building of the Los Angeles-San Pedro Railroad in 1869 established the community as a center of activity for the farming area south of Los Angeles. In 1876 the Southern Pacific Company bought the railroad and has retained the original franchise ever since. At the turn of the century, development of the San Pedro Harbor brought increased trade and transportation facilities which aided the growth of Compton. With the discovery of oil in the twenties, Compton, by the 1930s, became the second fastest growing city in the U.S. for its size.

Historical Committee: *Fine Arts and Historical Committee* of Carson. Formed in 1980s to try to maintain and preserve the history and fine arts of the area. 701 E. Carson Street, Carson.

Historians: *Mr. Paul Schneider,* 426 W. Carson Street, Suite 2, Carson, CA 90705. Mr. Schneider is the Executive Vice-President of the Chamber of Commerce. 213-320-0551.

Mr. Art Reeves. Dominguez Water Company, 21718 S. Alameda Street, Carson. 213-834-2625.

School: *Carson Street School,* since 1920. 161 E. Carson, Carson.

Sites: *Lone Pine Inn Restaurant,* 1900s. 110 W. Sepulveda Blvd., Carson. Very famous spot known by all the old-timers. Razed.

Businesses: *Dominguez Water Co.,* since 1911. 21718 S. Alameda Street, Carson.

Shell Oil Company, since 1922. P.O. Box 6249, Carson. 213-816-2000.

Atlantic Richfield, since 1922. (ARCO the refinery) 1801 E. Sepulveda, Carson. 213-548-8000.

CATALINA

History: Catalina is crammed with history; and like a tiny Madagascar that has been isolated from the mainland, much of its specialness, thank goodness, has been preserved.

After Spain and Mexico, the first American to own Catalina was Thomas Robbins. Even this acquisition was done with flare. Pio Pico was on his way to Mexico and as the Americans were coming, Robbins asked him to grant the small island to him. By the light of a candle on a piece of old butcher paper Pico did just that. Surprisingly that piece of paper was legally held up in a court of law. After Robbins, many owners came and went. Among them was George Shatto. He tried in 1887 to attract the new arrivals coming into Los Angeles to the lovely island off the coast. His sister-in-law had read Tennyson's Idylls of the King and liked the name Avalon in the poem, hence the name chosen for Catalina's one and only town. After Shatto, the Banning Brothers came, forming the Santa Catalina Island Company in 1892. They, too, had great hopes to build the island into a resort community. However a disastrous fire in 1915 altered their plans. In 1919, William Wrigley, Jr. of Chicago pur-

chased the island and it has been under the influence of the Wrigley family to some degree ever since.

Historical Society: *Catalina Island Museum Society, Inc.,* P.O. Box 366, Avalon, CA 90704. Located in the Casino Building. 213-510-2414.

Historical Landmarks: *The Casino,* 1927–29. P.O. Box 366, Avalon, CA 90704. Built by architects Weber and Spaulding, and engineer David M. Renton.

Mt. Ada–Wrigley's Summer Home, 1921. 213-510-2030. Now a bed and breakfast inn. Owned by Susie Griffin and Marlene McAdam, innkeepers.

Zane Grey Pueblo, 1924. 199 Chimes Tower Road, Avalon, CA 90704. 213-510-0966. Now a hotel.

William Wrigley Memorial and Botanical Gardens, 1924. At the head of Avalon Canyon. Open to the public. 213-510-2288.

Catalina Deagan Chimes, 1925. A gift to the City of Avalon in 1925 from Mrs. William Wrigley, Jr. Located in Chimes Tower.

Hollyhill House, 1890. On hill above Avalon Bay. Built by Peter Gano. Private residence but tours can be arranged through the museum.

Philip Wrigley's Home and *Ranch,*

Courtesy Mt. Ada Inn

1925. Overlooks Avalon Bay from the north. El Rancho Escondido (Rancho La Escondido). 1500 acre ranch home of Philip Wrigley, located near the Airport.

The Tuna Club, 1898. Cresent Avenue, Avalon. 213-510-0079.

Yacht Club, 1924. 30 Casino Avenue, Avalon. 213-510-0022.

Atwater Hotel, 1920. 125 Sumner, Avalon. 213-599-1010

Hermosa Hotel, 1896. 131 Metropole Avenue, Avalon. 213-510-0017.

Streets: *Avenida Le Crescenta,* 1920s. Wonderful curving brick and tile wall in the shape and appearance of a sea monster. (Look closely.) Look for its head and tail. Avalon Bay.

Churches: *Congregational Church,* 1888. Metropole and Beacon Street, Avalon. 213-510-1889.

Homes: *Wolfe House,* 1928. R.M. Schindler design. 124 Chimes Tower Road, Avalon.

Murdock House, 1929. 102 Maiden Lane, Avalon.

A House: or a Ship? 1910. In 1910 a real ship was brought to shore and over the years redecorated to look like a home. Downtown Avalon.

Schools: *First School.* Began classes in 1891 in the Congregational Church. Built school of two rooms 1901. Whittley Avenue, Avalon.

Post Office: *United States Post Office,* 1889. 228 Metropole Avenue, Avalon. 213-510-0281.

Library: *Catalina Library,* 1904. 215 Sumner Avenue, Avalon. 213-510-1050.

Airport: *Airport in the Sky,* 1946. First passenger service, sea, 1919. Buffalo Springs, Catalina. 213-510-0143.

Other Landmarks: *Samuel Prentiss Memorial.* First white man on Catalina, arriving 1824, died 1854. Overlooks Emerald Bay.

Cherry Valley. First gold in California discovered here, 1830. Capt. Yout.

Two Harbors: *Civil War Barracks,* 1863. Also windmill. Two Harbors. Now occupied by Isthmus Yacht Club.

Banning's Lodge, 1909. Beautiful lodge. Hacienda built by Banning family. Being renovated. Two Harbors.

Eagle's Nest, 1860s. Stagecoach stopped here, changed horses. Overnight guests' quarters here also. Goathunting headquarters. Stop over for people coming from Two Harbors to Avalon.

Motion Picture Set. From 1920s to present time. Two Harbors used to film dozens of motion picture and television films. The 1935 *Mutiny on the Bounty* was filmed in part here.

Indian Sites: Catalina is said to contain the greatest single number of Indian sites anywhere in California. Hundreds have been designated. Few have been extensively excavated.

Little Harbor. Site of an ancient Indian Village and in 1894 Dr. O.T.

Fellows built an Inn here as a stagecoach stop for passengers. Area is used today for camping.

White's Landing. Former Indian Village. Now a camp.

Events: World's *first wireless telegraph station* built here in 1902. The Pacific Wireless Telegraph. Razed 1972.

First flight in aviation history, by Glenn C. Martin, May 10, 1912. From Newport on the mainland to Avalon Bay.

First glass bottom boat, 1896. Charles Feige designed.

Trans Channel Races, held Jan. 1927. Won by 17 year-old Canadian man. In 1952 Florence Chadwick crossed channel. But most remarkable feat was Greta Anderson who in 1958 swam both to and from the mainland in 26 hours. Never attempted again.

In 1920 the Goodyear Company's *"Pony" blimp* began regular air service from its landing pad on South Main Street, Los Angeles to Avalon.

Syd Chaplin, brother of Charlie Chaplin began first regularly scheduled airline in California in 1919. It flew six round trips a day between Wilmington and Avalon.

Bed and Breakfast: *Mt. Ada-Wrigley's Summer Home.* See Historical Landmarks. 213-510-2030.

Gull House. 344 Whittley, Avalon, CA 90704. 213-510-2547.

Craftspeople: *Will Richards,* sculptor-artist. Marine Terrestrial Wildlife, P.O. Box 494, Avalon, CA 90704. Home 213-510-0805. Work 213-510-1714.

Museum: *The Casino.* See Historical Landmarks, and Historical Society. 213-510-2414. Mrs. Pat Moore, Historian.

Books: *The Catalina Story,* published by the Catalina Island Museum Society, Inc. Alma Overhold, 1962.

——— CHATSWORTH ———

History: Augusta Wagman came to the area and homesteaded in 1882. She married Karl Iverson. The area north and west of today's Chatsworth became Iverson Ranch in 1888. In 1911 Cecil B. De Mille shot scenes for the Squaw Man, first major motion picture shot in U.S. Over 2,000 films made there, not to mention television. Name came from Spencer Compton, VIII, Duke of Devonshire, after his English estate of Chatsworth.

Early Residents: Ann W. Johnson, homesteaded in area around 1870 and was one of the first English-speaking settlers to live in the area.

Chatsworth Historical Society: *Chatsworth Historical Society,* P.O. Box 102, Chatsworth, CA 91311. President, Lila Schepler. 818-341-3447.

Historic Landmarks: *Stoney Point,* #132 C.H.M. Site of an ancient Indian Village and also used by infamous bandit Tiburcio Vasquez as a hideout in the 1870s. East side of Topanga Canyon Blvd., Chatsworth.

Old Stagecoach Trail, #92 C.H.M. South of Chatsworth Park, north of Oakwood Memorial Park. West end of Devonshire Street, Chatsworth. From 1860 to 1905 stagecoach road provided a link between Los Angeles and San Francisco. Site also marks ancient Indian Villages.

76 Mature Olive Trees. Line both sides of Lassen Street. #49 C.H.M. Between Topanga Canyon Blvd. and Farralone Avenue, Chatsworth. Trees planted in the late 19th century by N.A. Gray family. Pioneer family came from Pennsylvania and purchased several hundred acres in Chatsworth.

Palmer Residence, 1913. #133 C.H.M. West end of Devonshire Street, Chatsworth. James D. Hill homesteaded property in Chatsworth in 1886, building this home, the second in the area, in 1913.

Chatsworth Lake, Lake Manor Drive, Chatsworth.

Chatsworth Community Church, 1903. 22601 Lassen Street, Chatsworth. #14 C.H.M. Formerly located at 10051 Topanga Canyon Blvd. Second oldest Protestant church in the valley. Moved to Oakwood Memorial Park in 1965. 818-341-0344.

Others: *Boy's Town of the West.* Rancho San Antonio. Founded 1933. 21000 Plummer, Chatsworth, CA 91311. 818-882-6400.

Historic Parks: *Santa Susana Mountain Park.* North of Oakwood Memorial Park, Chatsworth. Docent-led hikes which feature portions of the old Stagecoach trail. Call 818-882-4688.

Homes: Many of the present homes are built on the site of the old *Roy Rogers and Dale Evans* 110 acre ranch, now known as Indian Springs. 1917 home. 1121 Iverson Road, Chatsworth.

Victorian Homes. You might be surprised if you took a drive along Baden Street in Chatsworth. No, these are not old Victorians. They are new! What is unusual is that there are so many of them and their number is growing. Apparently Chatsworth has become a kind of new Heritage Square West. Remember: private residences! 22639 Ballinger, Chatsworth; 9525 Oakridge Place, Chatsworth; 9507 Baden, Chatsworth; 9505 Baden, Chatsworth; 9500 Baden, Chatsworth.

Historic Ranches: *Iverson Ranch,* dates from 1920s. It is not only the oldest ranch in the valley, but the owner, Robert Sherman, says it is also the oldest movie studio in the world! Augusta Wagman first purchased the 160 acre homestead in 1882. Augusta married Karl Iverson in 1888 and five children were born. In 1912 Hollywood came to the ranch and through the 1950s hundreds of movies were filmed here. The Iversons died in 1948. Young Joe Iverson continued the tradition with the making of dozens of T.V.

episodes. Today, Mr. Robert Sherman, great-great-great-grandson of Augusta Wagman plans to establish a museum on the property. Write to Mr. Robert Sherman, P.O. Box 3096, Chatsworth, CA 91313-3016 for more information. 818-700-9049.

Books: Sherman, Robert. *Quiet on the Set: The History of the Iverson Movie Location Ranch,* 1984.

Watson, Virginia, *Child's History of Chatsworth.* 818-341-3053.

Artists: *Nostalgic Graphics.* Artist Stan Cline, 9601 Owensmouth Avenue, Chatsworth, CA 91311. 818-998-1122. Old scenes of Los Angeles.

Courtesy Nostalgia Productions

Historians: *Iolene Cleveland,* 818-341-1529; *Virginia Watson,* 818-341-3053.

Historic Sites: *Chatsworth Reservoir Kiln Site.* #141 C.H.M. Southeast from intersection of Woolsey Canyon Road and Valley Circle Blvd. Here mission tiles were made for the San Fernando Valley Mission.

CHINATOWN

History: In 1850 two Chinese male house servants Ah Fou and Ah Luce were among Los Angeles' population of 1610. With the depletion of the gold fields, the completion of the transcontinental railroad, and growing hostility, the Chinese began to drift into Los Angeles. By 1870 their population was around 200. Most of these men were restricted to rundown areas southeast of the Plaza, hence creating the first "Chinatown."

In 1871 the worst incident occurred between the Chinese and the white population. Known thereafter as the *Chinese Massacre,* 19 innocent Chinese men and boys were killed. It was the most violent racial conflict until the Watts Riot in 1965. A white deputy was accidentally shot and killed during a dispute between two tong leaders. For the next five hours a mob surged through Chinatown stabbing, lynching, and shooting. Robert W. Widney, one of the founders of the University of Southern California, was among a number of citizens who rescued the Chinese. Armed with a large Colt revolver, he held back attackers and escorted many Chinese to safety. Judge Wilson Hugh Gray hid Chinese in the cellar of his house at Broadway and Seventh. For years afterward, on the Chinese New Year, he found anonymous presents at his door. The Chinese Massacre was the first Los Angeles event to make national headlines since the city's capture in 1846–47.

The Chinese workers performed most of the early Southern California agricultural labor, making possible the rapid expansion of the citrus industry. Cheap labor allowed investors to afford the heavy capital outlay necessary to establish a citrus grove, since it took seven years of cultivation to produce the first profitable crop. As late as 1920 over half of the 46,000 Chinese workers in the United States were employed by laundries or restaurants. Today, one out of every six Chinese in the United States works in or owns a restaurant.

In 1882 and 1892 the federal government passed the Chinese Exclusion Acts, barring Chinese immigration for ten years. In 1902 the act was made permanent. It was not repealed until 1943.

Today, one-fifth of the nation's 600,000 Chinese live in Los Angeles County. The percentage of Chinese men with college degrees is higher than any other ethnic group and twice as high as the general population's.

Historical Society: *Chinese Historical Society of Southern California,* 1648 Redcliff Street, Los Angeles, CA 90026. 213-828-6911.

Other: *Chinese Cultural Center,* 970 N. Broadway, L.A. 213-489-3827.

Chinese Chamber of Commerce, 213-617-0396.

Historical Landmarks: *Chinatown,* North Broadway and Hill Street, Los Angeles. In the mid 1930s all of Old Chinatown east of Alameda Street was torn down to make way for Union Station. New Chinatown features over 40 restaurants, dozens of shops, and other attractions. There is also a colorful celebration of the Chinese New Year.

Garnier Building, 1890. Corner Los Angeles Street and Arcadia Street, Los Angeles. Two-story building built by Philippe Garnier in 1890 specifically for Chinese commercial use. Until vacated in 1950, it was a busy center of the Chinese. Today it is part of the El Pueblo State Historic Park.

New Chinatown, 1938, Central Plaza, Gin Ling Way, Los Angeles. Plaque placed by Y.C. Hong in tribute to his Mother. Hong was the first Chinese-American lawyer in Los Angeles admitted to the bar. Facing gate is statue of Dr. Sun Yet Sen, founder of Republic of China. He led overthrow of Manchu dynasty in 1916.

Courtesy author.

New Chinatown opened in 1938. First planned urban Chinatown in the United States.

West Gate, Hill Street, Los Angeles. Bronze tablet commemorating part played by Chinese in California history. Placed by Governor Frank Merriam.

Historic Restaurants: *Yee Mee Loo,* 690 N. Spring Street, Los Angeles. Popular restaurant in the '30s.

Golden Palace Restaurant, 913 N. Broadway, Los Angeles. Mural reported to be one of the largest of its kind outside of China.

General Lee's, 1878–1986. 475 Gin Ling Way, Los Angeles. One of the earliest Chinese restaurants in Los Angeles continuously operated by the same family. Just closed in 1986.

Historic Stores: *Wing On Tong,* 1910. 701 N. Spring Street, Los Angeles. Chinese herb store, whose origin dates back 90 years to old Chinatown.

See Company, 1881. 507 Chung King Court, Los Angeles. One of oldest family owned Asian Art stores in Los Angeles. First opened in San Francisco in 1871, moved to Los Angeles in 1881. Still run by the Fong family.

Colorful Character: Homer Lea. Came to California in 1890; attended Occidental and Stanford University. Took an active part in trying to free China from despotism of Manchurian Dynasty. Went to China in 1900; returned as general in Chinese Army. Joined Dr. Sun Yat Sen. Wrote *The Valor of Ignorance.* Died in Ocean Park, CA 1912.

Pioneer Merchant: Chun Chick. Arrived in Los Angeles 1861.

Historic Newspapers: *New Kwong Tai Press,* 940 Chung King Road, Los Angeles. One of oldest Chinese newspapers in Los Angeles.

Historic Banks: *Cathay Bank,* 777 North Broadway, Los Angeles. First Chinese American owned bank built in Chinatown.

Historic Churches: *Chinese United Methodist Church,* 1887. 825 North Hill Street, Los Angeles. Organized first in Old China Town in 1887. Moved to its present location in 1947.

Historic School: *Castlelar School,* 1882. 840 Yale Avenue, Los Angeles. Second oldest continuously operating elementary school in Los Angeles Unified School District. First school in district with Trilingual instruction: English, Spanish and Chinese.

Historic Sites: *China City Site,* Ord Street Parking lot, Los Angeles. North Gate of China City located in present day parking lot. One can still see remains of Shanghai street shop fronts. During its heyday in 1940s China City had narrow twisting streets with almost 50 colorful stores. The House of Wong from the MGM film, "The Good Earth" was on display. China City lasted until a fire in 1949.

Sonora Town, 600 block of North Spring Street, Los Angeles. Called Sonoratown after the miners and families from the state of Sonora, Mexico who came to California. Chinese located here until late 1930s.

COMMERCE

History: The city of Commerce stands on what was once Indian land which later became part of the San Gabriel Mission in 1771. Don Antonio Lugo was granted approximately 29,500 acres between the Los Angeles City Limits (12th street) and what is now Lynwood. When one of Lugo's daughters died, he sold her acreage to Abel Stearns for $.16 cents an acre. Stearns acquired more land from other Lugo heirs until he owned the 6,000 Rancho Laguna which included all of present day Commerce. Fifty years later the Rancho Laguna was owned by Stearns' wife, Arcadia Bandini de Baker. It was then sold to a Whittier woman and still later 2,000 acres became Walter Vail's. The rest of the land stayed in the Bandini family until the 1920s. Gradually, the B.F. Goodrich plant, the UniRoyal Rubber Plant, Chrysler and other industrial giants built in the area. In the 1960s the city of Commerce was incorporated as the 67th city of Los Angeles County.

Historians: *Mrs. Eva Long,* 213-262-5063. Is a senior-citizen chairman in community. Councilman Arturo Markez was also very helpful. City Hall 213-722-4805.

Historic Landmarks: *Uniroyal Tire Company,* 1930. 5635 Telegraph Road, Commerce. Stiles O. Clements of Morgan, Wall & Clements, architects. The 35 acre landmark has been vacant since 1978 and has been owned by the city since 1983. It is famous for its 1700 foot Assyrian wall and facade, a replica of a palace for King Sargon II.

Plans for its future will include construction of a 10-story, 193 room Wyndham Garden Hotel, plus mixed-use development known as *The Citadel.* Restoration of the beautiful facade will be carried out as well!!

Union-Pacific Train Station, 1920s. Ferguson and Atlantic, Commerce.

Historic Sites: *B.F. Goodrich Company,* 1920s. Olympic and Goodrich, Commerce. Still there, however, is a 100 year old Morton Bay Fig Tree, deeded to the city.

Chrysler Building, 1933. Eastern and Slauson, Commerce.

Old Golden Gate Theatre, Corner Atlantic and Whittier, Commerce.

Books: At the *Central Library,* 5655 Jilson, Commerce (213-722-6660) there is a vertical file on the History of Commerce. The industrial counsel puts out an annual publication-report on the city, as well. Their telephone number is 213-723-9088.

CUDAHY

History: Part of the Rancho San Antonio granted in 1810 to Antonio Maria Lugo. In 1855 the Rancho was partioned and sold. It underwent many divisions, then in 1893 the Nadeau Ranch of 2,777 acres was sold to Michael Cudahy for $105 an acre. Bounded by Florence Avenue on the north, Santa Fe on the west and Manchester on the south.

Michael Cudahy was a merchant and manufacturer born in Ireland in 1841. Came to America in 1849. In 1873 Phillip Armour offered him a partnership with the firm of Armour and Company in Chicago. Eventually Cudahy left the company, forming his own Cudahy Packing Company, one of the largest concerns of its kind in existence. Finally he settled in Los Angeles and subdivided community later known as Cudahy in 1908. Streets named after his five daughters.

Book: A small book written on the 25th anniversary of Cudahy's incorporation. *25th Anniversary 1960–1985 City of Cudahy,* 1985. Available at Cudahy City Hall, 5220 Santa Ana, Cudahy. 213-773-5143.

Historic Buildings: *Cudahy Public Library,* 1913. 5218 Santa Ana Street, Cudahy. 213-771-1345.

Businesses: *Robie's Hobby Center,* since 1946. 7613 Atlantic, Cudahy, CA 90201. 213-560-3313.

Graham's Auto Electric, since 1930. 8216 Atlantic, Cudahy. 213-560-2557.

Scott Gasket, since 1940s. 8220 Atlantic, Cudahy. 213-560-1794.

Cudahy Building Materials, since 1930s. 8333 Atlantic, Cudahy. 213-560-1650.

Turner's Castings, since 1940s. 8333 Wilcox, Cudahy. 213-773-2363.

———— CULVER CITY ————

History: It all started when Harry H. Culver, a real estate developer from Los Angeles stopped his automobile to view the ninety-three acres of barley fields around him. The year was 1913. The city's first commercial structure was the real estate office of the Harry H. Culver Company. The first motion picture studio moved into the area in 1915.

Historic Society: *Culver City Historical Society,* P.O. Box 3428, Culver City, CA 90230. Marti Diviak, president. 213-398-8165.

Historical Landmarks: *Ince's Studio,* 1919. (second studio) 9336 Washington Blvd., Culver City. Also Selznick, DeMille, Culver City Studios, R.K.O. Studios, United Artist, Desilu, Laird and now *The Culver Studios.*

Mary Crest Manor. Once a private residence, 1930. Now a retirement home. Culver Crest, Culver City.

Legion Building, 1925. First club house in Culver City. 3620 Hughes, Culver City.

Citizens Building, 1929. 9355 Culver Blvd., Culver City. Built by the Donovan family, a Culver City pioneer. Still owned by family.

Culver City City Hall, 1928. 9770 Culver Blvd., Culver City.

MGM, 1924. (Thomas Ince's first studio, begun in 1915). 10202 Washington Blvd., Culver City.

Historic Hotels: *Culver Hotel,* 1924. 9400 Culver Blvd., Culver City. Built by Harry Culver. Once owned by John Wayne and Red Skelton. Used by the dwarfs during filming of the Wizard of Oz. 1939. Hotel currently in danger of being demolished.

Historic Parks: *Veterans' Memorial Park,* 1930s. Culver Blvd. and Overland, Culver City.

Historian: *Julie Lugo Cerro,* past president Historical Society. Culver City. 213-838-0215.

Historical Columns: *MGM Columns,* 1916. 10202 Washington Blvd., Culver City. MGM, now Lorimar Productions at 3970 Overland.

Historic Theatres: *Culver Theatre,*

1920s. Washington Blvd., Culver City. (Soon to be renovated by Filmcorp.)

Historic Hospitals: *Hull Building,* 1925. 9543 Washington Blvd., Culver City. 213-204-5590. Culver City's first hospital building. Later the Bank of Orange County. (Dr. Foster Hull) Now vacant.

Historic Schools: *La Ballona School* (third building). Dates from 1890. 10915 Washington Blvd., Culver City. First school in Culver City.

Historic Churches: *St. Augustine Church* (third church). 3950 Jasmine Avenue, Culver City. Land donated by Figueroa family in 1883.

Historic Depots: *Ivy Sub Station Pacific Electric,* 1920s. (The Castle) #182 C.H.M. 9015 Venice Blvd., Culver City.

Historic Sites: *Lookout Point* for Gabrielino Indians. On hill overlooking creek. Culver Park, Culver City.

Camp Latham, Civil War Camp, 1860s. Overland Avenue, south of Ballona Creek. Northern Soldiers. (Where Senior Citizen Housing is now) Culver City.

Site of *Hal Roach Studios,* 1920s. Washington Blvd. at National Blvd., Culver City.

Site of the *Burning of Atlanta* for filming of *Gone With the Wind,* 1939. North side of La Ballona Creek on Lucerne between Ince Blvd. and Duquesne Avenue, Culver City.

Site of Barney Oldfield Speedway, 1920s. Originally a horse-racing track. South of Carlson Park, Culver City.

Site of *1932 Olympic Villages.* South on La Cienega on Rodeo. Outside of Culver City limits.

Site of *Fatty Arbuckle's Famous Restaurant: The Plantation,* 1920s. A nightclub built in 28 days across from La Ballona School on Washington Blvd., Culver City.

Site of the *Roller Drome,* 1930s. Washington Place and Tilden Avenue, Tellefson Park. Drome was torn down in the 1960s. Culver City.

Historic Restaurants: Joe Petrelli's *Airport Cafe,* since 1920. 5614 Sepulveda Blvd., Culver City. 213-398-9777.

Ship's, 1950s. Overland Avenue at Washington Blvd., Culver City. 213-839-2347.

Businesses: *Betts-Sine Lumber Co.,* since 1920s. 8070 Washington Blvd., Culver City. 213-870-4721

Sam Slatter Lumber, since 1930s. 5850 Washington Blvd., Culver City. 213-839-2447.

Paul Heinley Shutters, since 1940s. 3550 Hayden Avenue, Culver City. 213-870-4895.

Stellar Hardware, since 1923. 3833 Main Street, Culver City. 213-839-2321.

Famous Streets: *Main Street,* 1913. Culver City. Listed in Guinness Book of Records as the shortest main street in country.

Books: L.W. Pennington and William K. Baster, *A Past to Remember: The History of Culver City,* 1976.

DOWNEY

History: John Gately Downey was Governor of California when the Civil War began and played a prominent part in placing the state on the side of the Union. When his gubernatorial term in Sacramento ended, he returned to develop his 17,000 acre Rancho Santa Gertrudes along the banks of the San Gabriel River. In 1873 the Southern Pacific Railroad tapped this rich agricultural area by building a spur line toward Anaheim. It ran between two small settled areas on the ranch between Gallatin and College Settlements. Downey plotted a town on the rail line between the two communities in

October of 1873 and called it Downey City.

Historical Society: *Downey Historical Society.* Los Nietos Valley Pioneers (part of the Historical Society) 12540 Rieves Avenue, Downey, CA 90242. 213-862-2777 or 213-928-4006. Mr. Don Vincent, president.

Historian: *Joyce Lawrence,* 9627 Chaddar, Downey, CA 90242. 213-803-5851.

Museums: *Downey History Center Museum,* 12540 Rieves Avenue, Downey, CA 90242. 213-862-2777 or 213-928-4006. Open Wed., Thurs. 9–2, 3rd Sat. 10–3 and by appointment. Also, museum is currently restoring 1887 pioneer cottage moved from Firestone and Paramount.

Art Museum, Furman Park, 10419 Rieves Avenue, Downey. 213-862-0918.

Historic Landmarks: *13 Mile Post,* 1906. Marks road from old Los Angeles County Court House to San Diego.

Historic Homes: *Casa de Parley,* 1926. On the National Register of Historic Places. Designed by architect Roland Coate. Florence Avenue at Rieves. Private Residence.

James C. Rieves Home, 1911. On the National Register of Historic Places. Paramount Blvd. and Third Street. Private Residence.

Historic Restaurants: *McDonald's Drive Inn,* 1953. 10207 Lakewood Blvd., Downey. Oldest existing original McDonald's Golden Arches. (August 18, 1953)

Other: *Rockwell International,* since 1929. 12214 Lakewood Blvd., Downey. Apollo space shuttle designs originated here.

Historic Churches: *First Baptist Church of Downey,* 1876 (Knott's Berry Farm). 8348 East Third Street, Downey. 213-923-1261. First church built in 1876 was later sold to St. Marks Episcopal. Later they donated it to Knotts Berry Farm. It is known there as

The Chapel of the Reflection.

Historic Parks: *Downey Cemetery,* 1868. Corner Lakewood and Gardendale Street, Downey. 213-869-5227.

Historic Sites: Site of the original *County Fair* 1884–1889. Forerunner of the Los Angeles County Fair. Downey and Brookeshire Avenue and Third and Fifth Streets. Where the present City Hall is now.

Site of the *Poor Farm,* 1888. 7601 Imperial Highway, Downey. Now a world wide center of catastrophic diseases. The Rancho Los Amigos Medical Center.

Site of *Gallatin,* 1865. Settlement prior to the town of Downey. Florence Avenue and Tweedy Lane, Downey.

Los Nietos Collegiate Institute, 1869. Paramount Blvd. and Alameda Street, Downey. One of the first Protestant colleges in 1869 when the area was called College Settlement.

Site of *Southern Pacific Depot,* 1874. Nance and La Reina, Downey. First depot built 1874. Torn down in 1968.

Businesses: *Sach's and Sons,* since 1926. 9515 Lakewood Blvd., Downey, CA 90241. Mrs. Sach's recently sold business, and it is today Downey Lincoln Mercury, 213-861-0721.

E. Waller's Appliances, since 1950s. (Furniture) 1112 S. Brookshire, Downey, CA 90241. 213-862-2201.

Kid Coy Barber Shop, since 1922. 10919 South Downey Avenue, Downey CA. 90241. 213-862-4884.

Craftspeople: *Mr. Larry Winans.* (Carpentry) P.O. Box 464, Downey, CA 90241. 213-560-3098. Larry is one of the finest men working in restoration in Los Angeles today.

Book: *The History of Downey,* by Charles Russell Quinn. Published by Elena Quinn, 1973.

Chamber of Commerce: *Downey Chamber of Commerce,* 11131 Brookshire, Downey, CA 90241. 213-923-2191.

─── DUARTE ───

History: The history of the city dates back to 1841 when Don Andres Duarte petitioned Governor Juan Alvarado for a grant of 6,000 acres of fertile land where Duarte now stands.

By 1880 *Rancho Azusa de Duarte* had experienced a shift from a thriving center for cattle, horses and sheep to a solid belt of citrus groves and avocado trees.

With the population boom that hit Southern California following World War II the groves of citrus were replaced by homes and businesses. Duarte was incorporated in 1957.

Historical Society: *Duarte Historical Society.* Monte Montgomery, president. 818-357-9419.

Historical Landmarks: *City of Hope,* 1500 East Duarte Road, Duarte, CA. 818-359-8111 (Hospital) Began in 1913 with two tents, five acres of land and a $130 subscribed by Jewish Merchants who wanted to stop the deaths in the garment industry. Oldest building still remaining is Maurice Hillquit Building.

Dr. Whalen and *Dr. Morrison Home,* 1890. Summer residence. Santo Domingo, one block off of Highland. Became a permanent residence of both doctors who were Chiefs of Staff for Sante Fe Railroad Hospital. Now known as Westminster Gardens Retirement Home for Presbyterian Missionaries. Private residence.

1903 Bridge. Oak Street above Huntington Drive. Used when the old Red Cars came into the area. Now used only for walking.

Historic Schools: *Duarte Unified School,* Administration Building, 1906. On the site of the first 1874 school. 1427 Buena Vista, Duarte, CA 91010.

Historic Restaurants: *The Way It Was,* 1930s. Originally the Sportsman Tavern. 1452 E. Huntington Drive, Duarte, CA 91010. (Recently closed).

The Cancun, since 1930s. Originally The Zanzibar. Mexican Food. 1501 E. Huntington Drive, Duarte, CA 91010. 818-357-8313.

The Trails, since 1950. 2519 E. Huntington, Duarte, CA 91010. 818-359-2850.

Historic Sites: Site of the former home of *Glenn Miller.* Originally a 1890 ice house. Had a tower. On Bettyhill and Las Lomas, Royal Oaks. Burned.

Books: *On the Duarte,* Aloysia Moore and Bernice Watson. Published by the City of Duarte, 1976.

Chamber of Commerce: *Chamber of Commerce of Duarte,* 2229 E. Huntington Drive, Duarte, CA 91010. 818-357-3333.

─── EAGLE ROCK ───

History: The history of Eagle Rock begins with the Indians. Unfortunately no one made a detailed description of the many stone pots, tools and assorted materials found in the canyons. Bernice Johnson's excellent book focuses on the Gabrielino Indians in California. She suggests that many excellent sites existed in the canyons of Eagle Rock, due in part to the lush streams that flowed most of the year.

During the Spanish period, Father Francisco Garcès passed through the area in 1776. On a trek from the San Gabriel Mission to the Tulare Indians near what is now Bakersfield, he probably crossed the hills around Eagle Rock.

In 1784, of the two earliest grants of land awarded by the King of Spain, a third was also granted in that same year to Jose Maria de Verdugo. *Rancho San Rafael's* 36,403 acres included the present day communities of Burbank, Glendale, Highland Park, Flintridge, Montrose, La Crescenta, La Canada, and Eagle Rock. Upon Jose Verdugo's death in 1831, the vast ranch passed to his son Julio and daughter, Catalina. The Verdugo claim was upheld by the United States Government in 1848, but because of a need of money, the family mortgaged the Rancho. Since the loan cost 3% per month, compounded every three months, it did not take long for the small amount of $3,445.37 to accrue to $58,750.00 Unable to pay, Julio Verdugo sold the Rancho at auction to Alfred B. Chapman. After many more court battles, the Rancho San Rafael was divided into 31 parcels among 28 people. The largest award went to Benjamin Dreyfus. It consisted of 8,000 acres and included all of Eagle Rock except the Rockdale area. Huntington's little Trolley system came to the area in 1906 and in 1911 Eagle Rock was incorporated.

Historical Society: *The Eagle Rock Valley Historical Society,* John Miller, president. 2035 Colorado Blvd., Eagle Rock, CA 90041. Old City Hall.

Historians: *Mr. Henry Welcome.* Can be reached through the Historical Society. 213-255-8780.

Donna Adams, historian and curator of the Museum at City Hall. 213-255-5807.

Historical Landmarks: *The Eagle Rock,* #10 C.H.M. Also known as The Bird. An important landmark used by the Indians, Spanish and Mexicans. During the 1890s the Rock was a popular spot for hikers. Around the turn-of-the-century, a beautiful park surrounded the rock. Northern end of Figueroa Street, Eagle Rock.

City Hall, 1922. #59 C.H.M. 2035 Colorado Blvd., Eagle Rock.

Historic Homes: *Mrs. C.W. Young Home,* 1878. Sierra Villa, Eagle Rock. Mrs. Young was a friend to early California writers and many of them spent time here.

Hickson Home, 1890. Mt. Royal and Hill Drive, Eagle Rock.

Valley Knudsen Home, Hill Drive, Eagle Rock. Mrs. Knudsen founded Los Angeles Beautiful in 1949. An outspoken advocate for preservation in our city.

Historic Churches: *United Church of Eagle Rock,* 1886. 5080 Maywood, Eagle Rock. 213-256-4230. Original 1886 structure still extant, but has been much altered. Church combined both the United and Methodist denominations. Today, it is a Korean church.

St. Barnabas Episcopal Church, 1915. 2109 Chickasaw Avenue, Eagle Rock. 213-254-7569.

Historic Library: *Eagle Rock Branch Library.* #292 C.H.M. Built 1927. 2225 Colorado Blvd., Eagle Rock.

Historic Theatres: *Eagle Rock Theatre,* 1924. Eagle Rock Blvd., Eagle Rock.

Historic Schools: *Eagle Rock School,* 1886. 2057 Fairpark Avenue, Eagle Rock. First school in Eagle Rock was founded on land donated by Mr. Galpin in 1884. The barn on which the school was founded still extant on Addison Way. Present location has buildings that date from 1920s.

Occidental College, 1886. 1600 Campus Road, Eagle Rock. 213-259-2500. Originally founded in Highland Park, the college was later moved to its present location. Founded by a group of Presbyterian clergymen. In 1896 fire destroyed many of the original buildings.

Other Buildings: *20th Century Women's Club,* 1914. Eagle Rock.

Historical Sites: Site of Original *Farm House* of Mr. Galpin, 1866. Mayfair Market, Eagle Rock. Plaque on the site placed by the historical society.

Businesses: *Trick's Hardware Store,* since 1920. 1620 Colorado Blvd., Eagle

Rock. 213-255-8222.

Eagle Rock Sentinel, 1910. 5420 N. Figueroa Street, Highland Park. Eagle Rock and other communities have joined other towns. This is a case in point. The newspaper was meant for Eagle Rock, but now serves a much broader area.

Books: Bernice Johnson, *California's Gabrielino Indians,* 1962.

Donald W. Crocker, *Within the Vale of Annandale,* 1968.

EL MONTE

History: Although *El Monte* was used as a campsite by the De Anza party in 1776 it was not settled until a group of pioneers bound for the gold fields arrived here. Following the old Santa Fe Trail they caught sight of the Rio Hondo and San Gabriel rivers and decided to stay. In 1851 the town was founded. One of the group's leaders, J.A. Johnson called the area Lexington after his home town in Kentucky. Known by the Spanish as "The Monte," in 1868 it was changed to El Monte. Incorporated 1912. El Monte is the oldest American town in Los Angeles.

Historical Society: *Historical Society of El Monte.* Helen Huffins, president. El Monte, CA 91731. 818-443-1097.

Museums: *El Monte Museum of History,* 3150 Tyler Avenue, El Monte, CA 91731. 818-444-3813. Lillian Wiggins curator. Located in 1930s W.P.A. building.

American Heritage Park and Military Museum, 1918 N. Rosemead Blvd., El Monte, CA 91722. 818-442-1776. Open 12–4:30 Saturday, Sunday.

Whittier Narrows Recreation Area & Legg Lake, 1000 North Durfee Avenue, El Monte. 818-444-1872. 227 acres. A museum of the ecosystem of San Gabriel Valley. Also Regional Park. 818-444-9305.

Historic Homes: *Victorian Home,* 1887. 3150 Lexington Street, El Monte. Designated as an historic landmark.

House, 1880s. Cypress and Kaufman, El Monte.

Historic Sites: Site of *Gay's Lion Farm,* 1900. Peck Road and Valley Blvd., El Monte.

1852 *Michael Johnson Home,* El Monte.

1850 *Nicholas Schmidt Adobe Home,* El Monte.

Courtesy Luis Hernandez, artist.

Site of 1880 *Jail.* South of present bridge. El Monte.

Site of *Willow Grove Inn,* 1853. First hotel. Located where City Hall is today.

Site of *first public school* in Los Angeles County. 1853–54. Granada Street, El Monte. Originally constructed of willows, then lumber from the San Bernardino Mountains, hauled by ox cart. One room. Larger structure burned down in 1979.

Historic Churches: *Presbyterian*

Church of El Monte, 1853. 11608 Valley Blvd., El Monte. 818-448-5974. A small hut was put up in 1852 at the end of the old Santa Fe Trail. The above church was built in the 1960s.

The Navtivity Catholic Church, since 1923. 3743 Tyler Avenue, El Monte. 818-444-2511.

Businesses: *Anderson's Photo Service* and *Camera Center,* 1922. 10839 Valley Mall. El Monte's oldest business. 818-448-5091.

Grant's Hardware, since 1938. 10944 Garvey, El Monte. 818-448-5363.

Casa Real Furniture. Victorian Furniture, 10720 Valley Mall, El Monte. 818-442-4234.

Artist: *Luis Hernandez,* 2110 Woodland Court, Walnut, CA 91789. Work: 818-580-2093. Luis does beautiful drawings of Victorian homes.

Books: *El Monte: From the Pioneer Days,* published by the United States public works project, 1936.

Chamber of Commerce: *Chamber of Commerce of El Monte.* 10820 Valley Mall, El Monte, CA 91731. 818-580-2049. Currently at City Hall because of '87 earthquake; will return to Valley Mall when repairs are done.

—— EL SEGUNDO ——

History: The year was 1911. Five men from Standard Oil Company came to a melon patch near the sea. The area they were looking for had to be adjacent to the seashore where tankers could transport oil to all parts of the world. The area they chose was part of a 1837 land grant. They named it *El Segundo,* the second. Why the second? There are two stories. One reason given is because this was the second refinery Standard Oil began. The first was located near Richmond in San Francisco. The other story for the origin of the name is attributed to a woman who exclaimed, "El Segundo is second to none." El Segundo became a city in 1917.

Historian: *Laura Bell.* 513 W. Sycamore Street, El Segundo. 213-322-0109.

Historic Landmarks: 100 and 200 block of Richmond is known as the Historic Block and is currently undergoing restoration.

Historic Theatres: *Old Town Music Hall,* since 1922. Also called W.C. Fields Theatre and Restaurant. 140 Richmond, El Segundo. Mr. Bill Kaufman, 213-322-2592. Only classic films shown. Theatre has also been restored.

Historic Hotels: *The Concord Hotel,* since 1913. 200 block Concord, El Segundo.

Historic Schools: *El Segundo High School,* since 1929. Main Street and Mariposa Street, El Segundo. Graduated its first class in '29.

Historic Church: *Methodist Church,* 1929. Main and Mariposa, El Segundo.

Other Buildings: *Women's Club* began in the original building which was the old school house. Prior to 1920. Moved from Richmond Street to its present address at 541 Standard Street, El Segundo.

Showboat Apts., 1913. 200 block of Concord, El Segundo.

The Lafayette Apts., 1929. Northwest corner of Grand and Main, El Segundo.

Businesses: *Standard Oil,* 1911 (Chevron since 1917). Now known as El Segundo Oil Refinery. 3240 West El Segundo Blvd., El Segundo.

Library: *El Segundo Public Library,* 111 West Mariposa, El Segundo. 213-322-4121. There is a Friends of the Library History Committee which organized information for the library. Mrs. Kirby is in charge.

Other: *El Segundo Chamber of Commerce,* 427 Main Street, El Segundo. 213-322-1220. Apparently El

Segundo has been selected as a typical example of "California Main Street" program. This means that the state will give matching funds to El Segundo to revitalize Main Street. Rather than redevelopment which destroys the past, this program maintains the Main Street flavor of 1960. Residents here want *more* tradition, not less.

Write: Downtown El Segundo, Inc., 111 W. Grand Ave., El Segundo, CA 90245.

——— ENCINO ———

History: Encino has one of the most exciting histories of any area in Southern California. In part this is due to the recent archeological find — the so-called "Lost Village of Encino." Actually what was found was the burial site, but it is still the very same Indian village Gaspar de Portolá saw in 1769. When his men crossed the area around Sepulveda Pass, they noted in the diary Father Crespi carried with him, the large Indian village. He also mentioned the springs and lovely oak trees in the area. They christened the area "El Valle de Santa Catalina de Bononia de Los Encinos." The Franciscan Fathers liked the spot so much they used it as their headquarters prior to the founding of the San Fernando Mission in 1797.

In 1845 after the Mexican period ended and the American era was just dawning, Pio Pico granted the 4,460 acre site to *Don Vicente de la Osa.* He built a beautiful adobe ranch house and established a cattle and sheep ranch on the grant. Across the street, in a small wayside stop, the stagecoaches sped past on their way to Monterey. (1858) Following Osa's death, the *Garnier* brothers, Philippe and Eugene purchased Encino in 1869. They created the lake, walled up the spring, and constructed the two-story French Provincial building in 1873. In 1878 the property was sold to *Gaston Oxarart,* then to *Simon Glass.* Finally Glass sold the ranch to his father-in-law, Domingo Amestoy in 1889. The *Amestoys* continued to run sheep, later turning to field crops of white wheat and barley.

In 1915 the ranch was sub-divided, part of it becoming Sherman Oaks. The Amestoys, however, retained the buildings and 100 acres. In 1944 they sold the remaining part of the ranch to Clarence Brown, a movie director. (See Calabasas). He in turn sold the property to a building syndicate and in 1945 their plans included the destruction of the entire historic structures. Thank goodness, *Maria Steward,* a resident of Encino for 15 years organized the Encino Historical Committee, and through her persistence, was able to turn area into a state park.

Historical Society: *Los Encinos Historical Society,* Los Encinos State Historic Park, 16756 Moorpark Street, Encino, CA 91436. 818-784-4849.

Historic Landmarks: *Old Oak Tree,* #24 C.H.M. About 1000 years old. Just a few yards back from Louise and Ventura Blvd., Encino.

Business District: *Tudor Shops,* 1920s. Corner Ventura Blvd. and Genesta, Encino.

Historic Streets: *Ventura Blvd.,* El Camino Real.

Magnolia Blvd.

Historian: *Mr. Ted Gibson,* 5033 Gaviotta Avenue, Encino, CA 91436. Mr. Gibson was Encino's first postmaster in 1938 and owned the first store in Encino. He also ran the service station. He has written his own story about the more than 60 years he spent in Encino. If you want a copy, write me: Jan Atkinson, 352 Innwood Rd., Simi Valley, CA 93065. Send $5 and I'll mail you a copy.

Honorary Mayors of Encino: Al

Jolson 1935–43; Phil Harris 1951; William Bendix 1953; John Wayne 1956; Jack Carson 1957; Ann Sheridan 1958; George Gobel 1959; Gesele MacKenzie 1962; Michael Landon 1965 and 1969; Dick Van Dyke 1966–67; Jerry Dumphy 1971; Tim Conway 1975.

Homes: During the '30s and '40s Encino was home to dozens of motion picture stars. Among them were:
Mickey Rooney Home, Densmore Avenue, Encino.
Broderick Crawford, Magnolia Blvd., Encino.
Al Jolson and *Ruby Keeler,* later *Don Ameche Home,* 4875 Louise Avenue, Encino.
Walter Brennan Home, Encino Avenue, Encino.
Mary Astor Home, Hayvenhurst, Encino.
Jane Withers Home, Hayvenhurst Avenue, Encino.
Roy Rogers and Dale Evans, Amestoy Avenue, Encino.
Edward Everett Horton, Encino.
Don the Beachcomber Estate, 17520 Embassy Drive, Encino.
Spencer Tracy Home, White Oak, Encino.
John Wayne Home, Louise Avenue, Encino.
Clark Gable and Carole Lombard Home. Originally the Howard Hawks Ranch home. Petit Street, Encino.
Bud Abbott Home, 4504 Woodley, Encino.
W.C. Fields Home, 4685 White Oak, Encino.
William Bendix, later *Marie McDonald Home,* Encino Avenue, Encino.
Dinah Shore and George Montgomery, White Oak Farm Home, White Oak Avenue, Encino.
Homeowner Group: *Homeowners of Encino,* Gerald Silver, 818-990-2757.
Historic Churches: *St. Nicholas Episcopal Church,* 17114 Ventura Blvd., Encino. Since 1938.

Sites: Site of *Frank* and *Vada Flowers,* and *Tropical Bird Farm,* 1927. 17555 Ventura Blvd., Encino.
Site of *Encino Gas Station,* 1925. Southeast corner of Ventura Blvd. and Oak Park Avenue, Encino.
Site of *Store* and *Fountain,* later Encino's First Post Office, 1938. Ventura Blvd., Encino.
Site of the *Encino Country Club,* 1925–29. Hayvenhurst Avenue and Adlon Street, Encino. First floor was locker rooms, pro shop, billiard and pool rooms. Second floor had offices, two large dining rooms. Third floor had 26 rooms and 26 baths for overnight guests. In front of the building was a lake, tennis courts and riding stables.
Site of *KNX.* Morrison near Gaynor Avenue, Encino. Originally a large hog ranch north of Morrison. Charlie Chaplin was the next owner.
Other: *Maria's Fruit Stand,* since 1943. Ventura Freeway and Hayvenhurst Avenue, Encino.
Encino Reservoir, 1936. Encino Avenue, Encino.
Flower Pavilion. 18013 Ventura Blvd., Encino. 818-788-8860.
Old Home, 1900. 17451 Ventura Blvd., Encino.
Within the Sepulveda Basin, a plan is afoot to turn the 2,097 acres into the largest recreation plan ever undertaken in the history of the basin. There will be the 160 acre park, called Bull Creek which will contain a lake, new trees and shrubs, and a home to more birds and wildlife. In addition there will be a wildlife refuge, polo fields, a fairground, an arts park and much more. Area bounded roughly by the San Diego and Ventura Freeways, Victory Boulevard and White Oak Avenue. Originally ground breaking for the basin took place in 1940 with the help of Jane Wyman and other Hollywood actresses.

GARDENA

History: Prior to the immigration of the Spanish, the Gabrielino Indian utilized the area, hunting and fishing close by. Skeletons and burial artifacts of this branch of the Shoshonean tribe were discovered near the lush area known as "Nigger Slough." Renamed in 1937 as *Laguna de los Dominguez,* the winding body of fresh water wandered through Gardena and Carson on its way to the mud flats at San Pedro.

Gardena's earliest beginnings as a community were in the late 1880s. The town started with a general store at the corner of Figueroa and 161st Street. In 1889 the Redondo Railway necessitated the moving of central Gardena to what is presently Vermont Avenue and Gardena Boulevard. From there the community expanded.

The city was incorporated in 1930.

Historical Society: None at the present time.

Historians: *Bill Gerber,* 2927 West 139th Street, Gardena, CA 90249. 213-323-6948.

Mr. Tom Parks, Exec. Vice President Chamber of Commerce. 1919 W. Redondo Beach Blvd., Suite 107, Gardena. 213-532-9905.

Historical Survey: The City of Gardena conducted a massive historical-architectural *survey* of Gardena in 1981. For a copy contact May Doi. 213-327-0220.

Historical Landmarks: *Horseshoe Club,* since 1949 (Casino). 14305 S. Vermont Avenue, Gardena, CA 90247. 213-323-7520.

Historic Homes: *Woodward Home,* 1888. Normandie Avenue North of Redondo Beach Blvd., Gardena. Oldest home in Gardena.

The Wills Home, 1909–10. Corner northwest Magnolia and Vermont, Gardena. Owned by Wills family since 1932.

Barbara Jones Home, 1908. 730 W. Alondra, Gardena, CA 90247. Recommended for local historical designation.

Private Residence. 16119 S. Brighton Avenue, Gardena. Recommended for local historical designation.

Isaac Ball Home, 1906. 739 West Gardena Blvd., Gardena. Recommended for local historical designation.

The Bathrick House, 1911. 1157 West Gardena, Gardena. Recommended for local historical designation.

The Wood House, 1912. 1154 West Gardena Blvd., Gardena. Recommended for local historical designation.

Byhower House, 1934. 1212 W. Gardena Blvd., Gardena. Recommended for local historical designation.

The Chapman House, 1910. 1304 West Gardena Blvd., Gardena.

The Hobbs House, 1900. 14703 S. Kingsley Drive, Gardena. Recommended for the National Register.

The Ybarra House, 1920. 16417 Manhattan Place, Gardena. Recommended for the National Register.

The Samuel K. Woodward Home, 1888. 15309 S. Normandie, Gardena. Recommended for the National Register.

The Morgan Home, 1907. 16229 S. Orchard, Gardena.

Miller House, 1908. 15625 S. Vermont, Gardena. Recommended for the National Register.

The Charles E. Wallin House, 1893. 1726 W. 145th Street, Gardena. Recommended for the National Register.

The Masuda House, 1742 W. 145th Street, Gardena. Recommended for National Register.

The Jeff Clark Home, 1926. 1203 W. 162nd Street, Gardena. Recommended National Register.

The Beri Fanning Home, 802 West 164th Street, Gardena. Recommended National Register.

The John W. Klasgye Home, 1892.

(Hark House) 835 W. 164th St., Gardena. Recommended National Register.
Stillman Gates Home, 1905. 1104 W. 164th Street, Gardena. Recommended National Register.
The Rentschler Home, 1908. 1110 W. 164th Street, Gardena.
DeHart House, 1913. 15927 S. Halldale Avenue, Gardena.
Abel Lewis House, 1892. 750 W. 167th Street, Gardena.
Historic Commercial Buildings: *Olsen's Grocery Store,* 1912. Today Cameo Chair, Inc. 16501 S. Western, Gardena.
Bathrich Hall, 1905. 1004 W. Gardena Blvd.
Ernst Sweet Shop, 1919. Today Trojan Room, 1005 W. Gardena Blvd.
Gardena Post Office, 1919. Today Martin's Jeweler's. 1007 W. Gardena Blvd.
Kurata Dept. Store, 1917. Now a laundry. 1024 W. Gardena Blvd.
George W. Flaer's Shop, 1918. Now Book Exchange. 1040 W. Gardena Blvd., Gardena.
Wednesday Progressive Clubhouse, 1912. 16121 S. Orchard, Gardena.
Historic Schools: *Peary Jr. High School,* 1906. Originally Gardena High School. 1415 W. Gardena Blvd.
Gardena Elementary School. Est. 1894. Present buildings—1949. 647 W. Gardena Blvd., Gardena. First school in Gardena.
Historic Churches: *First Methodist Church,* 1892–93, 1950. 812 W. 165th Place, Gardena. Oldest church.
St. Anthony's, 1900s. 1050 W. 163rd Street, Gardena.
First Methodist Church Rectory, 1900. 739 W. 167th Street, Gardena.
Historic Hotels: *Gardena Hotel,*

1900. 825½ West Gardena Blvd., Gardena. Jeffers General Store.
Historic Restaurants: *Bank Cafe.* 16522 Southwestern Avenue, Gardena, CA 90247. 213-324-1915. Formerly Moneta Bank. First bank in Gardena.
Historic Parks: *South Gardena Parksite.* Dominguez Slough. Entrance near corner of Vermont Avenue and Artesia Blvd., Gardena. Recommended for the National Register.
Businesses: *McMillian Mortuary,* since 1912. 1016 W. 164th Street, Gardena. 213-329-6333.
Hills Pet and Feed Store, since 1934. 1005 W. Redondo Beach Blvd., Gardena. 213-532-8755.
McCormick Mortuary, 1910. 1044 W. 164th Street, Gardena.
Donut King, 1950 Pop Fantasy Architecture. 15032 S. Western, Gardena.
Kobata Growers, Inc., since 1928. 1436 W. 139th Street, Gardena. 213-538-2552.
Gardena Valley News, since 1904 (garage). 16417 S. Western Avenue, Gardena. Present building—1920. 213-329-6351.
Horseshoe Club, since 1949. 14305 S. Vermont Avenue, Gardena. 213-323-7520.
Famous Streets: *Gardena Blvd.* Began in the 1870s. Palm Avenue moved when the railroad came to Gardena. Several old homes dating from 1890s still there.
Books: None. *Gardena Public Library,* 1731 W. Gardena, Gardena. 213-323-6363. Library has many historical pamphlets on file.
Other: *Old Timers.* Not a formal club. Rachael Adams (Ruiz) more or less heads groups. 15229 Haas Avenue, Gardena, CA 90249. 213-324-3777.

GLENDALE

History: One of the three original land grants awarded in Southern California. The *Rancho San Rafael* was granted to Jose Maria Verdugo in 1784. It lay about a league and a half from the San Gabriel Mission, on the old "Road to Monterey." Consisting of 36,000 acres by 1817, the ranch was pasturing 1,800 head of cattle, 1,000 calves, 600 unbroken horses, mules and other animals. In 12 years the number had doubled. For 40 years Jose Maria's wish to keep the ranch in the family was fulfilled. His two children, Julio and Catalina were unable, however, to maintain title to the San Rafael. With the coming of the Americans, Federal law demanded that title be proven. By 1861 Julio lost his share and in 1871 Catalina's Rancho La Canada was also broken up.

The Rancho San Rafael was important during the Fremont era when to this Verdugo Rancho, Fremont sent Jesus Pico—the Mexican guide whose life Fremont had spared when he was about to be executed at San Luis Obispo. His mission? To talk with the stubborn Californians and persuade them to deal with himself rather than Commodore Robert Stockton.

Historical Society: *Glendale Historical Society,* P.O. Box 4173, Glendale, CA 91202. 818-242-7447.

Historians: *Barbara Boyd.* Can be reached at the Glendale Public Library. 222 Harvard (East), Glendale. 818-956-2020.

Also, an Historic Landmark Committee appointed by Mayor Herman Barnes was set up in 1964. Its goal was to secure a list of places, sites identified with early history of Glendale. From this came an inventory of historic sites. Chairperson Glenn Cornwell. 837 Ridge Drive, Glendale, CA 91206. 818-242-0265.

Historic Landmarks: *Brand Library,* 1904. El Miradero, 1601 West Mountain Street, Glendale, CA 91201. 818-956-2051. Open 12–6. This original "castle" as it has often been called was built by a very flamboyant man, Leslie Brand who was responsible for much of the growth of Glendale.

The Doctor's House, 1888. Now at the Brand Library. Glendale. Formerly at 921 E. Wilson Avenue. Open. Contact the Historical Society for time.

Casa Adobe de San Rafael, 1865. 1330 Dorothy Drive, Glendale, CA 91202. 818-956-2000.

The beautiful Casa Adobe de San Rafael also is known as the *Tomas Sanchez Adobe,* the second oldest adobe home in Glendale. An excellent booklet is available on the adobe, by J. Marshall Miller who supervised its restoration in 1934–35. It is open for tours.

Landmarks: *Catalina Verdugo Adobe,* 1860. 2211 Bonita Drive, Glendale. This historic adobe is still privately owned. It was owned by Catalina Verdugo, daughter of the original owner of Rancho San Rafael, Jose Maria Verdugo.

Oak of Peace, 2211 Bonita Drive, Glendale. This famous old oak tree stands in front of the Catalina Adobe and was the site in 1847 of a treaty of peace between the United States and Mexico. Private property.

Cactus. Located at Randolph and Maryland, Glendale. Part of the original Casa Verdugo Restaurant Property.

Historic Homes: *W.C.B. Richardson House,* 1873. Glendale.

Courtesy artist Jim Gindraux

Colonial Mansion, 727 Kenneth Road, Glendale. Supposedly the inspiration for Tara in *Gone With the Wind.* Private.

The Henry and Joseph Goode Home, 1880s. 119 North Cedar, Glendale. Scene of a rigorous preservation contest. Hopefully the house won.

Somerset Farm, Verdugo Road at 1381 Windsor. Home of J.C. Sherer, early pioneer and scene of many early old-timers' picnics. Monument erected by Glendale Historical Society.

West Home, 1890. 815 South Central, Glendale.

Castle, 2707 Hermosita Drive, Glendale.

Castle, 431 Kempton Road, Glendale.

Castle, 330 Kempton Road, Glendale.

Castle, 721 East Mountain, Glendale.

United Presbyterian Home, 1890. 1230 E. Windsor, Glendale. Home of Spencer Robinson, early Glendale Mayor.

Historic Parks, Cemeteries: *Forest Lawn Memorial Park,* 1712 S. Glendale Avenue, Glendale, CA 91209. 213-254-3131.

Historic Libraries: *Carnegia Library,* 1907. 320 Glendale Avenue, Glendale. Moved in 1909 to this site.

Historic Schools: *Cerritos School,* 120 W. Cerritos, Glendale. Glendale's first school.

Historic Theatres: *First Glendale Theatre,* 520 E. Broadway, Glendale.

Historic Clubs: *Tuesday Afternoon Club,* Lexington and Central, Glendale.

Los Angeles Theatre Organ Society, P.O. Box 1913, Glendale, CA 91209.

Historic Sites: *Grand Central Airport site,* 1929. North off of the Golden State and Ventura Freeways. New business park. Glendale.

Talk about stupidity! When this fabulous nostalgic airport was torn down, with it went the memory of "Casablanca," the likes of men like Howard Hughes, Wiley Post, Will Rogers, Charles Lindbergh and hundreds of aviation hall of fame greats. To the women flyers as well, there was Amelia Earhart and a hundred female pioneering aviators. Gone too are the legends of aviation history that made Southern California the mecca for aviation's first steps. Despite all the plans to save it, only the Tower remains.

Site of the *Old Tropico City Hall.* S.W. corner of Brand and Los Feliz. Tropico was incorporated in 1911, annexed in 1918. Purchased by Mr. Richardson in 1868. The area was south of Chevy Chase Drive and extended from Los Angeles River on the southwest to hills of Forest Lawn on the east. The Santa Eulalia Ranch.

Site of *Glendale Depot* of the L.A. Interurban Railway of 1904–1922. At northeast corner of Brand and Broadway, Glendale.

Site of *Glendale High School,* 1903–1908. Southeast corner of Brand and Broadway, Glendale.

Site of the *First Hotel of Glendale,* 1887–1889. Then the first Glendale Union High School 1901–1903. Then Glendale Sanitarium 1905–1925. Today it is News and Press Building. 111 North Isabel, Glendale.

Site of *Glendale's First Fire Station,* Howard, south of the Public Service Building, Glendale.

Site of *Glendale's First Bank,* northwest corner of Wilson and Glendale Avenue, Glendale.

Site of *Glendale's First Presbyterian Church,* 1892. Northeast corner of Cedar and Broadway, Glendale.

Site of the *Egyptian Cafe,* 1920s. Glendale.

Other Buildings: *Utter-McKinley Mortuary,* 624 S. Central, Glendale. Was the original Glendale Country Club, then located at Brand and Wilson.

Hideout of Tiburcio Vasquez. Also site of an old Winery. Dunsmoore Avenue and La Crescenta Foothills, Glendale. Oldest frame house in the city. Le Mesnagner Ranch.

Businesses: *Interurban Press,* P.O. Box 6444, Glendale, CA 91205. 818-240-9130. Specializes in publishing books on old trains.

Southern California Music Co., since 1880s. 806 N. Glendale Avenue, Glendale. 818-240-2251

Vintage Parts, Inc., Volkswagen Restoration Parts. From 1967 and older. 5832 San Fernando Road, Glendale, CA 91202. 818-352-2833.

A Turquoise Nut, 321 North Verdugo Blvd., Glendale. 818-243-1001. Specializes in American Indian wares.

Hutchinson and Bloodcut, C.P.A., since 1922. 420 N. Brand Blvd., Glendale. 818-240-1437.

Godwin's Fabric, since 1920s. 315 N. Brand Blvd., Glendale. 818-243-4209.

Fancy Cleaners and Laundry, 1913. 3020 West Magnolia, Glendale. 818-848-9591.

Grand View Memorial Park, burial 1884, Memorial Park 1898. Bob Hepburn, 1341 Glenwood Rd., Glendale. 818-242-2697.

Chuck Reinie's Home Decorating Store, since 1945. 1801 W. Glenoaks, Glendale. 818-240-7700.

Virgil's Glendale Hardware, 1906–07. 520 Glendale Avenue, Glendale. 818-242-1104.

John Knight Insurance, since 1933. 145 N. Maryland, Glendale. 818-240-7670.

Doll Electric, since 1923. 1023 S. Brand, Glendale. 818-242-2108.

Books: George W. Kirkman, *Pictorial and Historical Map of Old Los Angeles County.*

R.F. Kittlerman, *Glendale — Its History and Romance.*

W.W. Robinson, *Glendale, A Calendar of Events in the Making of a City.*

Security Trust and Savings Bank. *First of the Ranchos, The Story of Glendale.*

J.C. Sherer, *History of Glendale and Vicinity.*

George Shochat, *The Casa Adobe de San Rafael* (The Sanchez Adobe) in Glendale, California. In the quarterly of the *Historical Society of Southern California,* December 1950.

——— GLENDORA ———

History: Nestled against the blue foothills of the San Gabriel Mountains, not only is the area home to oak trees, yucca, sand cactus and chaparral, but shelter as well to deer, rabbits, coyotes, bobcats, lizards and birds. It was sustenance to the Indians, and put clothes on their backs.

With the coming of the Spanish, trails were blazed from Mexico to California. Juan Bautista de Anza camped around the La Cienega (Mud Springs) in what is now San Dimas.

Among the earliest arrivals in the area was Henry Dalton who purchased the *Rancho Azusa* in 1844, before California became a state. He developed orchards, vineyards, cotton, cattle, sheep, tobacco, a cigar factory, a winery, a mill, dairy, the bee industry and brought water from the canyons. With statehood came land disputes. In 1868 the U.S. Government declared Rancho Azusa (land which included Glendora) open for homesteading. In 1874, John Bender and William Cullen settled in the Glendora area. Both men went to work buying out earlier homesteaders and cleared the land. They planted the area's first crops — beans, flax, wheat, potatoes and other vegetables.

Glendora Historical Society & Museum

Glendora Historical Society Museum
City Hall, Fire and Police Departments 1913

Glendora, California

Courtesy Glendora Historical Society.

Glendora's founding father was George D. Whitcomb, a retired fisherman. He arrived in 1875, purchased 200 acres which are today the heart of the community. The name "Glen" came from the glen behind his home and "Dora" from his wife's name, Leadora. Whitcomb convinced the Santa Fe Railroad to shift its proposed route from Pasadena to San Bernardino. Whitcomb and others formed the Glendora Land Company. On April 1, 1887 a public sale of lots was held.

The first lot purchased is on the northwest corner of Bennett and Glendora Avenue. The town was incorporated in 1911.

Historical Society: *Glendora Historical Society,* 314 N. Glendora, P.O. Box 532, Glendora, CA 91740. Home of city's first jail, city hall and fire station. Open 1–3 Sunday. Curator: Jackie Moody. 818-335-0408.

Historians: *Bobbi Battler,* author, historian. 813 W. Bagnall, Glendora. 818-335-0394.

Mildred Kobzeff, 228 W. Mountain View, Glendora, CA 91740. 818-335-1621.

Historical Landmarks: One hundred year old *Moreton Bay fig tree.* Big Tree Centennial Park at the corner of Santa Fe and Colorado, Glendora.

Largest growth of *Bougainvillea* in the United States. Bennett Avenue, between Pasadena and Cullen Avenue. Glendora.

Stone Marker, northeast corner of Glendora and Bennett Avenue, Glendora. Marks first lot sold in Glendora in 1887.

Big Dalton Dam, off Big Dalton Road, off of Glendora Mountain Road. Glendora.

Oblisque Century vault, in front of City Hall on Foothill Blvd., Glendora.

Historic Homes: *Bender Home,* 1883. 742 N. Rainbow Drive, Glendora. Oak tree in front is 400 to 600 years old. Early day founder of city.

Cullen Home, 1910. 554 N. Cullen, Glendora. Cullen was early day founder of Glendora. First home burned.

Singer Estate, 1920s. "Kregmont," 20749 E. Palm Drive, Glendora.

Bruebaker Home, 1908. 200 S. Vista Bonita, Glendora. Glendora's first mayor.

Scofield Home, 1887. 19151 Baseline Road, Glendora.

Mamlin House, 1910. 201 W. Bennett, Glendora. Presently the D.A.R. state headquarters.

Wood Ranch, 1893. 711 E. Virginia, Glendora.

Davis Homes, The Twins, 1886. 211 E. and 215 E. Virginia, Glendora.

The Jones-Felts Home, 1928. 18850 Gladstone Street, Glendora.

The West Family Home, 1880s. 250 N. Live Oak and 426 E. Bennett, Glendora. Home of the West brothers. The family kept rainfall figures for over 100 years.

Suydam Home, 1887. 645 N. Vista Bonita, Glendora.

Humphrey Home, 1886. 622 N. Vista Bonita, Glendora.

The Original Land Office, 1887. 403 N. Minnesota, Glendora.

Bradley Home, 1886. 736 N. Vista Bonita, Glendora.

Shank Home, 1880s. 316 W. Alosta, Glendora. Now serves as the Continental Restaurant. Original home inside of restaurant!

Former home of silent screen star *Mary Miles Minter,* 18849 Milton Drive, Glendora.

Rubel Home, 844 Live Oak, Glendora. Like a castle.

Miller Homestead, 1883. 539 E. Sierra Madre, Glendora.

Hamilton Home, 1900. 1030 E. Alosta Avenue, Glendora.

Odell Home, 1893. 403 Bennett, Glendora.

Pierce Home, 1902. 727 N. Vista Bonita, Glendora.

Detwiler Home, 1902. 325 E. Whitcomb, Glendora.

Gard House, 1910. 6735 N. Grand Glendora.

Funk House, 1908. 360 W. Juanita, Glendora.

Brunjes House, 1900–08. 301 Meda, Glendora.

Warren Estate, 1898–1915. Now a country club. Glendora.

Haas House, 1902. 229 W. Sierra Madre, Glendora.

Rogers House, 1890. 554 E. Whitcomb Avenue, Glendora.

Wilhite House, 1890. Dalton and Minnesota Avenue, Glendora.

Sunny Grove Ranch, 1907. (Needham Homestead) 617 Sierra Madre Avenue, Glendora.

Fickett House, 1886. 530 N. Wabash, Glendora.

Comstock Home, 1910. 864 E. Leadora, Glendora.

Engelhardt House, 1880s. 120 W. Colorado Street, Glendora.

Jack's Rock House 1899–1910. 1115 E. Bennett, Glendora.

La Chance House 1916. 1070 Leadora, Glendora.

Bank and Opera House, 1900–1902. 161 N. Glendora, Glendora.

Wilma Wright Lundh Home, 1900. 214 E. Foothill, Glendora.

Hopps House, 1910. 621 N. Pennsylvania, Glendora.

Herr House, 1910. 18717 Hicrest, Glendora.

La Fetra Home, 1886. 18708 Milton Drive, Glendora. Also the location of the 1875 Preston School.

Singer Mansion 820 N. Verano Drive, Glendora.

Historic Churches: *First Christian Church,* 1888. 300 N. Glendora Avenue, Glendora. Stone in front marks the first lot sold in 1887.

Methodist Church, 1888. 200 E. Bennett, Glendora. 818-335-4058.

Historic Cemeteries: *Fairmont Cemetery,* 1876. East of Baldy Vista, Glendora. Glendora's first cemetery. Caretaker Richard Davies. 818-963-3721.

Museum: *Glendora Historical Museum,* 1913. 314 North Glendora Avenue, Glendora. Call Parks & Recreation for tours. 818-335-4071. Home of the Historical Society.

Library: *Glendora Library and Cultural Center* 140 South Glendora Avenue, Glendora.

Other Landmarks: *Town of Alosta* 1887–1889. Now part of Glendora was located south of Foothill.

Indian Villages: *Ancient Indian trail and pond.* Artifacts found have been documented as having dated from 6,000 B.C.

Historic Sites: *Prestor Home,* 1869. 18537 Foothill Blvd., Glendora.

George Whitcomb Home, 1880s. End of Vista Bonita, Glendora.

Historic Restaurants: *Old Hickory,* 1920. Grand and Alosta Avenue, Glendora. Once a wayside stop, then a hangout for the high school crowd.

Now a gorgeous restaurant with wonderful historical pictures all around. 818-914-7791.

Notes: *Stagecoach Stop.* Live Oak, Glendora. This incredible building is in danger. Historian Bobbi Battler believes it was a stagecoach stop because of the many oldtimers that remember it being referred to as such. She is working to try to save it.

Historic Street: *Foothhill Blvd.* Once referred to as Minnehaha. Glendora.

Historic Colleges: *Azusa Pacific College,* 18527 Alosta, Azusa. Was once the site of the Harrison Feller Home. Much of what was originally in Glendora is now in Azusa.

Orange Tree Bazaar, 216 N. Glendora Avenue, Glendora. Early business still owned by descendants of the original owners. Was first a bicycle shop, then a funeral home, now an antique shop. 818-335-1524.

Businesses: *Faink-Biner's Grocery,* since 1940s. Meade and Glendora Avenue, Glendora. 818-335-1068.

The Gleaner, since 1920s. The Glendora Gleaner, then the Glendora Press, Azusa. 818-969-1711.

Other Facts: Glendora is the home of ex-football hero and movie star, *Woody Strode.*

Fan Dancer, *Sally Rand,* lived in Glendora most of her adult life. Her parents were early pioneers. Her son is still a resident.

Books: Bobbie Battler, *Remember When,* published 1986. Available by contacting Pat Sassone, P.O. Box 1986, Glendora, CA 91740. $9.50 including tax and postage.

Sheldon Jackson, *Beautiful Glendora,* 1982.

Donald Pflueger, *Glendora,* 1951.

Heritage Park: Scheduled for the near future. On Mauna-Loa Street.

——— GRANADA HILLS ———

History: Archeological remains have been found in the area which date from 1500 B.C.

Geronimio Lopez purchased a large portion of land in the area in 1855 building an adobe there in 1869. This later became the San Fernando Valley's first English speaking school—*Lopez Station.* The land on which the adobe once stood is now covered by the Van Norman Reservoir.

In 1874 the land was purchased by Charles Maclay and George Porter. In 1881 Porter kept a 20,000 acre portion located east of Zelzah, on what became Northridge. Land between Balboa and Zelzah was bought by J.H. Mosier in 1917. Mosier established the Sunshine Ranch Home, located on the north side of Rinaldi. In 1925 Sunshine Ranch was sold to Suburban Estates. The first houses were built in 1926 and still

known as Sunshine Ranch. In 1927 Granada was chosen as its official name and finally in 1942, name enlarged to Granada Hills.

Historical Society: *The San Fernando Valley Historical Society.* Andres Pico Adobe. #7 C.H.M. 10940 Sepulveda Blvd., Mission Hills, CA 91345. 818-365-7810.

Historian: *Ruth Benjamin,* Historian of Granada Hills, 11554 McLennan Avenue, Granada Hills. 818-368-3971.

Historical Landmarks: *Sunshine Ranch House,* 1917. West of Shoshone and North on Rinaldi (17563 Rinaldi). Granada Hills.

Van Norman Reservoir and Dam, 1913. Granada Hills.

144 Deodar Trees, 1932. #41 C.H.M. White Oak Avenue between San Fernando Mission Blvd. and San Jose

Street, Granada Hills. Historic Landmark #41.

Historic Homes: *Speer Home,* 1886–87. Victorian home originally located in Pacoima; moved by Speer family to Granada Hills and restored. Built originally for the Hoyt family. 17104 Mayerling, Granada Hills.

First Home in Granada Hills, 1927. Corner White Oak and Kingsbury. Captain J.L. Butler original owner.

James Cagney Ranch House, 1940s. Above Rinaldi West of Balboa, Granada Hills.

Mr. Culley's Home, 1927. (Thurlow Culley). San Fernando Mission Road, Granada Hills. Mr. Culley founded G.H. Culley and Smith Realtors.

Historic Churches: *First Presbyterian Church,* 1930s. 10400 Zelzah, Granada Hills. First church in Granada Hills.

Historic Schools: *Granada Elementary School,* 1927. 17170 Tribune Street, Granada Hills. First school in

the area still extant.

Historic Parks: *O'Melveney Park,* 714 acres. Donated by John O'Melveney, lawyer, who purchased land in 1937 as a cattle ranch. Granada Hills. Second largest park in county.

Businesses: *Mobil Station,* Corner Balboa and Devonshire, Granada Hills. First station in the area. Originally run by Mr. Eccles. 818-363-1213.

Roy Paul's T.V., since 1951. 17728½ Chatsworth Street, Granada Hills. 818-363-1102.

Chamber of Commerce: *Granada Hills Chamber of Commerce,* 10727 White Oak Avenue, Granada Hills, CA 91344. 818-368-3235.

Other Information: *Francisco* and *Maria Avila,* were caretakers of the old Lankershim Ranch. They lived on ranch until 1929. They were dedicated to saving memorabilia from that era. Many items given to Valley College Historical Museum and Campo de Cahuenga.

—— HAWTHORNE ——

History: Named after American author Nathaniel Hawthorne, author of *The Scarlet Letter.* Founded in 1905, incorporated 1922. Founders B.L. Harding and H.D. Lombard formed the Hawthorne Land Co. in 1905. Sold first homes in 1906.

Historical Society: None.

Historians: *Bob Hartman,* historian for city of Hawthorne. 4551 West Broadway, Hawthorne. 213-679-2310.

Tom Quintana, Hawthorne City Hall. 4455 W. 126th Street, Hawthorne. 213-970-7902.

Businesses: *Independent Lumber,* 1932. 12435 S. Hawthorne. 213-679-2565.

United Hardware, 1946. 13245 S.

Hawthorne Blvd., Hawthorne. 213-676-1173.

Phillips Plumbing, 1942. 13791 Hawthorne Blvd., Hawthorne. 213-676-1147.

Chaffee Motors, 1947. 13900 Hawthorne Blvd., Hawthorne. 213-644-0211.

Businesses: *Holly's 50s Coffee Shop,* 13763 S. Hawthorne, Hawthorne. 213-679-5509.

Chip's 50s Coffee Shop, 11908 S. Hawthorne, Hawthorne. 213-679-2947.

Books: Robert S. Hartman, *History of Hawthorne.* Published by the Hawthorne Chamber of Commerce, 1972.

——————— HIGHLAND PARK ———————

History: Highland Park was originally a part of the Rancho San Rafael. Although the land was sold to real estate speculators during the 1870s, development wasn't really begun until 1887, when the promise of a passenger railway in the area caused land values to skyrocket. Most of Highland Park and Mt. Washington was developed during the next forty years, between 1890 and 1930.

Highland Park was the first area to be annexed to the original Los Angeles city boundaries. The reason for this was a perceived need for law and order. The Sycamore Grove area was, in the 1890s, the site of several notorious roadhouses, stopovers for visitors to the red-light district in nearby Garvanza. The Arroyo in general was a favorite location for bandits who preyed on travellers. It was the inability of Highland Park residents to control the behavior of those loitering in the Arroyo that drove them to seek incorporation with the City of Los Angeles, with its crack police force.

Historical Society Groups: *Highland Park Heritage Trust,* Charles Fisher, P.O. Box 42894, Los Angeles, CA 90050. 213-256-4326.

Various groups have recently begun to designate homes, landmarks in the area. They have divided the community into several zones. There is the Mount Washington area, the San Rafael, Seaview Lane, Sycamore Grove, Echo and Hayes area. The group has published a brochure as well which lists addresses and dates of homes.

Historical Landmarks: *Heritage Square,* 1969. 3800 Homer Street, Highland Park. 213-449-0193.

Heritage Square got its start due in part to the demolition of Bunker Hill by the Community Redevelopment Association. A small group of preservationists from the American Institute of Architects came to Mayor Yorty and pleaded with him over the loss of so much of our old "gas light" circa 1860s homes. It was during that time that the Cultural Heritage Board was born. Plans were made to save two homes on Bunker Hill—The Castle and the Salt Box. Finally, the Redevelopment Corporation said the old homes would have to go. But where? Art Snyder, councilman of the 14th District offered to donate some surplus park land in his area to the newly formed Heritage Square Foundation. Funds were raised to move the old homes to the new Heritage Square. With much fanfare both the *Salt Box* and *The Castle* came to the square. Eight months later vandals broke into both of them and they were "mysteriously" burned to the ground.

As providence would have it, Channel 5 came out to the Square to cover the fire and so much sympathy was aroused for the "lost heritage" of Angelenos, that once again the Square began life anew. This time the Hale House was spied by a group who realized that it was destined for demolition. They were able to acquire the home and in the early 1970s it was moved to the Square and restored. Currently the Square has: (1) The Hale House 1887 #40 C.H.M. (2) The Palms Depot 1887 #22 C.H.M. (3) The Ford-Beaudry Home 1887 #108 C.H.M. (4) Mt. Pleasant Home 1876 #98 C.H.M. (5) The Shaw Home 1880s. (Valley Knudsen Home) #65 C.H.M. (6) The Lincoln Avenue Methodist Church 1898. #245 C.H.M. (7) The Carriage Barn 1890s. (8) The Octagonal House. Note: Salt Box was formerly located at 339 South Bunker Hill Avenue #5 C.H.M. The Castle was at 325 South Bunker Hill #27 C.H.M. Future plans for the square will include the addition of Angels Flight, a restaurant and cobblestone streets.

Heritage Square opens Sundays, 1–4.

213-449-0193.

Southwest Museum, 1907. #283 C.H.M. 234 Museum Drive, Highland Park, CA 90042. 213-221-2163; 213-221-2164. Open.

Northeast Police Station, 1925–26. #274 C.H.M. 6045 York Blvd., Highland Park.

The Charles Lumnis House 1898–1910. #68 C.H.M. 200 East Avenue 43, Highland Park, CA 90031. 213-222-0546. Note: The Southern California Historical Society has its headquarters here as well.

Casa de Adobe, 1914. 4603 N. Figueroa, Highland Park, CA 90042. 213-221-2163. This is not, as so many people believe, an authentic adobe. It is a replica of what an Hispanic Adobe looked like.

San Encino Abbey, 1915. #106 C.H.M. 6211 Arroyo Glen, Highland Park, CA 90042. This is a private residence.

Judson Studios, 1897–1920. #62 C.H.M. 220 S. Avenue 66, Highland Park, CA 90042. 213-255-0131. This is where all the gorgeous art glass came from that decorated Pasadena's homes for decades.

Historic Homes: *Queen Anne Eastlake Home,* 1887. #142 C.H.M. 5905 El Mio Drive, Highland Park, CA 90042. A private residence.

The Swiss Chalet, 1905. 3925 San Rafael, Highland Park.

The Hiner House, 1910. #105 C.H.M. 4757 N. Figueroa Street, Highland Park, CA 90042. Private residence.

Hoakum House, 1915. #287 C.H.M.

140 South 59th Street, Highland Park.

Munger Home, 1889. #107 C.H.M. 432 North Avenue 66, Highland Park.

Private Residence, 1895. #143 C.H.M. 6028 Hayes Avenue, Highland Park.

Judson Home, 1895. 216 Thorne, Highland Park.

Fargo House, 1908. 206 Thorne Street, Highland Park.

House, 1905. 5903 Echo Street, Highland Park.

House, 1910. 5915 Echo Street, Highland Park.

Bent House, 1909. Avenue 49, Highland Park.

Historic Schools: *Cathedral High School,* 1923. #281 C.H.M. 1253 Stadium Way, Highland Park. Oldest Catholic High School. Established by the Archdiocese of Los Angeles.

Other: *Hall of Letters,* 1904–1905. Old campus Occidental College. Northwest corner Figueroa and Avenue 50, Highland Park.

Masonic Temple #282 C.H.M. 104 North Avenue 56, Highland Park.

Highland Park Ebell Club, 1913. 131 South Avenue 57, Highland Park.

Mount Washington Cable Car Station, 1909. #269 C.H.M. 200 West Avenue 43, Highland Park.

Today, railroad station survives as a private residence.

Historic Photographs: *Peter Antheil,* 1951 Nolden Street, Los Angeles, CA 90041.

Old Los Angeles and Pasadena photographs. 213-255-7097.

—— HOLLYWOOD ——

History: The Gabrielino Indians are the first recorded residents of what is now Hollywood. They were noted in a diary on the 1769 expedition of Don Gaspar de Portolá. Camping overnight near what is now Elysian Park, the group made their way west across the foothill base of the Santa Monica

Mountains. The largest Village was located near the mouth of a canyon at the north end of what is now Sycamore Avenue.

The westerly half of today's Hollywood was once part of the *Rancho La Brea,* named for the swamps of tar noted by Portolá in 1769. *Rancho La Brea* was granted to Antonio Jose Rocha and Nemisio Dominguez. The first permanent resident of the rancho was James Thompson. After numerous title transfers, the rancho eventually ended up in the hands of John and Henry Hancock. Their portion became a large part of West Hollywood.

Another part of Hollywood was known as *Rancho Los Feliz,* a tract of nearly 7,000 acres, from what is now Gower Street on the west, to the Los Angeles River on the east, and from the top of the hills on the north, to the Los Angeles pueblo limits on the south. Eventually a large portion of this rancho came into the hands of Griffith J. Griffith in 1882.

It was a Kansas prohibitionist named Harvey Wilcox, however, that would develop the area known as Hollywood. He came to Los Angeles in 1883, opened a real estate office and began to buy and subdivide land. In 1886 he bought a 120 acre tract that ran from Whitley Avenue east on Sunset Boulevard to Gower, north on Gower to Hollywood Boulevard, west to Vine Street, north to Franklin Avenue, west to Whitley and south to Sunset. Harvey's wife, Daeida, while travelling East met a woman who described her summer home in "Hollywood." The name so pleased Mrs. Wilcox that upon her return from the East she christened her Cahuenga Valley ranch with the name. When Mr. Wilcox subdivided his ranch in 1887, he named it Hollywood.

Historical Societies: *Hollywood Heritage,* P.O. Box 2586, Hollywood, CA 90028. 213-465-5993. Don Hunt, president.

Historic Districts: *Hollywood Blvd.*

(Originally called Prospect). Extends from Gower to La Brea. Designated in 1986. Hollywood.

Whitley Heights National Historic District, 1902. See Historic Districts, p. 184.

Wilton Historic District, Wilton Place. See Historic Districts p. 184.

Las Colinas Heights.

St. Andrews Place, 200 block of St. Andrews and adjoining Gramercy Place. Area developed after 1910 when Cecil B. deMille began movie-making history one mile to the north. Currently seeking designation as an Historic District.

Historians: *Marian Gibbons,* founder of Hollywood Heritage. Member of the Central City Association. 213-463-1018.

Christy Johnson McAvoy, 3103 Lindo Street, Hollywood, CA 90068. 213-851-8854.

Don Hunt, President of Hollywood Heritage. 213-465-5993.

Historical Landmarks: *The Barn* (The Hollywood Studio Museum), 1913. 2100 North Highland, Hollywood. 213-874-BARN.

This is probably the most famous landmark in Hollywood, being the original barn where the Squaw Man was shot in 1913. Wonderful Hollywood memorabilia here.

Hollywood Bowl and Museum, 1922. 2301 N. Highland Avenue, Hollywood. 213-850-2000.

The pageantry movement was sweeping the country from 1914 to 1920. When the Bowl opened in 1922, its grand vision was to bring art and democracy into total fulfillment.

Hollywood Sign. 1923. #111 C.H.M. (Hollywoodland) Near the north end of Beachwood Drive, Mt. Lee, Hollywood. Each letter is about fifty feet high.

Hollywood Stone Gates, 1920s. Beachwood Drive, Hollywood. (Westshire and Belden Drives). #20 C.H.M.

The Janes House, 1903. (The Janes House Square 1987) 6541 Hollywood

Blvd., Hollywood.

Long a scene of controversy as to whether it would be saved or not, today the Janes home was been beautifully restored and is the main focus of attention in a new shopping center complex. It shows what can happen when developers utilize historic structures in their plans rather than tear them down. Developers Bamshaud & Edrehemian — Congratulations!

Charlie Chaplin Bronze, 1680 N. Vine Street, Hollywood (Lobby of the Taft Building).

The High Tower, 1920. North end of Hightower Drive, Hollywood.

Hollywood Murals, northwest corner Ivar, southeast corner Hudson; southeast corner Wilcox, Hollywood.

Hollywood Walk of Fame, 1950s. Designated 1986 #194 C.H.M. Between Gower Street and Sycamore Avenue and Vine Street, between Yucca Street and Sunset Blvd., Hollywood. Over 2500 names.

Crossroads of the World, 1936. 6671 Sunset Blvd., Hollywood. #134 C.H.M. 213-463-5611.

Capitol Records, 1954. 1750 N. Vine Street, Hollywood. 213-462-6252.

Hollywood Palladium, 1940s. 6215 W. Sunset Blvd., Hollywood. 213-466-4311.

William Stromberg Clock, 1927. #316 C.H.M. 6439 Hollywood Blvd., Hollywood.

Columbia Square, 1920. 6121 Sunset Blvd., Hollywood. Now CBS. 213-460-3000.

Farmer's Market, 1934. 6333 West Third Street, Los Angeles. 213-933-9211. A little too far southwest of Hollywood but within the original Rancho La Brea area.

Other Buildings: *Hollywood Post Office,* 1935. 1615 N. Wilcox, Hollywood. 213-464-2194. A W.P.A. art project 1937.

Bob Hope U.S.O. Headquarters, 1940s. 1641 Ivar, Hollywood.

Hollywood Reporter, 1930. 6715 W. Sunset Blvd., Hollywood. 213-464-7411.

Berwin Entertainment Complex. The old Hollywood Athletic Club, 1920s. 6525 Sunset Blvd., Hollywood. 213-464-0700.

Hollywood Masonic Temple. #277 C.H.M. 1922. 6840 Hollywood Blvd., Hollywood.

Fire Station No. 27. Built 1930. #165 C.H.M. 1355 North Cahuenga Blvd., Hollywood.

Y.W.C.A. Hollywood Studio Club, 1926. 1215 Lodi Place, Hollywood. #175 C.H.M. A Julie Morgan design.

Young starlets such as Marilyn Monroe, Kim Novak and a host of others stayed here for short times before making it "big."

Hollywood Legion Stadium, 1939. 1628 El Centro Ave., Hollywood.

Parva-Sed Apta Apartments, 1920s. 1817 N. Ivar Avenue, Hollywood. It was here that Nathaniel West prepared to write one of the most famous books on Hollywood, *The Day of the Locust.*

Alto-Nido Apts., 1920s. 1851 N. Ivar Avenue, Hollywood. Here, William Holden or Joe Gillis (as he was known in Sunset Boulevard) "lived."

Vedanta Temple, 1938. 6300 Vedanta Terrace, Hollywood.

Screen Actors Guild Headquarters. Formerly Hollywood Congregational Church. 7065 Hollywood Blvd., Hollywood. 213-465-4600.

Krotona, 1914. Between Argyle and Gower, north of the north end of Carmen and Vista del Mar Avenues. Hollywood.

Historic Churches: *Hollywood Presbyterian Church,* 1760 Gower, Hollywood. 213-463-7161. Lloyd Oglivie, Pastor. (1902, first structure 1909. Current buildings date from 1923).

St. Mary's of the Angel's Church, 1930. #136 C.H.M. 4510 Finley Avenue, Hollywood.

First United Methodist Church, 1929. (Hollywood Methodist) 6917 Franklin Avenue, Hollywood. #248 C.H.M. 213-874-2104.

Courtesy Hollywood Heritage

First Southern Baptist Church, 1922. (Originally a synogogue). 1528 Wilton Place, Hollywood.

Libraries: *John C. Fremont.* #303 C.H.M. 6121 Melrose, Hollywood.

Cahuenga Branch Library, 1916. #314 C.H.M. 4591 West Santa Monica Blvd., Hollywood.

Historic Theatres: *Cast Theatre,* 804 North El Centro, Hollywood. 213-462-0265. Oldest intimate theatre in Hollywood.

Huntington Hartford Theatre, 1926. Now the *James Doolittle Theatre.* 1615 N. Vine Street, Hollywood. 213-462-6666.

Warner Bros. Theatre, 1928. Now the *Hollywood Pacific.* 6433 Hollywood Blvd., Hollywood. 213-464-4111.

Grauman's Chinese Theatre, 1927. Now *Mann's Chinese Theatre.* #55 C.H.M. 6925 Hollywood Blvd., Hollywood. 213-464-8111.

John Anson Ford's Theatre, 1920s. The old *Pilgrimage Play Theatre,* 2580 Cahuenga Blvd. East, Hollywood. 213-972-7200.

The (Hollywood) Palace, 1927. 1735 N. Vine, Hollywood. 213-462-3000.

The (Hollywood) Pantages Theatre, 1929. #193 C.H.M. 6233 Hollywood Blvd., Hollywood. 213-216-6666.

The Greek Theatre, 1929–30. 2700 N. Vermont Road, Hollywood. 213-410-1062. (See Los Feliz)

El Capitan, 1926. Now Paramount Theatre Building. 6838 Hollywood Blvd., Hollywood. 213-463-3263.

Historic Studios: *Kalem, Essanay, Monogram* and *Allied Artist Studios,* 1912 on. #198 C.H.M. Now *KCET* Studios, 4401 Sunset Blvd., Hollywood.

Paramount Studios, 1927. (Original Gate on Bronson) 5555 Melrose Avenue, Hollywood. 213-468-5000.

Raleigh Studios, 1915. 650 N. Bronson, Hollywood. 213-466-3111. Believed to be the oldest continuously operating movie studio in Hollywood.

Charlie Chaplin Studios, 1918. (Now A & M) 1416 N. La Brea Avenue, Hollywood. #58 C.H.M. 213-469-2411.

Warner Bros. Studios, 1922. Southeast corner Sunset and Bronson, Hollywood.

Vitagraph, 1916. Today's *ABC,* 4151 Prospect, Hollywood.

Museums: *The Hollywood Studio Museum,* 2100 N. Highland, Hollywood. 213-874-BARN.

Hollywood Wax Museum, 6767 Hollywood, Hollywood. 213-462-8860.

Max Factor's Makeup Museum, 1666 Highland, Hollywood. 213-856-6297 (Bob Salvatori, curator).

Historic Hotels: *Highland Camrose Bungalow Village,* 1916–23. #291 C.H.M. 2103–2115 North Highland, Hollywood.

Montecito Apartments, 1931. 6650 Franklin Avenue, Hollywood.

Sunset Towers, 1930. (St. James Club) 8358 Sunset Blvd., Hollywood.

Chateau Marmont, 1924. #151 C.H.M. 8221 Sunset Blvd., Hollywood. 213-656-1010.

Sunset Plaza Apts., 1220 Sunset Plaza Drive, Hollywood. A Paul Williams design. #233 C.H.M.

Hollywood Roosevelt Hotel, 1929. 7000 Hollywood Blvd., Hollywood. 213-466-7000.

Site of the first academy awards, May 16, 1929. Beautifully restored! Also open is the Cinegrill Restaurant and Theodore's, both located in the Roosevelt Hotel. Much of Hollywood's recent revitalization is due in part to the remarkable restoration of this wonderful hotel.

Historic Schools: *Hollywood High School,* 1904. (Founded). 1521 Highland Avenue, Hollywood. 213-467-6191.

Historic Restaurants: *Musso & Frank's Grill,* 1919. 6667 Hollywood Blvd., Hollywood. 213-467-7788.

C.C. Brown's Ice Cream Parlor, 1929. 7007 Hollywood Blvd., Hollywood. 213-464-9726.

Yamashiro Restaurant, 1913. 1999 North Sycamore, Hollywood. 213-466-5125. Adolph and Eugene Bernheimer's former hilltop mansion. The Bernheimers were importers of fine oriental goods.

Tick-Tock Restaurant, 1930s. 1716 N. Cahuenga, Hollywood. 213-463-7576.

Cock "N" Bull, 1937. (just closed its doors after 50 years) 9170 Sunset Blvd., Los Angeles.

Brown Derby, 6301 Hollywood Blvd., Hollywood. 213-469-5151.

Historic Homes: *The Plummer Home,* 1878. 7377 Santa Monica Blvd., Hollywood.

This home has been moved, restored and is now located in, of all places, Calabasas. It stands in a beautiful park right next to the Leonis Adobe. See Calabasas.

Janes Home, 1903. (Janes House Square Open '87) #227 C.H.M. 6541 Hollywood Blvd., Hollywood. (Bamshaud & Edrehemian developers)

Hollyhock House, 1919. #12 C.H.M. 4800 Hollywood Blvd., Hollywood. 213-662-7272.

Hollyhock House was designed by Frank Lloyd Wright in 1921. Aline Barnsdall donated the entire area, home and land, to the city. Open.

Schindler Home, 1921. 833 N. Kings Road, Hollywood.

Taggart House, 1920s. 5423 Black Oak Drive, Hollywood. A Frank L. Wright design. (See Los Feliz)

Storer House, 1923. #96 C.H.M. 8161 Hollywood Blvd., Hollywood. A Frank Lloyd design.

Freeman House, 1924. #247 C.H.M. 1962 Glencoe Way, Hollywood. A Frank Lloyd design.

Novarro House, 1928. #130 C.H.M. 5609 Valley Oak Drive, Hollywood. (See Los Feliz) A Frank Lloyd design.

Sowden House, 1926. (See Los Feliz.) 5121 Franklin Avenue, Hollywood. A Frank Lloyd Wright design.

Craftsman Home, 1910–1915. 6407 Dix Street, Hollywood.

Craftsman Home, 1910–1915. 1931 Ivar, Hollywood.

The Lovell House, 1929. #123 C.H.M. 4616 Dundee Drive, Hollywood. (See Los Feliz) Richard Neutra design.

Ennis House, 1924. #149 C.H.M. 2607 Glendower Avenue, Hollywood. (See Los Feliz) A Frank Lloyd Wright design.

C.E. Toberman Estate, 1924. #285 C.H.M. 1847 Camino Palmero, Hollywood. Toberman was one of the early Hollywood movers and shakers.

The Buck House, 1934. #122 C.H.M. *Bollman House,* 1922. #235 C.H.M. 1530 North Ogden Drive, Hollywood. A Lloyd Wright design.

Arzner-Morgan Residence, 1931.

#301 C.H.M. 2249 Mountain Oak Drive, Hollywood. Home of Hollywood's first female director.

Rocha House, 1865. 2400 Shenandoah Street, Los Angeles. Listed now in Los Angeles, but part of the old Rancho La Brea area.

Will and Ariel Durant Home, 1920s. Briarcliff Road, Hollywood.

Wattles Gardens, 1912. 1859 North Curson, Hollywood. Beautiful estate, now the home to Hollywood Heritage.

Wolff's Lair, 1920s. Hollywood Hills. Developer of Hollywood land. Currently owned by Bob Crane, Realtor.

Villa San Guiseppe, 1927. (See Los Feliz area) Earle C. Anthony Home, 3412 Waverly, Los Angeles. Listed in Los Angeles, but part of the old Rancho Los Feliz.

Today home is known as the Sisters of the Immaculate Heart Retreat.

Castle Kalmia, late 1920s. 8311 Sunset Blvd., Hollywood (1468 Sweetzer). Recently purchased by a famous notable and has been beautifully restored.

Villa Carlotta, 1926. #315 C.H.M. 5959 Franklin Avenue, Hollywood.

Bernheimer Home, 1913. Now Yamashiro. 1999 N. Sycamore.

Holly Chateau, 1890s. Today known as the Magic Castle. 7001 Franklin, Hollywood.

Motion Picture Homes: *Charlie Chaplin,* 2010 De Mille Drive, Hollywood and 6147 Temple Hill Drive, Hollywood.

Pola Negri, 6533 Cahuenga Terrace, Hollywood.

Cecil B. deMille, 2000 De Mille Drive and 6136 Lexington Street, Hollywood.

W.C. Fields, 2015 DeMille Drive, Hollywood.

American Society of Cinematographer's Headquarters, 1903. 1782 Orange Avenue, Hollywood. This mission-revival building is rumored to have housed Frank Baum when he wrote "The Wizard of Oz."

Mae West 570 Rossmore Drive, Hollywood.

Fatty Arbuckle, 649 West Adams Blvd., Hollywood.

Theda Bara, 649 West Adams, Hollywood.

Raoul Walsh, 649 West Adams, Hollywood.

Norma Talmadge and Joe Schenck, also 649 West Adams, Hollywood.

Rudolph Valentino, 1436 Bella Drive, Hollywood. (Falcon Lair) (Also listed in Beverly Hills). Also 6776 Wedgewood Drive. (Demolished).

Mary Pickford, 1403 Western Avenue and 56 Fremont Place, Los Angeles.

Jesse L. Lasky, 720 Hillside Avenue, Hollywood.

Mack Sennett, 1141 Westmoreland Place, Hollywood.

Mabel Normand, 3089 Seventh Street, Hollywood. (Demolished)

Mary Miles Minter, 701 S. New Hampshire, Hollywood.

Barbara La Marr, 6672 Whitley Terrace, Hollywood.

Historic Sites: Site *Earl Carroll Theatre,* 1938. (today a T.V. facility) 6230 W. Sunset Blvd., Hollywood.

Site of the *Brown Derby Restaurant,* 1926. 1628 N. Vine Street, Hollywood. (Resurrected at 6301 Hollywood Blvd. See Restaurants).

Site of the *Franklin Garden Apts.,* 1820. #192 C.H.M. 6917–6933 Franklin Avenue, Hollywood.

Site of *Schwab's Drugstore,* 1930s. Sunset Blvd., and Laurel Canyon, Hollywood.

Site of *Glengarry Castle,* 1909. Northeast corner of Franklin and Argyle, Hollywood.

Sans Souci Castle, 1912. Across the street on Argyle, Hollywood.

Site of the filming of the *First Talking Feature Film, The Jazz Singer,* 1927. #180 C.H.M. 5800 Sunset Blvd., Hollywood.

Site of the *Garden of Allah,* 1921. 8152 Sunset Blvd., Hollywood.

Site of the *Masquers Club Building,* 1920s. #226 C.H.M. 1765 North Sycamore, Hollywood.

Site of the *Hollywood Hotel, 1903.*

Corner Highland Blvd. and Hollywood Blvd., Hollywood.

Site of the *Casa Don Thomas,* 1853. Franklin Avenue, west of Highland, Hollywood. First adobe house in Hollywood.

Site of *Taft House,* 1900 Farm House. Originally located on Hollywood Blvd. Moved to Sunset in 1919. Destroyed by fire in 1982.

Site of *The Cahuenga House,* or *Blondeau Tavern,* N.W. corner of Sunset and Gower, Hollywood. Hollywood's first motion picture studio, the Nestor Film Company began here.

Site of *Garden Court* Apt., 1919. 7021 Hollywood Blvd. Part of "old Hollywood." Demolished 1985. #243 C.H.M.

Site of the old *Pass Hotel* or *Eight-Mile House,* Cahuenga Pass, Hollywood.

Historic Parks, Cemeteries: *Hollywood Memorial Park Cemetery,* 1900. 6000 Santa Monica Blvd., Hollywood. 213-469-1181. Here lie Douglas Fairbanks, Rudolph Valentino, Tyrone Power and many more movie greats.

Hollyhock House Barnsdall Park, Art Gallery. #12 C.H.M. 4804 Hollywood Blvd., Hollywood. #33-34 C.H.M. Art Center and Art Park. 213-485-2116.

Griffith Park and Observatory, 2800 E. Observatory Road, Hollywood. 213-664-1191. Site of an ancient Indian Village.

DeLongpre Park, 1350 N. Cherokee Avenue, Hollywood. This park contains a Rudolph Valentino Monument.

Forest Lawn Hollywood Hills Memorial Park, 6300 Forest Lawn Drive, Hollywood. 213-254-7251. (Note: There is the *Mexican Heritage Museum* and the *Plaza of American Heritage* recently opened. 818-241-4151 Community Affairs.)

Historic Reservoir: *Hollywood Reservoir,* 1924. Hollywood Hills, Hollywood. The work of William Mulholland.

Other Historic Information: *Hollywood Photographers Archives.* A non-profit organization devoted to preservation, study and celebration of outstanding still photography, pertaining to the history of Hollywood. Organization created by famous world-reknown photographer Sid Avery. Located at 820 N. La Brea, Los Angeles, CA 90038. 213-466-5404.

Hollywood Miniatures, 1940s. Joe Pelkofer, a cabinet maker created a miniature of Hollywood in the 1940s. These remarkable miniatures, long out of public eye have recently been refurbished by Landmark Entertainment Group. Hollywood. For a time were at 6834 Hollywood Blvd., Hollywood.

Hollywood Arts Council, 1313 N. Vine Street, Room 121, Hollywood. 213-462-2355.

Businesses: *Larry Edmunds,* since 1955. 6658 Hollywood Blvd., Hollywood. 213-463-3273.

Hollywood Piano Rental Company, since 1928. 1647 North Highland Avenue, Hollywood. 213-462-2329.

Arrow Key Service, since 1923. 5517 Hollywood Blvd., Hollywood. 213-465-4134.

William Stromberg Jewelers, since 1920. 6439 Hollywood Blvd., Hollywood. 213-465-6115.

Bernard Luggage, since 1918. 1642 North Vine, Hollywood. 213-462-3296.

Baby Sitters, since 1948. 6362 Hollywood Blvd., Hollywood. 213-469-8246.

George Georges & Sons, since 1933. 1757 N. Highland Avenue, Hollywood. 213-464-3941.

Prime School, 1948. 7045 W. Sunset, Hollywood. 213-462-8498.

Haroutunian Oriental Rugs, since 1909. 7910 Santa Monica Blvd., Hollywood. 213-656-7575.

John's Pipe Shop, since 1908. 6765 Hollywood Blvd., Hollywood. 213-462-9013.

Party Stores, since 1934. 5969 Melrose, Hollywood. 213-467-7124.

Books: Bruce Torrance, *Hollywood: The First 100 Years,* published by the Hollywood Chamber of Commerce, 1979.

Emily B. Carter, *Hollywood: The Story of the Cahuengas,* 1926.

Mary Crosswell, *The Story of Hollywood,* 1905.

Beth Day, *This Was Hollywood: An Affectionate History of Filmland's Golden Years,* New York, 1960.

HUNTINGTON PARK

History: First European to arrive in the area was Don Jose Maria Lugo who first settled in Santa Barbara. His son, Antonio Maria Lugo applied for a grant of 29,500 acres known as the

Vicente Lugo. Permission, Helen Atkins.

Rancho San Antonio. The land encompassed present day cities of Vernon, Bell, Maywood, Cudhay, Bell

Gardens, Commerce, Montebello, and Monterey Park. Break up of this Rancho in the 1870s and the arrival of the Americans meant that the old road from Lugo's ranch to Los Angeles became Pacific Blvd.

Developers A.L. Burbank and E.V. Baker were among the first Americans in the area. In 1899 they had no intention of building a city; that was left for others. Weber-Garlow-Hubbard-Walters and Tate formed the Huntington Park Improvement Association and thereafter Huntington Park was off and running. In 1906 it was incorporated.

Historical Society: None.

Historical Landmarks: *Tweedy Home.* Moved from Southgate to Huntington Park. Right after move, burned.

Lugo Plaza, 2570 East Slauson, Huntington Park. (Opened November 1986) After the unfortunate loss by fire of the beautiful Lugo Adobe in Bell Gardens, the firm of Watson and Associates decided to build a replica of the Lugo Adobe incorporating it within the overall design of the shopping center.

Businesses: *Pacific Pumps,* 1923. 5715 Bickett Street, Huntington Park. 213-588-2201.

Sargent Industries, 1920. 2533 E. 56th Street, Huntington Park. 213-583-4161.

W.W. Henry Co., 1933. (Los Angeles) 5731 Bickett Street, Huntington Park. 213-583-4961.

Chamber of Commerce, 213-585-1155.

Other: *Huntington Park City Hall,* Redevelopment Dept. 213-582-6161.

—— INGLEWOOD ——

History: *Rancho Aguaje de la Centinela* was the name of the rancho that comprised the area later known as Inglewood. A home was built in 1834 by Ynacio Machado, one of the soldiers sent to protect the original settlers of Los Angeles. After several additions and several owners, the Rancho Centinela and Rancho Sausal Redondo were purchased by Sir Robert Burnett of Scotland. This land was leased and later sold to Daniel Freeman. Freeman settled in the Centinela ranch, and built a vast empire through dry farming.

Inglewood was the first settlement to be carved out of the 25,000 acre Centinela ranch in 1888. From 1920 to 1925 Inglewood was the fastest growing city in the United States. After 1923, the city became the chinchilla capital of the world when Mr. M.E. Chapman brought animals here from Peru.

Historical Society: *Historical Society,* 7634 Midfield Avenue, Inglewood, CA 90045. 213-649-6272.

Historical Landmarks: *Centinela Rancho,* La Case de La Centinela Adobe, 1834. Historical Museum and also where the historical society meets. 7634 Midfield Avenue, Inglewood, CA 90045. 213-649-6272.

Also on the Rancho grant is the 1887 Daniel Freeman Land Office and Centinela Valley Heritage and Research Center. Open Wednesdays.

Mines Fields, 1927. L.A.X. Andrew Bennett Ranch was converted into Mines Field. Charles Lindbergh flew the first passenger plane into Mines with Will Rogers and the National Air Races were initiated in 1928 with Lindbergh as one of the participants.

Hangar 1, 1929. L.A.X. 5701 West Imperial Highway, Inglewood. #44 C.H.M. Curtiss Flying Service con-structed hangar in 1929. Hangar 1 was renovated for offices in 1987.

Historic Theatres: *Loyola Theatre,* 1948. 8610 S. Sepulveda, Inglewood. #259 C.H.M.

Historic Parks: *Centinela Park Centinela Springs,* 700 Warren Lane, Inglewood. 213-412-5370. Oldest park in Inglewood.

Inglewood Park and Cemetery, 720 E. Florence, Inglewood. 213-412-6500.

Historic Churches: *First Presbyterian Church of Inglewood,* 1890. 100 N. Hillcrest, Inglewood. 213-677-5733. Oldest church in Inglewood.

First United Methodist Church of Inglewood. 304 E. Spruce, Inglewood. 213-677-7106.

Museums: *Aviation Library and Museum,* Northrop University, 1155 West Arbor Vitae, Inglewood. 213-776-5466. Open 8–4:30 Monday thru Friday.

Historic Restaurants: *Pann's.* 50s spaceage style coffee shop. 6710 La Tijera Blvd., Inglewood. 213-776-3770.

Historic Sites: *Site of Daniel Freeman Home.* Now the Daniel Freeman Hospital. 333 N. Prairee, Inglewood. 213-674-7050.

Site of *Sante Fe Passenger Station,* 1914. 322 N. Eucalyptus, Inglewood.

Businesses: *Troost Monument Company,* since 1870. 717 S. Florence Avenue, Inglewood. 213-678-3545.

Wise Tire and Brake Co., since 1923. 949 S. La Brea, Inglewood. 213-677-1515. Oldest business in the same family in Inglewood.

Sparling Buick, since 1920s. 217 N. La Brea, Inglewood. 213-677-1191.

Buffington Cadillac, since 1920s. 200 N. La Brea, Inglewood. 213-677-2117.

Harris Lumber Co., since 1909.

225 N. La Brea, Inglewood. 213-677-1301.

Other: *George Pepperdine Home,* 1912. 9550 Crenshaw Blvd., Inglewood.

This beautiful 14,850 square foot home built on a 35 acre site was destroyed in 1986. It was owned by the Crenshaw Christian Center who offered it to anyone who would move it. Alas, no one did.

—— LA CANADA-FLINTRIDGE ——

History, La Canada: In 1772 the story of La Canada began with the arrival of Don Jose Maria de la Verdugo. In 1784 he applied and received the Rancho San Rafael comprising almost 36,000 acres. It is today's La Canada, Glendale, Eagle Rock, Burbank and more.

Jose gave the name La Canada meaning Mountain Valley to the area known today as La Canada. Legends say that for a century and a half the padres travelled through these canyons from the Mission San Gabriel to the Mission San Fernando.

In 1859 Rancho La Canada was given as a separate grant to Jonathan Scott and Benjamin Hayes. Later Glassell and Chapman secured the Rancho and in 1876 Dr. Lanterman and his partner Colonel Williams purchased it. It was these two men that opened the area up for development. The La Canada Post Office was established in 1884, the Grammar School in 1889 and the La Canada Improvement Club in 1913. The various canyons still bear names of early settlers: Dunks, Hall, Beckley, Pickens, Price and Weber.

Historical Society: *La Canada Historical Society,* P.O. Box 541, La Canada, CA 91011. Russ Campbell, chairperson.

Historical Parks: *Descanso Gardens,* 1418 Descanso Drive, La Canada. 818-790-5571.

Park of the Rancho San Rafael granted in 1784 to Jose M. Verdugo. In 1937 Manchester Body purchased it. He built a 22 room home overlooking the gardens, and planted thousands of camelias, roses and many more beautiful flowers and plants. The County acquired the property in 1953. Open 9–5 daily.

Historic Homes: *El Nido, The Pink Castle,* 1911. (Private property) 5455 Castleknoll Drive, La Canada. One of the most famous landmarks as well. Built for California Lt. Governor Albert Wallace by Architect Arthur Benton. Occasionally the owners let special groups through.

Villa Elena, 1933. (Private Residence) 1618 Fairmont Avenue. Count Victor Wenzel von Metternick's home. Built originally for J.C. Penney. Purchased unseen by Metternick from an article in Esquire in 1929–30.

Lanterman Home, 1914. 4420 Encinas Drive, La Canada. 818-790-1421.

Recently deeded to city, however a controversy exists as to how the city can justify the cost of its operation. Recently received a $500,000 grant to restore home.

Homewood, Home of Dr. J.L. Lanterman built in 1877–78.

South side of Verdugo Blvd. West of Encinas Drive. The giant eucalyptus trees which line the south side of Foothill from Verdugo Boulevard west were planted by Dr. Lanterman.

Note: Paul Williams, noted black architect is reputed to have built about 23 homes in the area.

Historic Churches: *Church of the Lighted Window,* 1924. 1200 Foothill Blvd., La Canada, CA 91011. 818-790-1185.

Historic Schools: *St. Francis High School,* 1920s. The original Flintridge

Country Club. 200 Foothill Blvd., La Canada, CA 91011. 213-681-4251.

Flintridge Riding Club, 1920s. 4625 Oakgrove Drive, La Canada, CA 91011. 818-952-9287.

Flintridge Sacred Heart Academy, 1927. Once the Flintridge Biltmore. St. Katherine Drive, La Canada. 818-796-1134.

Other: *Eucalyptus Trees,* Gould Avenue. Will D. Gould, a Los Angeles attorney, acquired a lot from Col. Williams and planted these trees.

Historian: June Dougherty, 818-790-7301. Can be reached at the Lanterman Home. June has also written a pamphlet on the area. *History of La Canada,* published by the League of Women Voters.

Book: Grace Oberbeck, *The History of the La Crescenta and La Canada Valleys.* Montrose, 1938.

La Canada Library has more historical information as well. 818-790-3330.

History, Flintridge: In 1913 Senator Frank P. Flint purchased about 700 acres of the Turner Ranch, a portion of Rancho San Rafael. He subdivided it and named it *Flintridge.*

At about this same time, Edwin Earl a Los Angeles publisher, purchased 500 acres of Colonel Hall's ranch which adjoined Rancho La Canada on the north side and subdivided it, naming it Alta Canyada.

—— LA CRESCENTA ——

History: Historically the Foothills date back to 1784 when Don Jose Maria Verdugo established his 36,000 acre *Rancho San Rafael.* But it was not until the years between 1870 and 1920 that developers discovered the Rancho's fertile acreage and began to lay the foundations for communities that now make up the Foothills. While many of the other areas incorporated, La Crescenta and Montrose still remain as part of Los Angeles County. After World War II the area emerged from an agricultural economy to become a choice location for veterans seeking single family residences on hills overlooking the rest of the city.

Historical Society: None.

Historical Churches: *La Crescenta*

Presbyterian Church, 1886. 2902 Montrose, La Crescenta. 818-249-6137. Originally on Dyer Road.

St. Luke's of the Mountain 1924–54. Episcopal Church. 2563 Foothill Blvd., La Crescenta. 818-248-3639.

Historic Buildings: *Dunsmore Winery,* 1911. North end of Dunsmore Avenue, La Crescenta.

Castles: *Steve and Pat Holst,* 5526 Freeman, La Crescenta. This private residence has even got a dungeon!

Craftspeople: *Mimi McIntosh,* artist. La Crescenta. 818-241-4319.

Chamber of Commerce: *Crescenta Valley Chamber of Commerce,* 3131 Foothill Blvd., Suite M, La Crescenta, CA 91214. 818-248-4957.

—LA HABRA (ORANGE COUNTY) —

History: Meaning "Pass through the hills," La Habra stems from the early days of Spanish exploration. The land belonged first to the Mission San Gabriel. It was then granted to Mariano R. Roldan. The 6,698 acre

Rancho Canada de la Habra passed into Mariano's hands in 1839. It then went to Basque sheep ranchers; sold by Abel Stearns to English, Swiss and American settlers who dry-farmed it. The first store, post office and schoolhouse were built in 1896 as the community of La Habra came into being with the work of Willets J. Hole of Indiana. The first club was the Ladies' Mutual Improvement Club formed in 1898. These women held the first "Settlers Picnic" which in turn led to the formation of the old Settlers' Historical Society.

Historical Society: *La Habra Old Settlers Historical Society,* Bill Proud, president. 404 Magnolia Avenue, Brea. 714-529-4726. Secretary Edith Bee Bower, 213-697-2069.

Historical Landmarks: *Children's Museum of La Habra,* 301 S. Euclid, La Habra. 213-526-2227. Catherine Michaels, Director. The Children's Museum is located in a city park. On the grounds is the Union Pacific Railroad Depot, 1923, which has been restored. In the caboose there is an exhibit of the History of La Habra maintained by the Historical Society.

Pacific Electric Depot, 1909. 311 S. Euclid Street, La Habra.

Today this is used as the La Habra Community Theatre. It is next door to the Union Pacific Depot and Children's Museum. It is also on the National Register of Historic Places.

Landmarks: *Former President's Richard Nixon's First Law Office,* 1937. 135 West La Habra Blvd., La Habra.

As a young attorney, Nixon's career was launched here with a prominent law firm.

Historic Sites: *La Habra's Birthplace Site,* La Habra Civic Center. Southeast corner La Habra Blvd. and Euclid Street. The Post Office officially named the small settlement La Habra in 1896. The office was located in Z.T. Coy's Country Store.

Historic Churches: *La Habra Methodist Church,* 1898. Now known as the Vine Church. 631 N. Euclid, La Habra. Originally the church was on First and Main Street.

Books: Esther R. Cramer, *The Pass Through the Hills,* The Formative Years of a Southern California Community Fullerton: Sultana Press, 1969.

LA MIRADA

History: Once part of a vast Spanish land grant called *Rancho Los Coyotes,* the area that is now La Mirada was purchased by Andrew McNally of the Rand McNally map firm in 1895. McNally Ranch consisted of huge olive and citrus groves. It was sold for subdivision in 1953. A small community of fewer than 100 homes grew so rapidly that just seven years later, in 1960, La Mirada was incorporated as the 68th city in Los Angeles County.

Historical Landmarks: *McNally Ranch house and Neff Home,* 1893–94. Located between Biola and Valley View Boulevards, just off Stage Road at San Cristobal and San Esteban Streets.

The Neff Home. In 1880 Chicago atlas publisher Andrew McNally purchased the 2,378 acre Windemere Ranch in La Mirada. He planned to subdivide the area into 20 acre estates but the plan was abandoned in 1900. The remaining 1,500 acres were used to plant olive and citrus groves. In 1894 a ranch home was constructed for McNally, but his daughter and son-in-law, Edwin Neff were the first occupants. Ed Neff served as secretary and manager of the La Mirada Land Company. The Neffs lived in the house until McNally's death in 1904. Finally the family sold and/or donated 10 acres around the home to the Southeast Park District for a cultural center.

Historian: *Bob Camp,* La Mirada City Hall, 137 La Mirada Blvd., La Mirada, CA 90638. 213-943-0131.

Historic Farm: *Valley View Farms,* 1933 (El Monte) 13907 Valley View, La Mirada. 213-921-2561.

Books: C.W. Robert Camp, *La Mirada from Rancho to City,* 1970. Sultana Press, Fullerton.

——— LA PUENTE ———
CITY OF INDUSTRY

History: John Rowland and William Workman were both fur traders who had worked for the American Fur Trading Company owned by John Jacob Astor. Both men settled in Taos, New Mexico, a real jumping off place in the 1820s. Rowland had a flour mill and Workman a general store. Both men apparently became dissatisfied with Mexican rule then in effect and decided to come to California. It was a dangerous trip over the old Sante Fe Trail. About 25–30 people set out for the 1200 mile journey in wagon trains. It was an historic trip because when the group arrived in Los Angeles on November 5th, 1841, they were the first American wagon train of settlers in Southern California history.

Both men applied for a land grant and were given preliminary title to the 48,790 acre La Puente Rancho by Governor Alvarado. In 1869 the grant was equally divided between them. Both men raised a family, built homes and proceeded to become active participants in the life of the busy rancho. By 1858, 15,000 grape vines were bearing, 400 apple trees, and 2,000 head of cattle.

That their beautiful homes have been preserved today is unique. The Workman-Temple Homestead is the most beautifully restored landmark, as far as I'm concerned, in Southern California. The Workman-Rowland-Temple saga is one of the most tragic as well in the annals of San Gabriel history. Their stories can all be told today because the City of Industry restored this magnificent estate.

Historical Society: *La Puente Valley*

Historical Society, P.O. Box 522, La Puente, CA 91747. 818-336-7644; 818-336-2382 or 818-336-3384. President Flow Rutherford, 818-333-6505.

Historical Landmarks: *Workman-Temple Homestead, 1841.* La Casa Nueva, 1923. The Workman Home, 1844, 1869. El Campo Santo Cemetery, 1850. El Paseo de Memorial de Pio Pico, 1981. 15415 East Don Julian Road, City of Industry, CA 91744. 818-968-8492. On the National Register of Historic Places.

Heritage Square La Puente Historical Society, Rowland Home, 1855. 16021 Gale Street, City of Industry, 818-336-7644.

This two story brick home is the first such house of its kind built in Southern California. It is also the oldest brick house now standing, as well.

On this property are also the *Dibble Museum* and *Homestead*. The homestead is open to the public and special tours may be arranged. (The Round House) Also on the property is an 1855 adobe kitchen dating from the time of Rowland.

Rowland Adobe Ranch House, 1850. 130 Avenida Alipax, Walnut, CA 91789.

This is located in Lemon Creek Park. Built on the old La Puente Rancho for ranch hands.

Historic Buildings: *Stafford Milling* and Warehouse Co., 1925. 15566 E. Stafford, La Puente.

Beanery or Bean Warehouse, 1895. 15900 Old Valley, La Puente. Used for sorting and sacking dried beans. Later Mercantile and Post Office located in west end. First Walnut Packing House located at east end of building.

Courtyard, La Casa Nueva
WORKMAN & TEMPLE HOMESTEAD

Courtesy Workman-Temple Homestead

Faure Building, 1892. 15842 Old Valley, La Puente.

First a garage, then a restaurant; garage again, then *Puente Valley Journal* office. Masons have used upstairs since 1914.

Joseph Marcellin Home, 1904. 15835 Main Street, La Puente.

Casimir Didier Restaurant, 1896. Meat Market & Winery. 15858 Main Street, La Puente.

Also called Slaughter House. One of first bonded wineries in California. Started in 1906 in shed behind home and business.

Emile Alfhonse Rambaud Home, 1904. 144 N. Second Street, La Puente. One of first homes here. Barn extant.

La Puente's Women's Clubhouse, 1922. 200 First Street, La Puente.

Historic Sites: Indian Village of *Awingna* (Abiding Place) Located where the present La Puente High School is. 15615 E. Nelson Avenue, La Puente. 818-336-1241.

Site of *John Rowland Adobe,* 1841. ½ mile east of the William Workman Home. La Puente. Destroyed in 1850 when Rowland built his brick home.

Site of the *Rowland Hotel,* the Puente Hotel, 1886. Northeast corner of Main Street and Second, La Puente. Destroyed in 1956.

Site of the *William Workman Rodeo Grounds,* 1859. Corner of Proctor and Turnbull Canyon Roads, La Puente.

Site of the *First Public School* in Eastern Los Angeles. Northeast corner of Durfee and Santa Anita, La Puente.

Site of *1876 Depot,* Valley Blvd., and Glendora Avenue, La Puente.

Site of the *Rowland Reed Home,* 1865. Gale Avenue below Valley Blvd., La Puente.

The Historical Society tried everything they could to save this home. Finally were able to move it to the Square next to the Rowland Home. Then vandals and fire did their damage and the City of Industry said it had to be torn down. Too bad.

Site of *Francisco Grazide Home,* 1875–1878. East side of Batson, La Puente.

Site of *Hudson School,* 1887. Glendora Avenue and Rowland Street, La Puente. One room school house. Actually there were 4 schools on that site.

Site of the *Temple Sheep Ranch.* Corner Basedale and Peckham Dr., City of Industry.

Four Corners, Corner of Rosemead and Durfee, Los Angeles County. Just east of Montebello.

Once the site of Temple Hacienda, later an adobe, store and other buildings. Important as area where young Thomas Workman Temple found black gold (oil) coming from ground, enabling Temples to build La Nueva Casa.

For more information contact the Historical Society at 818-336-7644.

Other Buildings: Monument to the *First oil wells* in area 1885. Discovered in Puente Hills.

Masonic Lodge, 1910. 15845 Old Valley Road. La Puente, CA 91744. Town of Bassett.

Businesses: *The French American Bakery,* 1915. 15849 East Main Street, La Puente. 818-333-2293.

Keckter Moving Co., 2367 S. Almeza Ave., Rowland Heights. 818-964-5527. Re-location experts.

Other: Thomas workman Temple was the historian at the Mission San Gabriel for years. He also did a history of Temple City.

Book: Claire Radford, *Footsteps* 1984.

LINCOLN HEIGHTS

History: Originally the land was used for grazing sheep. The first settlers arrived around 1881. They were principally of German and Irish descent. North Broadway is the oldest commercial area. After World War I Italians moved into the area, and after World War II the Hispanic population grew.

Founding Families: Southland Pioneer *Esperanza Batz* Home was Rancho de Castilla, a 3,300 acre ranch that covered Alhambra, East Los Angeles, Monterery Park and El Sereno. The old adobe that she lived in was built in 1776. Her ancestry was Basque, having settled in Los Angeles in the 1850s. She moved from the old adobe in 1906 to a 12 room ranch home on Endicott Street in El Sereno. Esperanza Batz died in 1986.

Historian: *Michale Diaz,* 2652 Workman Street, Lincoln Heights, CA 90031. 213-223-6136.

Historical Society: None. There is however a *Lincoln Heights Preservation Association.* Contact Michael Diaz for more information.

Historical Landmarks: *Lincoln Heights Library,* 1910–19. 2530 Workman, Lincoln Heights. Mr.

Taylor, librarian. #261 C.H.M. This building was to be a replica of the Papal Palace. 213-225-3977.

Lincoln Park, 1874. Originally Eastlake Park. Plaza de la Raza, east corner Mission and Valley Blvd., Lincoln Heights.

Church of the Epiphany, 1913. 2808 Altura, Lincoln Heights. 213-227-9931. Designed by Arthur Benton. The 1888 Chapel designed by Ernest Coxhead.

Broadway St. Clock, 2434 N. Broadway, Lincoln Heights.

Historic School: *Farmdale School Building,* 1889. 2839 N. Eastern Avenue, Los Angeles.

Historic Churches: *Sacred Heart Church,* 1890. 2210 Sichel Street, Lincoln Heights. 213-221-3179.

Second Baptist Church Building, 1885. 2412 Griffith Avenue, Lincoln Heights. The present building of 1925 is a Paul Williams design.

Historic Homes: *Schieffelin Residence,* 1880s. 2419 Sichel Street, Lincoln Heights.

Old Castle, 3011 Minnesota Street, Lincoln Heights. Built by an Italian winegrower around 1915.

Home, 1887. 2054 Griffin Avenue,

Lincoln Heights. #144 C.H.M.

Villa Rafael, 1904 and 1920. 2123 Parkside, Lincoln Heights. #263 C.H.M.

Residence, 1913. 1443 North Martel, Lincoln Heights. #246 C.H.M.

Home, 1886. 3537 Griffin Avenue, Lincoln Heights. #145 C.H.M.

Private Residence, 1889. 2652 Workman Avenue, Lincoln Heights.

Sturgis House, 1889–90. 2345 Thomas Street, Los Angeles.

Home, 1885. 3110 North Broadway, Lincoln Heights. #157 C.H.M.

Other Buildings: *Old Jail,* 421 N. Avenue 19, Lincoln Heights.

Haden Building, 1888. Around Avenue 21 and 22. The oldest building in Lincoln Heights.

Dept. of Water and Power, 1920s. 2417 Daly Street, Lincoln Heights.

Historic Restaurants: *Le Blanc Cafe,* since 1930. 2824 North Broadway, Lincoln Heights. 213-222-5705.

Historic Site: *Lincoln Park Carousel,* Mission Road and Valley, Lincoln Heights. #153 C.H.M. This beautiful old Carousel was burned to the ground.

LITTLE TOKYO

History: Community began in 1884 when a sailor opened a tiny restaurant. The community grew up around it. By 1900 more than 100 Japanese people lived near downtown. There were many small shops. After the San Francisco 1906 earthquake more came.

By 1910 Los Angeles had more Japanese residents than any city in the United States, except San Francisco. During the 1920s they raised 90% of the produce consumed in Los Angeles. From growing produce, some Japanese moved onto handling it as wholesalers and retailers. In 1909 groups composed of Japanese and Chinese growers formed the City Market, a downtown wholesale produce exchange. A similar Flower Market was begun in 1914.

The Japanese also helped pioneer the fishing industry on the West Coast. (The Chinese fisherman had been active in California since the 1850s.) By 1929, together with Italian, Portuguese, and Croatian fishermen, they made San Pedro the nation's number one fishing port.

The third principal area of Japanese enterprise was small business, especially in the areas around First and San Pedro streets.

Historical Society: None. Japanese Chamber of Commerce, 213-687-7193.

Questions can be directed to the *Japanese American Cultural Center* 213-628-2725. The Japanese American National Museum is planned, and will be located on First and Central Street. 213-625-0414. Contact Dean Toji. Also Little Tokyo Community Redevelopment Association can arrange for tours of the area. Call 213-624-0837.

Historical Landmarks: *Asahi Shoe and Dry Goods Store,* 1909. First Street, Los Angeles.

Fugetsudo Confectionary Shop, 1903. First Street, Los Angeles. Oldest existing building in Little Tokyo.

Historic Sites: Site of the *Rose Hotel,* 1898. Little Tokyo.

Other Information: The Issei were first-generation Japanese whose hard work and success did not necessarily bring laurels of appreciation on the part of white businessmen. Rather, the Americans tended to prefer a docile labor force, not a new group of competitors. As a result, the Japanese found themselves more and more alienated from the mainstream. As labor-organizing movements grew in the 1920s and 1930s, the first and second generation of Japanese, the Nisei, remained to themselves rather than join white workers along class lines. The isolation increased antagonism and suspicions. By the time of Pearl Harbor, rumors ran wild. The demands of our political leaders over the protest of a few church and educational leaders prevailed, and on February 19, 1942, 112,000 Japanese were evacuated from the West Coast. Of these, two-thirds were American citizens. One community, that of Dayton Heights, located near the present site of Los Angeles City College on Vermont, composed of Japanese truck farmers, did not lose their property in the relocation. The neighborhood had been integrated with black and white families since the 1920s. During the relocation these people took care of the Japanese-Americans' property, renting out the houses to pay the taxes, until the owners returned. The way the people of Dayton Heights stood up for their Japanese neighbors suggests what might have been.

Landmarks Outside of Los Angeles: *Manzanar,* Owens Valley, Inyo County. #160 C.H.M.

Manzanar was a settlement that grew up in this area around the turn of the century. In 1942 it became the site of a Japanese War Relocation Center, housing 10,000 people. A pair of ornamental stone Japanese-style gates and a large garage remain beside the highway six miles southeast of Independence.

LOMITA

History: Once known as the "Celery Capital of the World", Lomita is 1.87 square miles of rich history. An important Indian village of Suangna still existed as late as the 1850s. In 1784 it became part of the vast Ranch San Pedro, later the Rancho Palos Verdes. Both the owners, the Sepulvedas and the Dominguezs disputed the land until 1834 when the property was finally divided. After the disastrous drought of 1862–64, delinquent taxes brought partitioning to all the ranches. By 1882 present day Lomita went to two owners—Nathaniel Narbonne and a Mr. Weston. In 1907 Lomita was born when W.I. Hollingsworth Company opened a tract for subdivision. Part of the old Narbonne Ranch, it was named Lomita, meaning Little Hill.

Historical Society: *Lomita Historical Society,* 24300 Narbonne Avenue, Lomita, CA 90717.

Historical Landmarks: *Lomita Railroad Museum,* 250th Street and Woodward Avenue, Lomita, CA 90717. 213-326-6255.

Books: Ella Ludwing, *History of the Harbor District of Los Angeles.*

Businesses: *Fanart Blacksmith,* 24800 Narbonne Avenue, Lomita, CA. 213-326-2141.

Lomita Lumber, since 1922. 1800 Pacific Coast Highway, Lomita, CA. 213-326-1437.

Historic Theatres: *Lomita Theatre,* (The Lomita Hotel) 1920s. Narbonne Avenue. (24329 Narbonne), Lomita. 213-326-9814.

Once leased in 1935 by Frank A. Gumm, Judy Garland's father. He had come to Lomita to manage the theatre and present his three daughters, Virginia, Suzanne and Judy.

Chamber of Commerce: 213-326-6378.

——— LONG BEACH ———

History: The old Rancho that covers this entire area dates from 1784. Originally, the King of Spain granted over 300,000 acres of land to Don Manuel Nieto in 1784. Later this ranch, simply called the *Nieto Rancho* was reduced to 185,000 acres. It was huge. When Don Manuel Nieto died, his land was divided into four parcels for his heirs. *Rancho Santa Gertrudes* upon which Downey, Rivera and Santa Fe Springs now stand; *Los Alamitos, Los Coyotes* and *Palo Alto* were the portion that went to Don Juan Jose Nieto. Los Bolsas to Dona Catarina Ruiz and *Los Cerritos* to Dona Manuel Nieto de Cota.

From this early Spanish beginning, two large ranchos emerged: The *Los Cerritos* owned by Juan Temple, and the *Los Alamitos,* owned by Abel Stearns.

With the arrival of the Americans, the land was sold to one family: the Bixbys. Carved out of this, the Bixbys sold 4,000 acres to the American Colony in 1880 under the leadership of W.E. Willmore. He called his new town: Willmore City.

William Willmore was born in 1855, an Englishman. He saw this area for the first time around 1870. His plans were to start an American colony like Pasadena's Indiana colony. By 1880 there appeared in the newspapers, the first account of his ideas. He planned excursions, he advertised, he had sales promotions. The first lots sold on Ocean Avenue for $100 in 1882. However, despite all his hopes, plans and dreams, only a dozen or so homes were built. He became bitter, and in 1884 abandoned his venture. Another man, A.T. Pomeroy, purchased Willmore's option and poured money into the area, whose name he had now changed to Long Beach. Advertising it as a sea-side resort, he built a large hotel, brought in a railway and water.

By the time the 1887 land boom hit, Long Beach was ready. What ever happened to Willmore? He died a pauper in an unmarked grave. Only recently were his remains removed and given a proper burial—his name honored as the man who founded a city.

Historical Society: *Historical Society of Long Beach,* 1150 East 4th Street, Suite 116, Long Beach, CA 90802. 213-435-7511 (Senior Center) William T.J. Harris, president.

Long Beach Heritage Foundation, P.O. Box 90007, Long Beach, CA 90809.

Willmore City Heritage Association, 631 Manila, Long Beach, CA 90814. Robert K. Ansorge. P.O. Box 688, Long Beach, CA 90801.

Historic Districts: *Drake Park Historic District.* Long Beach's original housing tract of 1881 was located in Knoll Park Tract, later named Willmore City after its founder. The Seaside Water Co. formed by Colonel Charles Drake also owned a small section of town known as Knoll Park which it gave to newly named Long Beach in 1904. It remained in this form until 1969. After Drake's death the Knoll Park district was renamed Drake Park. There is a brochure which lists 14 historic homes in this area. Check with the Historic Society for more information.

Bluff Park Historic District. It is the third such district to be proclaimed by Long Beach and the largest. It runs from Kennebec Avenue to Redondo Avenue and includes East Ocean Blvd., East First Street.

The Carroll Park Historic Landmark District. Located between Kennebec and Redondo Avenues, between Ocean Blvd. and Dodge Way.

Historic Landmarks: *Queen Mary,* 1930–34. Long Beach Pier, Long Beach, CA 90802. 213-435-4733.

The Queen Mary is the largest

passenger ship ever built. For more than three decades she sailed the North Atlantic between England and the United States. Most of that time, she sailed as a troopship. She completed her final voyage from Southhampton to Long Beach in 1967. By 1971 she was open to the public.

Spruce Goose 1942–47. Long Beach, 213-435-3511.

For years it was secluded away from public view, about as secretive as its builder, Howard Hughes. Now it is for everyone to marvel at and enjoy.

Oil Drilling Islands, 1967–68. Offshore from City of Long Beach. Named for astronauts: Grissom, White, Freeman and Chaffey.

Historic Homes: *La Casa de Rancho Los Alamitos,* 1806. 6400 E. Bixby Hills Road, Long Beach. 213-431-3541. Open Wednesday to Sunday 1–5. A wonderful place to spend the day. Excellent park-like grounds, museum, good docents, in one of Southern California's oldest adobes.

Rancho Los Cerritos, 1844. 4600 Virginia Road, Long Beach. 213-424-9423. Open Wednesday to Sunday 1–5. Both these adobes are must-see in Long Beach. Excellent information here, good exhibits.

Raymond House, 1918. Irving Gill design. 2724 Ocean Blvd., Long Beach.

Bixby House, 1920s. 11 La Linda Place, Long Beach. Long Beach is the story of three families: the Stearns, the Temples and the Bixbys.

Reeves House, 1904. (Moved to this location). 4260 Country Club Drive,

Long Beach. A Greene and Greene.

The Bembridge House, 1906. 903 Park Circle, Long Beach. Note: This is in the Drake Park Historic District.

The Heartwell/Lowe House, 1919. 2505 E. Second Street, Long Beach. Located in Bluff Park Historic District.

The Leonie Pray House, 1927. 4252 Country Club Drive, Long Beach.

The Skinny House, 1931. 708 Gladys Avenue, Long Beach.

The Tichenor House, 1904. A Greene and Greene. 852 E. Ocean Blvd. Long Beach.

William Frederick Prisk, 3001 E. Ocean, Long Beach. Mr. Prisk was the founder of the Press telegram 1911. Located in Bluff Park Historic District.

Note: Long Beach has three historic districts with dozens of homes in each district. For more information on these contact: Community Development Dept., 333 W. Ocean Blvd., Third Floor, Long Beach, CA 90802.

Also, the City of Long Beach has done an architectural survey of the city. This, too, lists hundreds of structures that have historical significance. Contact above. There is also a Long Beach Foundation for Cultural and Architectural Heritage. In addition there are several historical societies.

Finally, developer *Wayne Ratkovich* is currently in charge of 13.5 acres of downtown L.B. Renovation planned for mixed use.

Other Important Historical Information: *Long Beach Municipal Auditorium Mural,* South end of the new Mall and Third Street, Long Beach. W.P.A. mosaic. Also the front of the Auditorium marked the end of the Highway from Providence Town, Mass. to Long Beach, Calif. which was begun in 1911.

Willmore's Walk, 1870. 14th and Pacific. This is the area that Willmore walked down when he first made plans for Willmore City.

Marker, Ocean and Alamitos Avenues, Long Beach. This is the old division between the Rancho Los Alamitos and Rancho Los Cerritos, where horse races used to be held between the Stearns and the Temples.

Beach, Golden Avenue. Here Aviator Galbraith Rodgers made a trans-continental flight on December 11th, 1911 from sea to sea.

Historic Buildings: *Ocean Center Building,* 1928–29. Southwest corner Pine and Ocean, Long Beach.

The Pacific Coast Club, 1926. 850 E. Ocean, Long Beach.

The Villa Riviera, 1928. 800 E. Ocean, Long Beach.

Rancho Los Alamitos, 1806. 6400 E. Bixby Hills Road, Long Beach.

Rancho Los Cerritos, 1844. 4600 Virginia Road, Long Beach.

The Cooper Arms Apts., 1923. 455 E. Ocean Blvd., Long Beach.

The Long Beach Community Hospital, 1922–24. 1720 Termino Avenue, Long Beach.

Insurance Exchange Building, 1920s. (Middough Bldg.) 205 E. Broadway, Long Beach.

Recreation Park Golf Course Clubhouse, 1929. 5000 E. Anaheim Blvd., Long Beach.

Cherry Avenue Lifeguard Station, 1938. Foot of Cherry Avenue, Long Beach.

The Dr. Rowan Building, 1930. Art Deco. 201–209 Pine Avenue, Long Beach.

The St. Regis Building, 1926. 1030 E. Ocean Blvd., Long Beach.

Scottish Rite Cathedral, (Fraternal Organization) 1926. 855 Elm Avenue, Long Beach.

Fire Maintenance Station No. 10, 1925. (Now a Firefighters Museum) 1445 Peterson St., Long Beach. 213-597-0351. Mr. Herb Bramley, curator.

First National Bank of Long Beach, 1900/1906. 101 Pine Avenue, Long Beach.

The Masonic Temple, 1905. 228–234 Pine Avenue, Long Beach.

The Willmore Building, 1925. 315 West Third Street, Long Beach.

Farmers and Merchants Bank, 1922. Northeast corner Pine & Third, Long Beach.

The Breakers, 1923 (hotel) 200 E. Ocean, Long Beach.

The Heartwell Building, 1923. Northwest corner Pine and Ocean, Long Beach.

Historic Churches: *The First Congregational Church,* 1887/1914. Third Street and Cedar Avenue, Long Beach. First congregational church of Long Beach from 1887 to 1902 was located here. 213-436-2256. Founded in 1887 by the Bixby's. Present church dates from 1914.

Second Church of Christ, Scientist, 1916–25. Southwest corner of Cedar and 7th Streets, Long Beach.

Historic Cemeteries: *Long Beach Cemetery,* 1880s. (Also Sunnyside Cemetery) 1151 East Willow, Long Beach. Willmore is buried here.

Sunnyside Cemetery, (second one) 1920s. Cherry Street and St. Antonio.

Historic Parks: *Pacific Park,* 1882. Later Civic Center. This was the first park in area planned by Willmore himself. In 1915 became Lincoln Park, in the 60s Civic Center Park.

Historic Sites: *Naples,* 1903. The mud flats within Alamitos Bay, Long Beach.

Arthur Parsons envisioned the idea of creating a small community with canals, bridges and gondolas, much as Kinney did in Venice. He organized the Naples Land Company to buy the marshy slough from the Bixbys. The first houses were built in 1906 but a depression hit in 1907. In 1923 renewed development began and the canals were completed. A hotel was built and opened in 1929. The earthquake of 1933 destroyed much of the work. But in 1938–39 the canal walls and arched bridges were rebuilt. Guest of honor was Arthur M. Parsons, the founder of "Naples."

Hotel Naples, 1929. During the years when Parsons still controlled the Naples property, Miss Almire Hershey, of the famous chocolate family, erected the Hotel Naples. Was at: 103 Ravenna Drive, Long Beach.

Site of the *Old Long Beach Pier* and

Pike. Turn of the century. Visitors to the Pike in 1906 would have enjoyed the shocking thrill of a 85 foot salt water plunge where you could swim with the opposite sex!!!! In 1912 there was Looff's famous Merry-go-round and Magruder's salt water taffy. Magruder was the first to introduce it to the west coast. In 1930 the most famous of the Pike's attractions opened on Memorial Day 1930 — The Cyclone Racer. Also there were streets lit with 1000 lights on Horseshoe Pier. Then W.W. II came and thousands of soldiers and sailors flooded the area. Slowly, it declined as Disneyland drew crowds away. Then came the 1965 renewal plans. After that instead of the Pike reminding us of a romantic remembrance of times past and a great tourist attraction, we have windswept beaches of condominiums.

Note: *Naples:* Some exciting new things happening in this area. The *Hershey House,* 1916, at 213 Rivo Alto Canal spearheads a revival of the area. Gondola Service and much much more. See Books. Also L.A. Times article, "A Stroll Along Italian Canals in Long Beach," by Robert Pierson. December 20, 1986. pt. V.

Museum: *Long Beach Museum of Art,* 1912. 2300 Ocean Blvd., Long Beach, CA 90803. 213-439-2119. This building was originally constructed for Mrs. Elizabeth Anderson of New York. She used this 15 room mansion as a summer home where she housed her collection of notable paintings. Then in 1926 the building was used as the Club California Casa Real, the first athletic social and beach club in Long Beach. In 1950 the City of Long Beach purchased the property to be used as an art center, now a museum.

Businesses: *Morey's Music Store,* prior to 1900. 800 Pine Street, Long Beach. 213-436-2929. Recently moved to Lakewood.

Ward's Drug Store, 1930. 7th and Long Beach Blvd., Long Beach.

Long Beach Store Fixture Co., 1927. 895 West 5th Street, Long Beach. 213-435-6368.

Dooley's Hardware, 1920. 5075 Long Beach Blvd., Long Beach 213-428-1212.

Park Nursery & Florist, 1914. 3842 20th Street, Long Beach 213-439-6881.

Gallup Indian Shop, 429 Shoreline Village Drive Suite J, Long Beach. 213-435-5512.

Wehrman's Jewelers, 1922. 2108 Bellflower Blvd., Long Beach. 213-596-6572.

George Marmion and Co. (coffee nuts) 244 E. Third Street, Long Beach. 213-436-1754.

Egyptian Pharmacy, since 1922. 5128 E. Second St., Belmont Shores, Bob Wilson. 213-433-0456.

Craftsmen: *Peter Devereaux,* general contractor. 239 Grand Avenue, Long Beach. 213-439-1216.

Books: Sarah Bixby Smith, *Adobe Days,* Valley Publishers, 1974.

Robert Pierson, *The Beach Towns: A Walker's Guide to L.A. Beach Communities.* Chronicle Books, 1985.

Meyer, Larry and Kalayjian, Patricia. *Fortune's Harbor, A History of Long Beach,,* 1983.

Historian: *Zona Gale-Forbes,* 714-828-1171

LOS ALAMITOS (ORANGE COUNTY)

History: The history of Los Alamitos dates back to 1784 when Don Manuel Nieto was granted over 300,000 acres of land in the Southland. An incredible grant, it was later reduced to 185,000 acres. Through his descendants the rancho was divided into five separate ranchos. One of these was Rancho Los Alamitos. In 1842 Abel Stearns purchased the rancho and stock from the Nietos for $5,954.00! Stearns became the wealthiest landowner in Southern California until the terrible drought of 1863–64. He was forced to mortgage his holdings for $20,000.

In 1881 John W. Bixby purchased some of the former Stearns land, laying aside some portion of it for a town. Tied to the sugar beets when Montana Senator W.A. Clark built the Los Alamitos Sugar Works, the town prospered as a result of this industry. A small community formed. The tarring of an old dirt road, now Los Alamitos Boulevard brought development along with the first church and homes for workers.

After World War II and the arrival of the Los Alamitos Naval Air Station in 1943 the area witnessed a population boom. In 1960 Los Alamitos was incorporated.

Historical Society: *Los Alamitos Historical Society,* P.O. Box 15, Los Alamitos, CA 90720.

Los Alamitos Museum Association, 11052 Los Alamitos Blvd., Los Alamitos, CA 90720. 213-431-8836.

The museum is housed in a restored adobe built in 1943, which at one time was Fire Dept. Building. Open Tuesday–Sunday 2–4.

——— LOS ANGELES ———

Note: The following section gives the history of Los Angeles then lists landmarks and other information only for the *Downtown* area of the city. Also landmarks principally date from earliest times up to around 1930. Other areas covered under Los Angeles are: North University Park, Wilshire, Los Feliz, South Central, Alvarado Terrace, West Adams, LaFayette Square, and Country Club Park. For areas outside of Los Angeles see alphabetical listings of individual cities.

History: Eighteenth Century Spain was busy colonizing her lands in the New World, when an urgent dispatch from Spanish secret agents in St. Petersburg, Russia arrived. The Russians, it said were planning to establish colonies in North America. While the information has proved to be incorrect, the Russians did discover Alaska in 1741 and since that time had established fur colonies down the Northern Pacific Coast. That was sufficient to cause alarm in Spain.

What so many historians seem to leave out, however, is that the Spanish by this time had a small but stubborn hold in Southwest U.S. Father Francisco Kino founded 29 missions, far more than Father Serra would found, and had done so in a more difficult area terrain-wise and certainly far more hostile in terms of the Indians. Prior to that, the entire greater Southwest had been, since the 1540s, explored, charted, written about and fictionalized in legends of "Lost Cities." By 1757 Andres Burriel had gathered up 50 years of arguments into a three-volume book entitled *Noticia de la California* and bemoaned the fact that eternal blame would be placed on Spain if she did not colonize the coast of California. After Cabrillo's voyage of 1542, Sebastian Vizcaino sailed up the coast in 1602. He extolled Monterey Bay and soon after that plans were being made to colonize the area. Unfortunately Vizcaino was shunted into obscurity when another viceroy came to power, and even his mapmaker was hanged. So much for Monterey. By 1697 Lower California was sprinkled with a string of missions up to Loredo and these were thriving. By the time the now famous dispatch arrived in Mexico City, California was very much in the minds of a great many people.

Another item often over-looked in the colonization of California is Jose de Galvez. It was Galvez who had read Burriel's work. Before the now famous dispatch was ever received, Galvez was already preparing and organizing plans for a northern campaign. By 1768 when a copy of the dispatch reached him, Jose de Galvez was on his way to Baja, California. His plans were simply moved ahead faster than he had anticipated. He was also fortunate in having as the new military Governor of Baja, Gaspar de Portolá. Another fortunate change in circumstance was the expulsion of the Jesuits. When they left, the Franciscans replaced them. Father Serra was put in charge of the missions. Galvez met first with army engineer Miguel Costanso and naval captain Vicente Vila. The idea of a four-pronged expedition was authorized. When this group made their way to La Paz, they met Father Junipero Serra and Gaspar de Portolá for the first time.

Another often overlooked fact is the terrible supply problems the men had. Absolutely everything had to be carried by ship or mules. The missions in Lower California had been ransacked by the Jesuits when news reached them of their expulsion. The Franciscan monks inherited the chaos, and now were asked to draw upon these impoverished missions for further assistance in establishing yet more missions. Many thought the plan was doomed to failure. Father Serra did not. If it had not been for his constant encouragement, it is doubtful that Galvez's plan could have succeeded.

The first to start north was Captain Fernando Rivera y Moncada. January 9, 1769 Vila's vessel, the San Carlos started for San Diego. The San Antonio followed in February. Rivera began his trip from Velicata in March. It took him 52 days to reach San Diego. Back in Loreto, Father Serra, ill from a terrible infection in his leg, would have to catch up with Portolá, who had already left. By the time the soldiers reached San Diego in June, a heavy toll had been exacted in men lost. Ahead

lay the main thrust of the expedition — Monterey. Portolá started north on July 14th. With him were sixty-one skeletons, as he called them, yet they pressed on. Ironically, they could not find Monterey. The maps they carried, maps made 166 years earlier by Vizcaino, were all they had to go by. On October 29th they rested. Portolá ordered a party of scouts under Jose Ortega to ride ahead and try to find the elusive harbor. To their amazement they stumbled onto the largest harbor they had ever seen. It was San Francisco Bay. To Portolá it seemed impossible that so large a harbor had never been seen before. Eleven weeks later in January 1770, they dragged back to San Diego, discouraged, exhausted. As far as Portolá was concerned, the expedition was in serious jeopardy.

Worse, what they found when they reached San Diego was that a violent revolt had broken out among the Indians, and the little mission Father Serra had founded was burned. Not only that, the hoped for San Antonio and San Jose had not arrived with much needed supplies. The only thing to do was return to Velicata for more supplies. Portolá ordered the camp abandoned. On that very day however, in answer to the fervent prayers of the padres, the sails of the San Antonio appeared. The San Jose never made it. Thus Portolá and his men, with Father Serra, set out a second time to find Monterey. This time they were successful. On June 3, 1770 the mission and Presidio of Monterey were founded. Thus ended one of the most trying and difficult expeditions in the history of California.

Portolá returned to his work as military Governor of California. In his report he said it would be well to punish the Russians by letting them have California. Supply difficulties being what they were, he felt a province so far from Mexico would be impossible to maintain. If it had not been for the determination of Father Serra, that may have proved to be true. When conditions did not improve, and when the struggling little far-flung colony so far north began to starve for lack of supplies, Father Serra went back to Mexico City. In October 1772, sick and angry, Junipero Serra laid his case before Antonio Bucareli, new viceroy of New Spain. Among his most urgent pleas was that something be done to save the colony so many people had worked so hard to bring about. From this seminal meeting came the outline for a new policy toward California, and the founding of Los Angeles.

A new overland route had to be pioneered, a route that would make it easier to supply the far-flung outpost by land. For this hazardous task, 37 year old border captain Juan Bautista De Anza was chosen. In 1774 De Anza and one of the most outstanding priests in the southwest, Father Garcès began their overland quests. With them were 34 soldiers and a California Indian, Sebastian Tarabal.

Through the desert, they crossed the San Jacinto Mountains. On March 22, 1774 they knocked at the gates of the Mission San Gabriel. Delighted by this achievement, De Anza was promoted to the rank of lieutenant colonel. This time, a second expedition was ordered. It would be different than the first. Colonists would come, men and women, to settle California. They began their journey in October 1775 with 205 men, women, and children, and over 1,000 animals. Every item had to be packed on muleback and unpacked each morning and night. They reached Mission San Gabriel on January 4th, 1776.

Success, however, was not quite in hand. As each new establishment provided more crops and cattle, more Indians arrived, ready to abandon their seminomadic freedom in exchange for free food. The solution was, according to Felipe de Neva, the new Governor, the establishment of farming pueblos. He believed that one of these new pueblos should be in the north, the other in the south. Each village would receive four square leagues of land, about 17,500 acres. Within this area the head of each family would receive, close to the central plaza, one lot for his home and one for his garden, plus the right to graze his cattle and horses. While the town was getting underway, each settler would be paid a small salary for his service and be granted an allowance toward his family's daily rations.

Fourteen families, sixty-eight persons agreed to these terms and on November 29, 1777 San Jose was launched. Meanwhile Rivera had been charged with recruiting fifty-nine soldiers for the southern pueblo. He was only able to find eleven families, forty-four persons, including wives and children, fewer than half as many as Neve wanted. The husbands were mixed: two who claimed Spanish blood, four Christian Indians, two blacks, one mestizo, one mulatto, and one mix of Indian and black called a chino. Their wives were either Indians or mulattoes. This polyglot mixture Rivera sent north through Baja, California. Governor Neve met the eleven families at San Gabriel and led them to the site of the new town. There, borrowing the name of the little stream, on the evening of September 4th, 1781, El Pueblo de Nuestra Senora la Reina de Los Angeles de Porciuncula was founded. For a time the pueblo was called Porciuncula. Finally it simply became known as Los Angeles.

Downtown

Historical Society: *Historical Society of Southern California,* Ave. 43, Highland Park, CA 90031. Located in Charles Lumnis Home. 213-222-0546.

California Historical Society, 6300 Wilshire Blvd., Los Angeles. 213-937-1848. History Center.

Los Angeles Historical Society, P.O. Box 4106, Los Angeles, CA 90041. Christie M. Bourdet, President. 818-792-1048.

Historical Landmarks, El Pueblo: *El Pueblo State Historic Park,* 1781. Park Office, 845 N. Alameda Street, Los Angeles, CA 90012. Chief Curator: Jean Poole, 213-680-2525. Forty-two acres comprise the central core of Los Angeles history.

The Plaza, Main Street and Sunset Blvd., El Pueblo, Los Angeles. 1781/1815. #64 C.H.M.

The Plaza was laid out originally slightly northwest of its present location, but due to flooding, it was moved. The current Plaza dates from 1815.

Olvera Street, Paseo de la Plaza and Main Street, El Pueblo.

Originally known as Vine or Wine Street because of its location near vineyards and a winery, the street was renamed in honor of the first county judge of Los Angeles County, Agustin Olvera. Olvera fought on the side of Mexico in 1846–48 and was one of the signers of the Treaty of Cahuenga which ended the war in California.

Avila Adobe, 1818. 10 Olvera Street, El Pueblo.

Built around 1818, the Avila Adobe is the oldest existing residence in the city of Los Angeles. Constructed by Francisco Avila, an alcalde (mayor) of the pueblo, the adobe has undergone much restoration. During the Mexican-American War the Avila Adobe served briefly as the residence of Commodore Robert F. Stockton, commander of the U.S. Pacific Fleet. By the 1920s it was in ruins, and faced demolition. Due to the "heroic" efforts by Mrs. Christine Sterling, the historic structure was saved. Now part of the historic park.

Sepulveda House, 1887. (Visitor's Center) 420 Main Street, El Pueblo.

Built as residence, hotel and boarding house, it was named for its owner, Eloisa Martinez de Sepulveda. Currently undergoing restoration. 213-628-1274.

Pelanconi House, 1855. (*La Golondrina Restaurant*) W. 17 Olvera St., El Pueblo. 213-628-4349.

The builder, Austro-Italian named Guiseppe Covacichi, intended the building to be a wine cellar and residence. Ontonio Pelanconi, a gold miner originally from Italy purchased the building in 1865. The Pelanconi House was remodeled during the restoration of Olvera Street in 1929. Today it is home to La Golondrina Cafe, a wonderful Mexican Restaurant.

Fire House No. 1, 1884. Paseo de la Plaza, El Pueblo.

The first fire station built in Los Angeles. Used from 1885 to 1890s. Later it was used as a hotel, restaurant and salon. Today, it has been completely restored, and features fire fighting equipment from the 1880s.

Masonic Temple, 1853. 416 N. Main St., El Pueblo.

Pico House, 1870. 420 N. Main St., El Pueblo.

The Pico House was the first major three-story hotel in Los Angeles. Named for Pio Pico, the last Mexican governor of California, the hotel was commissioned by him in 1869. Built by Ezra F. Kysor, Pico intended for it to be the finest in the city.

Merced Theatre, 1870. 418 N. Main St., El Pueblo.

First theatre constructed in Los Angeles. Ezra F. Kysor, the architect.

Garnier Block, 1890. Los Angeles Street at Arcadia, El Pueblo.

Built by Phillipe Garnier who intended to rent space to the Chinese customers who lived in the area. The importing firm of Sun Wing Wo, operated by the Lew family conducted business here from 1890 to 1948. From 1900 to 1948 the Chinese Benevolent Society's headquarters were located on the second floor. It was acquired by the State of California in 1953.

Our Church of Our Lady Queen of the Angels, 1818–22. North Main St.

Courtesy, L.A. City Historical Society

at the Plaza (100 West Sunset Blvd.), El Pueblo. #4 C.H.M.

The Plaza Church is the oldest place of religious worship in the City of Los Angeles. Built by Franciscan fathers and Indian neophytes it was intended to serve worshipers in the pueblo. After 1852, when the Franciscan padres left San Gabriel, the church continued as a parish church. It was the first and only place of Catholic worship until 1876 in Los Angeles. The Claretian Missionaries were given charge of the church's administration in 1910.

Statues: *King Carlos III of Spain* 1759–1788. El Pueblo State Park. Carlos III was the man responsible for the settlement of California.

Governor Felipe de Neve. First governor of the Californias. Escorted first colonists to Los Angeles in 1781.

Historic Sites, El Pueblo: *Site of the Lugo Adobe,* 1830s. (LaFayette Hotel 1883–84) El Pueblo de Los Angeles. Today there is only a plaque marking the site of this magnificent adobe. Once it dominated the Plaza. Built for Vicente Lugo in the 1830s, it was donated by him to St. Vincent's College in 1867. St. Vincents relocated to Vincent's Square later becoming Loyola Univer-

sity. Lugo's adobe became LaFayette Hotel and was finally torn down in 1951.

Site of *First Cemetery of Los Angeles,* 521 North Main Street. Adjacent to Plaza Church. #26 C.H.M. 1823–44.

Historic Landmarks to 1917: *Elysian Park,* 1769. Elysian Park, Los Angeles.

The 1769 expedition of Don Gaspar de Portolá camped here on August 2.

Los Angeles River, named Porciuncula.

Portolá camped on the east side of the River, near today's North Broadway bridge. Juan Crespi noted in his diary of 1769, "After crossing the river we entered a large vineyard of wild grapes and an infinity of rosebushes in full bloom."

Capitol Milling Company, 1820–1880s. 1231 North Spring St., Los Angeles.

Perhaps the successor to a still earlier mill built there by Joseph Chapman who came to L.A. in the 1820s. It was a small mill then, run by water known as the Eagle Mills. This was owned by Abel Stearns among others. In the 1870s it was sold to J.D. Deming and by him to J. Loew in the 1880s.

Southern Pacific Railroad River Station, 1876. #82 C.H.M.

Bounded by North Broadway on the west, North Spring on the east, the Los Angeles River to the north, and the Capitol Milling Company to the south.

The Southern Pacific Railroad reached Los Angeles in 1876 and much of that construction can still be seen today at the River Station.

San Antonio Winery, 1917. #42 C.H.M. 737 Lamar St., Los Angeles, CA 90031. 213-223-1401.

Founded by Santo Cambianica in 1917 the San Antonio Winery is the oldest producing winery in Los Angeles. The original buildings, constructed from wooden boxcar sidings, remain intact. In the beginning, the winery obtained grapes from local vineyards in Sierra Madre and Burbank, but these have long passed into history. Open.

Chavez Ravine Arboretum, Stadium Way, Los Angeles. (Elysian Park) (also Grace E. Simmons Lodge 213-665-1155.)

Southern California's first botanic garden, Chavez Ravine Arboretum in Elysian Park was set aside in 1893.

Bradbury Building, 1893. #6 C.H.M. 304 S. Broadway, Los Angeles.

Pershing Square (La Plaza Abaja, Public Square, Central Park) Between Olive, Hill, 5th and 6th, Los Angeles.

This 5 acre park was originally public land of the pueblo. Set up as a public park in 1866.

Farmer's and Merchants Bank Building, 1868. #271 C.H.M. 401 S. Main Street, Los Angeles, CA 90013.

In 1868 two Los Angeles banks were founded. They were Hayward and Company, and Hellman-Temple & Co. Hellman left Temple and Company and formed along with John Downey the Farmers and Merchants Bank. It has survived down to the present time, a remarkable feat. In 1956 Farmers and Merchants Bank merged with the Security-First National Bank of L.A., which is now Security Pacific. This building on Main Street was built in 1904.

Barlow Hospital, 1902. Elysian Park, Los Angeles.

Founded in 1902 by Dr. Barlow prior to the days when wonder drugs were available. The land was owned by Isaac Lankershim who sold 25 acres to Barlow for $7,000, forgiving $1,000 of that as a gift to the hospital. Many interesting buildings here.

Alexandria Hotel, Palm Court, 1906. #80 C.H.M. 210 West 5th St., Los Angeles, CA 90013. 213-626-7484.

When the hotel opened in 1906 it was among the most luxurious in the West. Presidents Theodore Roosevelt, William H. Taft and Woodrow Wilson were guests here. It was especially popular among the early silent film greats such as D.W. Griffith.

Historic Parks: *Elysian Park Los Angeles Police Academy Rock Garden,* 1937. #110 C.H.M. 1800 North Academy Drive, Los Angeles.

Echo Park, 1894. Between Glendale Blvd. and Echo Park Ave. Between Park Ave. and Bellevue, Los Angeles.

Tied to Los Angeles's early water problems, beginning in the late 1860s. Area was chosen to build a dam site to catch winter rains from Coast Range. The Canal and Reservoir Company was organized in 1868 and a dam was constructed 20 feet high across the canyon where Echo Park is now located.

MacArthur Park (Westlake Park) 1865. 2230 W. 6th Street, Los Angeles.

In 1865 the area was an unsightly ravine with alkali cones. When surrounding land was auctioned off by the city at 50 cents an acre after the Civil War, no one would give even 25 cents an acre for it. In 1886 the City of Los Angeles received the 32 acres of land for a park in exchange for other city land. Mayor William Workman decided to create a lake thus covering the ugly alkali cones. The park's strategic location at the terminus of two streetcar lines attracted many visitors. Boating was introduced and Sunday afternoon concerts in 1896. Then in

1942 in recognition of the services of General Douglas MacArthur, the park was renamed MacArthur.

Lafayette Park, 1895. (Sunset Park) 2830 W. 6th St., Los Angeles.

Acquired by the City in 1895 as a gift from Mrs. Clara Shatto. Known as Sunset Park up to 1917, the name was changed during World War I to honor Marquis de la Fayette, the Frenchman who fought in the American Revolution.

Lincoln Park, 1874. East corner Mission and Valley Blvd., Los Angeles.

This 45 acre park contains an 8 acre lake and a carousel until the 1980s. The original carousel is now in Golden Gate Park in San Francisco. In the early years of the century the park was known for its ostrich farm and its alligator farm. Also known as Eastlake Park.

Historic Cemeteries: *Evergreen Cemetery,* 1877. First and Lorena St., Brooklyn and Evergreen Ave., Los Angeles.

Oldest existing cemetery in the city. The graves of the Workmans, Hollenbecks, Lankershims, Van Nuys, Coulters, Bixbys and many more rest here.

Rosendale Cemetery, 1884. 1831 W. Washington, L.A.

Home of Peace Cemetery, 1891. 4334 Whittier Road, East Los Angeles.

Historic Statue: *Stephen White* (see San Pedro) Hill and First St., Los Angeles.

Historic Homes: *Heritage Square,* 3800 Homer, Los Angeles, CA 90031. 213-449-0193 and 213-222-0556. See Highland Park.

Carroll Avenue, 1300 Block.

Carroll Avenue is a landmark of Los Angeles. It contains excellent examples of successful preservation and urban pioneering. Its collection of residences constitutes the highest concentration of Victorian homes in Southern California. The 1300 block of Carroll Avenue is listed in the National Register of Historic Places. Located in Angelino Heights, L.A.'s first suburb established in 1886. Over 300 structures were surveyed by the City as having architectural merit, and Angelino Heights is the first Historic Preservation Overlay Zone of Los Angeles. Although various individual restoration efforts had begun on the street in previous years, it was with the establishment of the Carroll Avenue Restoration Foundation in 1975 that efforts and planning took hold. With its annual House Tour the 3rd weekend in May, the Foundation has brought recognition to the street and surrounding neighborhood. The Carroll Avenue Restoration Foundation is a nonprofit charitable foundation established to restore, preserve and protect Carroll Avenue.

Aaron P. Phillips Home, 1887. #51 C.H.M. 1300 Carroll Ave., Los Angeles, CA 90026.

Ferdinand Heim House, 1887. 1320 Carroll Avenue, Los Angeles, CA 90026. #77 C.H.M.

Daniel Innes House, 1887. #73 C.H.M. 1329 Carroll Ave., Los Angeles, CA 90026.

Luckenback Residence, 1887. 1441–1443½ Carroll Ave., Los Angeles. #191 C.H.M. Sold to Mr. Cohn who established Kaspare-Cohn, forerunner of Cedars of Lebanon Hospital.

Horace M. Russell Home, 1887. #76 C.H.M. 1316 Carroll Ave., Los Angeles.

Residence, 1889. 1407 Carroll Ave., Los Angeles. #189 C.H.M.

Residence and Carriage House, 1411 Carroll Ave., Los Angeles. #190 C.H.M.

Charles Sessions House, 1888. #52 C.H.M. 1330 Carroll Ave., Los Angeles.

This splendid home is currently undergoing restoration. Built by the firm of Newsom & Newsom and is one of the most outstanding Queen Anne homes on the street.

Charles Haskins House, 1895. #79 C.H.M. 1344 Carroll Ave., Los Angeles.

Henry Pinney House. #75 C.H.M. 1887. 1355 Carroll Ave., Los Angeles.

Even has a beautifully restored Carriage Barn.

Residence, 1880s. 1325 Carroll Ave., Los Angeles. #109 C.H.M.

John Scheerer House, 1887. #78 C.H.M. 1324 Carroll Ave., Los Angeles.

The most outstanding home in 1887 was *801 East Edgeware Road* built by the developer William Stilson. It is today a victim of "modernization" which destroyed its Victorian grandeur.

Michael Sandes House, 1887. #74 C.H.M. 1345 Carroll Ave., Los Angeles.

Residence, 1880s. 1321 Carroll Ave., Los Angeles. #176 C.H.M. (Originally located at 1145 Court St.)

Private Residence, 1937. #257 C.H.M. 817 North Glendale Blvd., Los Angeles. (Overlooks Echo Lake.)

Homes, Greater Angelino Heights Area: *Private Residence,* 1887. #206 C.H.M. 724 East Edgeware, Los Angeles.

Private Residence, 1887. #216 C.H.M. 917 Douglas, Los Angeles.

Private Residence, 1908. #218 C.H.M. 945 E. Edgeware Road, Los Angeles.

Private Residence, 1887. #220 C.H.M. 1343 Kellum Ave., Los Angeles.

Private Residence and Carriage House, 1887. #221 C.H.M. 1347 Kellam Ave., Los Angeles.

Moses Wicks Home, 1894. #217 C.H.M. 1101 Douglas St., Los Angeles.

824 East Kensington Rd., Los Angeles. 1894. #223 C.H.M.

1239 Boston St., 1887. Los Angeles. #219 C.H.M.

1442 Kellam Ave., Los Angeles, 1887. (Now the Eastlake Inn) #321 C.H.M.

Carriage House, 1417 Kellum, Los Angeles. #166 C.H.M.

1334 Kellam Ave., Los Angeles, 1902. #207 C.H.M.

1405 Kellam Ave., Los Angeles. #222 C.H.M. Wonderful example of Mission Revival.

The *Carroll Avenue Restoration Foundation* has an open house tour every year on the third weekend in May at the culmination of Preservation Week. For its centennial celebration the Foundation published its "Picture Album of Historic Angelino Heights." The 21 page publication incorporates the history of Angelino Heights, Carroll Avenue, and the Carroll Avenue Restoration Foundation. For information regarding the annual tour or the picture album you may write to: *Carroll Avenue Restoration Foundation,* 1300 Carroll Ave., Los Angeles, CA 90026. Attention Tom Morales. Or you may call 213-250-5976 for a short message announcing the next tour.

Also, due to the enormous interest in "the hill" there is *The Angeleno Heights Community Organization.* The group is composed principally of homeowners on streets around Carroll Ave. They also have open house tours usually at Christmas. One year both these foundations got together and held a "joint" open house tour. For more information on Angeleno Heights contact: Angeleno Heights Community Organization, 601 East Edgeware Road, Los Angeles, CA 90026.

Mrs. Beverly Ellis is the newly elected president and can be contacted by phone at 213-481-0247.

Homes, Central Downtown Area: *The Foy House,* 1874. #8 C.H.M. 633 W. Witmer St., Los Angeles, CA 90017.

This home was originally located where the Hilton Hotel is today on 7th and Figueroa. Moved in 1906 to its present location, it is currently utilized as a business. The Foy home takes its name from the family who came here in 1854 and began a saddlery business. Their most famous relative was Mary Foy, whose life-long interest was the history of California. She helped to organize such groups as the First Century Families and the California Parlor of the Native Daughters of the Golden West. She was also the first woman to hold the position of city librarian.

Samuel Lewis Home, 1887. #39 C.H.M. 1425 Miramar St., Los Angeles.

Hard to believe that this lone survivor of the Victorian Era is still hanging on so close to downtown L.A. When built by the famous Newsom Brothers, there were two equally spectacular homes on either side, facing Third Street. The home belonged to the Lewis family who were employees of the Witmers. The Lewis daughter also married into the Witmer family. Once known as "Crown Hill" the original Witmer development was around 600 acres. Today this home is all that is left.

Mary Andrews Clark Memorial Home, 1912–13 (YWCA) #158 C.H.M. 306 Loma, Los Angeles.

Designed by Arthur Benton whose most famous architectural feat was Riverside's Mission Inn. This once spectacular private home was built in a very Missionesque mode for the mother of Andrews Clark: founder of the L.A. Philharmonic, mining mogul, lawyer and benefactor of libraries to U.C.L.A.

John A. Forthmann House, 1889. #103 C.H.M. 629 W. 18th St., Los Angeles.

Forthmann was president of the Los Angeles Soap Company.

House, 1896. #99 C.H.M. 1036–38 Bonnie Brae, Los Angeles.

House, 1897. 1047 S. Bonnie Brae Ave., Los Angeles.

House, 1905. 1053 S. Bonnie Brae Ave., Los Angeles.

House, 1897. 824 S. Bonnie Brae Ave., Los Angeles.

Flint House, 1888. 842 S. Bonnie Brae Ave., Los Angeles.

A Joseph Cather Newsom Home.

House, 1897. 1026 S. Bonnie Brae Ave., Los Angeles.

House, 1896. 1032 Bonnie Brae Ave., Los Angeles.

House, 1898. 1035 S. Bonnie Brae Ave., Los Angeles.

House, 1897. 1519 S. Hoover St., Los Angeles.

House, 1900. 1515 S. Hoover St., Los Angeles.

House, 1900. 1346 W. Constance St., Los Angeles.

House, 1898. 1030 Burlington Ave., Los Angeles.

House, 1905. 740 S. Union Ave., Los Angeles.

House, 1902. 1011 Beacon St., Los Angeles.

Hill House, 1911. 201 S. Coronado St., Los Angeles.

Bunker Hill. The last two Victorian homes which date from the late 19th century and survived the redevelopment of the 1960s may not last long. Between 3rd and 4th streets, south to Grand Central Market, Los Angeles.

Residence, 1890s. #167 C.H.M. 633 West 15th St., Los Angeles.

Garland Home, 1890s. #129 C.H.M. 767 Garland Ave., Los Angeles.

Built for oil executive Charles C.L. Leslie.

Bernard-Machado Home, 1902. (and carriage house) #208 C.H.M. Architect John Parkinson. 845 Lake St., Los Angeles.

Absolutely beautiful French Gothic home currently undergoing restoration.

Frederick Moore Home, 1894. #45 C.H.M. 818 Bonnie Brae, Los Angeles.

This home and the home next to it are unique in that they represent many architectural styles, including the Queen Anne, Colonial Revival and a touch of Islamic, stemming in part from the World's Columbia Exposition of 1893.

Bonnie Brae Street, 1000 block 1890/1905.

Go to the end of Bonnie Brae to 11th St. The L.A. Conservancy has submitted a nomination to the State Office of Historic Preservation in Sacramento to have this designated as the South Bonnie Brae Tract Historic District.

Historic Churches: *Plaza Church,* 1818. #3 C.H.M. North Main St., Los Angeles.

El Pueblo State Historic Park. Adjacent to the church is the site of the first cemetery in Los Angeles from 1823 to 1844. It also inters the remains of the aboriginal inhabitants of Yang-Na, the Gabrielino Indian Village.

Jesus Saves, Church of the Open Door, 1916. Hope St., Los Angeles. (Demolished 1988.)

Japanese Union Church of Los Angeles, 1923. #312 C.H.M. 120 North San Pedro St., Los Angeles.

First structure designed to house the Protestant congregation for Japanese Americans.

St. Vibiana's Cathedral, 1871 and 1876. 114 East 2nd St., Los Angeles.

Architect Ezra Kysor designed this second oldest Catholic church in downtown Los Angeles. John Austin designed the 1922 renovations.

Temples: *L.A. Hong Wanji Buddhist Temple,* 1924–25. #313 C.H.M. 355–369 East First St., Los Angeles.

Historic Sites: *Site of the Indian Village of Yang-Na,* North Main St., Los Angeles.

Village site first seen by Gaspar de Portolá in 1769. By 1836 it was gone. In that year Indians were put in a segregated area near southeast corner of Commercial and Alameda Streets. Pressure was put on the police to remove Indians. In 1845 police commission recommended that they be relocated on heights above the river. Village was called Pueblito. In 1847 it was razed. From then on people who hired them as servants were judged responsible for them. They drifted into the city. Prisoners were auctioned off to the highest bidder. By 1855, a majority of the Indians had syphilis. By 1871 huts of some Indians could still be seen scattered around Glendale. The last Indian raid in Los Angeles was in 1853.

Site of Bella Union Hotel, later *St. Charles,* North Main St., Los Angeles.

Site of the one-story adobe store of Isaac Williams who arrived in Los Angeles with company of fur-traders in 1832. Later the building was enlarged and became the famous Bella Union Hotel, first hotel in Los Angeles. Pio Pico's headquarters as Governor had been here as well. When area was demolished, remains of Yang-Na came to light.

Site of Fort Moore, 1847. 450 North Grand, Los Angeles.

After the bloody *Battle of San Pasquel* this fort was named in honor of Captain B.D. Moore, who was killed in the skirmish. The Fort held over 1,000 American soldiers. Is today occupied by the *Los Angeles City Board of Education.* A wonderful Pioneer Memorial bas-relief was sculpted in the 1950s.

Angel's Flight Site, 1901–1969. #4 C.H.M. Third and Hill St., Los Angeles. Called the World's shortest railway, its future is still "up in the air." Promised to Heritage Square, it is still waiting for a home.

Site of Hebrew Benevolent Society, 1854. Just recently, two carved stone blocks were dug up from Broadway, between 2nd and 3rd Streets, which were blocks from a temple completed in 1873 when the street was known as Fort Street. Congregation moved to Hope and 9th in the 1920s and later moved to Wilshire Blvd.

Site of Philharmonic Auditorium, 1906. #61 C.H.M. 427 West 5th St., Los Angeles.

Rochester House Site, 1897. #11 C.H.M. 1012 Temple St., Los Angeles. (Original location)

One of the truly magnificent Victorian Queen-Anne homes in downtown Los Angeles, the struggle that went on to save it is typical of the same struggles that continue today in spite of all the efforts of preservationists. Known also as the West Temple Apartments when the Van Nuys family divided the house into apartments in 1919. In 1970 the building was moved to Alameda and Bruno Streets, then demolished.

Los Angeles Star Newspaper Site, 1851. La Estrella de Los Angeles, Los

Angeles St., Los Angeles.

Founded by John Lewis and John McElroy, it was originally printed half in Spanish and half in English.

Site of Hebrew Benevolent Society, 1854. Cemetery.

First Jewish site in Los Angeles. The Society is today known as the Jewish Family Service.

Historic Restaurants: *Cole's P.E. Buffet,* 1908. 118 E. 6th St., Los Angeles, CA 90014. 213-662-4090. (Oldest Restaurant in L.A.)

Vickman's, 1919. 1228 E. 8th St., Los Angeles, CA 90021. 213-622-3852.

The Pantry, 1924. #255 c.h.m. 877 S. Figueroa, Los Angeles, CA 90017. 213-972-9279.

Little Joe's, 1927. 900 N. Broadway, Los Angeles, CA 90012. 213-489-4900.

Clifton's Cafeteria, 1935. 648 S. Broadway, Los Angeles, CA 90014. 213-627-1673.

This is the oldest of the six cafeterias founded by C.E. Clinton.

La Fonda, 1926. #268 c.h.m. 2501 Wilshire Blvd., Los Angeles.

Nostalgic Diner: *Elders Cafe,* 1230 Valencia, Los Angeles. 213-748-7897.

Clifton's Silver Spoon, 1922. (Originally Brock Jewelry Store) 515 West 7th St., Los Angeles. 213-485-1726.

Philippe The Original, 1924. 1001 North Alameda, Los Angeles, CA 90012. 213-628-3781.

Finney's, 1914. #137 c.h.m. Originally the Chocolate Factory. 217 W. 6th St., Los Angeles, CA 90014.

Schauber's Cafeteria, 1927. 620 S. Broadway, Los Angeles.

Pacific Dining Car, since 1921. 1610 W. 6th St., Los Angeles. 213-484-6000.

White Log Coffee Shop (Tony's Burger) 1932. 1061 S. Hill, Los Angeles.

La Golondrina Cafe, The Pelanconi House, 1855. West 17th Olvera St., Los Angeles, CA 90012. 213-628-4349.

St. Antonio Winery, 1917. #42 c.h.m. 737 Lamar St., Los Angeles, CA 90031. 213-223-1401. (Last remaining winery in the city of Los Angeles.)

Historic Hotels: *Hotel Cordova,*

1912. Northeast corner Figueroa and 8th. Los Angeles.

Apartment House, 1907. 928 S. Hope, Los Angeles.

The Stillwell Hotel, 1912. 838 South Grand, Los Angeles.

Biltmore Hotel, 1922–23. #60 c.h.m. 515 South Olive, Los Angeles. 213-624-1011.

Hotel Figueroa, 1925. 939 S. Figueroa St., Los Angeles.

Alexandria Hotel, 1906. #80 c.h.m. (and Palm Court) 210 West 5th St., Los Angeles, CA 90013. 213-626-7484.

Mayflower Hotel, 1927. #286 c.h.m. 535 South Grand Ave., Los Angeles.

Park Plaza Hotel, 1925. #267 c.h.m. 607 South Park View, Los Angeles. 213-384-5281. (Formerly Elks Building)

Charnock Block, 1888. (Pershing Hotel.) Southeast corner Main and 5th. Los Angeles.

Doria Apts., 1900s. 1600 S. Pico, Los Angeles.

Van Nuys Hotel, 1890s. #288 c.h.m. (Barclay Hotel) 103 W. 4th St., Los Angeles.

Lankershim Hotel, 1902. Broadway and 7th, Los Angeles.

Historic Bookstores: *Fowler's Bookstore,* since 1888. 717 West 7th St., Los Angeles. 213-627-7846.

Bed and Breakfast: *The Eastlake Inn,* 1887. #321 c.h.m. 1442 Kellam Ave., Los Angeles, CA 90026. 213-250-1620.

Historic Department Stores: *May Co.,* 1906. Southwest corner of 8th St. and Broadway, Los Angeles.

Originally Hamburger's Dept. Store.

J.W.R., 1883. Joseph Winchester Robinson. Spring St. and 7th, Los Angeles.

Boston Dry Goods Store originally. Was located where the present City Hall is. Moved to Spring St. location in 1887.

Harris and Frank, 1882.

Originally Harris & Jacoby, later London Clothing Co., Los Angeles.

Museums: *Well's Fargo History Museum,* 444 South Flower, Los Angeles. 213-683-7166.

Grier-Musser Museum (Bonnie Brae Museum), 1898. 403 S. Bonnie Brae, Los Angeles. 213-935-1664.

Historic Markets: *Grand Central Public Market,* 1917. 317 S. Broadway, Los Angeles, CA 90013. 213-624-2378.

Flower Market, 1920s. 755 S. Wall St., Los Angeles. 213-627-2482.

Produce Markets, 1900s. Central Ave. at 7th St. and San Pedro St. at 11th St., Los Angeles.

Ralph's Grocery Store, 1911. Pico and Normandie. 213-637-1101.

Bob's Market, 1910. #215 C.H.M. 1234 Bellevue Ave., Los Angeles.

Young's Market Building, 1924. 1610 West 7th St., Los Angeles.

Historic Streets and Districts: *El Camino Real,* 1769.

Mission Blvd., 1781. It was along the approximate location of this street that the families came in 1781. Until 25 years ago Pepper trees shaded the area for the padres as they walked over the old road.

Original Granite-Block Paving. Bruno St. between Alameda and North Main St., Los Angeles. #211 C.H.M.

The street is the last one in Los Angeles with the original paving of granite blocks hand-hewn.

Macarthur Park-Westlake District, 541 Parkview St., 537 Parkview St., 541 Parkview St.

These three colonial Revival Homes have been proposed as an Historic Preservation Overlay Zone.

Carroll Ave., 1300 Block.

An Historic Preservation Overlay Zone, Los Angeles.

Other Historic Buildings: *Union Station Terminal and Grounds,* 1939. #101 C.H.M. 800 North Alameda, Los Angeles.

Angelus Temple, 1922. Four Square Gospel Church, 1100 Glendale Blvd., Los Angeles, CA 90026. 213-484-1100.

Patriotic Hall, 1926. 1816 South Figueroa Street, Los Angeles.

Impressive array of Civil War, W.W. I and W.W. II items. Also the first American Legion Post in Los Angeles County.

Breed Street Shul, 1912. 247 N. Breed St., Los Angeles.

Here Al Jolson filmed Yom Kippur scenes from "The Jazz Singer."

Fire Station No. 28, 1912. 644 S. Figueroa St., Los Angeles.

Nelson Building, 1900. Northwest corner Broadway and 4th, Los Angeles.

Chapman Park Studio Building, 1929. #280 C.H.M. 3501-3519 West 6th St., Los Angeles. 213-857-6000.

Subway Terminal Building, 1925-55. #177 C.H.M. 417 S. Hill St., Los Angeles.

People still do not realize that Los Angeles really did have a subway system!

Fire Station No. 23, 1910. #37 C.H.M. 225 E. 5th St., Los Angeles.

Los Angeles Herald Examiner Building, 1912. 1111 S. Broadway, Los Angeles, CA 90015. #178 C.H.M. 213-744-8000.

Los Angeles Examiner founded here in 1903. Julia Morgan designed this building.

Mack Sennett Studios, 1912. #256 C.H.M. 1712 Glendale Blvd., Los Angeles.

Los Angeles Public Library, 1922-26. #46 C.H.M. 630 West 5th St., Los Angeles. 213-612-3200. Temporarily at 433 S. Spring St., L.A. Due to fires of 1986-87.

Bertram B. Goodhue designed this magnificent structure.

Pacific Mutual Building, 1912. 523 W. 6th St., Los Angeles.

Los Angeles Athletic Club, 1911-12. 431 West 7th St., Los Angeles. #69 C.H.M.

Jonathan Club, 1924. 545 S. Figueroa St., Los Angeles. 213-624-0881.

Municipal Water & Power Building, 1904. 207 S. Broadway, Los Angeles.

Pacific Stock Exchange, 1931. #205 C.H.M. 618 S. Spring St., Los Angeles.

St. Vincent's Jewelry Center, 650 S. Hill St., Los Angeles.

Walter Paul Story Building and Garage, 1916. Southwest corner Broadway and 6th, Los Angeles.

Hellman Building, 1903. (Banco Popular Center) 354 S. Spring, Los Angeles.

Brady Block, 1903. (The Continental Building) Southeast corner Spring & 4th, Los Angeles.

Stowell Hotel Building, 1913. (Pacific Grand Hotel) 416 S. Spring, Los Angeles.

Los Angeles City Hall, 1926–28. #150 C.H.M. 200 N. Spring, Los Angeles. Austin, Parkinson, Martin architects.

Merchants National Bank, 1915. (548 Building) 548 Spring St., Los Angeles.

Van Nuys Building, 1910–11. (Van Nuys Apts.) Southwest corner Spring & 7th, Los Angeles.

Union Oil Building, 1911. (Bartlett Building) Northwest corner Spring & 7th, Los Angeles.

Kerchkoff, 1907. (The Santa Fe Building) Northeast corner Main & 6th, Los Angeles.

Coca Cola Bottling Co., 1935. #138 C.H.M. 1334 S. Central Ave., Los Angeles. 213-746-5555.

Embassey Auditorium and Hotel, 1913. #299 C.H.M. 851 South Grand Ave., Los Angeles.

Title Guarantee Trust, 1931. #278 C.H.M. 401–411 West 5th St., Los Angeles.

Fine Arts Building, 1925. #125 C.H.M. 811 West 7th St., Los Angeles.

Oviatt Building, 1928. #195 C.H.M. 617 S. Olive, Los Angeles.

Variety Arts Center Building, 1924. #196 C.H.M. 940 S. Figueroa, Los Angeles.

Eastern Columbia Building, 1930s. #294 C.H.M. 849 S. Broadway, Los Angeles.

Cast Iron Commerical Building, 1900s. #140 C.H.M. 740–748 S. San Pedro, Los Angeles.

Wolfer Printing Co., 1929. #161 C.H.M. 416 Wall St., Los Angeles.

California Club, 1930. #43 C.H.M. 538 Flower St., Los Angeles.

Los Angeles Pacific Telephone Co. Building, 1911. 716 S. Olive St., Los Angeles.

Broadway Arcade Building, 1922–23. 542 S. Broadway, Los Angeles.

Commercial Block, 1889. 740–748 S. San Pedro St., Los Angeles.

Design Center (formerly Title Insurance and Trust Co.), 1928. 433 S. Spring, Los Angeles. John and Donald Parkinson, architects. Now home of the Los Angeles Conservancy. 213-623-CITY. Also temporarily housing the L.A. Public Library.

Pacific Electric Building, 1903. 610 S. Main, Los Angeles.

Historic Theatres: *Million Dollar Theater,* 1918. 307 S. Broadway, Los Angeles. 213-624-6272.

Mayan Theatre, 1926–27. 1040 S. Hill St., Los Angeles.

Pantages Theatre, 1911. (Now the Arcade) 534 S. Broadway, Los Angeles. 213-624-6272.

The Los Angeles, 1931. #225 C.H.M. 615 S. Broadway, Los Angeles.

Orpheum Theatre, 1911. 842 S. Broadway, Los Angeles. 213-624-6272.

Palace, 1911. 630 S. Broadway, Los Angeles.

Loew's State, 1921. 703 S. Broadway, Los Angeles.

Globe Theatre, 1912. 744 S. Broadway, Los Angeles. 213-624-6272.

California Theatre, 1918. 810 S. Main, Los Angeles. 213-624-6272.

Rialto, 1917. 812 S. Broadway, Los Angeles.

Tower, 1927. 802 S. Broadway, Los Angeles.

The Roxie, 1932. 518 S. Broadway, Los Angeles. 213-624-6272.

United Artists, 1927. 933 S. Broadway, Los Angeles.

Lunes Theatre (Cameo), 1910. 528 S. Broadway. Los Angeles. The oldest continuously operating movie-theatre in Los Angeles.

Note: For more information contact the Los Angeles Conservancy. 213-623-CITY.

Historic School: *Westlake School for Girls* (Founded here in 1904, moved to Bel-Air in 1928).

Businesses 100 Years Old: *Southern California Music Co.,* 1889. Originally Day's Music Store. Frank

J. Hart, 11 North Spring St. then Bradbury Building, then 585 Main St. Later moved to 637 S. Hill. Now located in Glendale and North Hollywood.
A. Ducommon, Inc., 1849. Originally a watch shop on Commercial St. between Main and Los Angeles Streets. Today is located at 1082A Hope St., Cypress. 714-952-2950.
Los Angeles Chamber of Commerce, 1887. 404 S. Bixel, Los Angeles. 213-629-0602.
Fowler Brothers, 1888. Booksellers. 717 West 7th St., L.A. 213-627-7846.
Los Angeles Soap Co., 1860. John Forthmann, East First St., Los Angeles. 213-627-5011.
California Hardware, 1880. 13085 E. Temple, Los Angeles. 818-369-9431 General Offices.
Isidore B. Dockweiler, 1889. Lawyer. 2650 West Temple, Los Angeles. 213-386-6888.
Farmer's and Merchants Bank, since 1868. Now Security Pacific. Oldest Bank in Los Angeles. 401 S. Main St., Los Angeles, CA 90013.
O'Melveny & Meyers, 1885. 400 S. Hope, Los Angeles. 213-669-6000.
Businesses 50 Years Old and Older: *Western Beverly Appliance and Plumbing Co,* Since 1906. 530 North Western, Los Angeles. 213-462-7281.
J.H. Minassian & Co., 1905. 401 S. Vermont Ave., L.A. 213-383-1397.
John Bloeser Carpet Co., since 1879 (begun elsewhere). 1325 Channing St., Los Angeles, CA 90021. 213-627-4738.
Gittelson Brothers Ticket Agency, since 1916. BonAventure Hotel, 5th and Figueroa, L.A. 213-624-3131.
Natick Store, since 1887 (begun elsewhere). 555 S. Flower, Los Angeles. 213-626-3339.
Schireson Brothers Music, since 1902. 344 S. Broadway, Los Angeles. 213-628-9161.
Bekins Van and Storage, since 1891. 1335 S. Figueroa, L.A. 213-749-4141.
Superior Marble and Granite Works, since 1900. 4161 Whittier Blvd., Los Angeles. 213-269-8788.
Bushnell Photo Studio, since 1904.

426 W. 8th St., Los Angeles, CA 90014. 213-629-8197.
Wolcott's Stationers, since 1893. 214 S. Spring St., L.A. 213-624-4943.
Rowan Jewelers, since 1907. 3656 E. 1st St., Los Angeles. 213-269-1106.
De Crestina, Joseph Jewelers, since 1919. 606 S. Hill St., Room 413, Los Angeles. 213-628-1000.
Thomas Brothers Maps, since 1915. 603 7th St., Los Angeles, CA 90017. 213-627-4018.
William Brothers, since 1910. 452 W. Hill St., L.A. 213-623-5948.
Gibbs Brothers Electric, since 1919. 1754 N. Main St., Los Angeles. 213-255-5945.
Darling's Flowers, since 1895. 1217 W. Temple, Los Angeles. 213-481-7100.
Broadway Florist, since 1910. 218 W. 5th St., Los Angeles. 213-626-5511.
California Floral Co., since 1916. 122 W. First St., Los Angeles. 213-624-0916.
Businesses Who Deal in Historical Products, Goods and Services: *The Ragmuffin,* Antique and Collectable Dolls, Toys. 1329 W. Washington Blvd., Los Angeles. 213-452-1268.
Katalin V. Slazer, Antique quilts. 2508 St. George St., Los Angeles, CA 90027. 213-661-0106.
Bob and Don Buckner, Color consultants specializing in Victorian Homes. 1862 Lakeshore Ave., Los Angeles, CA 90026. 415-922-7444.
Daley Papers, Connie Daley, Old prints, old ads. 2124 Lemoyne St., Los Angeles, CA 90026. 213-662-8566.
Caravan Book Store. Specializing in old and rare books. 550 S. Grand Avenue, Los Angeles. 213-626-9944.
Westgroup, Inc. A firm that specializes in remodeling older commercial properties in downtown areas. 523 W. 6th St., Suite 330, Los Angeles, CA 90014. 213-488-0111.
Cleveland Wrecking Co. 3170 E. Washington Blvd., L.A. 90023. 213-269-0633.
Organizations: *Cultural Heritage Commission,* Nancy Fernandez, Room 1500 City Hall, Los Angeles, CA 90012.

213-485-2433.

Los Amigos, dedicated to promotion of customs, culture of early California. John Bowles, President. Contact Los Angeles Historical Society.

Los Angeles Conservancy, Mary Kay Hight, President. 433 S. Spring St., Suite 1024, Los Angeles, CA 90013. 213-623-CITY.

Association of Historic Homeowners—Southern California. To belong to this group you must own an historic home. Contact: Richard Mouck 213-255-1526.

First Century Families, and *The Pobladores 200.* Both groups contacted through the *Los Angeles City Historical Society,* P.O. Box 4106, Los Angeles, CA 90041. Christie M. Bourdet, President. 818-792-1048.

The Register of Historic California Businesses, 2090 Jackson St., San Francisco, CA 94109.

Other: *Antiquarian Booksellers Association of America,* 50 Rockefeller Plaza, New York City, NY 10020. 212-757-9395.

A Southern California chapter exists but must contact them through current chairman. Call New York.

Historians: *Bill Mason,* 213-744-3357.

Books: Carey McWilliams, *Southern California Country,* New York, 1946.

Harris Newmark, *Sixty Years in Southern California,* L.A., 1984.

Lynn Bowman, *Los Angeles: Epic of a City,* Berkeley, 1974.

David Clark, *Los Angeles: A City Apart,* 1981.

Note: For these and other books on the History of Los Angeles, there is Dawson's Books, 535 N. Larchmont, Los Angeles, CA 90004. 213-469-2186. See Wilshire Area, Los Angeles.

West Adams—Arlington Heights

History: The historic West Adams district extends from Figueroa west to Crenshaw and south from Venice to Jefferson. When the area was developed, it was a time of transition in Los Angeles. Newfangled Pierce-Arrows and Packards lined the streets. Electric lights were replacing gas fixtures. The iceman came twice a week, and vegetables were delivered in horse-drawn carts. The strains of "Shine On, Harvest Moon" rippled down the street form the player pianos.

In 1896 Los Angeles had annexed Rosedale, and the Southern and Western Additions—the area that became Historic West Adams was being born. Land developers laid out tracts and neighborhoods in rapid-fire succession. On the maps were West Adams Heights, Kenwood Park, Garfield Heights, Belvedere Heights and Berkeley Square. A large section of West Adams was named Arlington Heights. Closely linked to the growth were the streetcar lines which permitted

people to live away from downtown. By 1904 the Pacific Electric Red Line had routes from the city center along Adams, Pico and Arlington westward to the beach.

Homes were being built less in the fading Victorian style than in the newer Colonial Revival and the very "classy" Craftsman style. Residents of the area included the rich and famous. There were Busby Berkeley, Theda Bara, "Fatty" Arbuckle, Leo Carrillo and dozens more. Wyatt Earp wrote his memories in a magnificent old home before he died. Then in the late 1940s change came. A black couple moved into the area. Other black families joined them. "White Flight" began. The 1970s brought more change. As homes soared in price, younger families began looking at West Adams as an area with enormous value. The old resentments were not important to couples looking for homes that were well-built and that had dozens of attractive features new housing could never offer. Today the area is experiencing new life. A wave of restoration is taking place throughout the West Adams area. There is the West Adams Heritage Association, formed to promote the restoration and preservation of vintage homes in the district. (Information from the West Adams Home Tour brochures 1985).

Historic Homes: *Miles Home,* 1909. 2143 West 20th St., Los Angeles.

Private Residence, 1906. #244 C.H.M. 1866 W. 14th St., Los Angeles.

Donavan Home, 1903. 2197 West 20th St., Los Angeles.

Gould Home, 1904. 2237 West 20th St., Los Angeles.

Minney House, 1909. 2273 West 20th St., Los Angeles. (Salisbury House–see Bed and Breakfast).

Marston Home, 1909. 2299 West 20th St., Los Angeles.

Wilcox Home, 1904. 2302 West 20th St., Los Angeles.

Cochran Guest Home, 1906. 2248 S. Hobart St., Los Angeles.

Bigelow Home, 1906. 2636 S. Kenwood St., Los Angeles.

Staples Home, 1904. 1656 West 25th St., Los Angeles.

Woods Home, 1905. 1660 West 25th St., Los Angeles.

Friend Home, 1903. 2302 S. Budlong St., Los Angeles.

Barton Home, 1906. Catalina St., Los Angeles.

Britt Mansion, 1910. 2141 West Adams, Los Angeles.

Chick Home, 2410 Fourth Ave., Los Angeles.

Dalton Home, 1912. 1823 S. Bronson Ave., Los Angeles.

Rector Home, 1908. 2280 West 21st St., Los Angeles.

Streetcar Home, 1908. 1715 S. Roosevelt St., Los Angeles.

Ducey Home, 1905. 2283 West 21st St., Los Angeles.

Salyer Home, 1902. 2712 S. La Salle St., Los Angeles.

Alexander Home, 1906. 2197 West 25th St., Los Angeles.

Bruner Home, 1894. 2723 S. La Salle St., Los Angeles.

Louise Beavers Home, 2219 S. Hobart St., Los Angeles.

Rindge Mansion, 1904. 2263 South Harvard, Los Angeles. Also listed in North University Park.

Butterfly McQueen Home, 2215 South Harvard, Los Angeles.

Hattie McDaniel Home, 2203 South Harvard, Los Angeles.

Library: *Washington Irving Branch Library,* 1926. #307 C.H.M. 1803 S. Arlington Ave., Los Angeles.

Other Buildings: *Fire Station No. 18,* 2616 S. Hobart Blvd., Los Angeles.

Bed and Breakfast: *Salisbury House,* 1909. 2273 West 20th St., Los Angeles. 213-737-7817.

The very first Bed and Breakfast in Los Angeles. Now owned by Elizabeth Henderson.

Salisbury Manor House, (The Ibbetson Mansion) at 1190 W. Adams, L.A. Kathy Salisbury has turned this into a delightful restaurant. 213-749-1190.

Realtors: *City Living Realty,* 2299 West 20th St., Los Angeles. (The Marston Home, 1909.) 213-731-3520.

Bob Borgfield began City Living Realty and his tragic death in 1986 left all preservationists saddened. Dave Rapossa has taken over the reins.

Books: For an excellent collection of books on architecture, historic restoration and preservation, contact: *Kathleen Pfeiffer,* 2143 W. 21st St., Los Angeles, CA 90018. 213-731-9376.

Artist: Mimi Stuart, 213-730-1588.

North University Park

History: Known originally as *Agricultural Park,* it was an area of vineyards and wide open country. Leonard J. Rose of San Gabriel loved horseracing and his racing stables were in the area. Rose and others formed the Southern District Agricultural Society for the development of Agricultural Park. Every year there were horse races at the park. John Griffin ran a hotel there for the devotees. Under the grandstand was the longest bar in Los Angeles. Nothing but beer was served. When a man stepped up to the bar, the bartender simply sent a schooner full of beer sliding down the bar's polished surface. In time however, more saloons appeared. The clapboard hotel became a "house of ill fame," and gambling went on. Civic-minded citizens did not like it. William Bowen made up his mind to take action. He sponsored measures that outlawed gambling in the community and ended racing at Agricultural Park. He launched another campaign to get governmental agencies to spend money to improve and beautify the park. He dedicated more than twenty years to the cause and eventually Agricultural Park became *Exposition Park* with a beautiful Coliseum, a museum, the *University of Southern California,* and many other significant structures.

After the boom of the 1887s a down spiral in the selling of real estate began. Carroll Avenue was already on its way to becoming one of the city's fine residential locations. In the south of town there was Bunker Hill and South Figueroa Street. By the 1890s people were ready to begin building again. This time they moved into a more westerly area along Adams Boulevard: Chester Place, and St. James Park. It wasn't until a streetcar line was built from downtown Los Angeles along Hoover Street to Exposition Park in the 1890s, however, that real interest began. At that time, Miller and Her-riott subdivided a new tract which thrived as a neighborhood of well-to-do families. By 1910 wealthier families began to leave the area. They moved to Hancock Park, and later Beverly Hills. The area turned sour. By 1940 multi-family units sprang up, and the demolition of the old houses was continuing at the rate of one per week.

Now that has changed. *The North University Park Community Association* formed and new blood entered the area. Art Curtis is President of the North University Park Community Association. He is also a graphic designer. Can be reached at 213-749-7347.

Historical Landmarks: The entire area is simply filled with outstanding landmarks and will be handled by categories. In many ways, Los Angeles' entire preservation thrust emanates from here, as we shall see.

Historical Homes: *Salisbury House,* 1891. #240 C.H.M. 2701 S. Hoover, Los Angeles, CA 90007. (Not to be confused with the Salisbury House Bed and Breakfast in the West Adams Area.)

Bradbeer and Ferris, architects. Once owned by businessman Alfred J. Salisbury it is now owned by Rafael Garcia, a very patient and wonderful young man who is restoring the home.

Cockins Home, 1894. 2653 S. Hoover, Los Angeles.

Sunshine Mission (Casa de Rosas) 1894. #241 C.H.M. 950 W. Adams (2660 Hoover), Los Angeles.

A Sumner P. Hunt design, this building was one of the really elegant buildings in Los Angeles. Originally the Froebel Institute, later a fashionable Girls School, then used as a dormitory by U.S.C., then for the military in W.W. II, and later by Sister West of the Foursquare Gospel Church. Today the structure is administered by the Old Time Faith, Inc. and is used for elderly women as a shelter.

Miller and Herriott House, 1890. #242 C.H.M. 1163 W. 27th St., Los Angeles.

This gorgeous home was the first, hence the oldest home built in the new tract. But through the years it had a succession of 27 owners and was pretty sorrowful. Then John Miller and Richard Mouck purchased the home and began to restore it during the 1970s. They sold it and the new owner then brought the house up to a standard which can only be described as beautiful! A real success story if one has the time, the patience and the money.

Casa Camino Real, 1924. #300 C.H.M. 1828 S. Oak St., Los Angeles.

Residential Buildings, 1920s. #297 C.H.M. 1158-1176 West Adams, Los Angeles.

Ibbetson House (now the Salisbury Manor House—see p. 97), 1899. 1190 West Adams, Los Angeles.

A.E. Kelly House, 1892. #295 C.H.M. 1140 W. Adams, Los Angeles.

Arguello-Wilcox House, 1899. 1110 W. Adams, Los Angeles.

A Frederick L. Roehrig design. Unfortunately this house has undergone "stuccoing" to modernize it but it is still an important feature of the area. It is believed that it was also the home of silent film star Marie Dreisler.

Kiefer House, 1895. 1204 W. 27th St., Los Angeles. A Eisen and Hunt design.

Home, 1895. 2671 S. Magnolia, Los Angeles.

A Frederick L. Roehrig design.

Harrison House, 1891. #296 C.H.M. 1160 W. 27th St., Los Angeles.

DePauw House, 1984. 1146 W. 27th St., Los Angeles.

Durfee Home, 1880s. #273 C.H.M. 1007 W. 24th St., Los Angeles.

Jim Burgess in partnership with Jack and Bob Deane has restored this old ranch house to real splendor. Sometimes called "The Pink Lady." When the owners got curious about its history they hired historian David Cameron to find out more about the house. What they found was that the house had been built in the early 1880s in Florence and moved to this location in 1899. The original owners never did know what happened to the home until David Cameron completed his research. Lots of families were brought together and many stories came to light. Research pays!!!

Private Residence, 1905. #117 C.H.M. 2218 South Harvard, Los Angeles.

Peet House, 1889. #272 C.H.M. 1139 S. Harvard, Los Angeles.

Note: There are dozens of homes in the North University Park area that rank historical significance. They are all listed in an excellent brochure published by the North University Park Community Association. Contact Art Curtis, 2647 Magnolia Ave., Los Angeles. 213-749-7347 or 213-748-4302.

Historic Schools: *University of Southern California,* 1879. #70 C.H.M. 650 Childs Way, U.S.C., Los Angeles.

In May 1879 Judge Robert Widney approached the Reverend A.M. Hough and many others regarding the project for a first Protestant institution of higher learning in Southern California. Land held by I.W. Hellman, J.G. Downey and O.W. Childs consisting of about 308 acres was accepted in trust as a gift from these men. The first building was built on Wesley Ave. The beginning of the institution was odd: its first department of arts was built in 1883 in Ontario. Its theological school in 1885 was opened in the San Fernando Valley. The oldest building is Widney Hall, 1880, built by E.F. Kysor. Oldest University Building in Southern California.

Also at U.S.C. is the *Hancock Memorial Museum* #128 C.H.M.

A four room display from the 42 room mansion owned by Major Henry Hancock, owner of Rancho La Brea has been moved here. The old mansion was on Wilshire Blvd. and Vermont Ave.

Historic Churches: *Second Church of Christ Scientist,* 1910. #57 C.H.M. 948 W. Adams Blvd., Los Angeles, CA

90007. 213-749-3761.

Design by A.F. Rosenheim, our city's first President of the American Institute of Architects.

St. Vincent de Paul Roman Catholic Church 1923–25. #90 C.H.M. 621 West Adams, Los Angeles.

Albert C. Martin design.

St. John's Episcopal Church, 1922–23. 514 W. Adams, Los Angeles.

Historic Libraries: *William Andrew Clark Library,* 1924–26. #28 C.H.M. 2520 S. Cimarron, Los Angeles. 213-731-8529. Robert Farquhar design.

Vermont Square Branch Library, 1913. #264 C.H.M. 1201 West 48th St., Los Angeles.

Historic Restaurants: *The Cloisters,* 1896. 2827 S. Hoover at 29th St., Los Angeles. 213-748-3528.

What's unusual is that this old Victorian has been turned into a restaurant! It represents a growing trend to provide people with something more than the typical dull surroundings to dine in.

Maison Magnolia, 2903 S. Hoover, Los Angeles, CA 90007. 213-746-1314.

This is more than a restaurant. It is a dining experience. Perhaps the most "prestigious" place to dine in L.A. and probably the least known. No menus, small parties of people who are introduced to each other, antique crystal service, etc. Simply very, very.

Salisbury Manor, 1899. 1190 West Adams, L.A. 213-749-1190.

Chester Place, 1895: (Doheny Mansion #30 C.H.M.) 8 Chester Place. Between 23rd St. and Adams, West of Figueroa. L.A. Today Mount St. Mary's College.

Chester Place was a private little world of 20 acres, laid out by Judge Silent. Silent named the park in honor of his young son, Chester, killed in a hunting accident. Originally there were 13 very elegant homes in the park. It was made famous when Lawrence Doheny Senior purchased the 1898–1900 Posey Home. When Doheny moved in, he purchased and then removed some of the homes. Today there are about eight structures remaining. Well worth a Sunday drive to see, walk around the grounds and note the incredible trees, plants, lighting fixtures, wrought iron grills marked Doheny.

Stimson Home, 1890. #212 C.H.M. 2421 S. Figueroa St., Los Angeles.

This truly spectacular private residence was built by Carroll H. Brown, a Chicago man who apparently was influenced by Richardsonian Romanesque when he had this home built for him. The property was owned by Mrs. Estelle Doheny who later donated it to the Sisters of St. Joseph of Carondelet who have lived in it since 1949. Called the Convent of the Infant of Prague.

De Camera Society, Chamber music at Historic sites. Call Sister Rose Ann at Mt. St. Mary's, 213-746-0450, ext. 2211.

Other Buildings: *Villa Maria,* 1908. #230 C.H.M. The Durfee Home, 2425 South Western Avenue, Los Angeles.

Designed by architect Frederick Roehrig, this home has quite a history. Nellie McGaughey fell in love with her mother's horse trainer. Forbidden to see him because he was married, Nellie waited. After a scandalous divorce and months after her mother died, Nellie married William Durfee. They bought this house, then tragically William died. Unable to accept this fact, Nellie became a recluse. Shrubs grew up around the house and most people thought it was abandoned. At 99 years of age Nellie died here in 1967. *The Brothers of St. John* now own it and the home has once again come to life. 213-734-0233.

Fitzgerald House, 1903. #258 C.H.M. 3115 W. Adams, Los Angeles.

Joseph Cather Newsom architect.

Adlai Stevenson Home, 1895. #35 C.H.M. 2639 Monmouth, Los Angeles.

Severance House, 1904. 650 W. 23rd St., Los Angeles.

Joseph Cather Newsome architect.

The Fremont Home, 1890s (Site) 28th and Hoover St., Los Angeles.

The incredible John C. Fremont did live in Los Angeles! The women of Los

The Rindge Home. Courtesy the artist, Mimi Stuart.

Angeles gave this home to Mrs. Fremont after her husband's death.

Automobile Club of Southern California, 1923. #72 C.H.M. 2601 S. Figueroa St., Los Angeles. 213-741-3111.

The Rindge Home, 1890s. #95 C.H.M. 2263 South Harvard, Los Angeles.

Mr. Rindge came to Southern California, fell in love with the Malibu and bought the entire land grant. He lived there in splendor but died in 1906. His wife, Rhoda Rindge fought the good fight to keep the Malibu intact but the U.S. Government wanted to build a highway through it. She fought for her rights all the way to the Supreme Court and lost. Broken, she began to sell parts of the Malibu. It became Malibu Colony. She finally retreated to her Los Angeles home on Harvard Street and died here in 1941. See Malibu.

Los Angeles Coliseum, 1913. 3911 S. Figueroa St., Los Angeles, CA 90037. 213-747-7111.

John Parkinson architect. At his own expense submitted designs to Times publisher Harry Chandler. He challenged bankers to underwrite the construction of the Coliseum. Begun in 1923. 1932 Olympics held here, and of course the spectacular 1984 Olympics as well.

Angelus Hospital, 1900s. 1925 S. Trinity, Los Angeles.

Shrine Auditorium, 1926. #139 C.H.M. 665 West Jefferson, Los Angeles.

Historic Parks: *Exposition Park,* 1872. (Exposition Club House, 1920s.) #127 C.H.M. Exposition Blvd., Figueroa St., S. Park Drive and Menlo Avenue, Los Angeles.

The 114 acre park was once used as a race track. Park established in 1910.

St. James Park, 1887. Chester Place, Los Angeles.

An historic 0.8 acre landmark considered one of the major tourist attractions of the city at the turn of the century. The Park and the adjacent area around Chester Place were once lushly landscaped and a botanical wonder to Easterners. Given to the city by developers of St. James Place tract, George King and Downey Harvey.

Museums: *California Museum of Science and Industry,* 700 State Drive, Exposition Park, CA 90037. 213-744-7400.

Natural History Museum of Los Angeles, 1913. 900 Exposition Blvd., Los Angeles, CA 90007. 213-744-3466.

Britt Museum, 1909. The Sports Museum. 2141 West Adams Blvd., Los Angeles. #197 C.H.M. (Amateur Athletic Foundation) 213-614-4111.

Architectural Preservation Group Victorian Register: *Jim Dunham,* 1308 West 25th St., Los Angeles. 213-734-1949.

Jim is a realtor who buys and sells historic properties. He probably knows more about homes in Los Angeles that have historic significance than any one else in town. He also holds seminars on every imaginable question regarding buying older properties. He has a bookstore which specializes in historic and architectural books on Los Angeles. Drop in anytime and he'll tell you what's new and how old it is!

Restoration Architect: *Martin Weil,* 2661 S. Magnolia Ave., Los Angeles, CA 90007. 213-747-4042.

Businesses 50 Years Old: *Abell Auctioneers,* since 1916. 1911 West Adams Blvd., Los Angeles. 213-734-4151.

Historic Districts: *Menlo Avenue National Historic District.* From Adams to 29th St. Currently in process of being designated a National Historic District.

Wilshire West

History: *Wilshire Boulevard* was created in 1885. Begins on Grand Ave. downtown, and ends at the beach in Santa Monica.

Gaylord Wilshire was born in Ohio in 1861. Educated at Harvard he left school to come to California in 1884. He became an avowed Socialist and had by 1887–89 founded the first Socialist paper in Los Angeles. He ran for Congress, became a gold mine speculator, publisher, inventor, lecturer, city founder, billboard owner, banker, real estate promoter and fruit grower. He inherited a fortune and lost it. He made another fortune in real estate and spent it. He and his father and half-brother founded Fullerton. He married a wealthy London widow and spent her money. He was able to promote three million dollars in a gold mining scheme and dissipated it. He made money on an electrically built gadget guaranteed to heal everything and spent all of that. Late in life he inherited another fortune. When he died, he was pennyless.

First lot sold on Wilshire went to Colonel Harrison Gray Otis, owner of the L.A. Times.

Historic Landmarks: *Otis-Parsons Art Institute,* 1898. 2401 Wilshire Blvd., Los Angeles. 213-387-5288/213-388-3128.

Harrison Gray Otis built a magnificent Mission Revival home in 1898. He asked that the property be used after his death to establish an art school. Otis Art Institute was begun in 1917 as a trade school. The Otis home was razed in 1954.

Bullock's Wilshire, 1926. #56 C.H.M. 3050 Wilshire Blvd., Los Angeles. 213-382-6161.

Arthur Letts came here from Canada with a few hundred dollars, purchased a bankrupt stock and from there went on to build the Broadway Dept. Store. John Bullock was a frugal Scotsman who had gotten a job as a salesman in Letts' Broadway store chain. Because Bullock was such a hard worker, Letts rewarded him by naming a new store at 7th and Broadway after him. He also gave Bullock $250,000 to outfit the store. Bullocks prospered. Bullock's, Inc. was formed to purchase the store from Letts' estate. Two years later, John Bullock opened the store on Wilshire Blvd. Everyone thought he was absolutely insane to open a store so far from downtown. The rest is history.

Cannell and Chaffin, 1929. 3000 Wilshire Blvd., Los Angeles. 213-

Courtesy Windsor-Square Historical Society.

380-7111. (Building vacant.)

Taken in trade for a home by silent film star Richard Barthelmess.

La Brea Tar Pits, 50,000 B.C.? 5801 Wilshire Blvd., Los Angeles, CA 90036. 213-936-2230.

George C. Page Museum contains excellent exhibits of this era. Archeological dig still continuing.

Ambassador Hotel, 1919. 3400 Wilshire Blvd., Los Angeles. 213-387-7011.

Because of recent anxiety over its fate, the L.A. Conservancy has moved to designate it an Historic Landmark.

Perino's Restaurant, 1932, 1949. Paul Williams design. 4101 Wilshire Blvd., Los Angeles. 213-487-0000.

Founded in 1932 on Gramercy by Alex Perino, the restaurant became a legend in L.A. In a town with practically no first rate restaurants, Perino's was outstanding. Moving in 1949 to the beautifully classic new structure designed by architect Paul Williams the Perino legend continued. Then in 1969 Perino sold the restaurant to Frank Esgro who ran it until 1983. In a disastrous move, the powers that be decided to open a second Perino's downtown. When it closed, Perino's Wilshire floundered. Today Perino's on Wilshire is back and looks better than ever.

The Wiltern Theater and *Pellissier*

Building, 1931. #118 C.H.M. 3780 Wilshire Blvd., Los Angeles. 213-388-1400.

A magnificent Zigzag Moderne theatre and office complex. Long the site of a dispute over whether to save it, Wayne Ratkovitch stepped in and showed everyone else how it's done. The Wiltern has been brought back to life and is again a showplace along Wilshire Blvd.

The Brown Derby, 1926. 3377 Wilshire Blvd., Los Angeles.

Well, the derby is gone, but the new shopping center that has taken the old restaurant's place will be topped with the original brown hat.

The Dark Room, 1935. 5370 Wilshire, Los Angeles. 213-271-9687.

Long a streamline Moderne landmark. In a city that moves on wheels the large camera on the storefront told passing motorists exactly what was sold inside.

Park La Brea Housing, 1941–42.

A 10½ acre development bounded by 3rd, Cochran, 6th and Fairfax.

Farmer's Market, 1934–37. Also the *Gilmore/Thompson Adobe,* 1834. Northeast corner Fairfax and 3rd. Los Angeles. 213-933-9211.

Historically, area goes back to the original Rancho days. The property then became part of the Earl B.

Gilmore land. Gilmore was a successful oil man who had one of the first gas stations in Los Angeles. The Adobe is located at 6301 West 3rd. Rarely opened to the public. Contact Windsor Square Hancock Park Historical Society.

Pan Pacific Auditorium, 1935. #183 C.H.M. 7600 Beverly, Los Angeles.

Long a city landmark, due to councilman Edleman's efforts, and preservationists, the Streamline Moderne edifice will be restored as a hotel/retail/office/Cinematheque project by the Somerset Company.

The Heinsberger Building, 1927. #275 C.H.M. 7415 Beverly Blvd., Los Angeles.

Museums: *The Los Angeles County Museum of Art,* 1964. 5905 Wilshire Blvd., Los Angeles. 213-857-6000.

Craft and Folk Art Museum, 5814 Wilshire Blvd., Los Angeles. 213-937-5544.

Holocaust Center, Los Angeles Jewish Federation, 6505 Wilshire Blvd., Los Angeles. 213-852-1234.

One of the most moving exhibits of the Jewish experience in Nazi Germany 1933–1945.

Historic Churches/Temples: *Wilshire United Methodist,* 1924. #114 C.H.M. 4350 Wilshire Blvd., Los Angeles, CA 90010. 213-931-1085. Office: 711 S. Plymouth.

Merging of other Methodist congregations as early as 1887. In 1927 other mergers formed this church. From this location church dates from 1924.

First Baptist Church, 1927. #237 C.H.M. 760 S. Westmoreland, Los Angeles.

Wilshire Christian Church, 1926–27. #209 C.H.M. 634 S. Normandie.

First Site of Temple Emanuel, 1925. 635 S. Manhattan Place, Los Angeles.

Today is occupied by Christ Church Congregation. Temple Emanuel is at 8844 Burton Way, Beverly Hills.

Originally on Fort Street, today's Broadway. Stone blocks of first temple recently recovered from original site.

Oldest site, *Sinai Temple,* 1909–1925. #173 C.H.M. (Welsh Presbyterian Church) 1153 S. Valencia, Los Angeles.

Oldest Conservative Synagogue congregation. Moved to Westwood 1961.

Second Site Sinai Temple, 1926. #91 C.H.M. 3412 West 4th St., Los Angeles.

Now the Korean Philadelphia Presbyterian Church.

Wilshire Blvd. Temple, 1862. (Founded) #116 C.H.M. Building dates from 1929. 3663 Wilshire Blvd., Los Angeles. (Congregation.)

Westminster Presbyterian Church, 1904. 2230 W. Jefferson Blvd., Los Angeles.

Historic Libraries: *Academy of Motion Picture Arts and Sciences Library,* 8949 Wilshire, Los Angeles. 213-278-4313.

You can find out all about your favorite motion picture stars here.

Memorial Library, #81 C.H.M. 4625 West Olympic Blvd., Los Angeles.

Dedicated to alumni of L.A.H.S. who died in W.W. I.

Historic Parks: *Hancock Park,* 5801 Wilshire, Los Angeles.

Originally this was the old Rancho La Brea owned by Antonio Jose Rocha and Dominguez. On November 16, 1860 Jose Rocha, son of Antonio deeded the rancho to Major Henry Hancock. He built a simple ranch house on the 3,000 acres. The tar pits contained extensive Pleistocene-era fossils, and he donated many of these to the Boston Society of Natural History. Land rich and money poor, his best stroke of luck was to marry Ida Haraszthy. She survived her husband by 30 years and leased the Rancho La Brea out for oil exploration. When the 350 wells yielded production of 4,535,000 barrels a day, she built a lavish Italian Villa on the corner of Vermont and Wilshire. Allen Hancock grew up to manage the fortune. He also founded the California Bank, now United California. The small ranch home was still visible into the 1950s.

The Villa was torn down in 1939 (see N.U.P. and U.S.C. where four rooms of villa remain). The park was created in the 1950s. The petrified bones uniquely preserved by the petroleum make the tar pits the greatest source of animal fossils in the world.

Hancock Park Residential Area: Bounded by Wilshire Blvd. on the south, La Brea on the West, Beverly Blvd. on the north, and Western on the East. For additional information on this, contact Windsor Square-Hancock Park Historical Society, 140 North Larchmont Blvd., Los Angeles, CA 90004.

Historical Societies: *California Historical Society,* 6300 Wilshire, Los Angeles. 213-651-5655.

Windsor-Square Hancock Park Historical Society, 140 N. Larchmont Blvd., Los Angeles, CA 90004.

Telephone Pioneers of America, L.A. Chapter, 1010 Wilshire Blvd., No. 460, Los Angeles. CA 90017. 213-975-7247. (A museum where L.A.'s old telephone directories are kept!)

Historic Areas: *Hancock Park Residential Area.* This area is one of the most historic in Los Angeles, but dates in terms of its development from the 1920s. Part of the Rancho Las Cienegas, the land grant extended from Wilshire Blvd. south to Baldwin Hills. It was Theodore Rimpau who developed the land which would become Hancock Park. Born in Germany, he was on his way to New York when the California gold strike changed his mind and he was lured to the Pacific Coast. When the gold in Yorba Buena didn't pan out, the young business graduate and linguist (he spoke six) struck out for Los Angeles. He set up a store, entered into the civic life of L.A. and married Francisca Avila, whose family owned Rancho Las Cienegas. The young Rimpaus built their first home near the Avila adobe on Olvera Street. Later, they again built on the ranch at what would become Vineyard and 23rd Streets at Washington Blvd. On the rancho, the Rimpaus operated a mer-

cantile store, raised grain and cattle and a large family. Much of the land was sold through the years. On the remaining several hundred acres, Adolf, the oldest son, joined in a mercantile business with Morris Goldman. In the 1920s Adolf and his brothers, Benjamin and Fred formed Rimpau Bros. Realty on Pico and subdivided part of Rancho Las Cienegas. When Los Angeles High School was built on Olympic Blvd., a connecting street was needed to Wilshire Blvd. It was named Rimpau. With the gradual subdivision of the estate and the establishment of Hancock Park, the last remaining parcel of the old rancho was sold in 1927. It was Edward Rimpau, one of Benjamin's sons, who assisted A.W. Ross in establishing the "Miracle Mile."

Larchmont Village, between First Street and Beverly Blvd., Los Angeles.

Three elements were responsible for this semi-secluded colony: a natural phenomenon called a hot springs, the trolley car and the farsightedness of one young man. First came the Hollywood Mineral Hot Springs at 5626 Melrose which brought people on excursions from Los Angeles prior to 1920. Until then Larchmont was just a wide street between two new residential developments called New Windsor Square and Hancock Park. With the advent of the streetcar came the development of Larchmont Heights. Mr. and Mrs. Julius LaBonte came to the area in 1920. By 1921 he had undertaken the construction of 70% of the commercial structures on the 100 and 200 block of North Larchmont. The first businesses were: (1) U.S. National Bank of Los Angeles; (2) LaBonte & Ransom Co., Ltd. Real Estate; (3) Clarence W. Bean Contractor (4) Larchmont barbershop; (5) Larchmont Printing; (6) A shoe repair shop; (7) The Larchmont Cafe; (8) Larchmont Electric Co.; (9) Albert Dippell real estate 1923; (10) W.H. Ledendecker, Wilshire Studios 1923; (11) Landis

Dept. Store 1933. Number 9, 10 and 11 are still in business.

The streets, Lucerne, Arden and Beverly Boulevards, take their names from the dairies that originally surrounded the area.

South Carthay, 1930s. Boundaries are Pico, La Cienega, Olympic and Crescent Heights.

While the area is composed chiefly of Streamline Moderne, period revival styles and others, it is of interest because of its being designated Historic Preservation Overlay Zone, the second in the city so named. A very active homeowners group was the core around which the HPOZ was eventually sought and approved. Spearheading this are Fred and Sandy Naiditch. 213-936-2206.

Historic Homes: *The Verbeck Mansion,* 1897. 637 Lucerne, Hancock Park.

This beautiful home was moved here in the 1920s.

Isaac Van Nuys Home, 1890s. (Van Nuys/Stuppy) 357 Lorraine, Hancock Park.

Mosier/Fifield/Willfong/Ali Home, Hancock Park.

Pickford/Minter/Howard/Layport/Qvale Home, Hancock Park.

Wilson/Phillips Home, Hancock Park.

Albertson/Ahmanson/Thomas Home, Hancock Park.

Davis Churchill Home, Hancock Park.

Boos/Marsten-Tibbett/Costell-Barrymore-Ruig/McConnell Home, Hancock Park.

Eisner/Copley/Shell/Miller Home, Hancock Park.

Janss/Stone/Chandler Home, "Los Tiempos", Hancock Park.

Davidson/Evans Home, #115 c.h.m. Hancock Park (419 S. Lorraine Blvd.)

La Casa de las Campanas, 1927. #239 c.h.m. 350 North June, Hancock Park.

Constructed in 1927 for Ruby Mead Lamb, this home has beautiful Spanish bells which hang in the Campanile. One is marked, San Juan-1790.

Paulson / Lockhart / Barrymore Getty Home, Hancock Park (home of Mayor Tom Bradley).

Stanton/Nigg Home. Hancock Park.

Apartments: *El Royale Apartments,* 1920s. #309 c.h.m. 450 N. Rossmore, Los Angeles.

Clubs: *The Ebell Club House and Theatre,* 1927. #250 c.h.m. 743 Lucerne, Los Angeles. 213-931-1277.

The Los Angeles Tennis Club, 5851 Clinton, Los Angeles, 213-464-3195.

The Wilshire Country Club, 301 N. Rossmore, Los Angeles. 213-934-1121.

Historic Firestation: *Firestation Engine Co.,* 1913. #310 c.h.m. 158 S. Western, Los Angeles.

Historic Trees: *Queen and Washington Palm Tree,* 1928. #94 c.h.m. Highland Ave. between Wilshire and Melrose, Los Angeles.

Moreton Bay Fig Tree, 1875. #19 c.h.m. 11000 National Blvd., Los Angeles.

Historic Adobes: *Rocha House,* 1865. #13 c.h.m. 2400 Shenandoah, Los Angeles.

Built for Antonio Jose Rocha II on the Rancho Rincon de los Bueyes.

Historic Schools: *Marlborough School for Girls,* 1889. 250 S. Rossmore, Los Angeles. 213-935-1147.

Moved to this location in 1916.

Bookstores: *Dawson's,* 1906. 535 N. Larchmont, Los Angeles, CA 90004. 213-469-2186. .

A wonderful bookstore in Los Angeles for historical material!

Zeitlin-Ver Brugge Bookstore, 815 North La Cienega Blvd., Los Angeles.

Jacob Zeitlin began his first shop at 567 S. Hope St. in 1928.

Later moved to former stables on the Earl estate on Cardondelet St. near Westlake Park. Finally he moved to the old Dutch Barn, long a familiar landmark on La Cienega. Mr. Zeitlin died in 1987. Store specializes in old, rare books, prints, art.

Historic Restaurants: *Cock "N"*

Bull, 1937–1987. 9170 Sunset Blvd., Los Angeles. Closed.

Marie Callender's Victorian Restaurant, 5773 Wilshire, Los Angeles. 213-937-7952.

El Cholo, 1921. 11215 Western Ave., Los Angeles. 213-734-2773.

Nostalgic Diners: *Johnny Rockets,* 7507 Melrose, Los Angeles. 213-651-3361.

Historic Cafes: *Tail of the Pup,* 1930. 329 North San Vicente, Los Angeles. 213-652-4517.

One of L.A.'s first fast food takeouts. Preservationists screamed loud enough and this was moved and saved!

Norms, 1950s. La Cienega Blvd. near Melrose Ave., Los Angeles.

Carney's, 1950s. 8351 W. Sunset, Los Angeles. 213-654-8300.

The Witchstand, 1950s. Slauson Ave. at Overhill Dr., Los Angeles. 213-293-5073.

Historic Buildings: *Sunset Towers,* 1930s. (St. James Club) 8358 Sunset Blvd., Los Angeles. 213-654-7100.

After years of disputes, lawsuits and real estate nightmares, this building has been beautifully restored.

Businesses: *Classic Wicker,* 8532 Melrose Ave., Los Angeles, CA 90069. 213-659-1121.

Western Costumes, 1912. 5335 Melrose Ave., Los Angeles. 213-469-1451.

D.W. Griffith went to this small company when he was filming Birth of a Nation. His meticulous standards put them forever in the realm of Hollywood legends.

Larchmont Chronicle, 542½ North Larchmont Blvd., Los Angeles, CA 90004. 213-462-2241. Jane Gilman, Publisher.

Auntie Mame, vintage clothing 1880–1980. 1102 S. La Cienega Blvd. 213-652-8430.

Movies and More Antique Clothes, 1882–1980. 3266 Cahuenga Blvd. West. 213-391-6206.

Play Back Antique Clothing, 622 N. Doheny Drive, Los Angeles. 213-273-5673.

Best of Yesterday Antique Clothing, 1519 W. Sunset, Los Angeles. 213-971-9074.

Feldman and Co., 1919. Lighting Fixtures, 853 N. La Cienega Blvd., Los Angeles. 213-652-1488.

Butterfield's Auctioneers and Appraisers, 1865. 808 N. La Cienega Blvd., Los Angeles. 213-657-5172.

Anawalt Lumber Co. 1912. 11060 W. Pico Blvd., West Los Angeles. 213-478-0324.

Greg's Antique Lighting and Collectables. American Gas & Electric Fixtures from 1850 to 1910. 12005 Wilshire, Los Angeles. 213-478-5475.

Modern Drapery Enterprise, 1917. 1914 S. Mariposa Ave., Los Angeles. 213-731-2538.

Luster Tile Co., 1900. 4912 Venice Blvd, Los Angeles. 213-931-1547.

Western Badge and Trophy, 1901. 1716 W. Washington Blvd., Los Angeles. 213-735-1201.

Crest Curtain and Drapery, 1918. 8972 W. Pico Blvd., Los Angeles. 213-271-5441.

Harris Doris Autographs, Historical Autographs, 5410 Wilshire Blvd., Los Angeles. 213-939-4500.

Karz Plumbing and Heating Co., 1919. 2007 Brooklyn, Los Angeles. 213-261-8131.

Better Built Robinson Roof Co., 1904. 2661 W. Pico Blvd., Los Angeles. 213-295-1013.

Jefferson Lock and Key, 1906. 2313 West Jefferson Blvd., Los Angeles. 213-731-1181.

The Junk Store, 11900 Wilshire Blvd., Los Angeles. 213-479-7413.

L.A.'s oldest fine vintage apparel.

The Next Stage, tours/travel, Marlene Gordon, P.O. Box 35269, Los Angeles 90035. 213-939-2688.

Craftsperson: *Designer Resource,* 5160 Melrose Ave., Los Angeles. 213-465-9235.

Other Historical Resources: *Southwest Oral History Association,* Kathryn Gallacher, Oral History Program U.C.L.A., 136 Powell Library, Los Angeles, CA 90024.

Mr. Gillingham, Historian. 5228

Holt Ave., Los Angeles, CA 90056. 213-645-5856.

Other: Two coalitions of businessmen and/or property owners and residential and community groups have formed within the last year. The Miracle Mile Civil Coalition and the Wilshire Shareholders Group. The L.A. Conservancy is also trying to get Wilshire Blvd. along Miracle Mile designated as an historic district. Wayne Ratkovitch, preservationist, developer, 3780 Wilshire, Los Angeles. 213-385-5600.

Alvarado Terrace

History: *Alvarado Terrace* was subdivided in 1902 on a land used as a putting course by the Los Angeles Golf Club, forerunner of the Los Angeles Country Club. In those days it was called "Windmill Links" after a windmill which remained from an earlier farm. The homes were built in 1902–06 as the exclusive residences of Los Angeles' most prominent citizens.

Historic Homes: *Edmund Barmore Home,* 1902. #83 C.H.M. 1317 Alvarado Terrace, Los Angeles.

Barmore was President of the Los Angeles Transfer Co.

Morris R. Cohn, 1902. #84 C.H.M. 1325 Alvarado Terrace, Los Angeles.

Cohn was the first garment manufacturer of Los Angeles beginning in 1893 with the production of work clothes. In 1897 he established the Morris Cohn Clothing Co. In effect, Cohn was the founder of the garment and sportswear industry of Los Angeles.

William F. Gilbert, 1902. #85 C.H.M. 1333 Alvarado Terrace, Los Angeles.

Pomeroy Powers Home, 1902. #86 C.H.M. 1345 Alvarado Terrace.

Pomeroy Powers was president of the Los Angeles City Council 1900–1904. He was also a real estate developer.

R.H. Raphael, 1902. #87 C.H.M. 1353 Alvarado Terrace, Los Angeles.

Today, this home is owned by Sandy and Shirley Spillman. They have turned their beautiful home into Terrace Manor, a Bed and Breakfast Inn. For more information call 213-381-1478.

A.W. Kinney, 1902. #88 C.H.M. 1401 Alvarado Terrace, Los Angeles.

Historic Parks: *Terrace Park and Powers Place,* 1904. #210 C.H.M. Powers Place and 14th St., Los Angeles. 1.17 acres.

This delightful park still has the original section of brick paving which is a reminder of the neighborhood's long history. It has been designated as an historic landmark.

Historic Church: *Central Spanish Seventh Day Adventist Church,* 1912. (Once housed Jim Jones congregation.) #89 C.H.M. 1366 S. Alvarado St., Los Angeles, CA 90066.

First Church of Christ Scientist.

Pico-Arlington Christian Church, 1927. 3405 Pico Blvd., Los Angeles.

The Church of Jesus Christ of Latter-Day Saints, 1928. 1209 S. Manhattan Place, Los Angeles.

Hebron Church (originally Forum Theater) 1921–24. 4050 Pico Blvd., Los Angeles.

Bed and Breakfast: *Terrace Manor,* 1902. #87 C.H.M. 1353 Alvarado Terrace, Los Angeles. 213-381-1478.

Note: Have you been enjoying those wonderful Pacific Bell T.V. commercials between two old friends? Well, one of the men is Sandy Spillman, owner of the Terrace Manor (and his wife, Shirley). The commercials are unusual because they are a first-time mini-series idea in which the concept of a story evolves. Congratulations Pacific Bell!!!! Drop by and see them sometime, or better yet, call and make reservations!

Country Club Park: Formerly the home of the Los Angeles Country Club (from 1889 through 1905), this 250 acre site today boasts some of the

finest homes in Los Angeles. The land was subdivided between 1906 and 1912 by Country Club Park, a real estate corporation headed by Isaac Milbank. Today, the neighborhood encompasses over 30 continuous residential blocks, bordered by Olympic, Pico, Western and Crenshaw. There are Mediterranean "villas," Tudor castles, Craftsman bungalows and late Victorian Queen Annes which line the streets. Credit to Ray Pendro and the Los Angeles Conservancy for above information. Their excellent brochure on this area can be obtained by calling 213-623-CITY.

Historic Homes, Country Club Park: *Milbank Mansion, 1913–14.* 3340 Country Club Drive, Los Angeles.

Reeves Mansion, Sisters of Social Service, 1913. 1130 Westchester Place, Los Angeles.

Alfred F. Rosenheim, architect.

West side of 3rd Avenue, south 1908–1912. From 1133 to 1271. Los Angeles.

Private Residence, 1912. 1229 3rd Ave., Los Angeles.

Private Residence, 1910. 1248 3rd Ave., Los Angeles.

Private Residence, 1907. 1255 Westchester Place, Los Angeles.

Private Residence, 1914. 1215 Westchester Place, Los Angeles.

Private Residence, 1925. 1230 S. Arlington Ave., Los Angeles.

Private Residence, 1915. 1245 S. Arlington Ave., Los Angeles.

Private Residence, 1925. 1236 S. Van Ness Ave., Los Angeles.

Private Residence, 1915. 1219 S. Van Ness Ave., Los Angeles.

Private Residence, 1921. 1225 S. Van Ness Ave., Los Angeles.

Private Residence, 1922. 1219 S. Gramercy Place, Los Angeles.

Private Residence, 1909. 1237 S. Gramercy Place, Los Angeles.

Private Residence, 1923. 1231 S. St. Andrews Place, Los Angeles.

Private Residence, 1924. 1215 S. St. Andrews Place, Los Angeles.

Private Residence, 1911. 1041 S. Gramercy Drive, Los Angeles.

Private Residence, 1909. 1035 S. Gramercy Drive, Los Angeles.

Private Residences, 1028 S. Gramercy Place, 1913. 1034 S. Gramercy Place, 1910. 1040 S. Gramcery Place, 1914, Los Angeles.

Country Club Neighborhood Association, Mr. Menion L. Carr.

Lafayette Square — St. Charles Place

History: Originally Lafayette Square was part of the Rancho Las Cienegas, subdivided in 1912 from barley fields and pastures, the square was the last and greatest of George L. Crenshaw's ten residential developments. Crenshaw was a midwest banker and a major real estate developer in our city. Lafayette Square was designed as an elegant residential park, with St.

Charles Place as its centerpiece. It is said that St. Charles Place imitated the Spanish park surrounding the Municipal Theater in Rio de Janeiro, Brazil. The neighborhood housed many prominent citizens such as W.C. Fields and Fatty Arbuckle, entrepreneur Norton Simon, boxer Joe Louis and Princess Pignatelli.

In the early days, restrictive convenants prohibited minorities from living here. Beginning in the late forties many eminent and professional black families moved to Lafayette Square. Residents included NAACP founder Paul Williams. (Above information from the L.A. Conservancy brochure on Lafayette Square).

Historic Homes: *Crenshaw House,* 1912. 1675 Buckingham, Los Angeles.

Actually the home was designed by Charles Wagner as a demonstration house for Lafayette Square. Its first occupants were the Grier family.

Private Residence, 1925. 1702 S. Buckingham, Los Angeles.

May Ormerod Harris Home, 1929. 1660 Virginia, Los Angeles.

Private Residence, 1921. 1681 Virginia, Los Angeles.

The McCoy Home, 1907. 1703 Virginia, Los Angeles.

McKinley Mansion (Hunt and Burns architects) 3rd and La Fayette Park Place, Los Angeles.

Edward Charles Hauser, 1916. 1717 Virginia, Los Angeles.

Private Residence, 1913. 1740 Virginia, Los Angeles.

Walter Albert Home, 1928. 1743 Virginia, Los Angeles.

Private Residence, 1922. 1820 Virginia. Los Angeles.

Henry Boss Home, 1916. 1651 Wellington, Los Angeles.

Henry Boos was the founder of Clifton's Cafeterias.

Private Residence, 1953. Designed by Paul Williams. 1704 Wellington, Los Angeles.

Paul Williams was the most famous black architect in Los Angeles. He was born in 1896 in Los Angeles, attended Polytechnic High School, the University of Southern California, and the Beaux Arts School of Design in New York City. He designed the W&J Sloane's Store, Saks Fifth Avenue, Perino's Restaurant, Sunset Plaza Apartments, and dozens of other buildings and homes throughout Southern California.

The Schummacher Home, 1922. 1705 Wellington, Los Angeles.

The Fisher Home, 1926. 1719 Wellington, Los Angeles.

Private Residence, 1913. 1725 Wellington, Los Angeles.

William Grant Still, 1936. #169 C.H.M. 1262 Victoria Ave., Los Angeles.

First black man to conduct a major symphony orchestra in U.S.

Private Residence, 1685 Victoria, Los Angeles.

Paul Williams Home, 1950. #170 C.H.M. 1690 Victoria, Los Angeles.

This is Paul Williams' own home.

Private Residence, 1912. 1705 Victoria, Los Angeles.

Private Residence, 1928. 1800 Victoria, Los Angeles.

The McGinley Home, 1926. 1821 Victoria, Los Angeles.

Granada Buildings, 1927. #238 C.H.M. 672 S. Lafayette Park Place, Los Angeles.

Joseph H. Small, 1925. 1752 Virginia, Los Angeles.

Note: For more information on the area and the L.A. Conservancy tour brochure dial 213-623-CITY.

Los Feliz

History: Corp. Jose Vicente Feliz was an escort on that historic journey of 1781 when the city of Los Angeles was founded. Six years later he became the Pueblo's first commissionado. Before he retired in 1800 he was given the use of land he named *El Rancho Nuestra Senora de Refugio de Los Feliz.*

In 1843 the Rancho Los Feliz was granted to Maria Ygnacia Verdugo but was occupied by her in 1841. The United States government issued a patent in her name for 6,647 acres. The rancho passed successively through the hands of Antonio Coronel, famous pioneer of Los Angeles; James Lick, founder of the Lick Observatory; and Colonel Griffith Jenkins Griffith, who in 1898 deeded 3,015 acres of the rancho to the City of Los Angeles. It is the largest city park in the United States.

Historical Landmarks: *Griffith Park*, 1896. Los Feliz Blvd. and Riverside Drive, Los Angeles. 213-665-5188.

When news of this outstanding donation to the city of Los Angeles was received, it was not greeted with open arms. Why? Major Horace Bell accused Griffith of bequeathing it solely to avoid paying taxes. As a result the park was not used in those early years. To make matters worse, Griffith was involved in a sensational trial for attempted murder in 1903. Griffith accused his wife of conspiring with the Pope to have him poisoned. He then turned a revolver on her and shot the fleeing woman in the eye. Griffith was sentenced to two years in San Quentin. After the prison term he came back home and generously offered a $100,000 gift to the city for an observatory. It was refused. When he died in 1919, he willed $700,000 to the city for an observatory and a Greek Theatre. By this time the gift was accepted. Today, there are more than 4,000 acres in the park.

In 1933, the park was the site of a disastrous fire and loss of life. Without warning as fires tend to begin in our city, one broke out in the hills around Mineral Wells Canyon. Thirty-six men, employees who had been working on a road system got trapped in a canyon. By the time they were found, it was too late. In terms of lives lost, it was the most disastrous fire in the history of Los Angeles.

Travel Town, Griffith Park, Atchison Topeka and Santa Fe Motor car are on view here. Los Angeles.

Griffith Park Observatory, 1935. #168 C.H.M. 2800 East Observatory Road, Los Angeles. 213-664-1191. For laser shows 997-3624.

It took two years and $225,000 to build the observatory. When it was completed it was only the third planetarium in the United States, the only one west of the Mississippi.

Griffith Park Zoo, 1966. Los Feliz Blvd. and Riverside Dr., Los Angeles. 213-666-4650.

The Los Angeles Zoo covers 110 acres in a natural setting. Note: Mr. Hjelte has written: *Footprints in the Park,* published by the Dept. of Parks and Recreation. All about Griffith Park.

Musuem: *The Gene Autry Western Heritage Foundation Museum,* 4700 Zoo Dr., Los Angeles. (In Griffith Park, opposite the zoo.) 213-460-5635.

Indian Sites: *Fern Dell Nature Museum,* #112 C.H.M. Site of Gabrielino Indian Village, 5373 Red Oak Dr., Los Angeles, CA 90068.

Archeological surveys reveal that at the mouth of Fern Dell canyon in Griffith Park there was a fairly large settlement of Gabrielino Indians. A plaque at the Los Feliz Boulevard entrance to the park names the area Mocohuenga Canyon.

Historic Theatres: *Greek Theatre,* 1929–30. Vermont Canyon Road, Los Angeles. 213-410-1062.

Los Feliz Theatre, 1940s. 1822 North Vermont, Los Angeles. 213-664-2169.

Historic Homes: *Feliz Adobe,* 1830s. 4730 Crystal Springs Dr., Griffith Park.

Villa San Guiseppe, 1927. 3412 Waverly Drive, Los Angeles.

This magnificent home was designed by Bernard Maybeck, interiors, Harold Grieve for radio and car mogul Earle C. Anthony. Today it is a Roman Catholic Retreat.

John Luckenbach, 1914. Hillhurst Park, Los Feliz.

Lovell Health Home, 1929. #123

C.H.M. A. Richard Neutra designed home. 4616 Dundee Drive, Los Angeles.

Walt Disney Home, 1932. 4053 Wrong Way, Los Angeles.

Vinmont Home, 1926. Roland Coate, Architect. 5136 Los Feliz Blvd., Los Angeles.

Farrell Home, 1926. 3209 Lowry Rd., Los Angeles.

Carr Home, 1925. S.E. corner of Lowry and Rowena, Los Angeles.

Historic Monuments: Memorial Fountain (Dedicated 1940) #162 C.H.M. Corner of Riverside Drive and Los Feliz Blvd., Los Angeles.

It was in this area that a young William Mulholland got his first job working on a zanya as a ditchdigger. He studied engineering at night and eventually became the superintendent of the Los Angeles Water Company. His single most stupendous task however was that of bringing water 230 miles away in the Owens Valley to a thirsty Los Angeles in 1913. It is still the single largest engineering feat ever undertaken by a single city. The fountain is dedicated to Mr. Mulholland.

Sunset Blvd. Bridge, 1934. #236 C.H.M. Crosses Silver Lake Blvd., Los Angeles.

Franklin Ave. Bridge, 1920s. #126 C.H.M. Between St. George and Myra, Los Angeles.

Glendon-Hyperion Bridge, 1929. #164 C.H.M. Over Los Angeles River Golden State Freeway and Riverside Drive, Los Angeles.

Historic Parks: *Laughlin Park,* off of Franklin from Los Feliz Blvd., Los Angeles.

Homer Laughlin was a builder in the tradition of Chester Place and Fremont Place. Here, in the 1920s came Hollywood's best and brightest. Cecil B. DeMille lived on DeMille Drive. (Of course). But then so did W.C. Fields.

Deania Derbin lived on Lindwood Drive. There is the beautiful Art Deco Home built in 1929 by Sherer, a home the Smithsonian says is the most beautiful Art Deco residence in the U.S. Several Lloyd Wright homes are in the area: Taggart House 1922–24 at 5423 Black Oak Drive; the Sowden House 1926 at 5121 Franklin; and the Samuels-Navarro House 1926–28 at 5609 Valley Oak. There is Frank Lloyd Wright's famous Ennis House 1924 at 2607 Glendower, sometimes open to the public on speical occasions. For more information, contact Mark Laska of the Laughlin Park Association. 213-660-108.

Historic Sites: *Site of Walt Disney's first studio* in Los Angeles, 1926, #163 C.H.M. 2725 Hyperion, Los Angeles.

At this location Snow White and the Seven Dwarfs was produced.

Historic Streets: Look at streets with names like Waverly Drive, Rowena, St. George, and Surry. When films like Ivanhoe and Robin Hood were made, so too were castles built and streets dedicated to the memory of knights in shining armor and a world Hollywood was trying to capture on the silver screen and promote at the box office. Los Feliz Blvd. to Griffith Park Blvd. and left at Rowena or St. George. There is also a Rowena Reservoir.

Historic Tree: *Cedars* #67 C.H.M. *Trees* at 4400 block of Avocado St., Los Feliz. Recently declared a historic landmark, these eight avocado trees are about 100 years old.

Los Feliz Blvd. between Riverside Drive and Western Ave., Los Angeles.

Historic Restaurants: *Tam O'Shanter Inn,* 1922. 2980 Los Feliz Blvd., Los Angeles. 213-664-0228.

Nostalgic Diner: *Millie's,* 3524 Sunset, Los Angeles. 213-662-5720.

Library: 213-664-2093. Los Feliz Branch.

South-Central

Area: Roughly south of downtown Los Angeles. South of Jefferson to Imperial. Watts on the East to Vermont on the West.

Landmarks: *Second Baptist Church,* 1926. #200 C.H.M. 2412 Griffith Ave., Los Angeles, CA 90011. 213-748-0318.

This is the second church—the first having been established in a room on Requina St. in 1885. This church was designed by Paul Williams, noted black architect.

Sojourner Truth Home, 1904, 1913. 1119 E. Adams Blvd., Los Angeles, CA 90011. 213-234-2037.

The Sojourner Truth Industrial Club was formed in 1904 in the First African Methodist Episcopal Church of Los Angeles. The organization was named after a former slave Isabella Baumfree.

Biddy Mason Center, 1152 E. Adams Blvd., Los Angeles, CA 90011.

Formerly a residence of Mrs. Jessis L. Terry, built by her husband, Woodford Terry, a pioneer black contractor. One of the most outstanding women in Los Angeles history, Biddy Mason represents the desire for freedom that we all have. The drama of her story began with Robert Smith, owner of a plantation in Mississippi. Bound for California (1850s) he bought a plantation style home where he settled down to a life much like the one he had left in the south. The new settlement did not work out, so he loaded up wagons and two black women, Biddy and a friend, and made his way to Texas. However, he had to stop in Los Angeles for supplies. Someone back in the colony realized that if these people went back to Texas, a slave state, they would be returning to a condition they would object to it if they knew about it. The sheriff of Los Angeles County was notified. The case went to court. The court found Smith guilty of misrepresentation. Meanwhile Robert Owens (who had aided families when they moved into town) invited Biddy Mason and her daughters to stay in his home. His son later married Biddy's daughter. Dr. John Griffin offered Biddy work. Biddy was able to save her money. She purchased two downtown lots for $250, between third and fourth streets. Her children also purchased land. In the 1880s when a

long and heavy rain drenched Los Angeles, Biddy placed a standing order with a grocery store on Spring Street to give free food to anyone who needed it. Today her descendants still live in Los Angeles. The copy of the 1856 court verdict has been saved by generations down to the present. It is a reminder of the stirring moment in Los Angeles history when, five years before the outbreak of the Civil War and seven years before Abraham Lincoln's Emancipation Proclamation, Biddy was given her freedom.

Biddy Mason Home, 331 Spring St., Los Angeles.

Also the First African Methodist Church, 1872. The building at 8th and Towne Ave. was the first Black Church in Los Angeles of any denomination. Home is an historic landmark.

Lincoln Theatre, 1924. 2300 S. Central Ave., Los Angeles, CA 90021. 213-232-7785.

Ebony Showcase Theatre, 4720 W. Washington Blvd., Los Angeles. 213-936-1107.

The Ebony Showcase is the oldest black-owned and independently funded legitimate theater in the U.S. In an era when theatrical outlets for blacks were almost nonexistent, Nick Stewart and his wife Edna established the Ebony to fill this void. Since 1950 the theater has been a place where up-and-coming actors and actresses could refine and exhibit their talents in a professional environment. In addition to stage plays, the Showcase also offers classes and workshops in the theater arts and has frequently hosted community groups and activities.

YMCA, 1926. 28th St., Los Angeles. 213-232-7193.

YMCA's black involvement dates back to 1900 when the Ministerial Alliance organized the first YMCA for black youth on the West Coast. Designed by Paul Williams.

Fire Station No. 30, 1942. #289 C.H.M. 1401 S. Central Ave., L.A.

Ralph Bunch Residence, #159 C.H.M. 1221–1223 E. 40th Place, Los

Angeles, CA 90011.

Ralph Bunch, Under Secretary of the United Nations; recipient of the Nobel Peace Prize lived here from 1919 to 1927. He studied at U.C.L.A. and Harvard, earning a Ph.D. in political science from that institution.

Mayme Clayton, 3617 Montclair St., Los Angeles.

Young Apts., 1921. #317 C.H.M. 1621 South Central, Los Angeles.

The Dunbar Hotel, Museum, 1928. #131 C.H.M. 4225 S. Central Ave., Los Angeles. 213-233-7168.

Originally named the Hotel Somerville by its builder, Dr. John Alexander Somerville, this historic hotel hosted the first national convention for the National Association for the Advancement of Colored People in 1928. In the 1930s the hotel was renamed the Dunbar when it was purchased by another prominent black community leader, Lucius Lomax.

Watt's Tower, 1921–1954. (Towers of Simon Rodia) #15 C.H.M. 1765 E. 107th St., Watts, CA 90002.

Probably the most remarkable piece of folk art in Southern California. Italian immigrant Simon Rodia erected the three immense concrete towers out of broken bottles, sea shells, china, wood and anything else he could find. In 1959 the city urged that they be demolished.

The towers, thank God, have remained, due to a great many art lovers, private citizens and many more who simply value this wonderful creative work.

Watt's Station, 1904. #36 C.H.M. 1686 E. 103rd St., Los Angeles, CA 90002.

One of the last remaining Pacific Electric stations in Los Angeles. As of '87 set for $310,000 restoration!

Historic Libraries: *Vermont Square Library,* 1913–19. #264 C.H.M. 1201 West 48th St., Los Angeles.

John Muir Library, #305 C.H.M. 1005 W. 64th St.

Businesses: *Batson's Laundry,* 1917. 6732 Crenshaw Blvd., Los Angeles. 213-759-9128.

Brockman Gallery, 4334 Degnan Blvd., Los Angeles. 213-294-3766. (Oldest black art gallery in Los Angeles.)

Lodge Memorials, 1915. 1247 S. Fairfax, Los Angeles. 213-931-1081.

Golden State Mutual Insurance Co., 1999 W. Adams, Los Angeles. 213-731-1131.

Advance A & Brass Sales Corp., 1912. 1001 E. Slauson, Los Angeles, CA 90011. 213-231-9301.

Broadway Federal, 4501 S. Broadway, Los Angeles. 213-232-4271.

Historic Sites: Site of the original *Vernon Branch Library,* #306 C.H.M. 4504 S. Central, Los Angeles.

Other: Black History, Western States, Black Research Center. Founder, Mayme Clayton. Black history tours during Black History Month. Our Authors Study Club, 213-295-0521.

Book: *City of Watts, 1907–1926.* Mary Ellen Bell Ray, Rising Publications, 1985.

——— LYNWOOD ———

History: Once part of the Rancho San Antonio, Lynwood may not be able to relate romantic stories of a glorious past, but it represents the development of many small towns in the southland.

In the beginning, this section of Los Angeles County was a barley field, with many willow trees and marsh land. In 1896 a man named Sessions bought a part of this tract and established a dairy. (See Angelino Heights for the beautiful Sessions home.) His family gave the name to the new area. His wife's maiden name was Miss Lynn Wood and together, they all agreed to call the dairy, the "Lynwood Dairy." The Southern Pacific Railway had a siding car here which they called "Lynwood Siding." Later three gentlemen, including H.V. Copeland, bought all the available acres and formed the Lynwood Company.

In 1913 two real estate subdividers, Harry T. Coffin and John Balliet opened up 800 acres for "suburban" home sites.

Historical Society: None. However the local Chamber of Commerce is working to organize one soon. Andrea Hooper, city clerk of Lynwood will be chairperson.

Chamber of Commerce, P.O. Box 763, Lynwood, CA 90262. 213-537-6484.

Historic Depot: *P.E. Depot,* Long Beach Blvd. and Fernwood, Lynwood.

Historic Schools: *Lugo School,* 1917.

4345 Pendleton St., Lynwood.
Lindbergh Lincoln, 1926. 11031 State, Lynwood.
Woodrow Wilson, 1917. 11700 School St., Lynwood.
Roosevelt School, 1924. 10835 Mallison Ave., Lynwood.

Historic Churches: *St. Emydius Catholic Church,* 1924. California St., Lynwood.
First Christian Church, 1925. 3340 Sanborn, Lynwood.
First Baptist Church, 1925. 11200 Pope St., Lynwood.

Businesses: *Lynwood Tribune,* 1922. 11148 Atlantic, Lynwood.
Earle Jorgenson and Co., 1923. 10700 Alameda St., Lynwood. 213-567-1122.

Other Buildings: *Post Office,* 1922. 11200 Long Beach Blvd., Lynwood.

Book: *Jack Willard Recalls: Lynwood All American City,* 1971. Author, Jack Willard.

—— MALIBU ——

History: A Harvard man, Frederick Hastings Rindge, fell in love with one of the most beautiful ranchos in Southern California. He bought the *Rancho Topanga Malibu Sequit* in 1891 for $133,150, a small fortune in those days. Bringing his young wife May (Knight) Rindge to live on the rancho with him, they both settled down to life in God's country at the end of the rainbow. Things did not work out quite the way they had both hoped. Frederick died early, in 1905, before realizing the extent of the problems their idealistic rancho would bring. The sea, with its gauzy veil of fog and breathtaking sunsets, the deep peaceful canyons were a world unto themselves. If one wanted to cross them however, one had to go by sea around the Malibu, or get permission to go through the Rindge gates and no trespassing signs. When Los Angeles had a small population

and few people had a reason to crisscross the property, all was well. But more and more people came to the area, more settlers moved into the canyons, more people wanted and demanded some kind of access road through the property. May would have none of it. This was *her* land, her rancho, private property, and in order to make sure people stayed out, she hired men with guns to patrol the Malibu. She even constructed her own railroad, becoming the only female railroad president in U.S. History. The reason, of course, was to make sure that a right of way was given Government sanctions so that no other railroad could gain access to the area. Even today there are no rail lines that extend through that section of Pacific Coast Highway. For twenty-seven years May Rindge fought the federal Government.

In the end, the U.S. Supreme Court awarded the right-of-way to the state and $100,000 to the family for damages. Knowing the inevitable, Mrs. Rindge began to sell the very exclusive beach front area called the Malibu Colony to film stars in 1936. With the depression, the Rindge interests went into bankruptcy. The unfinished mansion atop the hill was sold and May went to live in her home in Los Angeles. (See Los Angeles, North University Park section). May died there in 1941.

For a long time, the history of the Rindges was pretty much confined to researchers and those who took an interest in digging through records. However today, the beautiful Admanson Home is open to the public and with it, a wonderful museum which tells anyone who will spend the time, the story of the Rindges, the Malibu and the way things were, when the sea and the sky were all there was.

Note: First resident in the Malibu (after the Rindges) was silent film star Anna G. Neilsen in 1936.

Historical Society: *Malibu Historical Society,* Malibu, CA 90265. 213-457-9189. John Merrick, President.

Historical Landmarks: *The Malibu Lagoon Museum; The Adamson Home State Park,* 23200 Pacific Coast Highway, P.O. Box 291, Malibu, CA 90265. 213-456-8432.

There is the magnificent Adamson Beach Home built in 1928 by architect Stiles Clements, of the firm of Morgan Walls and Clements—famous as designers of the Hearst Castle at San Simeon. Rhoda Rindge Adamson was the last child of May and Frederick born in 1892. She married Merritt "Smoke" Adamson. Rhoda's mother promised she would help the young couple in any venture they chose. Someone recommended the dairy industry. They named the new business Adohr, a name derived from spelling Rhoda backwards. The home is open to the public.

Also here is the *Malibu Lagoon,* one of the oldest historic sites in Los Angeles County. The Malibu Creek flows to the coast in rainy weather and forms a natural lagoon. At the mouth of the creek is an archaeological excavation which has been worked on from time to time by U.C.L.A. The area is still pristine and a delight to view from busy Pacific Coast Highway. Also on the Adamson residence is an Indian midden.

Also off one of the rooms from the Adamson Residence is a wonderful museum with excellent photos of the Rindge family, the Malibu as it was before the coast was overgrown with people. It is very much a rare treat to view this.

The Serra Retreat, 1928/1971. Serra Rd., P.O. Box 127. Malibu, CA 90265.

The gates are sometimes closed, or there may be someone posted there to ask your business. The area is a private residential community. The Serra Retreat is now on the exact site where a palatial home of the Rindges once stood. An earlier home was located in the valley at the entrance to Malibu Canyon. Both homes were destroyed by fires that swept through the canyons. *Los Flores Canyon Road.* This is where the Rindge estate began.

Museum: *The J. Paul Getty Musuem,* 1953, 1974. 17985 Pacific Coast Highway, Malibu, CA 90265. 213-458-2003.

In addition to this spectacular Museum, there is an original Ranch House on the property. Mr. Getty expanded this house to provide more gallery space for his art collection. This first or "old" museum was opened to the public in 1953. The Ranch house is currently used as office space.

The Museum is modeled after an ancient Roman Villa, the *Villa of the Papyri* which was buried in the famous Mt. Vesuvius eruption of 79 A.D. It is the most ingenious way possible to view original Roman and Greek Art and have the ancient world come alive.

Note: The J. Paul Getty Trust will be embarking on a program to aid with

Historic Adamson House and Malibu Lagoon Museum. Courtesy Malibu Lagoon Museum.

preservation of architectural land-marks especially in the L.A. area.

Historic Homes: *Villa de Leon,* 1927. 17948 Porto Marina Way, Malibu.

As the Museum will tell you, this home has nothing whatsoever to do with the Museum. It is spectacular, however, and people always wonder who it belongs to. Story has it the famous Ali Khan and Rita Hayworth lived there.

Dr. Thomas Hodge Castle, 1977–79. 23800 Malibu Crest Drive, Malibu.

No one can miss this. It was built as a private residence and occasionally, the owners allow special groups to tour.

Gull's Way, 1940s. Pacific Coast Hwy. and Latiago Canyon Rd., Malibu. Private Residence.

Westfair House and Windmill, Meres Canyon, Malibu. Private Residence.

Arch Oboler House, 1940–41. A Frank Lloyd Wright Home. 32436 Mulholland Drive, Malibu.

Villa Casablanca, 16 acre site once part of the Serra Retreat, Malibu.

Historical Ranch: *Calamigos Ranch,* 1949. 80 acre ranch still owned by same family. 327 S. Latigo Canyon Rd. Malibu.

Historic Sites: *Marblehead Land Co.,* 1926–1933. Pacific Coast Highway, Malibu.

May Rindge began this high-grade ceramic tile factory in 1926 at the height of the Spanish craze in home building. Plant was located on the beach east of the Malibu pier. At one time there were over 127 employees involved in all

phases of operation from clay mixing, administration and sales. A L.A. display room and warehouse was located at 119 Larchmont Blvd.

Site of the Malibu Mountain Inn, 1930s and the *Malibu Archery Club,* Latigo and Escondido Canyons.

Site of the *Malibu Inn.* Originally a sandwich shop, then the *Inn* and a real estate office and market. Later became *Mayfair Market,* then *Colony Market,* now a new shopping center. 23900 Pacific Coast Highway.

Site of *Los Flores Inn.* Later *The Malibu Sea Lion.* See Historic Restaurants.

Site of the *SeaComber,* 1940s. Between Los Flores and Malibu Pier, Malibu.

Originally an Aquarium, later a restaurant was added.

A popular place for people to stop for a bite and watch the sea animals in the Aquarium.

Historic Restaurants: *Geoffrey's,* 1940s. 27400 Pacific Coast Highway, Malibu. 213-457-1519.

Used to be Holiday Inn.

The Malibu Sea Lion, 1940s. 21150 Pacific Coast Highway, Malibu. 213-456-2810.

Bed and Breakfast: *Malibu Hilltop Estate Bed and Breakfast.* So private the address is not even given. Upon inquiry the information I was given was that this is strictly for people looking for privacy and the ultimate in good service. Call 818-999-0857.

Casa Larronde, 22000 Pacific Coast Highway, Malibu.

Businesses: *Malibu Realty,* 1940s. Art Jones and Dave Duncan. 213-456-6431.

Pinnacle Vintage Antique Clothing, 28925 West P.C.H., Malibu, CA 90265. 213-457-5705.

Louise Busch Realty, 1941. 213-456-6477. Malibu's oldest realty.

Other Buildings: *Old Court House and Jail,* 1920s.

Los Flores Canyon and Pacific Coast Highway, Malibu.

Used at one time as a church. Now private offices.

Hindu Temple, 1600 Las Virgenes Rd., Malibu.

Books: Ron Rindge, *The Town of Canoes.*

Reeves Templeman, *Along the Malibu,* 1973.

Mr. Templeman is the publisher of the *Malibu Times,* who has been in the area over 40 years. 3864 Los Flores Canyon Rd., Malibu. 213-456-8016.

Frederick Rindge, *Happy Days in Southern California,* 1898.

W.W. Robinson and Lawrence C. Powell, *The Malibu,* 1958.

Unpublished Master's Thesis. *The History of Rancho Mailbu,* Doris Gilliland, 1947. U.S.C. Available at the Malibu Library.

Note: For more information on the Malibu area, see Santa Monica Mountains.

Railroad: Ran just east of the pier parallel to the highway, and to a barn which was used for hauling supplies on the ranch. No one is quite sure of the exact location.

MANHATTAN BEACH

History: Originally part of Rancho Sausal Redondo (Round clump of Willows). In 1900 Frank S. Daugherty and five Los Angeles businessmen incorporated the Highland Beach Co. and bought 20 acres in this area. They chartered a Sante Fe train and brought 500 people down to the grand opening. Known later as Shore Acres, a name Sante Fe used for a junction stop. A Stewart Miller came to the area in 1902. He owned the south portion of the old rancho naming his section Manhattan after his home in New York. Shore Acres and Manhattan were great names but which one would be chosen as the name for the growing community? A coin was tossed and Manhattan won. Incorporated in 1912 when the population was 600.

Historical Society: *Manhattan Beach Historical Society,* 425 15th St., Manhattan Beach, CA 90266. 213-545-1624.

Keith Roberson, President.

Historic Homes: *George Peck Home,* 1920s. 2620 Alma Ave., Manhattan Beach.

Mr. Peck was one of the founders of Manhattan Beach. His granddaughter still lives here.

Old Residence, 1906. Was at Manhattan Beach Blvd., now moved to Polliwog Park. Will be restored.

Victoriana: *Richard and Jean Anderson,* 400 Manhattan Ave., Manhattan Beach.

Victorian Condo, 708 Manhattan Ave., Manhattan Beach.

Other "Victoriana" homes 12th Street and 17th, 18th on the Strand.

Historic Pier: *Manhattan Pier,* 1917/1920. Manhattan Beach.

Businesses: *Ercoles Bar,* 1927. 1101 Manhattan Ave., Manhattan Beach. 213-374-9025. Still run by same family.

Manhattan Grocery, 1910. 1111 Manhattan Ave., Manhattan Beach.

Beckers Bakery, 1942. 1025 Manhattan Ave., Manhattan Beach. Before Beckers known as Webber's.

Metlox Potteries, 1927. 400 block Manhattan Beach Blvd., Manhattan Beach.

First manufacturing business in the area.

"Poppy Trail" Pottery, now a collectible.

Uncle Bill's Pancake House, 1305 Highland Ave., Manhattan Beach. 213-545-5177.

Business only 15 years old, but building is over 100 years old.

Poncho's Restaurant, 1930s. 3615 Highland, Manhattan Beach. 213-545-6670.

Historic Churches: *Community Church,* 1905. 9th and Highland, Manhattan Beach.

Has been extensively renovated.

Other Buildings: *Women's Club,* 1925. The Neptunian Society founded in 1909. Highland Ave., Manhattan Beach.

Historic Park: *Live Oak Park,* 1932. Valley Blvd., Manhattan Beach. Also a W.P.A. project. Boy Scout House here. 1937.

Polliwog Park. Was once the ranch of Benjamin Brown who let famous athlete Jim Thorpe use it. Made into a park in 1976. 1600 Manhattan Beach Blvd.

Craftsperson: *Todd Vander-Pluym,* architectural designer. 213-378-5559.

Mr. Vander-Pluym is the man who designed the two Victorian structures on the Strand.

Other: *Parque Culiacan,* 1923.

History was made here when the beach that was originally reserved only for blacks was turned into a new subdivision without their knowledge. A lawsuit followed and the blacks legally won the right to bathe wherever they liked.

Between 26th and 27th Streets on Highland Ave., Manhattan Beach.

Historic Sites: *Oldest House,* 1902. (Torn down 1987) 712 Manhattan Ave., Manhattan Beach.

——— MISSION HILLS ———

History: The San Fernando Valley was first seen by the Spanish in 1769. Father Juan Crespi called it *El Valle de Santa Catalina de Bononia de los Encinos.* By 1795 it was referred to as El Valle de los Encinos, the valley of the oaks. When the Mission San Fernando Rey de Espanã was founded in 1797, the entire "Valley" took the name San Fernando. As the area became subdivided, that name persisted. The Indians knew it as Achois Comihabit, or our place, our home.

The Valley as it is known today has a long and complex history. After the Mission and lands were leased by Pio Pico to his brother Andres, they were finally sold in 1846 to Don Eulogio de Celis, a Spaniard living in Los Angeles. It amounted to about 120,000 acres. Later the Valley was sold to the Lankershim group, many businessmen which included Isaac Van Nuys. They paid $115,000 for about 60,000 acres which included the southern section of the valley. In 1874 Charles Maclay purchased 57,000 acres in the northern end of the Valley.

The next big change came with the arrival of water in 1913. The land was subdivided, towns formed. The Maclay and Porter land became San Fernando Pacoima, Northridge, Granada Hills and Chatsworth. G.K. Porters' land became Sepulveda and Mission Hills.

Historical Society: *San Fernando Valley Historical Society,* 10940 Sepulveda Blvd. Mission Hills, CA 91345. 818-365-7810.

Mr. Robinson, President.

Andres Pico Adobe, 1834.

Historical Landmarks: *San Fernando Valley Mission,* #23 C.H.M. San Fernando Rey de Espanã, 1797.

Founded on Sept. 8 with Father Fermin Lasuen in charge. 15151 San Fernando Mission Blvd., Mission Hills. 818-361-0186.

San Fernando Valley Mission. Courtesy Geraldine Eddy Stinson, artist.

Open 7 days a week. Features an excellent museum, and an archival library.

Actually this is considered the site of the original mission, the present structure being a reconstructed version of the 1797 mission destroyed in the 1971 earthquake.

Andres Pico Adobe, 1834. 10940 Sepulveda Blvd., Mission Hills, CA 91345. #7 C.H.M. 818-365-7810.

Also home of the historical society. Built around 1834 by ex-mission Indians. It is the second oldest home in Los Angeles. In 1873 Andres Pico and his son Romulo built a second story. The adobe fell into neglect until 1930 when Dr. M.R. Harrington, curator of the Southwest Museum purchased it and the surrounding 20 acres. Restoration was begun in 1932. Today it houses not only the historical society but also a fine small library.

Elva Meline, curator.

Mission Dam, 1808. Mission Hills.

Masonry and boulder dam built by the San Fernando Valley Indians in 1808 to store water from the Mission wells. Between Laurel Canyon and Sepulveda Blvds., south of the Golden State Freeway on Rinaldi, north side of the street.

Historic Parks: *Brand Park 18th Century,* 15100 San Fernando Mission Blvd., Mission Hills, CA 91345. 818-361-1377.

Two foundations in park date from the mission period. Also vats for making tallow.

Businesses: *Mac's Electric,* Mac's Maintenance Service, General Contractor. P.O. Box 5577, Mission Hills, CA 91345. 818-908-1566.

Book: Lawrence Jorgensen, *The San Fernando Valley, Past and Future,* 1982.

——— MONROVIA ———

History: Monrovia had its beginning during Southern California's real estate boom of the 1880s. Due to its location and foresight of its founder it was more successful than many other towns in getting a foothold. Founded by W.N. Monroe in 1886 the town even had a newspaper called The Planet. A very active historical society, an active preservation group, and a strongly interested resident population all help to make Monrovia delightful to visit. Many open house tours as well.

Historical Society: *Monrovia Historical Society, 215 E. Lime* St., Monrovia. 818-358-3129. President Lynn Carter.

The Society meets here at the 1886 George H. Anderson Home. The home is also open for tours.

Preservation Group: *Old House Preservation,* 702 East Foothill Blvd., Monrovia, CA 91016.

Begun in 1980 by Lynn and Bruce Carter and Janet and Charles Manning. President: Charlotte Schamadan. 818-358-7634.

Historical Homes: *George Anderson Home,* 1886. 215 E. Lime Ave., Monrovia.

Gilbert Tillapaugh, 1906. 200 East Lime Ave., Monrovia.

Monrovia Planet, 1886. 240 East Lemon Ave., Monrovia.

Mr. Dorsey Bell, 1897. 517 South Ivy Ave., Monrovia.

Captain Albert Johnson, 1887. 210 West Colorado Blvd., Monrovia.

The Belmont, 1887. 210 West Lime Ave., Monrovia.

George Hutchins, 1896. 535 West Lemon Ave., Monrovia.

Mr. C.Z. Culver, 1887. 626 West Colorado Blvd., Monrovia.

General W.A. Pile, 1887. 255 North Mayflower Ave., Monrovia.

Studebaker Brothers, 1887. 447 West Hillcrest Blvd., Monrovia.

S.P. Metcalf, 1887. 404 West Hillcrest Blvd., Monrovia.

Mills View, 1887. 329 Melrose Ave., Monrovia.

Dr. Charles H. Stewart, 1888. 117 North Magnolia Ave., Monrovia.

The Oaks, 1885. 250 North Primrose Ave., Monrovia.

Note: I have listed only a small number of the homes that are truly outstanding in Monrovia. The Historical Society prints an excellent brochure with pictures and addresses of all the homes. Write to them for the brochure.

Celebrations: *Monrovia Days.* First held on May 17, 1886 when Monrovia was born. First parade 1892. Beginning in 1922 Monrovia Day Association holds a 4-day celebration. Contact Chamber of Commerce for more information. 818-358-1159.

Courtesy the author

Pioneers: *The Fisher Family,* 145 E. Pomona, Monrovia. 818-358-4666.

Mr. Fisher was brought from the South by Lucky Baldwin to be his blacksmith on the Santa Anita Rancho. Fisher family still lives here.

W.N. Monroe, founder of Monrovia in 1886 lived here until his death in 1935. His first home was at 225 Monroe Place, 1884. His second home was *"The Oaks"* at 250 Primrose Ave., 1885. How many towns in Southern California still have the homes of their founder intact?

Special Home: *Chateau Bradbury,* 1912. California St., Monrovia.

This home is really more connected if you will to Bradbury than Monrovia. It was built for Minerva and Isaac Polk, the daughter and son-in-law of Colonel L.L. Bradbury for whom the city of Bradbury is named. It was designed by noted Southern California architect Robert Farquhar.

See Bradbury.

Historic Hotel: *Leven Oak Hotel and Dining Room,* 1911. 120 S. Myrtle Ave., Monrovia. 818-358-2264.

Built in 1911 and the meeting place of the Monrovia Rotary Club since 1922.

The Wilson Hotel, 1904. Corner Olive and Myrtle, Monrovia.

Being restored by L.A. Design Center. In charge is Channa Grace, 213-629-2702.

Historic Parks: *Monrovia Library Park,* 1900. 321 S. Myrtle, Monrovia.

Monrovia Recreation Park, 1900. Mountain and Lemon St., Monrovia.

Historic Cemeteries: *Live Oak Memorial Park Cemetery,* 1887. Turner and Stevens, Monrovia. 818-359-5311.

Depots: *Former Sante Fe Depot,* 1925. Above Duarte on West side of Myrtle, Monrovia.

Historic Sites: *Indian Villages.* In many canyons in the San Gabriel Canyon area.

Site of Pottenger Sanitarium, 1911–1970. North Canyon Rd., Monrovia.

Site of Old Town Monrovia.

Between Colorado and Olive on the east side of Myrtle Ave., Monrovia.

Historic Restaurants: *The Aztec Hotel and Restaurant,* 1925. 311 West Foothill, Monrovia. 818-358-3231.

McBratney Building. Originally known as the B & C Block (Bartle and Corn). It was built around 1915. Gradually, it became known as the McBratney Building.

Wang's Restaurant, McBratney Building, 423 S. Myrtle, Monrovia. 818-303-3701.

The Thai Palace, in the McBratney Building. 618 S. Myrtle, Monrovia. 818-303-2643.

Businesses: *Monrovia Floral,* 1924. 432 W. Foothill Blvd., Monrovia. 818-358-1889.

Western Furniture Refinishers, 1550 S. Myrtle, Monrovia. 818-357-3798.

Chamber of Commerce: *Monrovia Chamber of Commerce,* 620 S. Myrtle, Monrovia. 818-358-1159.

This chamber is fortunate in having Jan Marugg, executive Vice President. She is very knowledgeable on the history of Monrovia.

Historian: Myron Hotchkiss, 818-358-3334.

Craftspersons: Rinson and Ware, 145 N. Mayflower Ave., Monrovia, CA 91016. 818-359-6113.

Books: John H. Wiley, *History of Monrovia,* 1927.

Charles F. Davis, *History of Monrovia & Duarte,* 1938.

T.M. Hotchkiss, *Selected Excerpts from the Monrovia Planet and the Monrovia Messenger. 1886–1891.* 2 Vols. 1979.

MONTEBELLO

History: After the Civil War an Italian immigrant Alessandro Repetto established a ranch of about 5,000 acres. Repetto built a ranch house on a hill overlooking his land in all directions about a ½ mile north of where Garfield Ave. crosses the Pomona Freeway. When he died in 1885 his brother sold the ranch to a group of men, Kaspare Cohn, J.D. Bicknell, I.W. Hellman, S.N. White and Harris Newmark for $12 an acre. These men in turn brought water to the area with William Mulholland's advice and sold the property in five-acre parcels locating the town site of Newmark near the tracks of the San Pedro, Los Angeles & Salt Lake Railroad. It later became *Montebello,* beautiful hills in Italian.

The discovery of oil by Standard oil in 1917 brought many changes. By 1920 Montebello oil fields were producing ⅛ of the state's crude oil.

There are many interesting stories related to Repetto. The most unusual is probably that of the bandit Tiburcio

Vasquez. One day in the spring of 1874 Vasquez and three of his companions appeared at the ranch of Repetto. Vasquez informed Repetto that he was organizing a revolution in Lower California and needed $800. He then compelled Repetto to write a check for that sum and dispatched it to town in the hands of a young boy. The young lad went to the bank of Temple & Workman scared to death. Temple grew alarmed and sent for the sheriff. The boy, however, pleaded so hard for Repetto's life that the Sheriff agreed not to accompany him back to the ranch. Sheriff Billy Rowland and several deputies took lookout points, so that as soon as Vasquez left Repetto's ranch they could pursue him. Unfortunately Vasquez had fresh horses and out-ran the posse.

Historical Society: *Montebello Historical Society,* 521 E. Los Amigos Ave., Montebello, CA 90640.

Ray Rameriz, President. This is Mr. Rameriz's home. 213-693-3102.

Historian: *Trent Steel,* 328 12th St., Montebello.

Mr. Steel is a collector as well of material on Montebello.

Historic Landmarks: *Battle of San Gabriel,* 1847. Washington Blvd. and Bluff Road, Montebello.

It was here, on January 8, 1847 that about 500-600 men under the command of General Jose Flores held this bluff while the Americans under Robert F. Stockton and General Stephen Kearny tried to ford the river. They had 600 men as well, but were carrying heavy artillery and the sand around the river was a problem for the heavy cannon. Within an hour the river was crossed and the Americans were pursuing the Californians to Los Angeles.

Soto-Sanchez Adobe, 1845. 946 Adobe Ave., Montebello.

Open Wed.-Sunday, 1-4.

This beautifully restored adobe is not only part of the history of Montebello but of La Puente as well.

Part of the La Merced Rancho of 2,363 acres that went to Juan Sanchez

in 1850, apparently Juan had known the Workmans and Rowlands in Taos, New Mexico before they had left for California. The next we hear of Juan is around 1850 when he turns up in the census that year as a mayordomo on the Workman Ranch, La Puente. Sometime around 1850-51 Mr. Workman made some kind of a "deal" with Sanchez, agreeing to a 50-50 split on any gold that Juan could find in the gold fields. Juan must have come back with something, because soon after that Workman deeded to him one-half interest in the La Merced Rancho. The first grantee of the ranch was Dona Casilda Soto de Lobo in 1844. When she went to William Workman for a loan he gave her the money with the stipulation that if she could not repay he would take over the ranch. In 1850 that's what happened, and the rancho reverted to Workman. Workman then granted ½ of the La Merced to Juan, the other half to his son-in-law Francis Temple.

The families were very friendly with each other. Francis Temple began a bank in 1868. In 1875 he ran into financial problems. He mortgaged his land, mortgaged the La Puente, and came to Sanchez for a loan on the La Merced. Sanchez agreed to it, and well, the rest is history. All was lost. Juan Sanchez died in his beloved home in 1885. His second wife died in 1892 and the land and adobe went to Lucky Baldwin to settle the loan against the Temple estate.

The property was sold after Baldwin's death in 1909 to a group of men. Among these men was W.B. Scott who chose the 45 acres upon which the adobe was located. He took title to it in 1915. By this time the home had greatly deteriorated. Upon Scott's death, his wife formed the W.B. Scott Investment Company and when she died the ranch and estate went to the children, Keith and Josephine Scott Crocker. It was Mrs. Crocker who in 1957 hired an architect, Eugene Hougham to restore the adobe to its original structure as it looked when Sanchez owned it. She then turned it over to the City of Montebello in 1971.

Taylor Ranch House, Montebello Ave. and La Merced, Montebello.

Historic Theatres: *The Old Vogue Theatre,* 1920s? 712 Whittier Blvd., Montebello.

It is now the Montebello Travel Agency.

Historic Churches: *The United Methodist Church,* 1905, 1928. 1220 West Whittier Blvd., Montebello. 213-728-8179.

Originally in 1905 church was at 4th and Los Angeles.

Historic Restaurants: *Marcel and Jeanne French Cafe,* 1930. S.E. Corner Whittier Blvd. and 22nd, Montebello.

Courtesy the author.

Historic Sites: *Original Site of the San Gabriel Mission,* 1771. Mission Vieja, Lincoln Ave. and San Gabriel Blvd., Montebello (See San Gabriel).

San Gabriel Mission founded on Sept. 8, 1771. Flooding caused the mission to be moved in 1775 to its present site.

Site of the old *Benedine Monastery,* 1913. 1600 West Beverly Blvd., Montebello.

Where the present City Hall is now located. Father Esplette set up this Monastery to minister to Basque sheepherders who had flocks of sheep in the area.

Site of *Simon's California City,* 1906–1952. Town borders City of Commerce and Montebello, Montebello.

An entire company town called Simon was located here 1906–1952. Walter Robbie Simon was from Eng-

land, came to California in the late 1880s, established brick plants throughout California. They even had their own script and their own police force. Entered the Rose Parade in 1923 and had their own band. Supplied brick to U.C.L.A. for Royce Hall.

Simon's home was located at 201 Plymouth, Hancock Park, Los Angeles.

Site of *Vail Air Field,* 1926. Montebello.

This is where *Western Airlines* began. Mr. Vail was an Arizona land-baron who came to Southern California. He and a Mr. Vickers bought acreage at the beach naming it Vickers City. Vail also owned land in Temecula and Warner Hot Springs at one time.

Site of *East Los Angeles Montebello Airport,* 1926. Montebello.

This was very close to Vail Airfield, and sometimes residents called it Vail II. Begun by Charles Ray in 1926 when sets for a film were placed there, including a hangar. The movie was completed and the hangar went to Vail I, but apparently someone stayed behind to begin the airfield. At one time it was owned by Edgar Bergen. Many movie stars learned to fly here including Clark Gable. Finally Western Air Express put up a hangar.

Site of *The Maple School,* Montebello.

It was here that a Japanese School was begun. In 1941 it was raided with a great deal of hoopla when one of the deputies held up a letter opener as being very suspicious. The unsuspecting children looked on in utter amazement.

Site of the *Old Montebello Ballroom Site.* Montebello.

This was designed by a female architect, still unusual enough that it warrants mention.

Montebello Oil Fields, 1914. Rio Hondo River.

It was here that young Thomas Workman Temple discovered black ooze floating to the surface. In 1917 Standard oil arrived.

—————— MONTEREY PARK ——————

History: Monterey Park's history is somewhat unique because Eulalia Perez was a Gabrielino Indian who inherited 12,000 acres in the area which would later become Monterey Park. Among the first ranchos was Rancho San Antonio, belonging to Don Antonio Maria Lugo. He was granted 29,500 acres in 1810. It passed through Spanish, Mexican and finally Italian hands when Alessandro Repetto, an Italian immigrant purchased 5,000 acres in 1866 from the Lugo heirs. (See Montebello) From the Repetto clan it passed to a number of different men, but it finally fell upon a most unlikely candidate to actually found the town. A young boy, 12 years of age came to the United States in 1850. A customs official gave him a job and help. The young Richard Garvey made his way in the world, finally coming to Southern California in 1880. He established a residence here, brought water to the area and began a subdivision in 1892. Garvey died in 1930 but his son Dick Garvey carried on.

Historical Society: There is an Historical Heritage Commission set up in 1984 formed by the *Monterey Park Historical Society,* P.O. Box 272, Monterey Park, CA 91754. Bea Rexius, President. 818-281-3015.

Historian: *Dr. Russ Paine,* 606 Hermosa Vista, Monterey Park, 818-281-9994.

Mr. Gribble, 818-573-1053.

Historical Landmarks: *Garvey Ranch Park,* 781 Orange Ave., Monterey Park.

Named for the city's founder. Observatory built before 1930. Ranch buildings and also a museum.

Historic Structures, 1928–29.

Built by Peter Snyder, real estate developer. At El Portal, Monterey Park.

Also known as El Miracado. Used during World War II as a U.S.O. Center. Waterfall also at same site. Used for weddings.

Historic Theatre: *Monterey Park Theatre,* 1920s. (Now Chinese Theatre) Garfield South of Hellman, Monterey Park.

Historic School: *Ynez School,* founded 1914. West Garvey, Monterey Park.

Historic Home: *Vanhusen Home,* 1920s. S.E. corner Baltimore & Hellman, Monterey Park.

Historic Church: *St. Stephens Church* (Built after W.W.I) Corner Ramon and Garvey, Monterey Park.

Historic Sites: Site of *first structure in Monterey Park,* the Alessandro Repetto adobe built in 1840. South Garfield, Monterey Park.

Owned originally by Jose del Lugo.

Businesses: *Monterey Park Drug Store,* 1934. The Ball Family, 101 West Garvey, Monterey Park. 818-288-2950.

Bank of America, 1920s. 100 West Garvey, Monterey Park.

Monterey Park Glass Co., 1940. 637 W. Garvey Ave., Monterey Park. 818-282-3191.

Browning Realty, 1922. 726 E. Garvey, Monterey Park. 818-280-8181.

Books: Margaret Dean, *The Story of Monterey Park,* 1965.

H. Russell Paine, ed., *History of Monterery Park,* a Bicentennial Report, 1976.

No author, no date. *Monterey Park History:* A collection of four articles bound together containing the cities and their history.

Available at the Bruggmeyer Library, 318 S. Ramona, Monterey Park. 818-307-1368.

Richard Garvey Adobe—later a bunkhouse. Courtesy Monterey Park Historical Society.

——— MONTROSE ———

History: Once called the "gem of the Verdugo Hills," Montrose was once part of the vast *Rancho San Rafael*. It was named Montrose in 1913 when the name was chosen as a winning entry for the new 300-acre tract of land newly opened for subdivision. There is a "Legend of Montrose" which Sir Walter Scott made famous. In any case by 1922 lots went for about $500, $10 down and $5 a month.

Historical Society: None.

Historian: *Anita Geyer.* Family founded Pete's Stationers at 2311 Honolulu St., 1935. 818-249-3211.

Chamber of Commerce: 818-249-7171.

Historic Marker: *Marker* to honor Viet Nam Veterans. Corner of Ocean View and Honolulu St., Montrose.

Marker: The Montrose-Verdugo City Chamber of Commerce has commissioned sculptor, William L. Gould to create a monument dedicated to the historic Rancho San Rafael.

Contact the Chamber for more information.

Historic Theatre: *Little Theatre,* 1930s. 2226 Honolulu Ave., Montrose.

Burned recently but being restored.

Historic Schools: *Montrose School,* 1930s. 2361 Florencita Ave., Montrose.

Historic Churches: *Holy Redeemer Church,* 2411 Montrose Ave., Montrose. 818-249-2008.

Businesses: *Pete's Stationers,* 1935. 2311 Honolulu St., Montrose.

Abril's Electric, 1940s. 2410 Honolulu St., Montrose.

Faye's, 1940. Honolulu St., Montrose.

—— NORTH HOLLYWOOD ——

History: It was back in 1847 that Lt. Col. John C. Fremont and General Andres Pico met at the Campo de Cahuenga — now a historical monument in North Hollywood — and signed the treaty that was to end the war between the United States and Mexico.

Twenty-two years later, in 1869, a Bavarian immigrant named Isaac Lankershim discovered the fertile lands lying just over the Cahuenga Pass from the City of Los Angeles and, with a friend named I.N. Van Nuys, purchased the entire southern half of the San Fernando Valley, some 59,500 acres, for $115,000 and began growing wheat. Lankershim died in 1882 but his name was to be perpetuated in the area. In 1889, as the land was being subdivided into small ranches and townsites, the Lankershim Ranch Land and Water Company spearheaded the establishment of a town to be named Toluca or "Fertile Valley." But the name Lankershim persisted and in 1896 became the official title of this unincorporated community. It was annexed to the City of Los Angeles in 1923, and the name Lankershim was officially changed to North Hollywood in 1927 by the Post Office Department.

In 1890, Wilson C. Weddington moved his family to Toluca/Lankershim and at the time there were only 10 families in the area. The Weddingtons were to play an important role in the emergence of North Hollywood as a flourishing Valley community. Weddington was named Postmaster of Toluca in 1893 and in 1910 founded the Weddington Investment Company which is still operated by his heirs.

In 1907 the City of Los Angeles commissioned engineer William Mulholland to construct a 230-mile aqueduct to bring water to its parched city from the High Sierras. The completion of this engineering marvel of its time in 1913 led to the annexation of the San Fernando Valley — bit by bit — to Los Angeles over the following years with North Hollywood following other Valley communities on December 29, 1923. Our valley had evolved from the cattle and sheep in the days of the Spanish Dons, to fields of wheat under Isaac Lankershim, to a small community of 4,000 in 1927.

The Lankershim Chamber of Commerce — which officially changed its name to the North Hollywood Chamber of Commerce in 1927 — was formed in 1914 and its roster of past presidents forms an honor roll of those who have worked, and who are working so diligently to shape the destiny and promote the future of the "Gateway to the Valley" for the past 6½ decades.

(Above information courtesy of North Hollywood Chamber of Commerce).

Historical Society: *Campo de Cahuenga Memorial Association,* 6026 Ensign Ave., North Hollywood, CA 91606. 818-761-2493. George Shipley, President.

Historical Landmarks: *Campo de Cahuenga,* 1847. #29 C.H.M. 3919 Lankershim Blvd., North Hollywood, CA 91602. 818-763-7651.

One of the most important historical landmarks in all of California, this simple adobe was the location of the signing of the Treaty of Cahuenga January 13, 1847.

A young, perhaps too brash, Lt. Col. John C. Fremont wrote out the agreement that ended hostilities between the U.S. and Mexico. Signing it was General Andres Pico. Fremont was later court-martialled for problems that had their beginning here.

Open Monday–Friday 8–4 grounds only. Activities held every January to commemorate peace treaty.

Historical Schools: *Campbell Hall,* 1944. 4533 Laurel Canyon Blvd., North Hollywood. 818-980-7280.

Historic Clubs: *Palomino Club,* 1952. 6907 Lankershim, North Hollywood. 818-764-4010.

Historic Home: *Amelia Earhart Home,* Valley Spring Lane, North Hollywood.

Famous flyer lived here with husband George Putnam from 1935 until her disappearance in the Pacific, 1937.

Historic Buildings: *El Portal Theatre,* 1939. 5269 Lankershim Blvd., North Hollywood. 818-769-4041.

No. 232 Dept. of Water and Power Building, 1939. #232 C.H.M. 5108 Lankershim Blvd., North Hollywood.

Historic Library: *North Hollywood Regional Library,* 1929. #302 C.H.M. 5211 Tujunga, North Hollywood. 818-766-7185. Sculpture of Amelia Earhart, 1979.

Historic Churches, Synagogues: *David Familian Chapel of Temple Adat Ariel,* 1938. #199 C.H.M. 5540 Laurel Canyon Blvd., North Hollywood.

First synagogue building in San Fernando Valley.

St. Charles Boromeo Catholic Church, 1959. Parish Hall, 1938.

S.W. corner Moorpark & Lankershim, North Hollywood.

Other Historic Sources: *Academy of Motion Picture Radio and T.V.* 5315 Lankershim Blvd., STE202, North Hollywood, CA 91607.

Businesses: *Dog Training School,* 1927. 10805 Vanowen St., North Hollywood. 818-762-1262.

Expert Reweaving, 1945. 6340 Coldwater Canyon Blvd., North Hollywood. 818-761-0522.

The Carpet Mill, 1913. 5156 Lankershim Blvd., North Hollywood. 818-762-1127.

Sterns Valley Furriers, 1933. 5112 Lankershim Blvd., North Hollywood.

818-761-1822.

Weddington Investment Co., 1910. 11222 Weddington St., North Hollywood. 818-762-3998.

Village Cycles, 1945. 5346 Laurel Canyon, North Hollywood. 818-761-6354.

Stevens Nursery and Hardware, 1943. 12000 Riverside Dr., North Hollywood. 818-763-6296; 818-763-6298.

Robert St. John & Associates, 10645 Chandler Blvd., North Hollywood. 818-769-1401.

J.E.S. Art Reproductions, P.O. Box 4335, North Hollywood. 818-782-3266.

They do very nice color reproductions of the California Missions.

Other: In the upper edges of North Hollywood, formally listed as Sun Valley, a now famous landmark, the Old Trappers' Lodge, stands in danger of being demolished. Its collection of folk art has long been a delight to the community. Owned originally by the Ehn family and opened in 1941, there were 20 towering statues of Old West characters. New homes are being sought for the art works, symbols of the Old West.

Craftspeople: *Sunland Wood Products,* Milling architectural woodwork. 7310 Ethel Avenue, North Hollywood, CA 91605. 213-875-3630.

Mario Jason, sculptor. 7309 Atoll Ave., North Hollywood. 818-765-2437.

Bed and Breakfast: *La Maida House Inn,* 1920. 11159 La Maida St., North Hollywood, CA 91601. 818-769-3857.

This is a super elegant home.

Pioneer Family: *The Weddington Family,* The Weddington Investment Co., 11222 Weddington, North Hollywood. 818-762-3998.

Historian: Mr. Lou Fisch, 818-508-0595.

—— NORTHRIDGE ——

History: Roscoe Boulevard was always the dividing line between the Northern and Southern San Fernando Valley. When the Maclays and Porters were dividing up the Valley between their interest and that of the

Lankershims and Van Nuys, Roscoe was the boundary between those divisions. George Porter and Benjamin Porter joined Charles Maclay for the purpose of purchasing 50,000 acres of Northern land. B.F. Porter claimed the area which included Northridge and Chatsworth. In 1887 Porter sold the 1,100 acre section known as Hawk Ranch. Then in 1910 this section was again subdivided. Area known as *Zelzah* when the Southern Pacific used it as a shipping point. Zelzah became North Los Angeles, later Northridge.

Historical Society: None. The Valley has one major historical society and that is the *San Fernando Valley Historical Society,* 818-365-7810.

Landmarks: *California State University Northridge,* Anthropology Museum.

Director: Lincija Baskauskas. Focus is on the Chumash Indians of Southern California. Many of the artifacts discovered in San Fernando Valley, Santa Clarita and Conejo are here.

Open 8–4 Mon.–Fri. 818-885-3331.

Historic Homes: *Mr. & Mrs. Jack Oakie Home,* 1936. Corner Devonshire and Reseda area, Northridge (18650 Devonshire). Remember, private residence!

This magnificent estate is almost unknown. Home designed and built by architect Paul Williams for actress Barbara Stanwyck. At that time Barbara Stanwyck and Mrs. Zeppo Marx began *Marwyck Ranch* as a horsebreeding farm. It consisted of about 125 acres. Later became Northridge Farms. The famous actor Jack Oakie purchased the home in 1938. Mrs. Oakie still lives in the home, and plans include leaving it to the Motion Picture Home.

Note: Many, many motion picture stars had homes in the area. Janet Gaynor and Adrian the dress designer, Clark Gable and Carole Lombard had a ranch in the area around Devonshire and Etiwanda. Ranch home of Clark Gable located around LeMarsh St. at Northridge Park.

Private Residence (around 1915), 17425 Nordhoff, Northridge.

Private Residence, 1915. 8803 Canby, Northridge.

Private Residence, 1900. 9000 Sunburst, Northridge.

Private Residence, 8136 Louise, Northridge.

Historic Churches: *Faith Bible Church,* 1917. #152 C.H.M. 18531 Gresham St., Northridge.

Businesses: *Northridge Glass and Mirror,* 1938. 18255 Parthenia, Northridge. 818-885-6266.

Historian: *Ginny Dill,* 7932 White Oak Ave., Northridge. 818-343-7579.

—— NORWALK ——

History: Once known as New River, Siete Alisos (the seven Sycamores), Sycamore Grove and Corazon de los Valles (Heart of the Valleys), Norwalk was finally referred to as "Corvalles" by Easterners who had great difficulty pronouncing Spanish names.

First settled in the latter 1850s the community did not begin developing until 1874 when railroad tracks crossed the North-Walk or Trail from Anaheim Landing for the first time. Concurrently, a town site was surveyed on the Corvalles acreage. Established as "Norwalk Station" by the railroad, the name Corvalles remained in favor until the town site was recorded three years later. With that recordation, the confusion of receiving mail for Corvalles at Norwalk Station ended and the two become one — Norwalk.

At the turn of the century, Norwalk was the dairy "Heart of the Valleys." Of the fifty local families recorded in

1900 census, most were involved with farming and dairying.

Historical Society: None.

The city has an *Historical Heritage Commission* however, headed by staff liaison Linda Alvarez. President of the commission is Arwilda Houston who can be reached at 213-864-3975. The Commission was formed in the 1960s and consists of 15 members.

Historical Landmarks: *Johnson-Hargitt House,* 1891. 12436 Mapledale St., Norwalk, CA 90650. 213-864-9663.

This house was built by D.D. Johnson who was the organizer of the Norwalk school system. Following the death of Johnson's grandson, Charles Hargitt, the property was donated to the City of Norwalk. It has the original furnishings, and is now a museum.

Gilbert Sproul Museum and Home, 1870. 12237 E. Sproul, Norwalk, CA 90650. 213-864-9663.

Gilbert Sproul was the founder of Norwalk. Town meetings were held in this house. Vida Sproul Hunter, Sproul's granddaughter donated the home to the City.

The Paddison Home and Farm, 1878. 11951 Imperial Highway, Norwalk, CA 90650. Private residence.

The last remaining extant original farm house in the area. Developers are banging at the door and the owners are trying to find ways to both preserve their home and make room for development.

Historic Homes: *Lindsay and Margaret Burke Home,* 1917. 12137 Sproul St., Norwalk.

Here last remaining Sycamore Tree native to area still survives.

Dean Clanton Home, 1894.

Corner Pioneer Blvd. and Ferina St., Norwalk.

Jack and Madeline Thomas Home, 1927.

Rosecrans Blvd., Norwalk.

Loomis Home, 1891.

Corner of Walnut and Elaine, Norwalk.

Historic Monument: *17 mile Stage Marker.*

Organized and operated by Samuel Bland in 1868. Marked mid-way point on old stage route between Los Angeles and Santa Ana. D.A.R. No. 303.

Historic Buildings: *Carter Hall,* 1939. Clarkdale St.

Community Hall since 1939. Still owned by the Methodist Church.

Metropolitan State Hospital, 1916. 11400 S. Norwalk Blvd., Norwalk.

Originally Norwalk State Hospital.

Bank of Norwalk, 1923. (Building about 1900) Now Bank of America, Front and Clarkdale, Norwalk.

Historic Cemeteries: *Little Lake Cemetery,* 1872. Lakeland Rd. off Norwalk Blvd., Norwalk.

Historic Sites: Site of *Seventh Day Adventist Church,* 1883. Corner Funston and Sproul, Norwalk.

Site of *Methodist Church,* 1871. Between corner of Firestone and San Antonio. Later moved to Clarkdale and Sproul 1922. Torn down 1966.

Site of *Gentry's Supper Club,* 1930s. 11957 Firestone, Norwalk.

Mr. Gentry still owns property.

Site of *Ostrich Farm,* 1887. Bloomington Ave., south of Firestone.

Edwin Cawston brought 52 ostrich from Australia to Norwalk.

Site of *Southern Pacific Depot,* 1875. Front Street. Torn down 1968.

Site of the *Eagle Hotel,* 1890. Foster Road, Norwalk. Torn down 1963.

Lone Star Hotel, Front St., Norwalk.

Site of *Excelsior Union High School,* 1903. Corner Alondra and Pioneer Blvd., Norwalk.

Site of *Dempsey Home.* Corner Imperial Highway and Pioneer Blvd. Famous as the setting of "The Postman Always Rings Twice," starring Lana Turner and John Garfield.

Site of *Cheese Factory,* 1882. Front St., Norwalk.

Produced Eagle Brand products. Responsible for development of dairy industry in city.

Historic Streets: *Firestone Blvd.* Originally called First St., then Broadway, then Church, in 1923 — Firestone.

Books: Richard Kahanek, *History of Norwalk,* 1960s. City of Norwalk, *Norwalk, California, Proud of Our Past,* 1984.

Disaster: February 1958, four-engine Air Force transport collided in mid-air with a twin-engine Navy bomber. Both planes fell near Firestone and Pioneer Boulevards. Forty-eight passengers and residents on the ground died. Plaque marks the incident.

Businesses: *Wong's Market,* 1939. 12125 Front St., Norwalk. 213-864-3252.

Fletcher Florist, 1930s. 12161 Firestone, Norwalk. Began in home, 1937. Opened store 1947.

——— PACIFIC PALISADES ———

History: People populated the mesas and canyons of what was to become Pacific Palisades as long as 10,000 years ago. The Indians were followed by land-grant owners of *Rancho Boca de Santa Monica,* the families of Francisco Marquez and Ysidro Reyes. They built a small community centered in the canyons. Marquez Road, fields of lima beans and a few ranch buildings were all that was here when a group of Methodists arrived in 1920 looking for a site upon which to establish "The Chautauqua of the West." The founders, led by Reverend Charles H. Scott purchased lots for $1,000 each, and built their first homes on the mesa above Potrero Canyon. The year was 1922. Development began in Temescal Canyon. As the Community grew it subdivided. Another group was named the *Huntington Palisades.* Another was known as the *Miramar Estates* and *Castellammare.*

Historical Society: *Pacific Palisades Historical Society,* P.O. Box 1299. Pacific Palisades, CA 90272. Bill Kelley, President.

Historian: *Betty Lou Young,* 550 Latimer Road, Pacific Palisades.

Betty Lou is one of those extraordinary people that Los Angeles is blessed to have. When, as a long time resident of the Palisades she decided to write down some brief information, what resulted were two first-rate books on the history, the life, the architecture, the stories and much more on the area.

See Books.

Historical Landmarks: *Will Rogers State Park,* 1921. 14243 Sunset Blvd., Pacific Palisades 213-454-8212.

Oh boy, where do you begin with this man? His death affected America as few other men's. Fifty-years later, his memory is still intact. Will Rogers gave us joy and a spirit deeply in tune with the country he so loved, in spite of his barbs. His life story is well documented at the Ranch, and there are many films which they have on his life, in addition to the 12-minute film they typically show the public. Rogers bought this ranch way out in the wilderness, after his own Beverly Hills home needed too much repair to warrant the work. Rogers also loved the idea of getting away as much into the back country as he could. In those days all you had to do was take an old dirt road to the beach. Rogers and his family moved to the ranch permanently in 1928. He added many structures through the years. It is absolutely the most wonderful, relaxing place to visit. Bring your lunch and stroll the grounds. Open 7 days a week.

Founders Oak, January 14, 1922. (Site of) #38 C.H.M. Community founded here between Temescal Canyon and Antioch St., 800 Haverford Road, Pacific Palisades.

The Uplifters Club, 1923. Haldeman & Latimer Rds., Pacific Palisades.

In 1913 a few members from the Los Angeles Athletic Club devoted themselves to what they labeled "High Jinks" and in the early 20s bought property on Latimer Road and began a kind of retreat. This clubhouse was built in 1913, burned in 1922 and was rebuilt again in a Spanish style in 1923.

First Forestry Station in the U.S., 1887. Latimer Road, Pacific Palisades.

Lush Eucalyptus Grove here plus many varieties of other trees, all in a unique setting of wilderness a la cabins, streams, and birds.

Marquez Family Plaque, 1827–Present. Elder St. near Entrada, Pacific Palisades.

The Marquez family still lives in the Palisades, and more unique, this is a rare private cemetery few people know anything about. Marquez came to L.A. from Mexico in 1825. His wife's family goes back even further, to 1781. The Marquez's were granted the Rancho Boco de Santa Monica, 6656 acres. Note: Jaconway and Marquez Ave. commemorate the joint ownership of this rancho.

Historic Homes: Note: there are several distinct historic areas in the Pacific Palisades area. There is the Uplifters Club area with dozens of old cabins and architectural wonders of contemporary design. In addition to this there is Castellammare, developed by Alphonzo Bell, Sr., and there is Huntington Palisades, developed by a group of Methodists in the 1920s. Each area is complex and has a variety of both old and new. Keep in mind that my emphasis is on historical homes. You may refer to Winter and Gebhard for their listing of the sepctacular designers homes of Lautner, Wright, Kappe, Moore, Neutra, Eames, Schlinder, Ellwood, Soriano and a dozen other outstanding contemporary architects.

Latimer Road Homes: "Hi" Lea's Home, 1923. 506 Latimer Rd., Pacific Palisades.

Designed by John Byers. He used timbers from the old Long Wharf and tiles from Marblehead Tile Co. in Malibu.

Gatehouse, 1921. 520 Latimer Rd., Pacific Palisades.

Was at the entrance of the Uplifters Ranch which occupied 150 acres north of here, established in 1921.

Uplifters' Clubhouse, 1923. 601 Latimer Rd., Pacific Palisades.

Original club of 1913 burned 1922. William Dodd built this in 1923. Used until 1947 for original Uplifters Club purposes.

Fred Kley, 1923. One Latimer Rd., Pacific Palisades.

James Harper, 31 Haldeman Rd., Pacific Palisades. Log cabin.

Dr. Luton, 1922–23. 33 Haldeman Rd., Pacific Palisades. Log cabin.

Westridge, Amalfi Drive, Pacific Palisades.

Home owned at one time by Douglas Fairbanks. Now owned by Steven Spielberg.

Tully Marshall, 1923. 34 Haldeman Rd., Pacific Palisades. Log cabin.

Leo Carrillo Home, 1920s. 439 E. Channel, Pacific Palisades.

Dr. Frank McCoy, 1927. 35 Haldeman Rd., Pacific Palisades.

Built for Dr. Frank McCoy of the "McCoy Health Systems" who advocated orange juice for movie stars.

Marco Hellman, 1923–24. 36 Haldeman Rd., Pacific Palisades.

One of three authentic log cabins made out of whole logs, acquired by banker Hellman from the movie set for "The Courtship of Miles Standish."

Marco Hellman's own log cabin, 1923–24. 38 Haldeman Rd., Pacific Palisades.

Occupied by Governor Warren and his family for several summers.

Albert C. Robbins, 1923–24. 39 Haldeman Rd., Pacific Palisades.

Purchased in 1929 by Hal Roach.

Feuchtwanger House, Sunset Blvd., 1920s. Pacific Palisades.

Hillkress.

Nothing remains but it was a fascinating house built on the canyon rim for Dr. Kress in 1922. The house was rented in 1939 to Aldous Huxley.

The above homes are only a fraction

of those in the Uplifters Club area. For additional information contact the historical society.

Historic Schools: *Canyon Elementary School,* 1894. Northeast of intersection of Ocean & Channel Rd., Pacific Palisades.

First public school in the city of Los Angeles begun by the Marquez family. The oldest structure in Pacific Palisades. (Now a children's library).

Palisades Elementary School, 1930. 800 Via de la Paz, Pacific Palisades.

Historic Churches: *Community United Methodist Church,* 1929. 801 Via de la Paz, Pacific Palisades.

Presbyterian Conference Grounds, 1922. North end of Temescal Canyon Rd., Pacific Palisades.

This once belonged to the Methodists and was the site of the yearly Chautauqua performances.

Historic Business Block: *Pacific Palisades Business Block,* Nov. 1924. Rededicated 1985. #276 C.H.M. 15300–15318 Sunset Blvd., Pacific Palisades.

Originally the Santa Monica Land & Water Co. Building.

Historic Sites: *Indian Sites:* The Indians always knew the best sites. Today the most expensive homes are typically located where Indian Villages once stood.

There are two known sites in Rustic Canyon below Mesa Rd. A village site was at the mouth of the Santa Monica Canyon. Man inhabited this area for at least 25,000 years. Settlements date from 7,000 to 6,000 B.C. When Gaspar de Portolá came through the area in 1769, mention was made of a prosperous Indian Village near the Springs of El Burrendo on the present site of the University High School, called Kuruvungna (the place where we are in the sun).

Site of the *Ysidro Reyes Adobe,* 1839–1890. Pampas Recas Blvd. meets Sunset Blvd., Pacific Palisades.

Site of the *Old Polo Field,* 1928.

Between Brooktree Rd. and Greentree Rd. off of Sunset Blvd. Actually there were 5 polo fields in the area.

Pacific Palisades.

Site of *The Bishop House,* 1920s. 15430 Sunset Blvd. (originally Temescal Canyon), Pacific Palisades.

One of first buildings constructed in area.

Site of *Lima Bean Fields.* Late 1880s–1930s. At Playa del Rey lima beans flourished because of the heavy dew at night.

Temescal Canyon Park, off of Sunset Blvd. Oldest area in Pacific Palisades.

Marker: Jacon Way and Marquez Terrace. Where adobe homes of the Marquez family once stood.

Historic Club: *Bel-Air Bay Club,* 1930s. 16801 Pacific Coast Highway, Pacific Palisades.

Businesses: *Norris Hardware,* 15140 Sunset Blvd., Pacific Palisades. 213-454-4116.

Pacific Palisades Drug Store, 1920s. 15300 Sunset, Pacific Palisades.

Oldest building in the area, built in 1912. Pictures here of the early days.

Colvey's, 1930s. 15306 Antioch, Pacific Palisades. 213-454-3017.

Palisades Letter Shop, 865 Via de la Paz, Pacific Palisades. 213-454-5316.

Books: Betty Lou Young, *Pacific Palisades: Where the Mountains Meet the Sea,* Pacific Palisades Historical Society.

_____, *Pacific Palisades and the Story of the Uplifters,* Casa Veja Press, 1975.

_____, *Rustic Canyon.*

These books can be found at the Pacific Palisades Library, 861 Alma Real Dr., Pacific Palisades. 213-459-2754.

The Santa Ynez Canyon and Vicinity Trail Guide. For a pamphlet write: Temescal Canyon Association, P.O. Box 1101, Pacific Palisades, CA 90272.

Other Historical Facts: Pacific Palisades producer Thomas Ince ran his studio here known as *Inceville.* When he needed extras for a western, Harry Culver enticed him to Culver City where there were plenty of actors and a "river." The rest is history.

——— PALOS VERDES ———

History: In 1784 Juan Jose Dominguez was granted the 75,000 acre *Rancho San Pedro*. Upon his death in 1809 Manuel Gutierrez, to whom Dominguez and his estate where heavily indebted, was made the administrator of the huge rancho. The rancho prospered under Gutierrez. Some years after his uncle's death, Cristobal Dominguez (nephew and heir of Juan Jose) tried to establish title to the Rancho San Pedro in his own name. Unfortunately Gutierrez flatly refused to surrender any part of the property. To make matters worse, he permitted a friend, Jose Dolores Sepulveda to graze his cattle on the western section of the land, a tract known as Rancho de Los Palos Verdes. All of these problems ended up in court, the result being that Sepulveda was recognized as legitimately entitled to the *Rancho Palos Verdes*. It amounted to quite a large portion out of the Rancho San Pedro—about 38,000 acres. Today, there are Palos Verdes Estates, Rancho Palos Verdes, Rolling Hills Estates, and the City of Rolling Hills.

Historical Society: *Rancho De Los Palos Verdes Historical Society,* P.O. Box 2447, Rancho Palos Verdes, CA 90274. 714-859-0641. Lee Belknap, president.

Historic Landmarks: *Point Vicente Lighthouse,* 1926. U.S. Lighthouse Service Coastguard, 1939. National Registered Landmark. Area first seen by Juan Cabrillo in 1542.

Glass Wayfarers Chapel, 1946–71. 5755 Palos Verdes Drive, Portuguese Bend, Rancho Palos Verdes, CA 90274. 213-377-1650. Designed by Lloyd Wright.

Malaga Cove Plaza, 1922. Palos Verdes Drive between Via Corta & Via Chico, Palos Verdes.

In 1913 the New York banker Frank Vanderlip acquired 16,000 acres of the Peninsula. He engaged Olmsted and Olmsted, Howard Shaw and Myron Hunt to lay out a "Millionaire's Colony." World War I intervened. After the war a pared-down version of the initial scheme was begun. Between 1922 and 1923 a master plan for 3,200 acres was begun. Four commercial centers were provided for: Lunada Bay, Miraleste, Valmonte and Malaga Cove. Only Malaga Cove was built. Neptune Fountain also here.

La Vinta Inn, 1924. 736 Via Del Monte, Rancho Palos Verdes, 213-378-9378.

Originally the Palos Verdes Inn was erected as a Club House by Pierpont Davies and Frederick Law Olmsted. Now used for weddings. Not open to the public.

Marineland of the Pacific, 1954–1987. (Now closed). Long Point; West Palos Verdes Dr., Rancho Palos Verdes.

Historic Schools: *Malaga Cove School,* Octagonal Tower, 1926. Corner Via Media & Via Arroyo.

Chadwick School, 1937. 26800 S. Academy Dr., Rolling Hills. 213-377-1543.

Historic Ranches: *Phillips Ranch,* 1894–1912. On Rolling Hills Rd. and Lariat Lane, Rancho Palos Verdes.

Rancho Elastico, 1885. A.E. Hanson developed northern part of Rancho Palos Verdes in 1930s. It became Rolling Hills.

Historic Libraries: *Malaga Cove Library,* 1926–30. 2400 Via Campacina, Rancho Palos Verdes.

Built by Myron Hunt, landscaping, Frederick Olmsted.

Other Important Buildings and Historic Sources: *Point Vicente Interpretative Center for Whale Watching,* 31501 Palos Verdes Drive West, Rancho Palos Verdes, 213-377-5370.

South Coastal Botanic Gardens, 26300 S. Crenshaw Blvd., Palos Verdes. 213-377-0468.

Malaga Cove School. Courtesy Palos Verdes Historical Society.

Palos Verdes Golf Course, 1922. 3301 Via Campesina, Palos Verdes.

Note: Club House designed by C.E. Howard has been heavily altered.

Historic Sites: *Site of Indian Village,* Malaga Cove, Palos Verdes.

This Village of Chowigna caused a lot of excitement when it was first excavated. Village dates from 8,000 B.C. One of the largest and richest sites in California.

Site of the old *Portuguese Bend Whaling Station,* 1820s. Palos Verdes Drive South, Rancho Palos Verdes.

Site has been marked by the Historical Society.

Jose Delores Sepulveda Adobe, 1818. Foot of Palos Verdes hill near Walteria off of Crenshaw Blvd., Palos Verdes.

Businesses: *Moore's Market,* 1930. 43 Malaga Cove, Palos Verdes, 213-375-2408.

Doyno Robin, Blacksmith. P.O. Box 143, Palos Verdes Estates, 213-373-8519.

Books: *E.G. Lewis,* promoter of Palos Verdes in the 1920s was apparently quite a colorful character. His 3200 acre parcel which his company purchased became the city of Palos Verdes Estates. There is a collection of his papers at the Palos Verdes Library. Call 213-377-9584.

Rolling Hills: The Early Years, A.E.

Hanson, City of Rolling Hills, 1978.

Homes: *Haggarty Home,* 1928 (Now the Neighborhood Church). 415 Paseo Del Mar, Palos Verdes (Malaga Cove).

32 room mansion modeled after an Italian Villa.

Cheney House, 1924. 657 Via Del Monte, Palos Verdes.

Schoolcraft House, 1926. 749 Via Somonte, Palos Verdes.

Palos Verdes Estates Project House, 1925. 408 Paseo Del Mar, Palos Verdes.

Goodrich House, 1928. 2416 Via Anita, Palos Verdes.

Gartz House, 1930.

Northeast corner of Via Almar and Via Del Puente, Palos Verdes.

Olmsted House, 1924–25.

Northwest corner of Paseo Del Mar and Via Arroyo, Palos Verdes.

Stein House, 1928. 2733 Via Campesina, Palos Verdes.

Gard House, 1927. 2780 Via Campesina, Palos Verdes.

Sias House, 1927. 3405 La Selva Place, Palos Verdes.

Visalia Sheraton, 1924. A home that represents a somewhat new phenomenon known as the "super" home. Increased from an original 2100 square foot home to about 15,072 square feet, the neighborhood is requesting a change in current ordinances.

—— PASADENA ——

History: Originally part of the San Gabriel Mission lands, Dona Eulalia de Guillen was awarded approximately 14,000 acres of this land. It next passed to Manuel Garfias and from there to American Dr. John Griffin. Eventually Benjamin Wilson and Griffin owned the Rancho San Pasquel between them, about 5,328 acres.

In Indiana the book by Nordhoff, *California, Land of Health, Pleasure and Residence,* was causing quite a stir among those who read it in 1873. One group in particular decided to abandon the snow for sunny California. They called themselves the *Indiana Colony* and choosing a representative to scout out property in the southland, they sent Daniel Berry West. He found exactly what he believed would make an ideal spot for the colony. However, just about that same time a letter arrived informing him of a financial panic in the east. The project would have to be abandoned. Berry was undeterred. He formed a new group, the *San Gabriel Orange Grove Association* and in 1874 purchased the 4,000 acre Rancho San Pasquel, for $25,000. On January 27, 1874 the 27 colonists gathered at their new property to choose lots. In an amazing example of harmonious accord, within twenty minutes each family was assigned the plot it had chosen with no altercations. Dr. Thomas Elliott, a member of the colony wrote to an eastern friend familiar with Indian lore and asked for an Indian word which might be appropriate for the name of the community. The friend suggested a Chippewa word for "valley" pronounced roughly Pasadena and it was this name which was adopted for the new settlement.

Historical Society: *Pasadena Historical Society,* 470 Walnut St., Pasadena, CA 91103. 818-577-1660. President, Margaret (Peg) Stewart.

They meet here at the beautiful Fenyes Estate. Designed by Robert Farquhar in 1905, additions in 1911. This beautiful estate contains a museum, bookstore and the historical society conducts tours through the mansion. Call for tour details.

Pasadena Heritage, 80 West Dayton, Pasadena. 818-793-0617.

Note: This group conducts excellent architectural tours.

Historical Groups: *Urban Conservation and Planning Dept.,* Pasadena City Hall, 100 N. Garfield, Pasadena. 818-405-4000.

Cultural Heritage Commission, 100 N. Garfield Ave., Pasadena. 818-405-4228.

Historic Districts: *South Marengo Historic District.* Nominated on the National Register of Historic Places by Pasadena Heritage in 1982. Twelve bungalows date from 1901 to 1916. South Marengo is located in the original city of Pasadena which was incorporated in 1886. Originally lined with pepper trees praised by President Teddy Roosevelt as a beautiful example of city planning. Street was widened in 1950 and the trees were replaced with Ash trees. Among its many outstanding structures one stands at 395 S. Marengo and is the last remaining frame hotel, *The Evanston Inn,* 1897.

Prospect-Armada Historic District. Predominantly Prospect and Armada bounded by Westgate, Forest and Orange Grove Boulevard.

Old Pasadena Historic District.

Predominantly Union, Colorado, Green, Raymond and Fair Oaks, roughly bounded at the north by Corson, east at Arroyo Parkway, south at Del Mar and at Pasadena Ave.

Pasadena Civic Center District, also *Pasadena Financial District.*

Other Historic Information, Sources: Pasadena Historical Society and Pasadena Heritage publish an outstanding group of brochures which encompass the plethora of historic structures within the city. The City of Pasadena publishes Ten Tours of Pasadena and The Treasures on Your Block, No. 1, 2, 3, and 4.

These four brochures each give maps of the area they encompass; they list dozens of homes, the outstanding features of these homes, whether they are on the National Register, etc. These brochures are published by the Architectural and Historical inventory of the Cultural Heritage Commission of the City of Pasadena, 1980.

Note: The Cultural Heritage Committee has a list of all their historically designated structures. Call or write them at the address listed at City Hall.

Historians: Pasadena is one of those rare cities whose residents are acutely aware of what they possess. I have yet to pick up the phone and call either the Historical Society, the Pasadena Heritage or Urban Planning and not be given, by the person I talk to, exactly the information requested. It's amazing! They seem to live, breathe, eat and enjoy their heritage. In other words, they are all historians.

Historic Landmarks: *City Hall,* 1926. 100 North Garfield Ave., Pasadena.

Colorado Street Bridge, 1913. Colorado Blvd., Pasadena.

Fenyes Estate, 1905. 470 West Walnut St., Pasadena.

Gamble House, 1908. 4 Westmoreland Place, Pasadena.

Pasadena Playhouse, 1925. 39 South El Molino Ave., Pasadena.

Wrigley Estate, 1905–14. 391 South Orange Grove Blvd., Pasadena.

Hotel Green Annex, 1887, 1898, 1903. 99 South Raymond Ave., Pasadena.

Rose Bowl, Brookside Park. 818-577-7208.

Historic Buildings: *The Fish Building,* 1887. 24–28 E. Colorado Blvd., Pasadena.

Chamber of Commerce Building (original), 1906. 109–125 E. Colorado Blvd., Pasadena.

Early City Hall, 1887. S.W. corner of Union St. and Fair Oaks Ave., Pasadena.

This was Pasadena's sixth City Hall.

Vandervont Block, 1894. 26–38 S. Raymond, Pasadena.

Doty Block, 1887. 103 S. Fair Oaks Ave., Pasadena.

Fire Station, 1889. 37 W. Dayton St., Pasadena.

Pasadena's first fire station.

Braley Building, 1906. 35 S. Raymond Ave., Pasadena.

Historic Homes: *Hillmont,* 1887. 1375 E. Mountain, Pasadena, CA 91104.

The Edwards Home. Private Residence.

J.M. Wood Home, 1894. 97 Bellevue, Pasadena. Now offices.

The Stoutenburgh House, 1893. 255 S. Marengo Ave., Pasadena.

(C.K.G. owners)

Private Residence, 1901. 569 South Marengo, Pasadena.

The Lukens House, 1886–87. 267 North El Molino Ave., Pasadena.

Mr. Roger Kislingbury. Private Residence.

The Lamphear Home, 1894. 346 Markham Place, Pasadena.

The Lamphears. Private Residence.

Private Residence, 1911. 405 Mira Vista Terrace, Pasadena.

The Farmhouse, 1887. 701 Oakland, Pasadena.

The Lows. Private Residence.

Victorian Home, 1894. 206 N. Grand, Pasadena.

Stu and Susie Clark. Private Residence.

Victorian Home, 1887. 311 Congress, Pasadena.

The Bogarts. Private Residence.

The Lowe Farmhouse, 1887. 919 Columbia, Pasadena. Private Residence.

The House Estate, 1913. 1284 South Oakland, Pasadena.

Recently owned by Dovie Beams de Villagran, designed by Sumner Hunt. Private.

Private Home, 1923. 645 Prospect Crescent, "La Miniatura," Pasadena.

Private.
A Frank Lloyd Wright Home.
Private Estate, 1913. 1365 South Oakland, Pasadena.
Blacker House, 1907. Greene and Greene. On National Register. At 177 Hillcrest, Pasadena.
Note: Greene and Greene Homes on Arroyo Terrace and Hillcrest are listed in separate brochures available from the Gamble House.
Note: The above is a fraction of the outstanding homes in Pasadena and lists only Victorians.
Historic Signs: Only in Preservation-conscious Pasadena would a new Historic Sign Ordinance be passed. As of September 1987, the following signs had been approved by the Cultural Heritage Commission for inclusion in the historic sign inventory: (1) Cornet Stores, 411 S. Arroyo Parkway; (2) Mark Allen Cleaners, 1707 E. Washington Blvd.; (3) Mission Liquors, 1801 E. Washington Blvd.; (4) Monty's Steak House, 592 S. Fair Oaks Ave.; (5) National Fabrics and Foam, 1368 N. Lake Ave.; (6) National Radiator Service, 1271 E. Green St.; (7) North Star Bakery, 1780 E. Washington Blvd.; (8) Parker's Office Furniture, 1155 E. Colorado Blvd.; (9) Sandwiches by Connal, 1505 E. Washington Blvd.; (10) Talbott's Electric, 1887 E. Washington Blvd.
Historic Churches: *Church of the Angels,* 1889. 1100 North Avenue 64, Pasadena.
Friendship Baptist Church, 1925. 80 West Dayton Ave., Pasadena.
First Baptist Church, 1925. 75 North Marengo Ave., Pasadena.
All Saints Episcopal Church, 1925. 132 North Euclid Ave., Pasadena.
Historic Schools: *California Institute of Technology,* 1930. 1201 E. California, Pasadena.
Westridge School, 1913. 324 Madeline Drive, Pasadena. 818-799-1153.
Polytechnic School, 1907. 1030 E. California at Wilson, Pasadena.
Mayfield Jr. School, 1931. 405 S.

Euclid, Pasadena.
Senior school moved to 500 Bellefontaine, to a 1917 estate in the 1950s.
Historic Theatres: *Pasadena Playhouse,* 1924–25. 37 S. El Molino, Pasadena. 818-356-7529.
David Houk, head of Pasadena Playhouse Associates is the man behind the resurrected Playhouse, so long "dark." It made its comeback April 19, 1986 with a new play. Support it!
Crown Theatre, 1920. 129 N. Raymond Ave., Pasadena.
Historic Hotels: *The Hotel Green,* 1887–91. 50 E. Green St., Pasadena, CA 91105. 818-793-7070.
(Privately owned) Originally at the S.E. corner of Raymond Avenue and Green St. Demolished in 1935; only the round corner entrance remains of the original hotel. On Raymond Avenue is the Hotel Green Annex. Jutting east from the hotel is a covered "Bridge of Sighs," which crossed Raymond Avenue to the original resort. Now the structure hosts apartments and senior housing.
Vista del Arroyo, South Grand Ave., Pasadena. (Now the 9th Circuit Court of Appeals).
Historic Museums: *Pacific Asian Museum,* 46 N. Los Robles Ave., Pasadena. 818-449-2742.
Once a private residence for Miss Grace Nicholson, an importer of Chinese Art. It then became the Pasadena Museum of Art. Now it is a museum specifically for Asian Art.
Norton Simon Pasadena Museum of Art, 1969. 411 W. Colorado, Pasadena. 818-449-3730.
Huntington Library Art Gallery & Botanical Gardens, 1904 on. 1151 Oxford Road, San Marino (See San Marino). 818-405-2275.
Pasadena Historical Society & Museum, 470 W. Walnut, Pasadena. 818-577-1660.
The Gamble House, 1908. Greene and Greene. 4 Westmoreland Place, Pasadena. 818-793-3334.
Historic Depots: *Santa Fe Railroad Station,* 1935. East side of Raymong,

"Hillmont"

Courtesy of the artist, Jim Gindraux.

North of Del Mar, Pasadena.

Historic Parks: *Singer Park,* 1920s. California Blvd. and John Ave., Pasadena.

Originally a home stood here. (No relation to Singer Sewing Co.) Upon death of the owner, she stated in her will that the home should be demolished and land donated to the city.

Arroyo Seco (Brookside Park). Holly Street Bridge to South Pasadena border, Pasadena.

When Teddy Roosvelt visited the site in 1911 he said it would make one of the greatest parks in the world. Unfortunately Pasadena spent more money investing in its commercial projects than in its parks.

Eaton Canyon Nature Center, 1750 N. Altadena Dr., Pasadena. 818-794-1866. Open Mon.–Sat. 9:30–5, Sun. 1–5.

Bed and Breakfast Inn: *DonnyMac Irish Inn,* 1920s. 119 N. Meridith Ave., Pasadena, CA 91106. 818-440-0066.

Historic Diner: *Rose City Diner* (50s nostalgia) 45 S. Fairoaks, Pasadena. 818-793-8282.

Historic Restaurants: *Dino's Italian Inn,* 1949. 2055 E. Colorado Blvd., Pasadena, CA 91107. 818-449-8823.

Dodsworth Bar and Grill. 1880s. Dodsworth Building, 2 West Colorado Blvd., Pasadena. 818-578-1344.

Harper's Livery. In the old Livery Stables. 110 East Holly, Pasadena. 818-796-8333.

The Raymond Restaurant, 1250 South Fair Oaks Ave., Pasadena. 818-441-3136.

Ernie Juniors, 1940s. 126 West Colorado, Pasadena. 818-792-9957. 213-256-9175 (Eagle Rock.)

Mijares, 1920. 12½ Palmetto Drive, Pasadena. 818-792-2763.

The Brown Derby (Since 1926). 911 E. Colorado Blvd., Pasadena, CA 818-796-7139.

Note: Old Pasadena, Fair Oaks and Colorado have perhaps a dozen old-fashioned looking restaurants.

Businesses: *Anderson Typewriter Co.,* 1912. 120 E. Colorado, Pasadena. 818-793-2166.

Jim Dickson, Realtor. 1471 E. Altadena Dr., Pasadena. 818-791-1000.

Jay's Antiques, 1947. 43 E. Colorado Blvd., Pasadena. 818-792-0485.

Arnold's Fine Jewelry, 1890. 865 E.

Del Mar Blvd., Pasadena, CA 91101. 818-795-8647.

Floyd S. Lee, 1926. Fireplace Furnishings. 1215 E. Walnut, Pasadena. 818-792-2136.

Parker's Office Supplies, 1921. 840 E. Colorado, Pasadena. 818-795-3307.

Jurgensen's Grocery Store, 1933. 842 E. California, Pasadena. 818-792-3121.

Cokesbury Bookstore. Since 1789 in the U.S. 476 E. Colorado Blvd., Pasadena. 818-796-5773.

Architectural Imports, 49 E. Colorado Blvd., Pasadena. 818-796-9019.

Businesses that sell goods related to history: *Vintage Cyclery of Pasadena.* Antique and Nostalgic Bikes. Steve Thomas, 93 North Grand Oaks, Pasadena, CA 91107. 818-440-1730.

Somewhere in Time, 98 East Colorado, Pasadena. 818-792-7503.

Classic Ceilings, Victorian Lamps, accessories, tin ceilings, Lincrusta. 166 W. Waverly Drive, Pasadena. 818-796-5618.

Plain & Fancy Tile, 714 E. Green St., Pasadena. 818-577-2830.

Sugar Daddy, vintage clothing. 18 S. Fair Oaks, Pasadena. 818-793-3532.

Craftspeople: *John Wallis & Association,* 2175 E. Foothill Blvd., Pasadena, CA 91107. 213-681-2387.

Jeffrey Spencer, Sculptor-glass, Pasadena. 818-449-1858.

Note: Pasadena Heritage keeps a list of craftspeople.

Books: *Talking About Pasadena:* Selections from Oral History Interviews, 1976.

Ann Scheid, *Pasadena: Crown of the Valley,* Windsor Publications, 1986.

Available at the Pasadena Historical Society bookstore.

Donald W. Crocker, *Within the Vale of Annandale,* 1968.

Additions: *Orange Heights Neighborhood Association,* P.O. Box 40484, Pasadena, CA 91104.

Fabulous Street: *Clubhouse Drive, Burleigh Drive.*

Developed around 1880s. Area has a magnificent private lake surrounded by spacious homes. There are an old Winery (The San Rafael Winery) and the remains of the old Beaudry Tunnel.

Pasadena began an *Oral History Project* in 1977. 285 East Walnut, Pasadena, CA 91101. 818-405-4060.

Note: Pasadena has just passed a new historic ordinance which will benefit financially owners of historic properties. These historic treasure owners will be given a variety of financial services. Check City of Pasadena.

——— SOUTH PASADENA ———

History: The *Rancho San Pasqual,* part of the extensive lands of the Mission San Gabriel. They were granted first to Juan Marine in 1835. The land was a gift in recompense for Marine's wife, Dona Eulalia, and her long service at the mission. Today, the cities of Pasadena, South Pasadena and Altadena cover the former rancho lands. Juan Marine and his wife only lived on the rancho three years. As a result, a cousin claimed the land. It was given to him in 1840. The next claimant was Manuel Garfias who paid for the improvements on the land. In 1843 he was

given a formal grant from Governor Micheltorena. Then came the Americans. The new owners of the San Pasqual was Dr. Griffin. He added to the original grant. He later sold half interest in his property to Benjamin Wilson. From time to time both Wilson and Griffin sold parts of their rancho. In 1873 they partitioned the San Pasqual. Griffin sold his section to the Indiana Colony, about 4,000 acres. Wilson held onto his for a while. It would be Griffin's portion, however, from which modern day Pasadena would emerge. City incorporated in 1888.

Historical Society: *Pasadena Historical Society,* 470 West Walnut St., Pasadena, CA 91103. Margaret Stewart, president. 818-577-1660.

Pasadena Heritage, 80 West Dayton, Pasadena. 818-793-0617.

Note: The Pasadena Historical Society and Pasadena Heritage are two of the more vociferous preservation voices in Southern California. Unlike most societies that are merely social groups, Pasadena Heritage especially works seriously to preserve the unique past of the area. They have gone about it in a very professional manner and much could be learned by other groups on "how to" from these people. It's also the only group I have ever encountered in the Los Angeles area that can be called any time of the day and asked just about any question on a house, or history and the person can rattle off the answer without so much as a pause.

South Pasadena Preservation Foundation, Kay Bowers, President. 818-799-5170.

Other: *Pasadena Urban Planning,* Pasadena City Hall, 100 N. Garfield, Pasadena. 818-405-4000.

Urban Conservation, 818-405-4228. They have been very helpful in answering questions regarding the history of homes, since they have records on file there.

Cultural Heritage Commission, 100 N. Garfield Ave., Pasadena. 818-405-4228.

Also, *Design Commission* and *Architectural Survey.* City Hall. 818-405-4228.

Historic Landmarks: South Pasadena has designated 25 sites as historic landmarks in their city:

The Adobe Flores, 1840. 1804 Foothill St., South Pasadena.

First house built on Rancho San Pasquel, also adobe was used by the Californians in 1847 as temporary quarters. Home is on the National Register of Historic Places.

Oaklawn Bridge and Waiting Station, 1906. Corner of Oaklawn Ave. and Fair Oaks, South Pasadena.

Built by Greene and Greene. Also on the National Register.

War Memorial Building, 1921. 435 Fair Oaks Ave., South Pasadena.

Built by N.F. Marsh to commemorate W.W. I veterans.

Garfield Residence, 1904. 1001 Buena Vista St., South Pasadena.

Built for Mrs. James Garfield, widow of President James Garfield by Greene and Greene. National Register.

Meridan Iron Works, 1890. 913 Meridan Ave., South Pasadena.

Currently being restored as a museum. Delightful area as well.

Wynyate, 1887. 851 Lyndon St., South Pasadena.

In 1876 three people, Margaret and Donald Graham and Margaret's sister Eliza Collier headed for California. Margaret sent letters home to Iowa. In 1877 the Grahams built their first home in Pasadena. Donald prospered and in 1887 they built their dream house, "Wynyate." The word was Welsh for vineyard. Donald was elected director of the Southern California National Bank of L.A. He was South Pasadena's first mayor. Then Donald died. Margaret was persuaded not to leave the home she loved so well, but to continue to write. She did, and the home stayed in the family for several generations. The letters that she wrote, and those she received were found in an old trunk in the attic. In 1974 they were published in a wonderful book called "Three Came West." It is a must-read for anyone who loves Pasadena.

Watering Trough, 1905 Wayside Station, Meridan Parkway between Mission and El Central St., South Pasadena.

South Pasadena Bank Building, 1904. 1019 El Centro St., South Pasadena.

First bank in the city of South Pasadena.

Oaklawn Portal, 1905. Entrance to Oaklawn Ave., South Pasadena.

Built by Greene and Greene.

South Pasadena Public Library, 1907. 1115 El Centro St., South

Pasadena.

Miltmore House, 1911. Chelton Way, South Pasadena.

Designed by Irving Gill. Also on the National Register.

Chelten Way and Ashbourne Drive, 1907. Private St., South Pasadena.

The Clokey Oak Tree, 1635 Laurel St., South Pasadena.

Ashbourne-Chelton Hybrid Oak Tree, 1997 Ashbourne Drive, South Pasadena.

Andrew O. Porter Residence, 1875. 215 Orange Grove Ave., South Pasadena.

Raymond Hill Waiting Station, 1903. Fair Oaks Ave. at Raymond Hill Road, South Pasadena.

Howard Longley Residence, 1897. 1005 Buena Vista St., South Pasadena.

For then Mayor of South Pasadena. A Greene and Greene home.

Also on the National Register.

Cawston Ostrich Farm Site, 1896. 105 Pasadena Ave., South Pasadena.

One remaining building is at the above address.

Cathedral Oak Monument. Opposite 430 Arroyo Drive, South Pasadena.

Erected in 1953 to mark site of towering oak tree famous for a cross carved in bark.

Fremont Ave. Brethren Church, 1887. 920 Fremont Ave., South Pasadena.

A Mission Revival from an earlier 1887 Pasadena Church.

Dr. John Tanner Residence, 1917. 225 Grand Ave., South Pasadena.

Lloyd E. Morrison Residence, 1923. 1414 Alhambra Road, South Pasadena.

Rialto Theatre, 1925. 1019 Fair Oaks Ave., South Pasadena.

Other Buildings: *The Original Carnegie Library,* 1908-09. El Centro and Diamond, South Pasadena.

Old Lawn St., 1906-20. Pillars and a bridge. South Pasadena.

Designed by Greene and Greene.

Eddy Mansion, prior to 1920. Eddy Park, South Pasadena.

Historic Sites: *Arroyo Hotel,* Mission Area, South Pasadena.

Manuel Grafias Adobe Site, 1853. 424-430 Arroyo Drive, South Pasadena.

Businesses: *Belks Hardware Store* since 1940s. 1518 Mission St., South Pasadena. 818-799-7146.

Swan's Stationary Store, 921 Fair Oaks, South Pasadena. 818-799-6119.

Gus's Barbecue, since 1920. 808 Fair Oaks, South Pasadena. 818-799-3251.

Craftspeople: *Will Tompkins,* wallpaper mechanic. South Pasadena. 818-799-9628.

Dan Reed, electrical. 20 N. Raymond, South Pasadena. 818-796-3247.

Historic Districts: *Mission St. Historic District.*

Books: Edited by Helen Raitt, Mary Collier Wayne, *Three Came West,* Tofua Press, 1974.

——— PICO RIVERA ———

History: In 1805 or 1806 Juan Crispin Perez began grazing cattle in the Pico Rivera-Whittier area. When Mexico gained her independence from Spain, those who held grazing rights could petition Monterey for actual ownership of land. The area granted to Perez in 1835 was called *Rancho Paso de Bartolo.* In 1843 700 acres of his land passed to Bernardino Guirado. After

Perez died another person entered the scene, one of the most important in our history. Pio Pico began dealing with the heirs of the Perez family for land in the area, eventually buying all the property. In 1852 he built an adobe known as the *Pico Mansion,* now in the town of Whittier.

California became a state. The land that was to become Pico Rivera evolved from two land grants. They were: *Rancho Paso de Bartolo,* and the *Rancho Santa Gertrudes.* The first American to own property in what is now Pico Rivera was Oliver Perry Passons. Others followed. The earliest settlement was known as *Gallatin.* The second was *Ranchito,* and a third *Rivera.* Pico and Rivera were separate towns before they merged. Finally in 1958 the two names were combined.

Historical Society: *Pico Rivera Historical and Heritage Society,* P.O. Box 313, Pico Rivera, CA 90660.

Historian: *William Loehr,* 8227 Cravill, Pico Rivera, CA 90660. 213-949-4690.

Historic Homes: *The L.W. Houghton Home,* 1920s. Burke St., Pico Rivera.

Houghton built the first hotel in town.

Chauncey Clark House, 1912. 8310 Orange Ave., Pico Rivera.

Judson Wells Home, 1914. Passons Blvd, Pico Rivera.

Shade House, 1895. Shade Lane, Pico Rivera.

The Burke Mansion, 1922. 7814 Passons Blvd., Pico Rivera.

Charles Warren-Ray Reese Home, 1898. 9022 Whittier Blvd., Pico Rivera.

Cate Home, 1905. Durfee Ave., Pico Rivera.

James Barlow-George Haag Home, 1897. 8612 Dunlap Crossing Road, Pico Rivera.

Charles Chandler Home, 1870/1904. 9220 Mines Blvd., Pico Rivera.

Originally Methodist Church built in 1870, and in 1904 was converted to this home.

Historic Churches: *First Baptist Church of Rivera,* 1888. Pico Rivera.

Since 1888 to 1916 church was located on the S.E. corner of Slauson Ave. and Rosemead Blvd. In 1916 moved to: 9141 E. Burke St., Pico Rivera. 213-698-0095.

Presbyterian Church, Dunlap Crossing Rd. and Passon's. Served as a clubhouse for Pio Pico Women's Club. Pico Rivera.

Historic Schools: *The first school* in Pico Rivera, 1866–1883. 1866 Shugg School.

Then Maizeland School. It was moved to Knotts Berry Farm.

Second School in Pico Rivera, 1883–1915. Serrapis and Old Rivera St., Pico Rivera.

Became a meeting place for Rivera Women's Improvement Club.

Historic Depots: *Santa Fe Depot,* 1884–1888. Serapis, Pico Rivera.

In 1974 this depot was moved to: 9122 Washington Blvd.

Currently the Chamber of Commerce is housed here.

Historic Restaurants: *The Tamale,* 1928. Now CasaGrande, 6420 Whittier Blvd., Pico Rivera. 213-948-3776.

Historic Sites: *George Caralambo,* "Greek George" died at Whittier Narrows in 1913. Greek George was very famous as one of the drivers of the old Camel Corp. He is buried at Mt. Olive Cemetery in Whittier.

Site of *Awigna Indian Village,* Pico Rivera.

Settlement of *Gallatin, Rivera.*

Site of *Mt. Baldy Inn,* 1930s. Whittier Blvd., Pico Rivera.

Destroyed in 1986. A popular restaurant and example of "pop" architecture.

Founders: First American to own property in what is now Pico Rivera was Oliver Perry *Passons.* In 1855 he acquired 100 acres. The Ford Motor Co. located on that property.

Other founders, the *Cate* family arrived in 1856. Cate home (1905) located Durfee Ave. adjacent to present North Park Jr. High School.

Another interesting person who worked here was former President Nixon's father, *Frank Nixon.* He was a motorman on the Pacific Electric Big Red Cars circa 1904 between Whittier and Rivera.

And finally, this was home to *Sebastian Tarabal,* who in the 1770s left the San Gabriel Mission with his Awigna wife to return to Mexico. His wife perished in the Borrego desert. Tarabal reached Mexico just as Bautiste de Anza was ready to embark on the first overland expedition to California. Tarabal was persuaded to guide the expedition across the desert.

Books: Martin Cole, *Where the World Began: Pico Rivera,* published by Rio Hondo College, 1981.

———— REDONDO BEACH ————

History: The first people in the area were the Chowigna Indians who resided near the old Salt Lake. Next came the Spanish, led by Gaspar de Portolá. In their expedition was Sergeant Juan Jose Dominguez, who was granted the vast *Rancho San Pedro*. It included present-day Redondo Beach.

As part of the 43,000 acre Dominguez Rancho of 1784, Redondo Beach remained a rich farming and grazing area until the late 1800s. Later came settlements, the advent of the railroads and an epic battle for the "Port of Los Angeles." There were the legendary Hotel Redondo, the Plunge, the Pavilion, the Mandarin Ballroom, the lightning racer roller coaster, the many piers and the beautiful fields of carnations. By the late '20s Redondo Beach was changing. Not all of the changes were beneficial. Storms lashed the beach front, property values declined. Finally breakwaters were built, and oil drilling revenues helped bring Redondo Beach back to life. Today, it is a thriving community of over 58,000 residents. Incorporated 1892.

Historical Society: *Redondo Beach Historical Society,* 320 Knob Hill Ave., Redondo Beach, CA 90277. 213-372-1171. Ext. 252. President Sandra Dyan, 213-379-3087.

Historians: *Toni Phillips.* 213-373-0456.

Pat Dreizler, Community Resources Dept. City of Redondo Beach, 320 Knob Hill, Redondo Beach.

Other Historical Organizations: *Redondo Pier Association.*

Check with Historical Museum for current person in charge. Note: George Freeth Centennial Celebration 1883–1983. Bust of George Freeth, located on Redondo Pier.

Historical Society Board. See Historical Museum. Meets 7:30 P.M. third Thursday of the month.

Historical Commission Meeting. See Historical Museum. Meets 6:30 P.M. fourth Thursday of the month.

Historical Society. See this under its own heading.

Home Tours. The Historical Society is very active in conducting yearly historical home tours. They publish excellent brochures, booklets on these. Call Historical Society.

Courtesy Redondo Beach Historical Home & Building Tour

Historical Landmarks: *Old Salt Lake.* First street at Harbor Drive (North Edison Entrance). Redondo Beach.

Important to newcomers and Indians.

Redondo Pier, 1888. Torrance Blvd., Redondo Beach. Fire of 1988 destroyed much of pier but it will be rebuilt.

Historic Museum: *Redondo Beach Historical Museum,* 320 Knob Hill, Redondo Beach.
Open Wed.–Fri. 1–4 P.M. 213-372-1171, Ext. 252 for information. Home of the Historical Society.
Historic Homes: *Victorian Home,* 1894–95. 402 South Broadway, Redondo Beach.
Victorian Revival, 1892 (original owners, Thomas family). 323 South Francisca, Redondo Beach.
Two-Story Saltbox, 1890 (original owner, Dr. Burns). 411 Emerald, Redondo Beach.
Victorian, Edwardian, 1906. 413 Emerald, Redondo Beach.
Victorian, Edwardian, 1905. 415 Emerald, Redondo Beach.
Victorian, Edwardian, 1910. 417 Emerald, Redondo Beach.
Farm House, 1905. 2604 Fisk, Redondo Beach.
Victorian Beach Cottage, 1880. 816 Emerald, Redondo Beach.
Bungalow Home, 1898–1902. 218 South Helberta, Redondo Beach.
Craftsman Bungalow, 1912. 513 Garnet, Redondo Beach.
Original Beach Bungalow, 1910. 417 South Broadway, Redondo Beach.
California Bungalow, 1911. 409 South Gertruda, Redondo Beach.
California Bungalow, 1915. 500 Camino Real, Redondo Beach.
Craftsman Bungalow, 1910. 201 South Helberta, Redondo Beach.
Craftsman/Colonial, 1910. 303 North Francisca.
Victorian, 1885–95. 200 Diamond, Redondo Beach.
Mission Revival, 1912. 732 South Catalina, Redondo Beach.
Italian Renaissance, 1928. 124 Via Monte de Oro, Redondo Beach.
Early California Clapboard, 1924–27. 629 North Lucia, Redondo Beach.
Beach Cottages, 1923. 207–11 South Broadway, Redondo Beach.
The Sweetser House, 1921. 417 Beryl, Redondo Beach.
The Charles Lindbergh Home, 408 South Catalina, Redondo Beach.

This is the house where the famed Charles Lindbergh lived while he attended Redondo Union High School.
Craftsman Style, 1922. 626 Elvira, Redondo Beach.
Spanish Colonial Revival, 1929. 217 Avenue F, Redondo Beach.
Restored Spanish/Tudor, 1928. 413 Pearl, Redondo Beach.
Other Historic Buildings: *Redondo Beach Women's Club,* 1922. (Founded 1908) 400 South Broadway, Redondo Beach. (Also on the National Register)
Redondo Beach Public Library, 1930. 309 Esplanade, Redondo Beach (On the National Register).
Salvation Army, 1930s. 125 Beryl, Redondo Beach.
The Fire House, Renovation: Victorian. 2103 Havemeyer, Redondo Beach.
Here is a 7,000 square-foot showplace for a remarkable collection of fire engines and antique cars.
Historic District: 300 Block of *North Gertruda;* 400 Block of Emerald; 600–700 Blocks of Elvira; 400–800 Blocks of El Redondo (original gas lamps); 500 North Block of Guadalupe; 400 South Block of Broadway; The Esplanade and Catalina. Weddle Woodcraft Site on Catalina.
Historic Churches: *First United Methodist Church,* 1887. 243 S. Broadway, Redondo Beach.
Christ Church Episcopal, 1887. 408 S. Broadway, Redondo Beach.
South Bay Bible Church, 1887. 101 S. Pacific Coast Highway, Redondo Beach.
First Baptist Church, 1912. 100 N. Pacific Coast Highway, Redondo Beach.
Historic Parks: *Veterans Park,* by the seashore on the Esplanade, Redondo Beach.
Moreton Bay fig tree over 90 years old.
Historic Trees: *OMBU trees,* Pacific Coast Highway and Ave. A, Redondo Beach.
Unusual native trees of South America.
Historic Schools: *Redondo Beach*

Union High School, 631 Vincent Park, Redondo Beach.

Pipe organ inside auditorium installed around 1916.

Historic Sites: *Hotel Redondo,* 1890–1920. Basin Three in King Harbor on the north to Sapphire Street on the south. Redondo Beach.

225-room hotel was the queen of hostelries.

Southern California Edison Offices, 1897 (Site) 310 South Catalina, Redondo Beach.

Historic Restaurants: *Old Tony's on the Pier,* 1952. Foot of Torrance Blvd., Redondo Beach. 213-374-9246.

"Millies" Millie Riere's, 1946. Corner Ave. 1 and Esplanade, Redondo Beach.

Historic Businesses: *D and D Drug Store,* 1897. 316 North Harbor Drive, Redondo Beach. 213-372-3360; 213-379-1486.

Wardrobe Cleaners, 126 North Catalina, Redondo Beach. 213-372-2442.

Located where the railroad station once stood. Old railroad ties and part of the station still located inside.

Willie Glen's Family Shoe Shine Parlor, 1948. 129 South Pacific Coast Highway, Redondo Beach.

Adams Iron Works, 132 North Catalina, Redondo Beach.

Originally the first blacksmith shop in Redondo, Adams Iron Works is still operating in a similar capacity.

Historic Person: *George Freeth.* First surfer in the United States. Located Redondo Beach Pier-Bust.

George Freeth born in Honolulu 1883 of royal Hawaiian and Irish ancestry. As a youngster he revived lost Polynesian art of surfing while standing on a board. Henry Huntington was so amazed at his abilities, he induced George to come to Redondo Beach in 1907 to help promote the building of the "largest warm saltwater plunge in the world." Thousands came to see George "walk on the water." George Freeth introduced the game of water polo to this coast. He trained many champion swimmers and divers. He was our first "official" lifeguard. He invented the torpedo-shaped rescue buoy that is now used worldwide. On December 16th, 1908 he rescued six Japanese fisherman from a capsized boat. He died at the age of 35 in 1919, as a result of exhaustion from strenuous rescue work.

Books: *Old Redondo, A Pictorial History of Redondo Beach,* Legion Press, 1982.

Note: The city of Redondo Beach has just completed an architectural survey. Contact City Hall for additional information. 213-372-1171.

RESEDA

History: Part of historic San Fernando Valley Mission land. In 1913 Valley was subdivided by the Suburban Homes Association. Harry Chandler visited Mexico City, fell in love with the Paseo de las Reforma, and returned to the Valley to design *Sherman Way* after the Paseo.

Community of *Marion* laid out and named for the daughter of General Otis, one of the officers of the Suburban Homes Association. But in 1921 when a Post Office was established, the name conflicted with Mariana, California. Reseda selected instead. In Latin, it meant, "to give aid or comfort."

Central business district began in 1915. Lee's Hardware Store was first business at the corner of Reseda Blvd. and Sherman Way. That is still the oldest corner in Reseda. In 1930s Reseda was the foremost producer of lettuce in the United States. In 1950–56, Reseda was also the fastest growing city in the U.S.

Historical Society: None. (See San

Fernando Valley Historical Society Mission Hills).

Historical Landmarks: *Pony Country,* Tampa Ave. near Roscoe, Reseda.

Once part of a 200 acre alfalfa farm owned by Zelzah family. During 1920 farm sold to General Moses Hazeltine Sherman. Barn dates from 1915 and was once a walnut processing area.

Pioneers: *Mr. & Mrs. W.J. Lausen,* 1920s. 7008 Baird St., Reseda.

The Chamber of Commerce calls them the founders of Reseda.

Businesses: *Lewis for Books,* 1948. 7119 Reseda Blvd., Reseda, CA 91335. 818-343-5634.

Allyn Flowers, Corner Sherman Way and Reseda Blvd., Reseda.

The oldest corner and building in Reseda.

Historic School: *Reseda Elementary School,* 1926. 7265 Amigo St., Reseda. 818-343-1312.

———— ROSEMEAD ————

History: In 1852 John Guess and his wife Harriet arrived in the San Gabriel Valley via an ox-drawn wagon. They pitched camp about where the present Savannah School is located. In 1867 John purchased 100 acres of a 164 acre ranch which he named Savannah.

Following in his footsteps were Frank Forst and Leonard J. Rose. Rose and his wife Amanda purchased about 700 acres of land increased to 1300 acres around today's Rosemead Blvd. He named his ranch "Rosemeade" meaning Rose's meadows. The ranch thrived and eventually became known as Rosemead.

In 1959 the town of Rosemead was incorporated.

Historical Society: None. However, *Mr. Hugh Foutz* is the City Historian and can be reached at: 8838 E. Valley Blvd., Rosemead, CA 91770. 818-280-2266 (Home); 818-288-6671 (The City Hall).

Historical Landmarks: *The Dinsmoor Heritage House Museum,* 1929. 9642 Steele St., Rosemead.

In 1926 the D.A.R. marked this home as an historic landmark.

Historic Homes: *The Richardson Farm House,* Mission Drive, Rosemead.

An old barn, wagons which Mr. Richardson rents to the motion picture studios. Home is board and batten.

California Christian Home, 1927. Now an Old Folks Home. Mission Drive, Rosemead.

Leonard J. Rose
Inspired
Rosemead Name

Courtesy Rosemead Chamber of Commerce.

Historic Schools: *Garvey School,* 1893. 2720 Jackson Ave., Rosemead. 818-572-4677.

First graduate was Dick Garvey (Montebello).

Historic Cemetery: *Savannah Memorial Cemetery,* 1850. 9263 Valley Blvd., Rosemead.

First cemetery at the end of the old Santa Fe Trail.

Historic Sites: Site of the J.W. Robinson (Department Store) family. Had a large ranch and summer home here. Built a large three story Victorian home around the corner of Rio Hondo and Valley Blvd. It was purchased by Dinsmoor. Home demolished.

Site of *L.J. Rose's Home,* 8941 Valley Blvd., Rosemead. (where First American Bank is today).

Founder of Rosemead.

Original ranch was about 1300 acres and included parts of San Gabriel. 1862 Rose home is on La Presa Ave. 7020 San Gabriel. See San Gabriel.

Site of *Fletcher Aviation,* 1910–1950. East of Rosemead Blvd., Rosemead.

Dr. Fletcher was an inventor. Now area is an industrial park.

Other: *Cork Oak Tree,* rare, indigenous to area. Mission Drive, Rosemead. (In front of Richardson Home).

Businesses: *California Brick and Tile Co.,* 1927. 8632 E. Valley Blvd., Rosemead. 818-288-2010.

Harry & Son's Radiator Shop, 1919. 9344 Valley Blvd., Rosemead. 818-288-0644.

Reliable Lumber Co., 1930. 8614 Valley Blvd., Rosemead. 818-288-0860.

Books: *L.J. Rose of Sunnyslope,* by L.J. Rose, 1959.

Rosemead: An Historical Sketchbook, 1859–1985. Beth Wyckoff and Joan Walton.

Special Collection of historical papers on Rosemead at the library, 8800 Valley Blvd. 818-573-5220.

SAN FERNANDO

History: In 1846 Pio Pico, our last Mexican Governor owned almost the entire San Fernando Valley. He deeded all of this land except for the San Fernando Valley Mission, to a Spaniard, Don Eulogia De Celis, for $14,000. It consisted of 120,000 acres. De Celis returned to Spain and Andres Pico, brother of Pio, acquired a half-interest in the area in 1854. In 1862 Andres transferred his interest, which was in the southern portion of the valley to his brother Pio. This 60,000 acre portion then was sold for $115,000 to the Lankershim and Van Nuys company known as *San Fernando Homestead Association.* The Northern portion was purchased by Senator Charles Maclay in 1874. Mr. Maclay laid out the town of San Fernando that same year.

Historical Society: *San Fernando Valley Historical Society,* Andres Pico Adobe, 1834. #7 C.H.M. 10940 Sepulveda Blvd., Mission Hills, CA 91345. 818-365-7810.

The Historical Society resides here,

in this beautifully restored adobe. There is a small but exceptionally good library. Open.

Andres Pico Adobe. Courtesy San Fernando Valley Historical Society (Mission Hills).

Historical Landmarks: *La Casa de Lopez Adobe,* 1882. 1100 Pico St., San Fernando. 818-365-9990.

This charming adobe was built by Valentin Lopez. Open.

Griffith Ranch, 1912. Foothill Blvd. and Vaughn St., San Fernando.

It was here that D.W. Griffith, famous silent film maker, filmed his epic "The Birth of a Nation." Many other films were shot here as well. A monument marks the site.

Other: *Home of the Franciscan Sisters,* 11306 Laurel Canyon Blvd., San Fernando.

Businesses: *Cassell's Music Store,* 1947. 901 North Maclay, San Fernando. 818-365-9247.

Dunn's Super Service, 1915. 233 N. Maclay, San Fernando. 818-361-8686.

Brown Printing, 1920s. 926 N. Maclay, San Fernando. 818-361-4233.

Mission Jewelers, 1019 San Fernando Rd., San Fernando. 818-361-5128.

San Fernando Hardware, 211 S. Maclay, San Fernando. 818-361-0178.

Weaver Bros. Auto Repair, 647 San Fernando Rd., San Fernando. 818-361-4928.

Oswald Mortuary, 1001 North Maclay, San Fernando. 818-361-6283.

Chamber of Commerce: *San Fernando Valley Chamber of Commerce,* 519 S. Brand Blvd., San Fernando. 818-361-1184.

Books: Lawrence C. Jorgensen, *The San Fernando Valley Past and Present,* 1982.

Derward P. Lommis, *San Fernando Retrospective: The First Fifty Years,* 1985. San Fernando Heritage, Inc.

——— SAN GABRIEL ———

History: On August 6, 1771 a party set out from San Diego, which consisted of two priests, Pedro Benito Cambon and Angel Somera, ten soldiers and assorted gear to found a mission to the north. On September 8, 1771, the *Mission San Gabriel Arcangel* was founded. In 1774 Bautista de Anza reached the old Mission and stayed for nearly three weeks. In 1781 the Rivera Expedition stopped at the Mission, on their way to found a new pueblo—Los Angeles. Jedediah Smith stopped in 1826 as he pioneered the first American routes into the Southland. William Workman and James Rowland brought the first American settlement over the Santa Fe Trail in 1841, stopping at the mission. In 1852 San Gabriel became one of the first Townships in the County of Los Angeles. Today, the San Gabriel Mission is the only one of the 21 California Missions to be in continuous use throughout its more than 200 year history.

Historical Society: *San Gabriel Valley Historical Society,* 318 S. Mission Drive, San Gabriel, CA 91776.

Bill Bauld, president. 818-308-3223.

San Gabriel Museum Association, 318 S. Mission Drive, San Gabriel.

Historian: *Kit Williams,* San Gabriel Historical Society, 818-282-0749.

Historical Landmarks: *Mission San Gabriel Arcangel,* 1775. 537 W. Mission Drive, San Gabriel. 818-282-1775.

Present Building dates from 1815. Original site of the old, original Mission has been marked, about five miles south of the present site, corner of San Gabriel Blvd. and Lincoln Ave. Open 9:30–4 daily.

Mission San Gabriel. Courtesy of the artist, Gerry Stinson.

San Gabriel Civic Auditorium, 320 S. Mission Drive, San Gabriel.

Built in 1926 to give Mission Plays written by Steven McGroaty from 1912 to 1932. The facade of the auditorium was destroyed in the 1987 earthquake but will be rebuilt.

Historic Homes: *Las Tunas, The Cactus,* 1770s? 315 Orange St., San Gabriel.

Perhaps the oldest adobe in this area is the former home of Colonel Purcell. It is said to have been built as a home for the mission friars three years before the mission church was erected. The history of Las Tunas Ranch is uncertain. In 1852 it was purchased by Judge Volney Howard. It was occupied earlier by Henry Dalton. Hugo Reid was once its owner as well. Lots of history here.

Casa Vieja de Lopez, 1790s? 330 North Santa Anita, San Gabriel.

The Grapevine Adobe. One block west of the Mission, corner of Santa Anita Ave. and Mission Drive. San Gabriel.

Adobe has been torn down, but its grapevine remains.

Vigare Adobe (Ortega-Vigare 1792–1805), 616 Ramona St., San Gabriel.

For years the home of Dona Luz Vigare, great-granddaughter of a soldier of the mission guard.

Vovard Home, 1887. (private residence) Pine St., San Gabriel.

E.J. Rose Home, 1862. *"Sunnyslope."* La Presa Ave. and Huntington Drive, 7020 La Presa Drive, San Gabriel (See Rosemead)

Historic Church: *Church of Our Savior,* 1867. 535 West Roses Rd., San Gabriel. 818-282-5147.

Businesses: *Mission Super Hardware,* 1924. 501 West Valley Blvd., San Gabriel. 818-284-7021.

San Gabriel Florist and Nursery, 1920. 632 South San Gabriel Blvd., San Gabriel. 818-286-9787.

Star Tup's Social Catering, Five generations of Starup Family. 323 S. Mission Drive, San Gabriel. 818-570-1233.

Historic Restaurants: *El Encanto,*

formerly The Newman's. 100 E. Old San Gabriel Rd., Azusa. 818-969-8877.

Originally this structure was known as Camp One in the San Gabriel Canyon. After death of Mrs. Newman's husband, she began a restaurant. Oldest in the area. See Azusa.

The Original Petrillo's Italian Cuisine, 1950s. 833 E. Valley Blvd., San Gabriel 818-280-7332.

Panchito's Restaurant, 161 S. Mission Drive, San Gabriel. 818-284-8830.

Located in San Gabriel's First City Hall.

Other: Descendants of Pioneer Families hold get-togethers each year since 1934. San Gabriel is blessed to still have so many of these descendants still living in the area. Held at the Mission. Contact Kit Williams 818-282-0749.

Additions: *Plaza Park.* Original site of the "Mission Play" 1912–1926. San Gabriel.

Sister City Plaque, marked by a Jacaranda Tree, San Gabriel. Sister city is Celaya, Mexico.

Site: where City Hall now stands. This land was originally donated by Walter P. Temple. Also there is a *millstone* near the steps which commemorates Joseph Chapman's Mill which he built in 1823.

First Bank, 1913. Used today by local Fine Arts Assocation. San Gabriel.

Salido Store, 1915. Dept. of Parks and Recreation now occupy building. For years this was the only establishment for miles in which supplies could be had.

Old Grape Vine, originally planted in 1861. Mission San Gabriel.

Also a 1000 gallon wine cask here which is among the largest in the world.

There is an historical walk which the historical society gives and an excellent brochure as well. Contact historical society.

SAN MARINO

History: Originally part of the San Gabriel Mission lands, it was Benjamin Wilson who came West in 1841 not to stay, but to continue his journey to China. He remained in the Southland and built up a small empire. One of these was an area later to become known as Pasadena. Wilson set aside about 2,500 acres adjoining that area on its eastern boundary and called it *Lake Vineyard.* It was a section of this thereafter known as the San Marino Ranch, which would be developed by Wilson's son-in-law, James de Barth Shorb. His ranch was purchased by Henry E. Huntington in 1903 and is today the site of the Huntington Library, Art Gallery and Botanical Gardens.

Historical Society: *San Marino Historical Society,* 1867 Windsor Rd., P.O. Box 80222, San Marino, CA 91108. 818-284-2130. President, Midge Sherwood.

Midge Sherwood founded this society in 1973. Her book, *Days of Vintage, Years of Vision,* has become a classic.

Historical Landmarks: *The Huntington Library and Home, Botanical Gardens,* 1151 Oxnard Rd., San Marino. 818-405-2275.

Henry Edwards Huntington purchased the 600 acre ranch in 1903. Began serious collecting of art around 1911. Mr. Huntington is, of course synonymous with the P.E. cars in Los Angeles. The Huntington Library has just about the best collection of California research sources than any library in the world. Many scholars here who specialize in Southland history.

The Huntington Hotel, 1907. 1401 S. Oak Knoll Ave., San Marino, CA 91109. 818-792-0266.

Scheduled for demolition. A replica to be opened 1990, Ritz-Carlton.

Old Mill, El Molino Viejo, 1816. 1120 Old Mill Rd., San Marino, CA 91108.

818-449-5450.

(San Marino Society of the California Historical Society).

Constructed by Indians this old mill was the first of its kind in the area. When a new mill was constructed in 1823, this less-efficient mill was relegated to an auxiliary role.

Following secularization, the mission lands surrounding the Old Mill were sold to William Workman and Hugo Reid. Finally after some legal disputes, the land went to Dr. Thomas White in 1859. Dr. White deeded the property to his daughter, and she and her husband, state Assemblyman Colonel Kewen, converted the old adobe into a residence with a garden, orchard and vineyard amid 500 acres. Finally the property came under the control of Henry Huntington. When the Hotel Huntington opened, the Old Mill served as a clubhouse for the hotel golf course. In 1927 it passed to Mrs. James Brehm, and she decided to rescue the structure and preserve it as an important legacy of California's past. Upon the Brehms' deaths in 1962 the mill went to the City of San Marino. Open Tues.–Sun. 1–4.

Historic Homes: *Michael White Adobe,* 1845. 2701 Huntington Drive, San Marino, CA 91108.

Oldest residence in the area. Has been recently restored. Open.

Collis Huntington Holladay, 1931. 1125 Rosalind Rd., San Marino.

Private Residence, 1928. 1985 Orlando Rd., San Marino.

Private Residence, 1932. 708 Winston Ave. at S.E. Corner Lombardy, San Marino.

Roland Coate designed this gorgeous two-story Monterey Style home. There are many of his homes in the area.

Note: many estates in the area, but like other exclusive districts, it is difficult to see them. Watch paper for Designer Home Open House Tours and/or join the Historical Society.

Historic Sites: *George Stoneman Adobe,* 1870s. 1890 Montrobles Place, San Marino.

This was the site of "Los Robles," the 400 acre estate of Governor George Stoneman. Here in 1880, Pres. Rutherford B. Hayes was entertained. The first schoolhouse in the San Gabriel Valley, California's first tennis club, and the first municipal Christmas tree of San Marino located here.

Historic Restaurants: *Colonial Kitchen,* 1940s. 1110 Huntington Drive, San Marino. 818-289-2449.

Cycle World, 1948. 2523 Huntington Drive, San Marino. 818-793-9065.

Other Organizations: *Pacific Railroad Society,* P.O. Box 8726, San Marino, CA 91106.

Book: Midge Sherwood, *Days of Vintage, Years of Vision,* 2 vols., 1976.

Wallace Neff: Architect of California's Golden Age, compiled and edited by Wallace Neff, Jr. Capra Press.

Wallace Neff designed many of the homes in San Marino.

——— SAN PEDRO ———

History: In terms of exploration, this area was first seen by the Spanish in 1542 when *Juan Rodriguez Cabrillo* sighted the coast first in San Diego and later, San Pedro. It was Sebastian Vizcaino in 1603 who chose the name *St. Peter.* Early on called the Bay of Smokes by the Spanish (probably from the early campfires of the Indians or the burning of brush as they chased game into an open area). Today the name seems very appropriate when smog clouds the harbor.

In 1784 three Spanish land grants were awarded in Southern California. One of these was Rancho San Pedro, 75,000 acres, granted to Juan Dominguez.

With the coming of the American sailing vessels in the 1820s, a small landing was built for the sailing ships that made their way around the horn. The first Stagecoach took passengers from this crude wharf to Los Angeles, some twenty-six miles away.

San Pedro Bay is rich in historical folklore. It is recorded that during the waning days of Mexican domination and the deportation of Governor Micheltorena, Pio Pico was convinced that the capitol of California should be moved from Monterey to Los Angeles, just to be close to the Port of San Pedro.

Historical Society: *San Pedro Bay Historical Society,* 1159 Amar St., San Pedro, CA 90732. Arthur A. Almeida, President. (his home)

Also: 638 S. Beacon No. 505, P.O. Box 1568. San Pedro, CA 90733.

These are where the archives are kept—in the municipal building. 213-548-3208. Monday–Wed. 1–4.

Historical Society: *Note:* The San Pedro Historical Society is currently in the process of restoring the old *1897 Muller Home.* The Mullers owned the home from 1906 to 1963, and donated it to the society. It is located at: 1542 S. Beacon St., San Pedro.

Historian: *Kay Schultz.* Can be reached at 213-548-3208. (Archives, City Hall).

Historical Landmarks: *Point Fermin Lighthouse,* 1874. Gaffey St. and Paseo Del Mar. Point Fermin Park, San Pedro.

Phineas Banning was the first to petition Congress for an appropriation to begin work on a breakwater and lighthouse. Banning asked for $100,000 and got $30,000. The Lighthouse was

Courtesy the artist, Sharon Adler

begun and opened in 1874. It has stood for over 100 years.

Fort MacArthur, 1888/1914. Pacific Street between 22nd and 36th. San Pedro.

This area was the center of the early shipping activity of the harbor. In 1796 Father Lasuen built an adobe shelter here where the present post engineers building now stands. Later, the land was involved in a legal dispute with the intermarriage between the Sepulvedas and the Dominguez family. It needed the U.S. Land Grant Commission to sustain the Sepulveda's claim which said that San Pedro was owned by the Sepulvedas. During the Mexican-American war, (1845–47) Commodore Robert Stockton used the area for storing of ordnance and supplies for his march on Los Angeles. It was on these grounds that the now-historically famous dispute arose in 1847 between Kearny and Stockton into which John Fremont became embroiled and later courtmartialed. Historical research has shown that three U.S. Presidents:

Grant, Cleveland and Woodrow Wilson were concerned about the Fort. It was commissioned by Grover Cleveland as a military reservation in 1888. Lots of history here. 213-831-7211.

St. Vincent Thomas Bridge, 1961–63. North of the Catalina Terminal. Named after one of San Pedro's "own."

Young Thomas, class of '28 was an orphan from the streets and wharves of San Pedro. He sold newspapers, pies and other sundries to get by. While a student at SPHS he became active in student government. He loved sports and received an athletic scholarship to Loyola. He got a law degree, ran for State Assembly. In 1978 he had served longer in Sacramento than any other elected official in California history.

Cabrillo Museum, 3720 Stephen White Drive, San Pedro, CA 90731. 213-831-3207; 213-548-7562.

Named in honor of Juan Cabrillo who sailed past this coast in 1542, the street *Stephen White* is also important. White was a United States Senator from California. His brilliant oratory and debating skill literally saved the Port of San Pedro from being overshadowed by Santa Monica where Collis Huntington and the Southern Pacific Railroad were convinced it should be. White knew their interests were purely selfish and he convinced the Senate as well. In Los Angeles, there is a life-size bronze statue of White at Hill and First Streets.

Municipal Ferry Building, 1941. #146 C.H.M. (Now the Maritime History Museum). Main Channel, San Pedro.

A wonderful W.P.A. streamline Moderne building.

Korean Bell and Belfry of Friendship, #187 C.H.M. (Dedicated 1976) Angel's Gate Park, Gaffey and 37th St., San Pedro.

Ports of Call Village, Berth 77, Los Angeles Harbor.

I suppose I must include this, though a replica of a New England Whaling Village is not exactly my idea of good representation of the rich California sea-faring traditions the designers could have utilized. 213-831-0287.

Historic Homes: *Dodson House,* 1888. #147 C.H.M. 859 West 13th St., San Pedro.

Harbor View House, 1926. #252 C.H.M. 921 Beacon St., San Pedro.

Danish Castle, 1880s. 324 West 10th St., San Pedro.

Peck House, 1887. 380 West 15th St., San Pedro.

Private Residence, 1899. #253 C.H.M. 575 19th St., San Pedro.

Private Residence, 1898. 918-20 Centre, San Pedro.

Muller Home, 1897. 1542 S. Beacon St., San Pedro.

Home to the San Pedro Historical Society. '87.

Historic Ships: *S.S. Catalina,* 1924. #213 C.H.M.

The great white streamer built by William Wrigley carried passengers to Avalon for over 50 years.

Historic Churches: *Old St. Peter's Episcopal,* 1884. #53 C.H.M. 24th and Grand Ave., San Pedro.

Oldest church in San Pedro. Located since 1884 on Beason St., then moved in 1956 to above address.

Historic Parks: *Harbor View Memorial Park,* 1879. 24th and Grand Street, San Pedro.

Historic Theatres: *Fox-Warner Theatre,* (now Juarez), 1931. #251 C.H.M. 478 West 6th St., San Pedro.

Historic Restaurants: *The Grand House and Folk Art Shop,* 809 S. Grant St., San Pedro. 213-548-1240.

They publish their own newsletter, have art shows, films, walking tours.

Olsen's Restaurant, 1938. 589 9th St., San Pedro. 213-832-7437.

Historic Buildings: *U.S. Post Office,* 1935. 839 S. Beacon St., San Pedro. 213-548-2747. A W.P.A. Building.

The Arcade, 1925. 479 West 6th St., San Pedro. 213-833-4813.

Just recently completed, this building has been rehabilitated by Mr. Gary Lawson, owner and project manager.

Morgan House, 1918. #186 C.H.M. Harbor Area YWCA, 437 West 9th St., San Pedro. A Julia Morgan design.

Fireboat No. 2 and *Firehouse No. 112,* 1925. (no. 112 demolished) Berth 227 Foot of Old Dock St., San Pedro. No. 2 Fireboat is #154 C.H.M.

Historic Sites: *Site of the old Hide Adobe,* 1823.

About where Fort MacArthur is. British Traders and American traders stopped here. Richard H. Dana wrote about it in 1835 in "Two Years Before the Mast." Abel Stearns built a small hide house in the 1830s. Temple and Alexander Stage began here in 1845. It was Los Angeles' first mail stop. It was the beginning of San Pedro.

Timm's Landing and Sepulveda's Landing Site, 1835. #171 C.H.M. Plaque at 14th and Beacon St., San Pedro.

Historic School: *San Pedro High School,* 1935-37. Leland St. between 15th and 17th, San Pedro.

Historical Monuments: *U.S.S. Los Angeles Naval Monument,* #188 C.H.M. (1979) Harbor Blvd. between 5th and 6th, San Pedro.

Famous Street: *Beacon St.,* San Pedro.

Businesses: *King's Bicycle Store,* 1925. 1209 S. Pacific, San Pedro. 213-833-2835.

Christensen's Norwegian Bakery, 13th and Pacific, San Pedro. 213-832-6965.

Halverson-Leavell Mortuary, 1914.

576 W. 6th St., San Pedro. 213-832-4221.

Williams Book Store, 1909. 708 S. Pacific, San Pedro. 213-832-3631.

Books: Hank Silka, *San Pedro: A Pictorial History,* 1983.

Oliver Vickery, *Harbor Heritage,* 1979.

SANTA FE SPRINGS

History: Originally part of the enormous 1784 *Los Nietos* land grant, later became known as the smaller *Santa Gertrudes* Ranch. A fort was built here when California belonged to Mexico. Thanks to many people, especially Mrs. Hathaway, much of this historic property will be restored.

Historical Society: *Sante Fe Springs Historical Commission,* P.O. Box 2120, Santa Fe Springs, CA 90670.

Also an Historical Committee was appointed by the city in 1965 whose purpose was to disseminate historical information on the city to young school children.

Historic Landmarks: *Heritage Park,* 1830s. Norwalk Blvd. and Telegraph Rd., Santa Fe Springs.

Long a controversy as to its fate, at last this really exciting area will be restored. It comprises about six acres and has an 1830 adobe (the largest residential adobe in all of Southern California), an 1890 Windmill, an 1870 Carriage Barn, Botanical Hawkins gardens of 1867, a Tank House, an Aviary, and a Conservatory.

Historic Homes: *The Hathaway Home,* 1932, *Library-Museum,* 11901 E. Florence Ave., Sante Fe Springs.

This unique home was built by the Hathaways, who arrived in 1876. They have one of the most unique private libraries I have ever seen and a private museum which tells the history of the area.

Open. You must call 213-944-6563.

Houghton Home, Telegraph Rd., Santa Fe Springs.

Marie Rankin Clark Estate, 1912. Off of Pioneer Blvd., Santa Fe Springs. Recently acquired by the city, this home was built by Irving Gill! Plans are to renovate home, open it for parties, weddings, etc. Contact Monica at the library. 213-868-0511.

Churches: *Catholic Church,* Orange and Los Nietos, Sante Fe Springs.

German Baptist Church Cemetery, 1890s. Corner Los Nietos and Painter. Santa Fe Springs. Now a Bible Missionary Church.

Historic Sites: Site of the *Santa Fe Springs Hotel,* 1880s. Two blocks North of Telegraph, and two blocks East of Norwalk. Sante Fe Springs.

Four Corners. Originally known as Fulton Wells, later Four Corners. Norwalk Blvd. and Telegraph Rd., Santa Fe Springs.

A Banning Stage Coach Stop at one time.

Craftspeople: *Mr. Stoterau,* Gifted woodwork, Santa Fe Springs.

Books: *History in the Making,* Santa Fe Springs, 1976. Nadine Hathaway, chairman, Santa Fe Springs Bicentennial Commission.

Note: *Heritage Park,* 1987 up-date. Ontiveros St., Santa Fe Springs.

This wonderful 6 acre park opened in March 1988. Staff peson to contact is the librarian, Monica Penninger at 213-868-0511, Ext. 250. There is an archeological dig which goes back to Mission days, and the city of Santa Fe has big plans to utilize the park for theatres, plays, weddings, receptions, etc.

—— SANTA MONICA ——

History: Name appeared for the first time on a land grant, *San Vicente y Santa Monica,* made by Don Francisco Sepulveda and Augustin Machado, 1827.

Beginning with the 1870s attention was focused on this beach area as a possible summer resort. In the summer of 1871 about twenty families, the majority in tents, sojourned there among the sycamore groves where a J.M. Harned had a bar and "refreshment parlor."

In 1874 Senator John P. *Jones* and Colonel R.S. *Baker* became interested in the area and laid out the new town of Santa Monica in 1875. The area was advertised as "The Zenith City by the Sunset Sea." Tom Fitch was the "Silver-tongued Orator," and he painted a gorgeous vista of the day when the white sails of commerce would dot the placid waters of the harbor, and the products of the Orient would crowd those of the Occident at the great wharves! Few people took him seriously. The year 1887 witnessed the completion of the Arcadia Hotel, named after *Dona Arcadia,* wife of Colonel Baker, former wife of Abel Stearns. The hotel became one of the first fine suburban hotels in Southern California. Senator Jones built a long wharf and the brand new Los Angeles & Independence Railroad with its opening to the coast was expected to bring much development to the area.

By 1880 Santa Monica had shrunk to but 350 people. In 1890 the Santa Monica Land Company was pushing its sales of real estate and the area was again off and running.

Between 1928-38 gambling ships floating from the Santa Monica Bay south to Long Beach caused much consternation on the part of city officials. The Queen of the fleet was Tony Cornero's *Rex.* One of his ships was able to carry 7,000 cases of whiskey. The operation was brought down by then State Attorney General Earl Warren.

Historical Society: *Santa Monica Historical Society,* P.O. Box 3059, Santa Monica, CA 90403. 213-394-2605. Louise Gabriel, President.

Historic Landmarks: *Heritage Square,* 2612 Main St., Santa Monica, CA 90405. 213-392-8537. (Roy Jones Home). Open Thurs.–Sat. 1–4, Sun. 1–4.

Santa Monica Pier, foot of Colorado Ave., Santa Monica. Originally built in the late 1800s. Rebuilt in 1906.

Originally called "Looff Pier."

Serra Springs, 1769. (State Historic Landmark) 11800 Texas Ave., Santa Monica.

Miramar Moreton Bay Fig Tree, (circa 1879–1889). Planted by Georgina Sullivan Jones. Ocean Ave. at Wilshire Blvd., Santa Monica. Plaque placed by D.A.R.

Rapp Saloon, 1875. (Oldest building in Santa Monica). 1438 Second St., Santa Monica.

Marion Davies Estate, 1929. (The Sand and Sea Club) North Guest House, 415 Palisades Beach Rd., Santa Monica.

Julia Morgan design.

Angel's Attic, 1887. 516 Colorado Ave., Santa Monica. 213-394-8331.

(Originally at 4th and Wilshire).

The Miramar Hotel, 101 Wilshire Blvd., Santa Monica. 213-394-3731.

(Originally the private home of the Jones family, then a military school, then a Hotel).

Historic Homes: *The Roy Jones Home,* 1905. See Heritage Square.

Crenshaw House, 1925–26. 1923 La Mesa Drive, Santa Monica.

Thompson House, 1924–25. 2021 La Mesa Drive, Santa Monica.

Byers House, 1924. 2034 La Mesa Drive, Santa Monica.

Zimmer House, 1924. 2101 La Mesa Drive, Santa Monica.

Bundy House, 1925. 2153 La Mesa

Drive, Santa Monica.

Tinglof House, 1925–26. 2210 La Mesa Drive, Santa Monica.

John Byers Office, 1926. 246 26th St., Santa Monica.

Fuller House, 1920–22. 304 18th St., Santa Monica.

Laidlow House, 1924. 217 17th St., Santa Monica.

Carrillo House, 1925. 1602 Georgina Ave., Santa Monica.

MacBennel House, 1921–22. 404 Georgina Ave., Santa Monica.

Weaver House, 1910–11. 142 Adelaide Drive, Santa Monica.

Gorham-Holliday House, 1923–24. 326 Adelaide Drive, Santa Monica.

Gorham House, 1910. S.W. corner Adelaide Drive and 4th St., Santa Monica.

Private Residence, 1907. 130 Adelaide, Santa Monica.

Roy Jones second home. Robert Farquhar, architect.

Minter House, 1915. 142 Adelaide, Santa Monica.

Milbank House, 1910–11. 236 Adelaide, Santa Monica.

Byers House, 1917. 547 7th, near Alta, Santa Monica.

Witbeck House, 1917. 226 Palisades Ave., Santa Monica.

Gussie Moran Home, 1890s. Ocean Ave., Santa Monica.

About the only old home left on Ocean Ave. Gussie Moran was a famous tennis star and not the first owner of this home.

Gillis House, 1906. S.E. corner of 4th St., Santa Monica.

Worrel House, 1923–24. 710 Adelaide Drive, Santa Monica.

Vauter House, 1900. 504 Pier, Santa Monica.

Historic Churches: *First Methodist Episcopal Church,* 1875–76. 2621 Second St., Santa Monica.

Santa Monica's Roman Catholic Church, 1925. N.W. Corner of California Ave. and 7th, Santa Monica.

Historic Schools: *Roosevelt School,* 1935. 801 Montana Ave. and Lincoln Blvd., Santa Monica.

Historic Buildings: *The Miles Play House,* 1929. 1130 Lincoln Blvd., Santa Monica.

Ocean Park Library, 1917–18. 2601 Main St., Santa Monica.

Parkhurst Building, 1927. 185 Pier Ave., Santa Monica.

On the National Register.

Horatio West Court Apts., 1919–21. On National Register. 140 Hollister Ave., Santa Monica. Irving Gill design.

Santa Monica City Hall, 1938. John Parkinson, architect. 1685 Main St., Santa Monica.

The Old House Antiques, 1887. 528 Colorado Ave., Santa Monica.

Remember radio star Dennis Day? His wife ran an antique store here for years. Recently used for law offices.

Merle Norman Building, 1935–36. 2521–29 Main St., Santa Monica.

Two Bungalows, 1910. N.W. corner of Main St. and Pier Ave., Santa Monica.

Keller Block, 1890. N.W. corner Broadway & 3rd, Santa Monica.

Historic Theatre: *Elmiro Thearea* (now cinema) 1933–34. 1443 Santa Monica Mall, Santa Monica.

Museums: *Donald Douglas,* 2800 Airport Ave., Santa Monica, CA 90405. 213-390-3339.

Historic Sites: Site of the old *Marquez Rancho,* near end of 7th Ave., Santa Monica. (See Pacific Palisades).

First house, *Adobe of Ysidro Reyes,* 1839. 7th St. and Adelaide Dr., Santa Monica. Destroyed 1906.

Arcadia Hotel, 1887. Ocean Ave. between Colorado & Pico, Santa Monica.

Rindge Home, 1895. 454 Ocean Ave., Santa Monica.

Site of the *Long Wharf.* #831 C.H.M. 1893. Will Rogers State Beach. 1800 feet long.

Businesses: *H.C. Henshey's,* 1920s. 402 Santa Monica Blvd., Santa Monica. 213-394-6751.

The Chronicle Restaurant, 2640 Main St., Santa Monica. 213-392-4956. (Originally a 1890 home).

Helen's Cycles, 1936. 2501 Broadway, Santa Monica. 213-829-1836.

Courtesy Santa Monica Heritage Square Museum Society.

Swartz Glass Co., 1933. 1726 Colorado Ave., Santa Monica. 213-870-1331.
Frank's Flowers and Plants, 1939. 3232 Wilshire Blvd., Santa Monica. 213-829-6766.
Wounded Knee Indian Gallery, 2413 Wilshire Blvd., Santa Monica. 213-394-0159. (for fine Indian fare).
The Outlook, established Oct. 13, 1875. (Called the Santa Monica Evening Outlook. A weekly newspaper).

1920 Colorado Ave., Santa Monica. 213-829-6811.
Out of the Past, Vintage Clothing. 130 Broadway, Santa Monica. 213-394-5544.
Hennessey and Ingalls, Inc. Specializing in Art and Architecture Books. 1254 Santa Monica Mall, Santa Monica. 213-458-9074.
Historian-Researcher: *David Cameron,* architectural researcher, historian. P.O. Box 611, Santa Monica, CA 90406. 213-452-0914.
Craftsperson: *George Martin,* Creative Metal Craft. 1708 Berkeley, Santa Monica, CA 90404. 213-829-0079.
Other Important Facts: After 1895 South Santa Monica became known as *Ocean Park.*
Light House of 1912 is now at Pepperdine University Campus in Malibu.
Glover Field, 1924. Named after Grier Glover, a W.W. I pilot.
Topanga Canyon was first settled in 1875. Opened in 1925.
Sawtell, first called *Barrett.*
Book: Charles Warren, *The History of the Santa Monica Bay Region,* 1934.

— SANTA MONICA MOUNTAINS —

History: The area is extremely rich in Indian sites, and follows pretty closely the same Spanish-Mexican-American exploration—conquest-settlement pattern that the rest of Southern California experienced. In addition, it tends to be slightly more complex because the mountain areas were places for weekend cabins and retreats; for the film companies to shoot a variety of movies; for the building of ranches, and a host of other activities. Fortunately there has been an excellent book written on the area by Linda Greene for the National Park Service. The area has become embroiled in the same kind of preservation/conservation problems that we hear about elsewhere, but here,

I feel there is more at stake. There is much wildlife, beautiful trees and flowers and wild roots, and many Indian sites. The need to preserve it is very important.

There are state beaches; there are county parks. There are canyon preserves and there are scenic corridors. There is the Santa Monica Mountain Conservancy, the group which one hears so much about in the newspapers, battling to save some important acreage on the one hand, while struggling to secure funds to acquire it. All of these groups work under different administrative heads, though you will not notice this unless you want to utilize the parks for special occasions.

For general information call: The National Park Service Headquarters at 22900 Ventura Blvd., Woodland Hills, CA 91364. 818-888-3770.

Parks: *Point Mugu State Park,* 15 miles southeast of Oxnard on Pacific Coast Highway, Ventura. 818-706-1310.

Rancho Sierra Vista, Potrero Rd. off Wendy Drive, 818-888-3770.

Malibu Springs, National Park Service. Off Mulholland near Ventura Los Angeles County Line. 818-888-3770.

Leo Carrillo State Beach. 21 miles S.E. of Oxnard at the intersection of Pacific Coast Highway and Mulholland Highway. 804-499-2112 or 818-706-1310.

Charmlee County Park. Entrance on Encinal Road, four miles inland from Pacific Coast Highway. 213-738-2961.

Rocky Oaks, National Park Service. Corner of Mulholland and Kanan Rd., 818-888-3770.

Cheeseboro Canyon. National Park Service. Located north of 101 Ventura Freeway, off of Cheeseboro turnoff. 818-888-3770.

Paramount Ranch, National Park Service. Near Mulholland on Cornell Rd. 818-888-3770.

Malibu Creek State Park. Entrance corner of Mulholland and Cornell Roads and on Las Virgenes-Malibu Canyon Rd. 818-706-1310.

Castro Crest, National Park Service. Corral Canyon Rd. off of Pacific Coast Highway. 818-888-3770.

Diamond X Ranch, National Park Service. Mulholland Highway, east of Las Virgenes/Malibu Canyon Rd. 818-888-3770.

Tapia County Park, Located 5 miles south of 101 Freeway on Las Virgenes/Malibu Canyon Rd. 213-738-2961.

Cold Creek Canyon Preserve, Nature Conservancy. Stunt Rd. off Mulholland Highway. 818-880-5800.

Stunt Ranch, Santa Monica Mountains Conservancy. 818-706-8380.

Satwina Loop Trail and Nature Con-servancy, Indian Cultural Center. Pine Hill Rd. & Potrero.

Will Rogers State Historic Park, Amalfi Drive and Brooktree Rd. off of Sunset Blvd. Pacific Palisades. 213-454-8212.

Topanga State Park, Topanga Canyon Boulevard to Entrada Rd. 213-455-2465 or 213-454-8212.

Cross Mountain Park, Coldwater Canyon, Mulholland and Franklin Canyon Rd. 818-888-3770.

Wildacre Estate, City of Los Angeles. 818-769-2663.

Coldwater Canyon Park, 818-769-2663.

Upper Franklin Canyon Reservoir, 213-271-2222 or 213-858-3834.

Franklin Canyon Ranch, National Park Service. 818-888-3770.

Fryman Canyon, Santa Monica Mountains Conservancy, 213-620-2021.

Griffith Park, Golden State Freeway and Los Feliz Blvd. 213-665-5188.

Peter Strauss Ranch/Lake Enchanto, Ventura Freeway to Kanan Rd. to Troutdale Rd. to Mulholland Highway. Large gates. 818-991-9231.

Roberts Ranch, Contact Santa Monica Conservatory. (New acquisition).

Book: *A Historical Survey of the Santa Monica Mountains of California: Preliminary Historic Resource Study.* Santa Monica Mountains National Recreation Area. Linda Greene. Published by Historic Preservation Branch Pacific Northwest/Western Team Denver Service Center National Park Service. U.S. Dept. of the Interior, Denver, Colorado. August 1980.

Also, Santa Monica Mountains National Recreation Area, National Park Service, 22900 Ventura Blvd., Suite 140, Woodland Hills, 91364. They publish excellent booklets on the numerous activities held within all of the parks. Get on their mailing list!

SEAL BEACH (ORANGE COUNTY)

History: Originally a 28,000 acre Spanish Land grant, Rancho Los Alamitos given to Manuel Nieto, later sold to Abel Stearns. It was Major J.C. Ord however who became the father of Seal Beach. In 1901 he was the only resident in the area. He came here after the Civil War, settling in Los Alamitos in 1894. In 1901 he hired a 30 mule team to bring his small general store building from Los Alamitos to "Bay City."

Historical Society: *Seal Beach Historical Society,* P.O. Box 152. Seal Beach, CA 90740. Barbara Roundtree, president. 213-431-7435.

Historians: *Virginia Hadley,* 237 8th St., Seal Beach. 213-598-0954.

Cliff Evans, 221 8th St., Seal Beach. 213-430-4558.

Historical Landmarks: *Red Car Heritage Square,* 707 Electric St., Seal Beach (Old Town).

This car, No. 1734 placed here to commemorate the Pacific Electric Railroad built in 1904. 213-596-2579.

The Tower House, 1940. Pacific Coast Highway to its intersection with Anderson St. in the Sunset Beach portion of Seal Beach. Dr. George Armstrong.

This abandoned water storage tank was converted to a private residence and caused quite a stir. What a view!

Anaheim Landing, 1857. Electric Avenue and Seal Beach Blvd., Seal Beach.

Soon after founding of Anaheim Colony in 1857 Anaheim Landing became a port of entry for all Santa Ana Valley.

Seal Beach Municipal Pier, 1906. Main St. and Ocean Ave., Seal Beach.

Longest pier South of San Francisco, 1865 feet long. Destroyed by El Nido, 1983. Rebuilt 1985.

Historic Homes: *Judge J.C. Ord Home,* 1920s. 202 10th St., Seal Beach, Old Town.

Civil War Veteran, first mayor of Seal Beach.

Mr. Proctor, 1905. 227 10th St., Seal Beach, Old Town.

Krenwickle Home, 1920s. 160 12th St. Seal Beach.

Home originally at Anaheim Landing and moved here in 1944.

George Morrison Home, 1910. 111 13th St., Seal Beach.

Robert Lufberry Home, 1910. 141 13th St., Seal Beach.

Two Story Home, 1910. 1515 Seal Way, Seal Beach.

One of two identical homes built in 1910. One of oldest in Seal Beach.

Commander Sleeth Home, 1938. 404 Ocean Ave. Seal Beach.

This was the man who broke the Japanese code in World War II.

John Nance Home, 1910. 413 Ocean Ave., Seal Beach.

The Lothian Home, 1905. 117 Ocean Ave., Seal Beach.

The Little Blue House, 1895. Originally on ocean, moved in 1920s to 12th Street. Now has been donated to the historical society who are tyring to find a new location for it.

The Girl Scout Home, 1946. Electric and 7th St., Seal Beach.

Other Buildings: *Main Street Business District.* The old town business district is the oldest commercial area in Seal Beach. Main St., Seal Beach.

Seal Beach City Hall, 1929. 202 8th St., Seal Beach.

On the National Register of Historic Places.

Post Office, 223 Main St., Seal Beach.

Historic Churches: *The First United Methodist Church,* 1915. Central Ave. and 10th St., Seal Beach.

Historic Schools: *Mary E. Zoeter Elementary,* 1933. Pacific Coast Highway and 12th. Seal Beach.

Historic Restaurants: *The Glide'er Inn,* 1930. 1400 Pacific Coast Highway,

Seal Beach.

Contains lots of memorabilia.

The Irisher and Clancy, an historic Irish pub since the 50s. 121 Main St. 213-596-1427.

Other: *1,000 acre National Wild Life Refuge.* Pacific Coast Highway, Seal Beach Blvd. Westminster Ave. and Edinger, Seal Beach.

Under auspices of the Naval Weapons Station.

Books: Jean Deorr, *The Story of Seal Beach,* published by the city.

SHERMAN OAKS

History: This area belonged originally to the San Fernando Valley Mission. It passed to Pio Pico, and from the Pico Brothers to Eulogio De Celis and back again to the Picos.

Later the Southern portion was sold to the *Suburban Homestead Association,* to be turned into wheat and barley fields. This area was owned by the Van Nuys and Lankershim interest. The Northern portion went to Senator Charles Maclay in 1874 and several small towns were begun at that time. In the South, both Lankershim and Van Nuys sold their portion and the areas took on new names. In 1880 Lankershim took the easternmost section and divided it into the Lankershim Orchard Tract. The wheatfields vanished and North Hollywood was born. Van Nuys organized his section into the *Los Angeles Farm and Milling Company.* When wheat production declined in the 1890s, Van Nuys sold his section in 1910 to the Los Angeles Suburban Home Co. The men that purchased this 47,500 acre section then began subdividing their portions into towns. Moses H. Sherman called his own 1,000 acre ranch *Sherman Oaks.*

Historic Homes and Places: *Horace Heidt Magnolia Estates,* 1945. 14155 Magnolia Blvd. Sherman Oaks.

This 10 acre area was owned first by Laurel and Hardy, the famous comedy team of the 20s, 30s and 40s. Horace Heidt was an equally famous band leader, known mainly over radio.

La Reina Movie Theatre, 14626 Ventura Blvd., Sherman Oaks. 1938.

#290 C.H.M. Now La Reina Fashion Plaza. 818-783-3100.

After much controversy, Developers Equity saved the facade of the old theatre. 213-277-9696.

Lou Costello Home, 4121 Longridge, Sherman Oaks.

"Western Town," 14322 Ventura Blvd., Sherman Oaks.

Fossil Ridge, a 100 acre ridge which contains 10-million year-old fish fossils. Beverly Glen Blvd. and Mulholland Drive, Sherman Oaks and Santa Monica Mountains.

Kerry's Coffee Shop, 14846 Ventura Blvd., Sherman Oaks. 818-783-1889.

Example of 50s pop architecture.

Kathy's Diner. 50's Nostalgia. 4609 Van Nuys Blvd., Sherman Oaks. 818-906-1955.

Courtesy Sherman Oaks Chamber of Commerce.

The Magnolia, 1929. #293 C.H.M. 13242 Magnolia, Sherman Oaks.

Streets: *Mulholland Highway,* 1924. 55 miles of scenic beauty, beginning in Hollywood, ending at Pacific Coast Highway near Leo Carrillo State Beach.

Historic School: *Notre Dame High School Building,* 1938. N.E. corner of Woodman Ave. and Riverside Dr., Sherman Oaks.
Businesses: *Baron's Italian Cuisine,* 1945. 14151 Ventura Blvd., Sherman Oaks. 818-784-6226.
Jerry Berns & Associates, 13756 Ventura Blvd., Sherman Oaks, CA 91423. 818-788-0446.

Mr. Berns writes the column "Valley Landmarks" in many local newspapers. Excellent source of historical information on the Valley.
Other: *Tower of Wooden Pallets.* See Van Nuys.

——— SIERRA MADRE ———

History: In February 1881, Nathaniel C. Carter purchased from E.J. Baldwin some eleven hundred acres of the *Santa Anita Ranch.* This he subdivided, piping water from the hills and with much advertising he established Sierra Madre, appropriating the name already selected by a neighboring colony.
Historical Societies: *Sierra Madre Historical Society,* P.O. Box 202, Sierra Madre, CA 91024. Richard Johnson, president.
Sierra Madre Preservation Society, 430 Grandview Ave., Sierra Madre. 818-355-3928. Phyllis Chapman, president.
Cultural Heritage Commission, appointed by the mayor. City Hall. 818-355-7135.
Historian: *Phyllis Chapman,* 430 Grandview Ave., Sierra Madre. 818-355-3928.
Historic Landmarks: *Mt. Wilson Observatory,* Mt. Wilson, Sierra Madre. (See Altadena).

Named in honor of Benjamin Wilson who cut a path here seeking timber for his wine casks. In 1889 Harvard University astronomers brought a 13" telescope to the summit and until 1929 operated it on the peak. The Observatory itself dates back to 1903 with the work of astronomer George E. Hale. The 60" telescope began in 1909 and the 100" in 1917. By the time the 200" telescope was developed, it was decided that the lights of a growing city would make Mt. Wilson an unlikely place to put it. As of 1976, the park and the access road to the observatory were closed to the public. The side road to Mount Wilson and the Observatory branches from the Angeles Crest Highway at the Red Box ranger station. Just south of Red Box a dirt road leads west into the canyon of the West Fork of the San Gabriel River. About 6 miles along this road is *"Old Short Cut."* It is the oldest building in the Angeles National Forest, erected in 1900. The log structure was the original West Fork ranger station and is said to be the first U.S. Forest Service ranger station.

It was also true that both Henry Ford and Andrew Carnegie came to Mt. Wilson for the view.
Lizzie's Trail End, 1880s. Mount Wilson, Sierra Madre.

Refreshment stand established here since end of the 1880s. Next to Richardson's House. Historical society maintains both of these.
Historic Homes: *Richardson House,* 1870s. 167 E. Mira Monte, Sierra Madre. Next to Lizzie's Trail. Home maintained by Historical Society.
Jameson House, 1908. 481 W. Highland, Sierra Madre.
Originally the C.H. Baker Home.
Russell House, 1917. 171 West Orange Grove, Sierra Madre.
The Fletcher House, 1890. 89 Olive, Sierra Madre.
Carriage Home of A.L. Sumans, 1914. 300 Sturtevant Drive, Sierra Madre.
The Pinney House, 1887. 225 Lima

Street, Sierra Madre. Built by the famous Newsom Brothers.

Hallberg House, 470 West Highland. Sierra Madre.

Ocean View House, 1886. 93 West Mira Monte, Sierra Madre.

Casa de Monte Lado, 1906. 49 East Alegria, Sierra Madre.

C.J. Pegler House, 1900. 375 East Grandview, Sierra Madre.

William Deutsch House, 1887. 229 North Baldwin, Sierra Madre.

E. Waldo Ward Ranch, 1903. Barn 1901. 273 E. Highland. Sierra Madre.

J.C. Pegler House, 1893. 419 East Highland, Sierra Madre.

Tucker Home, 1906. 43 Sierra Place, Sierra Madre.

William Paul Caley, 1898. 233 Ramona, Sierra Madre.

Valley Hunt Club Home, 1887. 145 South Lima, Sierra Madre.

Note: The Sierra Madre Historical Society sponsors home tours. They publish a brochure on their outstanding gems. Contact them for further information.

Historic Churches: *Church of the Ascension,* 1888. N.E. corner of Baldwin and Laurel, Sierra Madre. On National Register of Historic Places.

Congregational Church, 1890. 170 W. Sierra Madre Blvd., Sierra Madre.

Passionist Fathers Monastery and Retreat House, 1928-31. And Mater Dolorosa Retreat, north end of Sunnyside. Sierra Madre.

St. Alverno Convent, 1925. N.E. corner Michillinda and Highland. Sierra Madre.

Designed by Wallace Neff.

Historic Hotels: *Ocean View House,* 1882. 93 West Mira Monte, Sierra Madre.

First hotel in Sierra Madre. Built for Nathaniel Carter, founder of Sierra Madre.

Renaissance Plaza Hotel, 1920s. 38 West Sierra Madre Blvd., Sierra Madre. 818-355-0242.

Historic Parks: *Park Sierra Madre.* Property purchased by John Hart in 1885. Adobe built shortly after that. A Winery was also established here, the *Montevina Winery.* Adobe still stands and has been faithfully restored.

Historic Site: *Abbot Kinney's Kinneyloa,* 1870s. A housing subdivision now, the home was quite elaborate, built by the founder of Venice. Located on a mesa on top of the hill.

Business: *King's Closet,* vintage clothing. 129 W. Sierra Madre Blvd., Sierra Madre. 818-355-5513.

——— SIGNAL HILL ———

History: Originally part of the vast 1784 Rancho Nietos, the land was eventually divided among the heirs. This area became known as the *Rancho Los Alamitos.* Owned by Abel Stearns in the 1840s, it was later sold to the Bixby family. The name Signal Hill came from the old hill which was an ancient landmark used by the Indians, Spanish and Mexicans.

Historian: *Doris Miller,* 3315 Falcon Ave., Signal Hill, CA 90807.

Doris can also be reached at the *Signal Hill Chamber of Commerce,* above address, 213-424-6489.

Historical Landmarks: *Signal Hill.* Between Hill and Willow Streets, Cherry and Redondo, Signal Hill.

Discovery Well No. 1, 1921. Hill St. and Temple Ave., Signal Hill.

The oil well "Alamitos" discovery well of the important Signal Hill fields, takes its name from the old rancho. Drilled to a depth of 3,114 feet in 1921 it was the largest single oil find in American history up to that time.

1915 Bridge, 2100 California, Signal Hill.

It was here the famous *Pearl White* made many of her "heroic" silent films.

City Hall, 1920. 2176 Cherry, Signal Hill.

Historic Homes: *McQuinnes Family Home,* 1920. 2445 Rose Ave., Signal Hill. A Greene and Greene.

Historic Schools: *Walnut Elementary School,* 1920. Walnut St. Between Hill St. and Cherry, Signal Hill.

Southern California Military Academy, 1924. (Founded Long Beach) 1900 Cherry St., Signal Hill. 213-595-7112. (Closed 1987).

Historic Depots: *Old Depot,* 1910. California St., Signal Hill. Now *Wanda Green* blow out equipment firm.

Historic Cemetery: *Sunnyside Cemetery,* Corner Orange and Willow, Signal Hill. (See Long Beach) Early Indian Cemetery, also Chinese. Established prior to 1900. William Willmore, founder of Long Beach died a pauper and was buried here by friends.

Historic Sites: *Pala Mansion,* 1920s. Hill St., Signal Hill.

Famous in the "old days." Razed.

Businesses: *Tribune Newspaper,* 1913. 2400 Gundry St., Signall Hill. Now the Star Tribune. Every copy of this paper extant.

Library: *Library,* 1770 E. Hill St., Signal Hill. Booklet *Never by Chance* is available here. A book on the 50th Anniversary of Signal Hill. Also seven large scrapbooks and articles on the area. 213-424-5383.

STUDIO CITY

History: Prior to 1920 this was a rural area. *Republic studios* was opened by *Mack Sennett* in late 1920s. At that time the area had a drug store, a small bank, a hamburger stand. By 1935 the Company had 400 employees. Stars who got their start on Republic's back lot were: Ronald Reagan, Gene Autry, Jack Benny, Tony Curtis, Bette Davis, Joan Fontaine, Rita Hayworth, Ray Milland, John Wayne and Jane Wyman.

Historic Church: *The Little Brown Church,* 1941. 4418 Coldwater Canyon, Studio City, CA 91604. 818-761-1127.

Here Nancy Davis and Ronald Reagan were married.

Historic School: *St. Savior's Chapel and Harvard School,* 1914. #32 C.H.M. 3700 Coldwater Canyon Blvd., Studio City, CA 91604. 818-980-6692. Moved to this location in 1937.

Historic Homes: *Chemosphere Home,* 1961. John Lautner Design. Studio City.

Lankershim Home, 3706 Berry, Studio City.

Historic Restaurants: *Tiny Naylor's* pop archtirecture, 50s. 12056 Ventura Blvd., Studio City.

Historic Buildings: *Laurelwood Apartments,* 1948. #228 C.H.M. 11833–11837 Laurelwood Drive, Studio City. R.M. Schindler design.

New Victorian Office Complex, 4400 Coldwater Blvd., Studio City. Ebbe Vidercksen, architect.

Courtesy Studio City Chamber of Commerce.

Businesses: *Indian Art Center of California,* 12666 Ventura Blvd., Studio City. 818-763-3430.

Roger's Shoes (50 years in L.A.), 12117 Ventura Blvd., Studio City.

The Victorian Garden, 12180 Ventura Blvd., Studio City. 818-505-9809. Vintage Clothing.

MacEnerney's Stationers, 1946. 12202 Ventura Blvd., Studio City. 213-877-4621; 818-762-6566.

Studio City Jewelers, 1938. 13192 Ventura Blvd., Studio City. 818-762-2331.

Claudia, vintage clothing. 11930 Ventura, Studio City. 818-980-3473.

Isabelle's Clothing, old-fashioned clothing. 12132 Ventura Blvd., Studio City. 818-760-2788.

Chamber: *Studio City Chamber of Commerce,* since 1944. 12174 Ventura Blvd., Studio City. 818-769-3213.

——— SUNLAND-TUJUNGA ——— SUN VALLEY, LAKEWOOD TERRACE

History: The land boom of 1887 brought many settlers into the Sunland, Tujunga, La Crescenta and La Canada areas. *Dr. Jacob Lanterman* and *Colonel A.W. Williams* purchased Rancho La Canada in 1876, subdividing the land between Pickens Canyons and Arroyo Seco. In 1882 Phillip Beque Senior homesteaded Tujunga. A Post Office was established in Sunland in 1887 and in La Crescenta in 1888. Development of Sunland began in 1900 by *F.H. Barclay* and *William E. Smythe. The Little Landers Colony* of Los Terrenitos began in 1913.

Historical Landmarks: *Friends of McGroarty Cultural Arts Center,* 1923. Rancho Chupa Rosa. 7570 McGroarty Terrace, Tujunga, CA 91042. 818-352-5285. #63 C.H.M.

The area had at one time an Association whose purpose was to gather together the papers of McGroarty. Once that was accomplished, the group disbanded.

The McGroarty home was the residence of John Steven McGroarty and his wife, prominent figures in Southern California history. He was author of eleven books and seven plays; his *Mission Play* ran for several years. He also served as a respresentative in Congress. In 1933 he was named *poet laureate* of the state. In 1953 his home and 12 acres were purchased by the City and have since been used as a Cultural Arts Center. Open.

Hansen Dam. Near 210 Foothill Freeway and Osborne St. in Lakeview Terrace.

Historical Society: *Bolton Hall,* 1913. #2 C.H.M. 10110 Commerce Ave., Tujunga.

This served as a meeting place for the Little Landers Colony, the first residents of the Tujunga area. They were a colony that intended to raise their own food and be self-supporting.

Little Landers Historical Society. President Sally Walker. 818-353-7417.

Historic Homes: *Tierra Del Sol,* 1920s. 9919 Sunland, Tujunga.

Once a private home, then Frog-Jump, now a home for autistic adults established by Eddy Cantor. 818-353-0777; 818-352-1419.

Weatherwold Castle, 1923–24. 10633 Commerce St., Tujunga.

Built by Eddy Brien who inherited enough money to send him to Switzerland and back here to build.

Blarney Castle, 1920–21. 10217 Tujunga Canyon Blvd., Tujunga.

Private Residence, 1925. 10142 Samoa Ave., Tujunga.

Elmer Reavis Home, 1924. 10620 Samoa Ave., Tujunga.

R. Lee Heath Home, 1924–25. 10420 Fairgrove, Tujunga.

Mr. Heath was L.A. Chief of Police.

Craftsman Style Home, 1915. 6944 Apperson, Tujunga.

Private Residence, 1925. 10428 Tujunga Canyon Blvd., Tujunga.

Adobe Home, Walnut and Clyborn, Tujunga.

Private Residence, 1913. 10004 Clybourn Ave., Sunland.

George Harris Home, 1920s. 7320 Foothill Blvd., Tujunga.

Harris was a prominent architect who designed many homes in the area. *The Cronks,* 9701 La Tuna Canyon Rd., Sun Valley.

Francis X. Bushman Home, 1924. 9601 Foothill Blvd., Lakeview Terrace.

Private Residence, 1915. 6915 Day St., Tujunga. This could have been an old Wells Fargo Station.

Old House, in back of Villa Rotunda, 8624 La Tuna Canyon Rd., Sun Valley.

Private Residence, 1922. 8642 Sunland Blvd., Sunland.

Private Residence, 1920s. 8436 Hillrose, Sunland.

Private Residence, 10071 Weatha Ave., Sun Valley.

August Furst Castle, 1936. 9983 Johanna Ave., Sunland.

Old Areas: Roscoe, an old colony, now Stonehurst, north of Valley. *Stonehurst Recreation Center Building,* #172 C.H.M. 9901 Dronefield, Sun Valley.

Historic Restaurants: *Villa Cinzano,* 1928. The Old Vienna Restaurant, 9955 Sunland, Sunland.

Villa Rotunda, 8618 La Tuna Canyon, Sun Valley.

Other: *Old Store,* 10103 Thelma, Sun Valley.

Folk Artist John Ehn's Monument to the Old West. 10340 Keswick St., Sun Valley. Old Trapper's Lodge. A

residential motel decorated with a flamboyant wild west tableau. See North Hollywood.

Historic Cemetery: *Hill of Peace Cemetery,* 1922. Parson's Trail, Tujunga.

Historic Church: *34th Church of Christ Scientist* (Christadelphian Society), 10210 Commerce, Tujunga.

Our Lady of the Rosary Catholic Church, 1930s. 7800 Vineland, Sun Valley.

Historic Sites: Site of *Captain Charles Farr's Ship,* 1884/1930. 10324 Samoa, Tujunga.

Built in 1884 for use between Wilmington and Catalina Islands, the tug boat warrior was condemned in 1901. Captain Farr created an unusual residence utilizing the boat. It was again condemned, however, and demolished.

George Harris, *Moon Festival, Garden of the Moon,* 1921. 7200 Foothill, Tujunga.

Largest semi-open dance hall in California. Sponsored by the American Legion. Torn down 1933. Several such dance halls were built in the area in the 20s during prohibition Twin Pines and others along Foothill Blvd.

Hi-Yn-Ka, 1920s. 9918 Redmont, Tujunga.

Built by a Mr. Phillips, these were walk-ways built up into the side of the hill. Archway and barbecue are still there. Torn down in 1971.

——— SYLMAR ———

History: *Sylmar* was once the site of the world's largest olive groves, hence its name which means "Sea of Trees." The old Stetson Ranch located below the mountains was dedicated to the City as an *Equestrian Trails Park* containing miles of horse trails for riding.

Historic Landmarks: *Mission Wells,* 1800. #50 C.H.M. Bleeker St. and Havana Ave., Sylmar.

Built around 1800 by the Indians from the San Fernando Valley Mission. This water is the oldest existing water supply source in the City of Los Angeles.

Los Angeles Aqueduct Cascades, 1907–13. Balboa Blvd. to Interstate 5 turning left onto Foothill Blvd., Sylmar.

William Mulholland, one of the

most gifted and also tragic figures in our history, engineered this remarkable aqueduct. Without water the southland would never have become the urban center of today.

Other Buildings: *Merle Norman Classic Beauty Collection* (San Sylmar), 15180 Bledsoe St., Sylmar. 818-367-1085.

Ed Cholakian World's Largest Collection of Antique Cadillacs. 12811 Foothill, Sylmar. 818-361-1147.

Historic Cemeteries: *Pioneer Cemetery–Morningside Cemetery,* 1880s.

Foothill Blvd. at Bledsoe St., Sylmar. Oldest nonsectarian cemetery in the Valley.

Craftspeople: *Gerry Stinson,* artist. 15455 Glenoaks No. 61, Sylmar, CA 81342. 818-362-3506.

Her work can be seen at all the California Missions. Also designed tile.

Library: *Sylmar Library,* 13059 Glenoaks Blvd., Sylmar. 818-367-6102. Research paper by Doris Vick 1981 on Sylmar.

Other: *Sylmar Earthquake,* 1971. Tunnel Disaster Sylmar June of 1971.

——— TARZANA ———

History: This area was part of the wheat fields of Lankershim and Van Nuys from 1876 to 1900. When these men sold out to the Los Angeles Suburban Home Company, the modern day towns of Van Nuys, Marion (Reseda) and Owensmouth (Canoga Park) began. The remaining principals set aside portions for themselves in the rest of the Valley. *Mr. Sherman* kept 1000 acres which became Sherman Oaks. *Harrison Gray Otis* liked an area further west which he later sold to a young writer whose novel, *Tarzan of the Apes,* had become a best seller.

Edgar Rice Burroughs was born in Chicago in 1875. He failed at just about everything he did. He tried half a dozen private schools before finally graduating from a military academy. He couldn't even secure a commission in the Chinese Army. He tried the U.S. Cavalry, but when he was discharged, he was still a private. Then came dozens of jobs, business ventures and marriage. By 1911 he was pawning a watch to buy food for his family. His first love? He liked to doodle and sketch and write poetry. Finally he wrote a story on the back of an old letterhead from a bankrupt business. It netted him $400. But the historical novel that energetically followed was rejected.

Broke again, he almost quit. Then a friend told him "Don't give up." He sat down and wrote "Tarzan of the Apes." It appeared in 1912 in a magazine. Rejected by practically every major book publisher in the country, it was finally printed in book form. It became a best seller in 1914.

About this same time, clear across the country in the San Fernando Valley, General Harrison Gray Otis had just purchased a 1000 acre ranch which he called the *Otis Ranch.* In 1919 Edgar Rice Burroughs purchased the ranch. It was later renamed *Tarzana.*

Landmarks: Sad, but there is almost nothing that commemorates the old ranch that Burroughs made so famous. There is a *Bungalow,* at 18354 Ventura Blvd., Tarzana. 818-344-0181. This home was built in 1927 and is the office headquarters of the Edgar Rice Burroughs Foundation.

Edgar Rice Burroughs Office, 1927. 18354 Ventura Blvd., Tarzana.

The ashes of E.R. Burroughs are buried in the old Walnut tree in the front yard.

Museum: Not really a museum, but at *Valley Federal Savings* in Tarzana there are some wonderful exhibits of pictures, and posters from the Tarzan films.

18801 Ventura Blvd., Tarzana. 818-708-3553.

Historic Sites: *Harrison Gray Otis Home,* 1919–1940.

Until 1924 this was the Otis home, then it was turned into the Caballero Country Club. It was razed in 1940.

Homes: *Burroughs Home* on part of original ranch. 1926. 5046 North Mecca Ave., Tarzana.

John Huston Estate, Vanalden, Tarzana.

Forest Hills, 1920. End of Oakdale. Remote, gated, exclusive area.

Tarzana Design Home, 1939. (Cranberry Knoll) 500 Ventura Blvd., Tarzana.

Businesses: *Jimmy K's Place,* 18752 Ventura Blvd., Tarzana CA 91356. 818-344-1223.

Best selection of fine antiques anywhere in the Valley.

Antique Ford Shoppe, specializing in Model "A"s only. 18318 Oxnard, Tarzana. 818-996-1666.

The Gibson Girl. Victorian Clothes and Bridal Ware. 18527 Ventura Blvd., Tarzana, CA 91356. 818-345-8066.

Wall Street Plaza, '86–87. Corner Yolanda and Ventura Blvd. Brand new and uniquely Victorianesque.

——— TOPANGA ———

Historical Society: *Topanga Canyon Historical Society,* P.O. Box 1214. Topanga, CA 90290. Mr. Kenneth York, President.

Historian: Louise York is currently working on a History of the area. Is also looking for old photographs for her book. P.O. Box 860, Topanga. 213-455-1111.

Drawing of 1920 post office. Artist, Charlotte Melcher Gutshall, one of the first white babies born in the canyon.

Chamber of Commerce: P.O. Box 185, Topanga, CA 90290. 213-455-2021.

Historical Landmarks: *Fernwood Market,* 1930. Fernwood Cafe and Tavern. Now the Country Natural Food Store, 415 South Topanga Canyon Blvd., Topanga.

Topanga Shopping Center, 1947. 131 S. Topanga Canyon Blvd., Topanga.

Opened originally by Fred Solomon.

Theatricium Botanicum, 1911 Will Geer Theatre, 1973. 1419 North Topanga Canyon Blvd., Topanga. 213-455-2322.

Originally this was the *Julian Ranch* of 1911. Then Will Geer, popular actor for years, made more popular from "The Waltons" T.V. series. (1973). A wonderful outdoor theatre.

Camp Wildwood, 1919. 500 S. Topanga Canyon Blvd., Topanga 213-455-1050.

Begun in 1919 by Frank Amlar and is the oldest continuously operating business in Topanga.

Historic Restaurants: *The New Discovery Inn,* 1930. (Drug Store 1930) 156 S. Topanga Canyon Blvd., Topanga. 213-455-3125.

Originally The Discovery Inn. Building was first the Drug Store.

Inn of the 7th Ray Restaurant, 1940. 128 Old Topanga Canyon Rd., Topanga. 213-455-1311.

Originally the Four Square Church. Founded in 1940.

Shemrun Restaurant, 1925 (school) 1104 North Topanga Canyon Blvd., Topanga. 213-455-2222.

Originally a 1925 school, then American Legion.

Historic Churches: *Baptist Church,* 1933. First a hardware store (1933). 506 S. Topanga Canyon Blvd., Topanga.

Opened by George Williams in 1933 and rebuilt after 1943 fire. Opened as a church 1963.

Community Church, 1940. Old Topanga Canyon Blvd., Topanga.

Historic Sites: Site of *Tank Site,* Indian Archeological find. Excavated 1940 by U.C.L.A. and U.C.B. Dig is estimated to be 8,000 years old. Santa Monica State Park, Topanga.

Site of *Mineral Springs Hotel,* 1920s. Horseshoe Bend, Topanga.

Craftspeople: *Lisa Hamilton,* general contractor. 2440 Minard Rd., Topanga, CA 90290. 213-737-4300.

Lisa is very active moving homes, and a dozen other projects connected with Preservation, Restoration.

Tom Braverman, woodworking. 213-455-1184.

——— TORRANCE ———

History: In 1911 *Jared Sidney Torrance,* a land developer from Pasadena purchased over 3,530 acres from an original land grant of the Dominguez family known as Rancho San Pedro. Mr. Torrance wanted a well planned community, similar to the towns in Western Europe. He hired *Frederick Law Olmsted* to landscape area. El Prado Park aligned to afford a view of Mt. San Antonio.

Historical Society: *Torrance Historical Society,* 1345 Post Ave., Torrance, CA 90501. 213-328-5392. Or P.O. Box 10304, Torrance, CA 90505. President, Janet Payne 213-328-7549; also Bill Henderson 213-370-0589.

There is also an *Olde Torrance Neighborhood Group,* 213-328-5392.

Historical Homes: *Private Residence,* 1922. 1329 Engracia Ave., Torrance.

Private Residence, 1940. 1329 Arlington Ave., Torrance.

Private Residence, 1914. 1313 Cota Ave., Torrance.

Private Residence, 1919. 1551 Post Ave., Torrance.

Private Residence, 1924. 1518 Post Ave., Torrance.

Private Residence, 1925. 1620 Post Ave., Torrance.

Private Residence, 1928. 1507 El Prado, Torrance.

Casa Del Amo, 1912. 1860 Torrance Blvd., Torrance.

An Irving J. Gill home.

Irving J. Gill Bungalow, 1920 Gramercy Ave., Torrance.

Private Residence, 1936. 1318 Engracia Ave., Torrance.

Private Residence, 1916. 1323 Cota Ave., Torrance.

Private Residence, 1920. 1434 Post Ave., Torrance.

Private Residence, 1922. 1444 Post Ave., Torrance.

Private Residence, 1927. 1448 Post Ave., Torrance.

Private Residence, 1918. 1511 Post Ave., Torrance.

Private Residence, 1915. 1525 Marcelina Ave., Torrance.

The Isabel Henderson Home, 1912. 1804 Gramercy Ave., Torrance.

James Post Home, 1928. 1541 Post Ave., Torrance.

Judge Post Home, 1919. 1503 Post Ave., Torrance.

The Whyte Home, 1925. 1620 Post Ave., Torrance.

Schindler Home, 1932. 408 Via Monte d'Oro, Hollywood Riviera.

Private Residence, 1931. 628 Calle Miramar, Hollywood Riviera.

Reid Mansion, 1928. 124 Via Monte d'Oro, Hollywood Riviera.

Private Residence, 1929. 624 Calle Miramar, Hollywood Riviera.

Historic Hotels, Apts.: *El Roi Tan Hotel,* 1912. 1211 El Prado, Torrance.
Murray Hotel, 1912. Irving Gill design. 1210 El Prado, Torrance.
Brighton Hotel, 1912. Irving Gill design. 1639 Cabrillo Ave., Torrance.
Mayfair Apts., 1927. 2014 Torrance Blvd., Torrance.
Historic Churches: *St. Andrews Episcopal Church,* 1927. 1432 Engracia Ave., Torrance.
Nativity Catholic Church, 1939. 1447 Engracia Ave., Torrance.
First Lutheran-Methodist Church, 1923. 1551 El Prado, Torrance.
St. Joseph's Mission, 1919. 2314 Del Amo Blvd., Torrance.
Historic Schools: *Torrance High School Campus,* 1917. 2000 Carson St., Torrance.

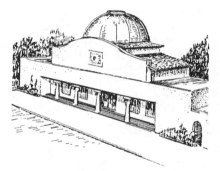

Pacific Electric Depot, Irving Gill, 1912. Courtesy Torrance Historical Society.

Historic Depots: *Southern Pacific Railroad Station,* 1912. 1300 Cabrillo Ave., Torrance. Designed by Irving Gill. 213-328-6322.
Historic Bridge: *The Bridge,* 1912. Torrance Blvd. and Santa Clara St. Irving Gill design.
Other Historic Buildings: *Post Library,* 1936. 1345 Post Ave., Torrance.
A W.P.A. building.
Tared Sidney Torrance Memorial Hospital, 1924. 1425 Engracia Ave., Torrance.

Stove and Myers Mortuary, 1924. 1221 Engracia Ave., Torrance.
United California Bank, 1918. 1403 Sartori Ave., Torrance.
Credit Bureau of Torrance, 1928. 1266 Sartori Ave., Torrance.
J.J. Newberry Co., 1930. 1315 El Prado, Torrance.
U.S. Post Office, 1935. 1433 Marcelina Ave., Torrance.
City Hall, 1936. 1511 Cravens Ave., Torrance.
Historic Sites: *Reynolds Metals Co.,* 1916. 2311 Dominguez Ave., Torrance.
U.S. Steel, 1912. 401 Van Ness Ave., Torrance.
Armco Steel, 1912. 1524 Border Ave., Torrance.
Historic Restaurants: *Vince's Italian Restaurant,* 1945. 23609 Hawthorne Blvd., Torrance, CA 90505. 213-375-1455.
Ed Debevic's Nostalgic Diner, 50s. 23705 Hawthorne Blvd., Torrance. 213-378-5454.
Tommy's Restaurant, 50s nostalgia. Second of the chain of Denny's restaurants begun by Harold Baker and designed by the firm of Arnet, Davis and Newland. "Googies" style architecture. 1882 West Torrance Blvd., Torrance. 213-320-3740.
The 94th Aero Squadron (Doolittle's Raiders) Dine in a 1918 French Farm house. 2780 Skypark Drive, Torrance. 213-539-6203.
Businesses: *Paul Freiler's Historical Models,* 19510 Hawthorne Blvd., Torrance. 213-542-6391.
Bubble Bath Car Wash, 1950s nostalgia. 1888 W. Torrance Blvd., Torrance. 213-618-1706.
Torrance Pharmacy, 1933. 1411 Marcelina, Torrance. 213-328-1655.
Other: *Alpine Village,* 833 West Torrance Blvd., Torrance. 213-323-2872.
Book: *Historic Torrance,* published by Legends Press, Redondo Beach, 1984.
Parks: *Torrance Madrona Marsh,* 8.5 acres. Friends of Madrona Marsh, Torrance.
Another controversial legal issue

involving preservation of rare marsh-land with varieties of wild life, and the developers who want to build homes. Contact City Hall.

——— UNIVERSAL CITY ———

History: *Carl Laemmle* purchased a chicken ranch in this area in 1915 converting it to a film studio. (See Studio City.) Only city in the world dedicated to movie production.

Historic Landmarks: *Universal Studios,* 1915. 100 Universal City Plaza, Universal City, CA 91608. 818-777-1000.

James B. Lankershim Plaque, 1850-1931. #181 C.H.M. North end of Nicholas Canyon Rd., Universal City.

Historic marker which marks site of the burial place of J.B. Lankershim. Lankershim and Van Nuys were the first to make a large scale attempt to grow grain in the San Fernando Valley in 1876-1890. Sold their interest to Suburban Homes.

Battle of 1845 Cahuenga Pass, marker north end of Nicholas Canyon, Universal City.

This skirmish occurred before John C. Fremont set foot in California. General Micheltorena, who was rather unpopular, met the forces of Pio Pico at the top of Cahuenga Pass. After shots rang out, the cannons were fired, the loses amounted to one horse and a mule. Contented after counting the casualties, everyone went home. Micheltorena fled black to Mexico, and the Battle of Cahuenga was over.

——— VAN NUYS ———

History: It began with the birth of the *Los Angeles Suburban Homes Company.* Thirty local businessmen, among them Otis, Chandler, Sherman, Brant and Whitley invested $25,000 each for a total of $750,000. With it they purchased the 47,000 acres of land from the *Farming and Milling Company* owned by Lankershim and Van Nuys. Beginning around 1910, several towns were laid out as planned communities. Among them was Van Nuys. Why Van Nuys? It was Paul Whitsett who is truly entitled to be called the father of the Valley. Whitsett was born in 1875 in Whitsett, Pennsylvania. At least one town in the U.S. took its name from the family. In 1910 he became associated with the syndicate that had purchased the southern half of the Valley. Three sites had already been chosen as townsites — Van Nuys Owensmouth, and Marion. It was Whitsett who really promoted the area. He enticed people to buy lots by throwing in free livestock. He would go down to the train station and pay the baggage boys to put "Try Van Nuys" stickers on the luggage of all incoming passengers. The population grew from 20,000 before the War, to hundreds of thousands by 1950.

Historical Society: None. See *San Fernando Valley Historical Society,* Andres Pico Adobe, 10940 Sepulveda Blvd., Mission Hills. 818-365-7810.

Note: Due to the celebration of Van Nuys' 75th Anniversary, the Chamber of Commerce has gathered together a list of names of "pioneers," those who were here as early as 1911 and are still around to tell the tale. Contact Marsha Mednick at the Chamber of Commerce. 818-989-0300.

Museum: *Dr. James L. Dodson,* curator Historical Museum at the Los Angeles Valley College, 5800 Fulton Ave., Van Nuys, CA 91401. 818-781-1200, extension 373.

Dr. Dodson has begun this small museum of the San Fernando Valley and gives voluntarily of his time. Some excellent exhibits and a library.

Historical Landmarks: *Picover Railway Station,* 1912. Abner's Yellow Barn, 16710 Sherman Way, Van Nuys. 818-785-4303.

The old *Pacific Electric* stopped here. And when the Saylor family purchased the old station they did not modernize it but kept it intact. Today, Phil Saylor, son of founder of the *Yellow Barn* believes very much in preservation. He will talk with anyone about the history of the old building which has been beautifully restored, and is a delight to wander through. The area too around the Barn is still slightly reminiscent of a past era.

Historic Homes: *"The Magnolia,"* 1929. 13242 Magnolia, Sherman Oaks (but often listed in Van Nuys).

Magnolia Street is worth a look. Many Motion Picture Stars chose this as a residential area.

The Baird House, 1921. #203 C.H.M. 14603 Hamlin St., Van Nuys. 818-785-4134.

Private Residence, 1930s. 6845 Louise Ave., Van Nuys.

This magnificent Colonial home was built by Warmington Bros. Once owned by Al Jolson and later Shirley Temple, it represents many of the kinds of homes built in the Valley. Originally faced South before Louise Ave. was built.

Greer House, 1940. 9200 Haskell Ave., Van Nuys. Lloyd Wright design.

Victorian Home, 14108 Erwin, Van Nuys.

Original Farm House and Ranch, 1920. The Fleming-Devlin Home, 17320 Hart Street, Van Nuys. Foreman's cottage in the back.

Research may indicate this was once a stagecoach stop. Was also heart of a breeding ranch for race horses. Entrance to the ranch in those days was Hart Street, with a gate along a dirt road which is now Louise. Street was lined with poplar trees. *Earl Carroll's Turkey Ranch* also here. Fronted on Sherman Way to Hart St.

Castle. Replica of 13th century Scottish castle. Chandler and Fulton Ave. Private residence. Owner, Robert Bond.

Other Buildings: *The Van Nuys News,* later the Van Nuys News and Green Sheet, now the Daily News, 1911. 14539 Sylvan, Van Nuys, 818-997-4111.

Van Nuys City Hall, 1932. #202 C.H.M. 14410 Sylvan. (Now Valley Municipal Building).

Carnation Research Building, 1938. 8015 Van Nuys Blvd., Van Nuys.

Van Nuys Post Office, 1926. 14540 Sylvan, Van Nuys.

L.A. City Council just voted to restore facade of the Post Office and convert it into a 360 seat theatre. Project qualified for a $600,000 grant from the state office of Historic Preservation. Plans not official yet.

Old Patio Court Building, 1927. 6410 Van Nuys Blvd., Van Nuys.

Built by Whitsett himself, this beautifully restored structure came from an idea Whitsett had seen in Milan, Italy. During the 60s and 70s building sadly in need of repair. In the 80s it was restored and scroll-work came to light.

Van Nuys Women's Club, 1912. #201 C.H.M. 14836 Sylvan St., Van Nuys.

Club founded 1912, building 1917.

Van Nuys Original Library. Now the Fire Dept. Corner Sylvan and Vesper, Van Nuys.

Schools: *Van Nuys High School,* 1911. 6535 Cedros, Van Nuys. 818-785-5427.

Historic Churches: *St. Elizabeth Catholic Church,* 1949. 6628 Cedros Ave., Van Nuys. 818-785-0105.

Van Nuys First Baptist Church, 1914. 14800 Sherman Way, Van Nuys.

Founded Dec. 17, 1914 in a "chapel" railroad car. Relocated here 1965.

Church will be moving to Chatsworth in 1989. Church on the way has purchased property.

Courtesy Phil Saylor, The Yellow Barn. Artist: Maua.

When original town-site of Van Nuys laid out (Oxnard to Vanowen and Hazeltine to Kester), two parcels of land given to two churches. They are still extant.

Van Nuys Presbyterian, 1911. 14701 Friar, Van Nuys.

Van Nuys Methodist, 1911. 6260 Tyrone Ave., Van Nuys.

First Foursquare Church of Van Nuys (Church on the Way), 1930s. 14300 Sylvan, Van Nuys. 818-786-7090.

Historic Hotel: *Van Nuys Hotel,* 1911. 6209-13 Van Nuys Blvd., Van Nuys. (Recently building undergoing renovation. Will be an office-complex.)

Airport: *Van Nuys Airport,* 1942. Between Woodley and Hayvenhurst, between Roscoe and Victory. 6950 Hayvenhurst, Van Nuys. 818-785-8838.

There's still much discussion about it, but the airport swears that scenes from *Casablanca* were filmed here. (So do Glendale Airport, and Burbank Airport).

Note: Mrs. Lois Lacey is making plans to get a historical museum started here. Contact Clay Lacey Aviation. 818-989-2900.

Historic Theaters: *Fox Theatre,* 1930s. 6417 Van Nuys Blvd., Van Nuys. 818-780-9212.

Now the Van Nuys Fox Theatre.

Historic Parks: *Sherman Oaks War Memorial Park,* Van Nuys Blvd. South of Magnolia, Van Nuys. 818-783-5121.

Other: *Tower of Wooden Pallets No. 184.* 1950s. #184 C.H.M. 15357 Magnolia Blvd., Van Nuys.

Purportedly covers the grave of a child buried in 1869.

Restaurants: Theme of *94th Aero Squadron Headquarters Restaurant* is historic, hence here listed. 16320 Raymer, Van Nuys. 818-994-7437.

Historic Depot: *Pacific Electric Depot,* 1911–12. Corner of Friar and Van Nuys Blvd., Van Nuys.

Depot moved to Tyrone St. and is now a private home.

Mrs. Dorothy Kidd's father-in-law, Mr. Ralph Kidd, was stationmaster here and she remembers the big old tree next to the station where everyone gathered to share news.

Businesses: *King's Western Wear,* 1946. 6555 Van Nuys Blvd, Van Nuys. 818-785-2586.

Abner's Yellow Barn, 16710 Sherman Way, Van Nuys. 818-785-4303.

Sam's U Drive, 1930s. Sam Greenberg, 14540 Oxnard, Van Nuys. 818-785-1507.

Van Nuys Upholstery, 1927. 14532 Vanowen St., Van Nuys. 818-344-9671.

Grant Studio, 1940. 14625 Victory, Van Nuys. 818-785-6554.

Van Nuys Awning Co., Inc., 1918. 5661 Sepulveda, Van Nuys. 818-782-8607.

Polly's, since 1950. 14424 Vanowen, Van Nuys. 818-781-5970.

Hart's Jewelers, 1915. 6362 Van Nuys Blvd., Van Nuys. 818-785-4558.

Peterson Lumber Co., 1934. 7610 Woodman, Van Nuys. 818-782-9320.

Precision Locksmith, 1941. 13641 Vanowen, Van Nuys. 818-781-2618.

Van Nuys Savings and Loans, 1912. Now Valley Federal Savings, 6842 Van Nuys Blvd., Van Nuys. 818-786-7220.

Whitsett Family Co., Feb. 1912. 5 Pembroke Place, Menlo Park.

Historical Sites: Site of the *Whitley Mansion* (Praisewater) 1913. 5849 Van Nuys Blvd., Van Nuys. Beautiful old home of one of the founders of Van Nuys razed.

Site of the *Southern Pacific Depot,* Bessmer and Van Nuys Blvd., Van Nuys.

Site of *Skytrails Restaurant.* Corner Hayvenhurst and Sherman Way.

Artist: *Margaret Fleming,* 17320. Hart St., Van Nuys, CA 91406. 818-881-0929.

VENICE

History: Abbot Kinney was one of the most remarkable men that ever came to the Southland. He had a dream and saw it come to pass. He did not live long enough to see Venice, the city by the sea, fall into disrepair and ruin.

Abbot Kinney was born in New Jersey. He studied in Europe before making his fortune as a cigarette manufacturer. Due to his health, he settled near Sierra Madre in the San Gabriel Valley in 1880. Kinney was amazing. He wrote books on sociology, child-rearing, metaphysics and lots of other things before turning his attention to the beach. He purchased coastal land near present-day Santa Monica. He drained the marshy area and created a fifteen-mile network of canals based on those of Venice, Italy.

He built an auditorium and booked Sarah Bernhardt to appear in *Camille.* What he didn't count on and apparently did not understand was that visitors preferred the beach to the educational theatre, the side-shows rather than the lecture hall. The new businesses took their cue fast enough from the public and refused to build in the Venetian style. Then a disastrous fire burned it all to the ground. Kinney's son rebuilt it, but the old gusto had waned. By 1930 most of the canals were filled in. A few survived.

Historical Society: *The Venice Historical Society,* contact either Tom Moran or Tom Sewell. The Society was just getting underway in 1986.

Historian: *Tom Moran.* Tom has written extensively on Venice. 218

Howland Canal, Venice. 213-832-5516. *Tom Sewell.* Tom also is a writer. 213-392-5721; 213-392-7441.

Courtesy Fantasy by the Sea. Tom Moran & Tom Sewell.

Historic Homes: *Private Residence,* 1904. (University of the Arts). 1304 Riviera, Venice.

Private Residence, 1907. N.W. corner Andalusia & Rialto, Venice.

Private Residence, 1907. Cabrillo near intersection with Market. Former home of silent film stars *Rudolf Valentino, Mae West and Francis X. Bushman?* Anchorage St. and Speedway, Venice.

Venice Beach House, 1911. No. 15 30th Ave., Venice, CA 90291. 213-823-1966.

The Venice Beach House is also a Bed and Breakfast Inn.

Abbot Kinney Home, 1908. Originally on Windward and Main. Moved to 6th and Santa Clara. Kinney left home to his chauffeur, Irving Talbot.

Businesses: *Golyester,* Victorian and Antique Clothing. 1356 Washington Blvd., Venice.

Merchant of Venice, Mike Sake, 1345 Washington Blvd., Venice. 213-457-1553.

The Native American Art Gallery, 215 Windward Ave., Venice. 213-392-8465.

Books: Tom Moran and Tom Sewell, *Fantasy by the Sea,* Culver City, 1979.

Jeffrey Stanton and Annette Del Zoppo, *Venice, 1904–1930.* 1978.

Unpublished Doctoral Dissertation, Lynn Cunningham, Venice California: "From City to Suburb," U.C.L.A. 1976.

Historical Landmarks: *Venice Canals,* 1905. #270 c.h.m. 72 year old canals still intact. Can be seen around Carroll, Linne, Howland, Sherman, Eastern, Grand and Ballona, Venice.

There is also a special homeowners group organized to restore the canals. *Venice Canals Resident Homeowners Association.* Tom Moran, 213-832-5516.

Arches, 1905. 1516 Pacific, Venice.

One of the earliest arched buildings built by Kinney. Originally housed the station for Huntington's little "Red Cars," then the Security Pacific Bank, now is home to a variety of shops known as the Flea Market.

Hotel St. Charles, 1905. 25 Windward, Venice.

Now the home of a youth hostel on the second and third floor, and downstairs, *St. Marks Bar and Grill.*

Windward Farmers Building, 105 Windward, Venice.

Now *Best Produce Market.*

Circle, corner of Windward and Pacific, Venice.

Soon to be the location for a new major sculptor.

Main St. Design Center, 1918. 228 Main St., Venice.

Old Factory where the Ford dealership was housed, then it became the Rose Milk Hand Lotion company. Today, it houses architects' offices. Tom Sewell responsible for renovation.

Bungalow Island, 1925. Known as the United States Island. Originally 48 bungalows here and the canals went around the island. Today about 20 bungalows left. Voltaire and Andalusia Streets, Venice.

Historic Restaurants: *72 Market Street,* Venice.

Building dates from 1920s. Was artist Bob Erwin's studio, then Ace Gallery, site of where Orson Welles' movie *Touch of Evil* was filmed. Restaurant owners include among others, Dudley Moore.

The Rose, 220 Rose, Venice. 213-399-0711.

The Fire House Restaurant, Rose and Main, Venice.

Originally the old Fire House, 1920s.

Historic Fire Station: *Police and Fire Station of Venice,* 1930. N.E. corner of Venice Blvd. and Pisani Drive, Venice.

Historic Sites: *St. Marks Hotel,* 1905. Razed 1956. Corner of Windward and Speedway, Venice.

Other Buildings: *Apartment Building,* 1905. 235 San Juan Ave., Venice.

Murals: *Mural of the St. Charles,* Windward Ave. Fine Arts Squad.

Icarius Rising, at the Fern Violet Building, Market St.

The Day it Snowed in Venice. Ocean Front and 26th St., Venice. L.A. Fine Arts Squad.

The 25¢ Wash, Brooks and Main, Venice.

Artists: Terry Schoonhoven, Leonard Koran, Victor Henderson. L.A. Fine Arts Squad.

——————— **VERNON** ———————

History: Originally part of the old *Rancho San Antonio* granted to the Lugo family in 1810. Dozens of towns emerged when the Spanish, then Mexican lands were sold and subdivided.

With the coming of the Americans and what they do best: advertise — *Vernon* and *Vernondale* were names given to subdivisions on Central Avenue near Jefferson Street. The advertising ran like this:

> Go, wing thy flight from star to star,
> From world to luminous world as far
> As the universe spreads its flaming wall,
> Take all the pleasure of all the spheres,
> And multiply each through endless years,
> One Winter at Vernon is worth them all!

Historical Society: None.

Historical Landmarks: *Battle of La Mesa,* 1846. 4500 S. Downey Rd., Vernon.

It's hard to imagine any more what the area was like in 1846 when Commodore Stockton and General Kearny brought their troops against General Flores. Growing Los Angeles has engulfed the old mesa. While called a battle, at best it was a skirmish.

Farmer John Mural, 1957. 3049 E. Vernon, Vernon.

Murals are becoming very popular in our city, but when these were executed they stood alone in their splendid outrageous depiction of pigs. Begun around 1957 by artist Les Grimes, a scenic artist who had worked for a local movie studio, these murals have become an historical landmark. They should be visited. It cost Mr. Grimes his life when he fell 50 feet to his death from a scaffold in 1968. I hope the pigs were worth it!

The Terminal Building Tower, 1920s. 4814 Loma Vista Ave., Vernon.

——————— **WHITTIER** ———————

History: *John M. Thomas,* Indiana farmer came to California in 1859, and to Los Angeles in 1868. He purchased 1,275 acres of ranch land, then in 1886 deeded it to others. The same year

midwestern Quakers made plans to establish a colony of Friends on the coast, they chose the Thomas ranch to lay out their townsite. In 1887 the corp. of *Pickering Land and Water Co.*

began. That same year residents built their homes and moved in. By 1898 the town was incorporated.

Historic Landmarks: *Pio Pico Mansion,* 1850 (state owned). 6003 S. Pioneer Blvd., Whittier, CA 90606. 213-695-1217. Open Wed.–Sun.

Following the Mexican War, Pio Pico acquired the 9,000 acres known as *Rancho Paso de Bartolo* and referred to it as his "El Ranchito" because it was so small. The first adobe built on the banks of the San Gabriel River was destroyed by the floods of 1883. The second adobe is still standing. Until a few years prior to his death in 1894, Pio Pico lived at his beloved ranch. In 1898 the City of Whittier puchased six acres of the Pico ranch. In 1903 the East Whittier Woman's Club sponsored a project to preserve the home.

Whittier Arch, Whittier Blvd.

The Bailey House Museum, 1888? 13421 E. Camilla St., Whittier. 213-696-9048. Tours: Wed. and Sun. 1–4. Note: Due to 1988 earthquake home presently closed.

Whittier College, 1891. 13406 E. Philadelphia Ave., Whittier. 213-693-0771.

The Nixon Papers are here, Mr. O'Brien, Librarian at College.

Museum: *Whittier Museum (and Historical Society),* 6755 Newlin Ave., Whittier. 213-945-3871.

Tours: Sat., Sun. 1–4. Tues.–Fri. by appointment.

Courtesy Whittier Historical Society

Historian: *Virginia Mahoney,* 213-945-3871.

Historic Homes: *Simon Murphy Home,* 1895. 7758 South College, Whittier. (Private Residence).

Dorland Home & Barn, 1888. 12348 Dorland St., Whittier. (Private Residence).

The Charles House, 1893. 6537 S. Washington, Whittier.

The Strong Ranch, 1900s. 1114 Orange Drive, Whittier. (Private Residence).

C. W. Harvey Home, 1888. 5854 Painter Ave., Whittier. (Private Residence).

Historic Depot: *Southern Pacific Railroad Station,* 1888. 11825 Bailey St., Whittier.

Other Structures: *Old Mill Winery,* 1870. 1955 S. Workman Mill Rd., Whittier.

East Whittier Women's Improvement Club. Originally the pumping station of the late 1880s. 2nd St. corner of California, Whittier.

Historic Schools: *Fred C. Nelles School for Boys,* 1888. 11850 E. Whittier Blvd., Whittier.

Historic Parks: Note: *Whittier Narrows* is located in El Monte.

Founder's Memorial Park, 1900. Citrus Ave. and Broadway, Whittier. Greek George was buried here.

Rose Hills Memorial Park, 3900 S. Workman Mill Rd., Whittier. 213-699-0921.

Historic Tree: *The Whittier Hybrid Walnut Tree,* 1907. 12300 E. Whittier Blvd., Whittier.

Planted by George Weinshank as an experiment for the University of California, Los Angeles.

Other Groups: *Founder's Day Picnic,* begun to celebrate the founding of Whittier in 1887. Begun on first Founders' Day, May 11, 1894.

Friends of the Bailey House, Nellie Counts, 6522 Washington Ave., Whittier, CA 90601. (Tours Wed. and Sun. 1–4 P.M.)

Swedish American Historical Society of California. Mrs. Carl Johanson, 8477 E. Enramada St., Whittier.

Other: *Whittier Hills,* Vic Hodgin flew from here in 1910. Whittier.

Historic Restaurants: *Cafe Rene,* restored. 6754 W. Greenleaf, Whittier.

213-693-3775. National Bank of Whittier, 1920.

Businesses: *Birean Christian Bookstore,* 1925. 8416 S. Quadway, Whittier. 213-698-9981.

The Daily News, 1900. 7037 S. Comstock Ave., Whittier. 213-698-0955.

Historic Sites: *Picoville,* 1867. (Never materialized).

Mr. H.W.R. Strong purchased 320 acres a short distance from the Pico Mansion on the old County Rd., now Whittier Blvd. It was a part of Pico Ranch. The home is still at 1114 Orange Drive. Private residence. Whittier.

Site of Whittier Hotel, 1888. Corner of Philadelphia St. & Bright Ave. (S.W.) Replaced by St. John's Building. Still standing.

Book: Benjamin Arnold, *History of Whittier,* 1933.

There is an *Historical Room* on Whittier at the Whittier Public Library, 7344 S. Washington Blvd., Whittier. 213-698-8949.

WILMINGTON

History: Wilmington is the result of one very remarkable man: *Phineas Banning.* Of all of the talented men who came to Southern California few can compare to Banning's sheer energy, will and determination to make Los Angeles a great city. When Banning first laid eyes on San Pedro in 1851 little was there. A shack, a crude landing and a stagecoach took the rare visitors 26 miles away, along a dusty road to the pueblo of Los Angeles. It was not exactly what Banning had imagined. He went to work, and before long was a driver for one of the stages. Then he became a partner and eventually owned the stage line. He purchased 2400 acres of marshy land in what people thought was the worst possible place to begin a business, but Banning had plans for a harbor. Some thought him insane. He changed the name to *Wilmington* and began dredging the sand bars. He worked hard and was able to bring in light steamers to a dock he had built. He then convinced the Federal Government to build a barracks there as the Civil War got underway, and when it was over, more men were stationed at Drum Barracks than lived in Los Angeles. He died in 1885, not long enough to see his dream of a major harbor become a reality. Today, it is one of the largest man-made harbors in the world.

Historic Landmarks: *Banning Home and Museum,* 1864. #25 C.H.M. 401 East "M" St., Wilmington, CA 90744. 213-548-7777.

Banning built this palatial home for his growing family. It had a clear view of the Wilmington Harbor. Today, it houses an excellent museum of the entire history, not only of Wilmington, but of the harbor as well. Very much worth the trip to see this extraordinary home. Open.

Courtesy Banning Home and Museum.

Drum Barracks and Officers quarters, #21 C.H.M. Museum Society for the Preservation of Drum Barracks. 1860–62. 1053 Cary Ave., Wilmington. 213-518-1955.

This is absolutely amazing, and so few people know it's even here. Over 7,000 troops were stationed here during the Civil War. It is also the only major Civil War landmark in California.

Powder Magazine, 1860s. Camp Drum. #249 C.H.M. 561 Opp St., Wilmington.

For Drum Barracks.

Historic Churches: *St. John's Episcopal Church,* 1876 to 1883. #47 C.H.M. Later moved to 422 North Avalon Blvd. In 1943 moved to present location at: 1537 Neptune Ave., Wilmington. 213-835-7870.

Calvary Presbyterian Church, #155 C.H.M. From 1869–1937 on Fries Ave. and G Street. Moved to present location in 1939. 1160 N. Marine Ave., Wilmington. 213-835-8333.

Historic Cemetery: *Wilmington Cemetery,* 605 East "O" Street, Wilmington. 213-834-4442.

Many of the Banning family members are buried here, also some of the first Indian families as well.

Historic Homes: *Lucy Banning Home,* 1900. S.W. corner of Anaheim St. and King Avenue, Wilmington.

Historic Library: *Wilmington Branch Library,* 1926. #308 C.H.M. 309 West Opp St., Wilmington. Note: A Wilmington Historical Society is planned. Loraine Roberts of the Banning Park neighborhood is spearheading group.

——— WOODLAND HILLS ———

History: George Platt purchased 1100 acres around the *old Rancho El Escorpion* and established the Platt Ranch in 1912. It was not subdivided until 1945. *The Otto Brant* ranch, about 845 acres, was also in the area. *Harry Show* had a 500 acre ranch south of Ventura Blvd. *James Irvine* and his associates owned about 886 acres of walnut trees and other agriultural products. But it was a young man named Victor Girard who was responsible for founding what became known as Woodland Hills.

He was born Victor Kleinberger. He got his first job as a young boy selling imitation Persian rugs. His sales pitch was unique. He knocked on a door and just as it opened, in flew the rug, then a leg. Immediately Victor would begin coughing. He would mumble something about a priceless genuine Persian rug, something about tuberculosis, and the naive and surprised witnesses would hand over far more than the rug was worth. Girard became known as the investor's Messiah. An early 20s slogan was "Follow Girard." He was an inspiration for the quick-buck land investor. He was bankrupt by the time he was 20. His entry in the West San Fer-

nando Valley amazed everyone, especially when he attempted to sell over 6,000 lots—some as small as 25 feet in width. He purchased 2,886 acres of land south of Ventura Blvd. He imported over 120,000 young sycamore pine and pepper trees and planted them along Canoga Ave. Twenty years later they would name the area Woodland Hills.

On February 23, 1923, the townsite of *Girard* was opened to the public. The ads boasted of over $300,000 of improvements. Victor did not bother to explain that the would-be investors would be the people who paid for them. Girard knew the only way to get to the area was over Cahuenga Pass, so he and a group of other businessmen worked to push through a scenic highway. In 1924 *Mulholland Highway* opened. Girard opened the *Girard Country Club* in 1925. He told his salesmen take anything you can get for a down payment. But in 1929 the dream died. By 1932 only 75 families were living in the little townsite. Lawsuits were filed. Victor Girard disappeared. Around 1945 the name of the area was finally changed to Woodland Hills.

Businesses: *Green's Drug Store,*

1930. Originally at 21928 Ventura Blvd. Now located at 21602 Ventura Blvd. Woodland Hills. 818-340-4333.

Rudy's Hardware, 1946. 21142 Ventura Blvd., Woodland Hills. 818-348-4844.

My Brother's Barbecue, 1948. 21150 Ventura Blvd., Woodland Hills. 818-348-2020.

Westbound, Inc. Barbara Dysart, 23105 Hatteras St., Woodland Hills. 818-887-9887; 818-346-9048.

Book: Richard Cacioppo, *The Dream City: Woodland Hills.* Available at the Pierce College Library, The Beachy Room.

Other: *Motion Picture Home,* 1946. 23450 Calabasas Rd., Woodland Hills, CA 91364. 818-347-1591.

The idea to care for its members in times of distress was begun in 1921. Known at that time as the Motion Picture Relief Fund. From the original financial assistance of 18 people and $700, today the budget is $21,000,000. This 41 acre facility was begun July 7th, 1946.

Historian: *Lowell Krauf,* Woodland Hills. 818-347-4944.

Historic Landmarks: *Pierce College,* 1943. 6201 Winnetka Ave., Woodland Hills. 818-347-0551.

Once a remote agricultural area, in 1943 the Board of Education voted to buy 400 acres for an agricultural college in the West Valley. Today there are about 427 acres which comprise Pierce College, named after Dr. Pierce. A few of the original structures remain. Today they are utilized as Faculty Offices.

Chalk Hill, long a landmark in the area. It has been bulldozed for a 663 unit luxury apartment project.

Rows of Pepper trees, along Canoga Ave. Planted by Girard in the 1920s. Name of area also known as *Walnut Acres,* then *Girard,* then Woodland Hills. Trees have been designated as an historic landmark. #93. C.H.M. Torn down 1986!

Homes: *Victor Girard Home,* 1920s. Medina St., Woodland Hills.

Griffith Ranch House, 1936. 4900 Dunman Ave., Woodland Hills. A Lloyd Wright design.

Cyclops Silo Home, Saltillo St. and Canoga Ave. Al Struckus Home designed by Bruce Goff. Woodland Hills.

Spectacular new *Victorian Home,* 20645 Wells Drive, Woodland Hills.

Country Club of Woodland Hills. 1930s. Canoga Ave. and Morror Drive near Dumetz, Woodland Hills.

Sites: *Harry Warner Home,* Desoto and Oxnard, Woodland Hills.

This 3,000 acre ranch sold to Warner Center in 1955.

Baby J. Ranch, 1949. Betty Grable and Harry James. Ventura Blvd., Woodland Hills.

Hertz Ranch Stables Training Ranch, located where Pinecrest School is today on Shoup, Woodland Hills.

Kay and Walter Beachy Ranch and Home, 1938. Also located on property where Pinecrest is today on Shoup. Woodland Hills.

Site of *Page Military Academy.*

Historic Realtors

Victorian Register, Jim Dunham, 1308 West 25th St., Los Angeles, CA 90007. 213-734-1949.

Jim was the first in that exclusive field of realtors who turned to "real" value, and began buying and selling Victorian as well as other historical properties. He found that it took far more to sell these homes than closing escrow. It took education, knowledge about tax structure, maintenance, repair, restoration, community affairs and a dozen other matters. Jim conducted seminars, published a newsletter, moved an old house himself which he restored, invited the public into his office and more. Jim now has a bookstore and sells publications which inform the public regarding the pro's and con's of buying and selling older real estate.

City Living Realty, 2299 West 20th St., Los Angeles. 213-731-3520.

Jim Dickson Realty, Astrid E. Ellersieck, 1471 E. Altadena Drive, Pasadena, CA 818-791-1000.

Formerly at 2245 N. Lake Ave., Altadena.

**The
VICTORIAN
REGISTER**

1314 West 25th Street

Los Angeles, California 90007

(213) 734-1949

for irreplaceable real estate

Courtesy Jim Dunham.

Mossler Randall Deasy & Doe Realtors, 858 Doheny Drive, Los Angeles, CA 90069. 213-275-2222.

Architecture for Sale, Mark Schaye and Toni Karnes, 2306 Hyperion Ave., Los Angeles, CA 90027. 213-662-0300.

Houses for Sale (Housing Solutions). Cathy Davis, 3605 Laury Rd., Los Angeles, CA 90027. 213-665-4145.

Alvarez, Hyland & Young, 210 N. Canon, Beverly Hills. 213-278-0300.

Jerry Berns, 13756 Ventura Blvd., Sherman Oaks. 818-788-0446.

Historic Districts, Areas

West Adams Historic Area: Two mile area starting at Harbor Freeway extending west beyond Crenshaw Blvd. Bounded on the south and north by Jefferson and Venice Blvd. Bisected by Santa Monica Freeway. During the 1900s West Adams was the place for the rich and famous. An historically significant area architecturally it is also an historically important area for breaking the "color" barrier in 1947. As wealthy upper class blacks moved into the area after World War II, white families left. Today, just the opposite is happening. White families seeking well-built modestly priced homes are moving into the area in larger numbers since 1962.

West Adams Heritage Association: Jerry Mendelsohn 213-935-6335; president 1987.

Angelino Heights Historic District: Located approximately one mile from Civic Center, off the Hollywood Freeway, Hwy. 101, east of Glendale Boulevard and Echo Park, the Historic Preservation Overlay Zone (HPOZ) encompasses an area of approximately 110 acres in Angelino Heights. Angelino Heights, subdivided in 1886 by William W. Stilson and Everett E. Hall, is considered the first suburb of Los Angeles. The boundaries of the HPOZ are confined within the Kensington Road loop and Bellevue Avenue, which runs parallel to the Hollywood Freeway to the south. The area was designated an HPOZ, the first of the City, in August of 1983. An appointed commission of five preserva-tionists administer the Angelino Heights Historic Preservation Association, primarily concerned with the preservation of 26 City Monuments and over 300 structures surveyed architecturally significant and with design review for modifications and new construction in the area. Carroll Avenue with its excellent collection of Victorian residences forms the core of the district. Inquiries regarding the HPOZ should be directed to the Angelino Heights Historic Preservation Association, 1300 Carroll Avenue, Los Angeles, CA 90026. Information regarding the Carroll Avenue Restoration Foundation and the Angeleno Heights Community Organization can be found by calling 213-250-2869.

Hancock Park: There is a park known as *Hancock Park* on Wilshire Blvd. However, while not marked on the maps, the area from Western Ave. on the east, Wilshire, south, La Brea on the west and 3rd on the north, acts as a boundary for this very elegant residential neighborhood. Fremont Place is marked along Wilshire Blvd., as well. The area has its own *Windsor Square-Hancock Park Historical Society,* publishes a newsletter, and information seems to emanate from *The Larchmont Chronicle,* a newspaper whose publisher, Jane Gilman, knows what is going on. 213-462-2241.

Larchmont: Is a street within the Hancock Park Area, between 3rd and Beverly, between Rossmore and Van Ness. It is a special street defying the modernization which has destroyed so many other neighborhoods. This is still pretty much the way it was in the 1930s.

Lafayette Square Area: Originally part of Rancho Las Cienegas subdivided in 1912 from barley fields. The Square was the last and greatest of George Crenshaw's 10 residential developments. Area home to many greats: Founder of Pepperdine University, George Pepperdine, actors W.C. Fields, Fatty Arbuckle. Boxer Joe Louis lived here as well as famous black architect Paul Williams. Bounded by Adams on the south, Crenshaw on the east, La Brea on the west and Pico on the north. There is a Lafayette Square Homeowners Association.

North University Park (Menlo Avenue National Historic District): Vermont on the west, Harbor Freeway on the east, Jefferson on the south and the Santa Monica Freeway on the north. This beautiful area of Victorian gems began in the 1890s, and by the turn-of-the-century was "the" place to reside. In fast moving Los Angeles, the tide turned by 1910, 1915. Wealthier residents moved out of the area. By 1940 North University Park was facing demolition and ruin. Today it is much sought after as a place to have a really elegant Victorian home.

North University Park Community Association, 1080 W. Adams Blvd., Los Angeles, CA 90007. 213-749-7347. Art Curtis is head of organization.

Wilton Historic District: The area along Wilton Place and Wilton Drive between 3rd Street and First Street in Hollywood was developed during the early 20th Century. About half of the 65 structures were built before the beginning of the first World War. Remaining houses were completed in decade after the war with only two exceptions, these built in the 1930s. Around 1900 it was an area used as a chicken ranch and vegetable garden by the Plummer family to supply food for restaurants in Plaza area of Los Angeles. In July 1979, the Wilton Historic District became the third in the City of Los Angeles to be so designated.

Whitley Heights National Historic District: Owned and developed by one of the founding fathers of Hollywood, Hobart J. Whitley. In 1918 Whitley determined to create a Mediterranean village in Hollywood. He began to subdivide hills he had owned since 1902. Whitley hired architect Arthur Barnes. Barnes toured Europe and the Mediterranean, studying architecture and landscaping and returned to build. Located just minutes from the early film industry, it made it desirable for filmdom's rising stars to live here. Rudolph Valentino, Francis X. Bushman, Marie Dressler and later came a youthful Bette Davis, Gloria Swanson and Tyrone Power to reside in the fashionable district.

Whitley Heights Association formed and in 1982 area placed on the National Register. Highland Ave. on the west, Franklin Ave. on the south, Cahuenga Blvd. on the east and north. Also contact Hollywood Heritage.

South Carthay Historic District: Fred Naiditch was the man responsible for establishing this HPOZ. The area is predominantly Spanish Colonial Revival near Olympic and Crescent Heights Districts.

Note: *Virginia Ernst Kazor,* architectural historian, was instrumental in forming the Wilton Historical District. She is now the curator of Hollyhock House and has restored her own home. She has spoken to large groups about the National Register of Historic Districts.

Also *Alma Carlisle* is an architectural associate with the City of Los Angeles Dept. of Works, Bureau of Engineering. She is the city's principal resource for cultural surveys which potentially lead to formation of Historic Districts and overlay zones.

Christy McAvoy works with Johnson Research Associates and has been very active doing architectural surveys for many cities in the Southland. She serves as a consultant for the National Register Designation, tax certifications and Cultural Resources Surveys.

For the other Historic Districts, see Long Beach, Pasadena, and Redondo Beach.

Historic Restaurants

C.C. Brown's 1906/1927. 7007 Hollywood Blvd., Los Angeles. 213-464-9726.

The Miramar, 1920s. 101 Wilshire Blvd., Santa Monica. 213-394-3731.

Lobster House, 1910. 4211 Admiralty Way, Marina Del Ray. 213-923-5339.

El Encanto, 1930s. 100 E. Old San Gabriel Rd., Azusa. 818-334-2311.

Pancho Villa, 239 Foothill Blvd., Azusa. 818-334-0512.

In and Out, 1947. 13502 E. Virginia Ave., Baldwin Park. 818-338-5587.

The Chronicle Restaurant, 1898 Home. 2640 Main St., Santa Monica. 213-392-4956.

Carney's, 8351 West Sunset Blvd., Los Angeles, 213-654-8300.

Panchito's Restaurant, 261 South Mission Drive, San Gabriel, 818-284-8830.

The Raymond Restaurant, 1250 South Fair Oaks Ave., Pasadena. 818-441-3136.

Gus's Barbecue, 1920. 808 Fair Oaks Ave., South Pasadena. 818-799-3251.

Cafe Rene, 1920. 6754 South Greenleaf, Whittier. 213-693-3775.

Dino's Italian Inn, 1949. 2055 E. Colorado Blvd., Pasadena. 818-449-8823.

Doolittle's Raiders. A 1918 Farmhouse. 2780 Skypark Drive, Torrance. 213-539-6203.

Vince's Italian Restaurant, 1945. 23609 Hawthorne Blvd., Torrance. 213-375-1455.

Olsen's Restaurant, 1938. 589 9th St., San Pedro. 213-832-7437.

The Original Petrillo's Italian Cuisine, 1950s. 833 E. Valley Blvd., San Gabriel, 818-280-7332.

The Derby, 1922. 233 E. Huntington Drive, Arcadia. 213-447-8173.

Mijares Mexican Food, 1920s. 145 Palmetto Drive, Pasadena. 818-794-6674.

The Grand House, 809 S. Grand Ave., San Pedro. 213-548-1240.

White Log Coffee Shop (Tony's Burger), 1932. 1061 S. Hill St., Los Angeles.

Schauber's Cafeteria, 1927. 620 S. Broadway, Los Angeles.

Cole's Buffet, 1908. Oldest restaurant in Los Angeles. 118 E. 6th St., Los Angeles. 213-622-4090.

El Cholo Restaurant, 1920s. 1121 S. Western Ave., Los Angeles. 213-734-2773.

Yamashiro, 1913–1914. 1999 N. Sycamore Ave., Los Angeles. 213-466-5125.

Pacific Dining Car, 1924. 1610 W. 6th St., Los Angeles. 213-484-6000.

Musso and Franks, 1919. 6667 Hollywood Blvd., Los Angeles. 213-467-7788.

Tick Tock, 1930s. 1716 N. Cahuenga, Los Angeles. 213-463-7576.

The Hollywood Roosevelt Hotel, 1920s. 7000 Hollywood Blvd., Los Angeles. 213-469-3802.

Bel Air Hotel, 1920s. 701 Stone Canyon Rd., Bel Air. 213-472-1211.

La Costera, 1925. 8711 Long Beach Blvd., South Gate. 213-569-1662.

The Colonial Kitchen, 1110 Huntington Dr., San Marino. 818-289-2449.

Mimi's Cafe, 500 W. Huntington Drive, Monrovia. 818-359-9191.

187

The White House, 1909. 8875 Anaheim Blvd., Anaheim, CA 92807. 714-630-2812.

Warner's Dinner House, 1910. 1001 West Lincoln Ave., Anaheim. 714-535-5505.

Leven Oaks Hotel, 1911. 120 S. Myrtle Ave., Monrovia, CA 91016. 818-358-2264.

Landmark Cafeteria, 500 W. Temple, Los Angeles. 213-617-1232.

Little Joe's, 1927. 900 North Broadway, Los Angeles. 213-489-4900.

St. Antonio Winery, 1917. 737 Lamar St., Los Angeles. 213-223-1401.

Le Blanc Cafe, 1930. 2824 North Broadway, Lincoln Heights, CA 90031. 213-222-5705.

Clifton's Cafeteria, 1935. 648 S. Broadway, Los Angeles. 213-627-1673.

Clifton's Silver Spoon, 1930s. 515 West 7th St., Los Angeles. 213-485-1726.

The Cloisters, 1895 Victorian Home. 2827 S. Hoover at 29th St., Los Angeles. 213-748-3528.

Maison Magnolia, Turn of the Century Home. 2903 S. Hoover, Los Angeles. 213-746-1314.

Bullock's Tea Room, 1926. 3050 Wilshire Blvd., Los Angeles. 213-382-6161.

La Golondrina Cafe, The Pelanconi House, 1855. West 17 Olvera St., Los Angeles. 213-628-4349.

Philippe The Original, 1918. 1001 North Alameda, Los Angeles. 213-628-3781.

Finney's, 1914. 217 W. 6th St., Los Angeles.

Chasen's, 1940s. 9039 Beverly Blvd., Los Angeles. 213-271-2168.

Perino's, 1920s. 4101 Wilshire Blvd., Los Angeles. 213-487-0000.

Tom O'Shanter, 1922. 2980 Los Feliz Blvd., Los Angeles. 213-664-0228.

Vickman's, 1930. 1228 E. 8th St., Los Angeles. 213-622-3852.

The Pantry, 1924. 877 S. Figueroa, Los Angeles. 213-972-9279.

The Ambassador, 1921. 3400 Wilshire Blvd., Los Angeles. 213-387-7011.

The Grand Tradition. A new Victorian Masterpiece. 1602 S. Mission,

Fallbrook, CA 92028. 714-728-6466.

Glen Tavern, 1911. 134 N. Mill St., Santa Paula, CA 93060. 805-525-6658.

Griswold's, 555 W. Foothill Blvd., Claremont, CA 91711. 714-247-9252.

Rutabagor's, 158 W. Main St., Tustin, CA 92680. 714-731-9807.

The Edwards Mansion, 1887. 2064 Orange Tree Lane, Redlands, CA 92373. 714-793-2031.

The San Dimas Mansion, 1887. 121 North San Dimas Ave., San Dimas, CA 91773. 714-599-9391.

The Hotel Del Coronado, 1888. 1500 Orange Ave., Coronado, CA 92118. 619-522-8011.

Glorietta Inn, 1908. 1630 Glorietta Blvd., Coronado, CA 92118. 800-432-7045.

The Twin Inn's, 1887. 2978 Carlsbad Blvd., Carlsbad, CA 92008. 714-729-3131.

San Ysidro Ranch, 1769. Montecito, CA 93108. 805-969-5046.

Pierpont Inn, 550 Sanjon Rd., Ventura, CA 93003. 805-653-6144.

The Cancun, 1930s. 1501 E. Huntington Drive, Duarte. 818-357-8313.

The Trails, 1950. 2519 E. Huntington, Duarte. 818-359-2850.

Jack's Plaza Bakeshop, 1930s. 57 Maluca Cove, Palos Verdes, CA 90274. 213-378-3016.

Saddle Peak Lodge, 1940s. 419 Cold Canyon, Calabasas, CA 91302. 818-340-6029.

Baron's, 1945. 14151 Ventura Blvd., Sherman Oaks, CA 91423. 818-784-6226.

California Fettuccini Bar, 1930. Formerly A Matter of Taste. 29008 W. Agoura Rd., Agoura, CA 91301. 818-991-3000.

Pelican's Retreat, 1924. Schoolhouse. 24454 Calabasas Rd., Calabasas, CA 91302. 818-710-1550.

The Palomino, 1940s. 6907 Lankershim Blvd., North Hollywood. 818-764-4010.

The Smoke House, 1946. 4420 Lakeside Drive, Burbank, CA 91505. 818-845-3731.

My Brothers Bar-B-Q, 1957. 21150

Ventura Blvd., Woodland Hills. 818-348-2020.

A 1928 Ice Cream Parlor, 14058 Burbank Blvd., Van Nuys, CA 91401. 818-782-1928.

Shemrun Restaurant. A 1925 school. 1105 North Topanga Canyon Blvd., Topanga. 213-455-2222.

The New Discovery Inn, 1930s. 156 South Topanga Canyon Blvd., Topanga. 213-455-3125.

Inn of the 7th Ray Restaurant, 1940s. 128 Old Topanga Canyon Rd., Topanga. 213-455-1311.

The White Horse Inn, 1957. 17710 Roscoe, Northridge. 818-343-1987.

Gaetano's, in the old Kramer's Store, 1900. 23536 Calabasas Rd., Calabasas. 818-716-6100

Sagebrush Cantina, 23527 Calabasas Rd., Calabasas. 818-888-6062.

The Old Place, 29983 Mulholland Highway, Agoura (Cornell). 818-706-9001.

The Salisbury Manor Restaurant (1899 Ibbetson Home). 1190 W. Adams, Los Angeles. 213-749-1190.

Bed and Breakfast Inns

Salisbury House, 2273 West 20th St., Los Angeles, CA 90018. 213-737-7817.

Eastlake Inn, 1442 Kellam Ave., Los Angeles, CA 90026. 213-250-1620.

Terrace Manor, 1353 Alvarado Terrace Manor, Los Angeles, CA 90006. 213-381-1478.

Seal Beach Inn and Gardens, 215 5th Street, Seal Beach, CA 90740. 213-493-2416.

Gull House, P.O. Box 1381. 344 Whittley, Avalon, CA 90704. 213-510-2547.

The Inn on Mt. Ada, Avalon, CA 90704. 213-510-2030.

The Venice Beach House, No. 15 30th Street, Venice, CA 90291. 213-823-1966.

Donny Mac Irish Inn, 119 Meridith Avenue, Pasadena, CA 91106. 213-440-0066.

Malibu Hilltop, 31131 Via Colenas, Suite 606, Westlake Village, CA 91362. 818-999-0857.

La Maida, 11159 La Maida St., North Hollywood, CA 91601. 818-769-3857.

Christmas House, 9240 Archibald Ave., Rancho Cucamonga, CA 91730. 714-980-6450.

The Knickerbocher Mansion, P.O. Box 3661, 869 S. Knickerbocher, Big Bear Lake, CA 92315. 714-866-8221.

Gold Mountain Manor, 1117 Anita, Big Bear City, CA 92315. 714-585-6997.

Bluebelle House, 263 South Highway 173. Lake Arrowhead, CA 92352. 714-336-3292.

Storybook Inn, 28717 Hwy. 18. P.O. Box 3621. Skyforest, CA 92385.

Ojai Manor Hotel, 210 East Matilija, Ojai, CA 93023. 805-646-0961.

Roseholm Inn, 51 Sulphur Mountain Rd., Ventura, CA 93001. 805-649-4014.

The Lemon Tree Inn, 299 West Santa Paula St., Santa Paula, CA 93060. 805-525-7747.

Ballard Inn, 2436 Baseline, Ballard, CA 93463. 805-688-7770.

Solvang Castle, 1210 Mission Drive, Solvang, CA 93463.

Laurelwood Bed and Breakfast, 232 North 8th Street, Santa Paula. 805-525-3087.

Union Hotel, 1880. P.O. Box 616, Los Alamos, CA 93440. 805-928-3838.

Bittersmith Hill, P.O. Box 1295, Vista, CA 92083. 619-724-4407.

Halbig's Hacienda, 432 South Citrus Ave., Escondido, CA 92027. 619-745-1296.

Bed and Breakfast at Rivendell, P.O. Box 1082, Julian, CA 92036.

Pine Hills Lodge, P.O. Box 701, Julian, CA 92036. 619-765-1100.

Sea Star, P.O. Box 434, Julian, CA 92036. 619-765-0502.

Shadow Mountain Ranch, P.O. Box 791, Julian, CA 92036. 619-765-0323.

Whispering Pines Manor, P.O. Box 1048, Julian, CA 92036. 619-765-2048.

WoodHaven, P.O. Box 497, Julian, CA 92036. 619-765-0243.

Patra Sraub, P.O. Box 1306. Carlsbad, CA 92008. 619-729-7519.

Scripps Inn, 555 Coast Blvd. South, La Jolla, CA 92037. 619-454-3391.

Rock Haus, 410 15th St., Del Mar, CA 92014. 619-481-3764.

Whale House, P.O. Box 574, Cardiff-by-the-Sea, CA 92007. 619-942-1503.

Heritage Park Bed and Breakfast, 2470 Heritage Park Row, San Diego, CA 92110. 619-295-7088.

Edgemont Inn, 1955 Edgemont St., San Diego, CA 92102. 619-238-1677.

Del Mar Inn, 720 Camino Del Mar, Del Mar, CA 92014. 619-755-4411.

Brookside Farm Bed and Breakfast Inn, 1373 Marron Valley Rd., Dulzura, CA 92017. 619-468-3043.

Balboa Park Inn, 3402 Park Blvd., San Diego, CA 92103. 619-298-0823.

Le Petite Chateau, 1491 Via Soledad, Palm Springs CA 92262. 619-325-2686.

Eiler's Inn, 741 South Coast Highway, Laguna Beach, CA 92651. 714-494-3004.

Prospect Park Inn, 1110 Prospect St., La Jolla, CA 92037. 619-454-0133.

Abigail Bed and Breakfast, 6310 Raydel Court, San Diego, CA 92120. 619-583-4738.

Bea Hive Enterprises, 4703 59th St., San Diego, CA 92155. 619-286-4571.

Britt House, 406 Maple St., San Diego, CA 92103. 619-234-2926.

The Cottage, P.O. Box 3292, San Diego, CA 92103. 619-299-1564.

Harbor Hill Guest House, 2330 Albatross St., San Diego, CA 92101. 619-233-0638.

Belmore Bed and Breakfast, P.O. Box 5124, San Diego, CA 92105. 619-584-0715.

Circa 1900. P.O. Box 203, Coronado, CA 92118.

Anaheim Country Inn, 856 S. Walnut, Anaheim, CA 92802. 714-778-0150.

Casa Laguna Inn, 2510 South Coast Highway, Laguna, CA 92653.

South Coast Bed and Breakfast, P.O. Box 388, San Juan Capistrano, CA 92693. 714-496-7050.

Cheshire Cat, 36 West Valerio St., Santa Barbara, CA 93101. 805-569-1610.

Simpson House Inn, 1874. 121 East Arrellaga St., Santa Barbara, CA 93101. 805-963-7067.

The Parsonage, 1600 Olive St., Santa Barbara, CA 93101. 805-962-9336.

The Old Yacht Club, 431 Corona Del Mar, Santa Barbara, CA 93103. 805-962-1277.

The Glenborough, 1327 Bath St., Santa Barbara, CA 93101. 805-966-0589.

The Bath Street Inn, 1720 Bath St., Santa Barbara, CA 93101. 805-962-9680.

The Red Rose Inn, 1416 Castillo St., Santa Barbara, CA 93101. 805-966-1470.

The Bayberry Inn, 111 W. Valerio, Santa Barbara, CA 93101. 805-682-3199.

Blue Quail Inn and Cottages, 1908 Bath St., Santa Barbara, CA 93101. 805-687-2300.

Tiffany Inn, 1323 De La Vina St., Santa Barbara, CA 93101. 805-963-2283.

The Arlington Inn, 1136 De La Vina, Santa Barbara, CA 93101. 805-965-6532.

The Upham, 1871. 1404 De La Vina, Santa Barbara, CA 93101. 805-962-0058.

Weddings, Receptions, Christmas

Dorothy Chandler Pavilion Music Center, 135 N. Grand, Los Angeles. 213-972-9211.

Eldorado Room and the Blue Ribbon Room.

Flower Pavilion, 18013 Ventura Blvd., Encino. 818-788-8860.

L.A. State and County Arboretum, 301 N. Baldwin Ave., Arcadia. 818-447-8207.

Queen Anne Cottage available for weddings.

Los Encinos State Park, 16756 Moorpark St., Encino. 818-784-4849.

Adamson House Malibu Lagoon, 23200 Pacific Coast Hwy., Malibu. 213-456-9497.

Casa de Adobe San Rafael, 1330 Dorothy Dr., Glendale. 818-956-2000.

Charter Concepts, Shipboard Weddings. 213-823-2676; 213-491-1999.

Muckenthaler Center, 1201 W. Malvern Ave., Fullerton. 714-738-6340.

Orcutt Ranch, 23600 Roscoe Blvd., Canoga Park. 818-785-5798.

Peter Strauss Ranch, 3000 Mulholland Hwy., Agoura. 213-620-2021; 818-760-8380.

Marilyn Jenett Locations, 213-852-1651.

Can arrange marriages and receptions in mansions around the Southland.

Padua Hills Theatre. Now owned by Pomona College, Claremont. 714-621-8000.

Avenue, Alta Loma. 714-987-7551.

Heritage Park, Santa Fe Springs.

Call Library for more information or City of Santa Fe, both at 213-868-0511.

Marie Rankin Ranch Estate. An early Irving Gill, only recently acquired by the City of Santa Fe Springs, this lovely home will now be utilized for weddings, receptions, and other special events. Call 213-868-0511 (Library).

Heritage Square, 3800 Homer Ave., Los Angeles, CA 90031. 213-449-0193.

There is an annual Christmas Fair. Check the newspapers for time. The Hale house is open for tours. Someone is usually playing the old organ, docents are dressed up Victorian Style, and a good time can be had by all. Each year the Square looks different. More homes are completely restored, furnished, and there are always new acquisitions. Music in the Main Square, food, Santa makes an appearance, lots of antiques.

Lumnis Home, 200 E. Ave. 43, Highland Park. 213-222-0546.

Just around the corner from Heritage Square is the wonderful Lumnis Home. All dressed up for Christmas.

Casa de Adobe, 4602 North Figueroa, Highland Park.

For a very Hispanic holiday, try the Adobe, also just down the street from the Lumnis Home and Heritage Square.

The Southwest Museum, 234 Museum Drive, Highland Park. 213-221-2164.

Festive decorations, refreshments, and a Christmas tree.

Olvera St., El Pueblo State Historic Park.

For the Posadas and the colorful blind-folded game played by Hispanic children all over Latin America. Call 213-687-4344.

Huntington Beach, The Newland House, 19820 Beach Blvd., Huntington Beach. 714-962-5777.

They have a candlelight reception here.

Rancho Los Cerritos, 4600 Virginia Rd., Long Beach. 213-424-9423.

Rancho Los Alamitos, 6400 Bixby Hill Rd., Long Beach. 213-431-2511.

Whittier Museum, 6755 Newlin Ave., Whittier. 213-945-3871.

Montebello Sanchez Adobe, 946 Adobe, Montebello. 213-721-3487.

Banning Home, 401 East "M" St., Wilmington. 213-548-7771.

A Victorian Christmas.

Heritage Hill Historical Park, 25151 Serrano Rd., El Toro. 714-855-2028.

Muckenthaler Cultural Center, 1201 W. Malvern, Fullerton. 714-738-6595.

The Christmas House, 9240 Archibald Ave., Rancho Cucamonga, CA. 714-980-6450.

With a name like Christmas House, well....

Irvine Historical Museum, 5 Rancho San Joaquin, Irvine.

Y.W.C.A., 16 East Olive Ave., Redlands. 714-793-2957.

Each year they sponsor an Open House Tour held the first Sunday in December. This is the best time to see the gorgeous Victorian homes here— all decorated for Christmas.

Morey Mansion, 190 Terracina Blvd., Redlands. 714-793-7970.

This is one of the real masterpieces in the Southland. Contact the YWCA for time, cost of open house tours.

Riverside Heritage House, 8193 Magnolia Avenue, Riverside. 714-787-7273.

Olivas Adobe, 4200 Olivas Park Drive, Ventura. 805-644-4346.

Ojai. They have a very, very "in" Christmas Tour held each year by the Historical Society. Few outsiders know anything about it. Well worth looking into. Contact: *Visitors Guide,* Ojai Valley News, Inc. 1016 W. Ojai Ave., P.O. Box 277, Ojai, CA 93023. 805-646-1476.

The Visitors Guide is wonderful to know what's happening in this delightful little town. *Mr. Dave Mason* is the man who heads up the Ojai Cultural Heritage Board and knows everything that goes on in the town. 805-646-6381.

The *Parade of Lights* held each year at various harbors is growing. Every harbor has one of these, from Santa Barbara down to San Diego. Check with the local Chamber of Commerce.

Harbor Cruises Balboa Pavilion, 400 Main St., Balboa. 714-673-5245.

Queen's Wharf Sport Fishing, Roberta Klugman, 555 Pico Ave., Long Beach, CA 90802. 213-432-8993.

Pioneers Skippers Association, Marina Del Rey Christmas Boat Parade. 213-821-7614.

Huntington Harbor, 714-846-5551.

Huntington Harbor Philharmonic Office, 714-846-9216; 714-846-3589.

Huntington Harbor Yacht Club, 714-846-7766.

Marina Del Rey, Fun Fleet Fisherman's Village, 13755 Fiji Way, Marina Del Rey, CA 90291. 213-822-1151.

22nd St. Landing, Berth 36, 141 West 22nd St., San Pedro, CA 90731. 213-832-8304.

Sundowner Yacht Charters, 5974 Buckingham Parkway No. 202, Culver City, CA 90230. 213-392-2327.

Charter Concepts, 13757 Fiji Way, Marina Del Rey, CA 90291. 213-823-2676.

Note: I try to list the more unusual, more private attractions. But Los Angeles has a *Visitors and Convention Bureau* which publishes a booklet on where to go, what to do. It lists hundreds of places to see and visit, as well. They are located at 505 S. Flower St.,

Los Angeles, CA 90071. 213-488-9100. Also check each city—practically all the historic "Heritage Squares" are open during the holidays.

Janet Irene Atkinson Victorian Productions. Video on Unusual Places to Get Married in Southern California. Also list of bridal shops, caterers, jewelers, flowers, etc. Write: Janet I. Atkinson, 352 Innwood Rd., Simi Valley, CA 93065. For questions on the *Directory* write me, Janet Atkinson, at the above address.

Selected Bibliography

Banham, Reyner. *The Architecture of Four Ecologies.* Pelican Books (paperback), 1973.

Bowman, Lynn. *Los Angeles: Epic of a City.* Berkeley, CA: Howell-North, 1974.

Caughey, John W. and LaRee. *Los Angeles: Biography of a City.* Berkeley, CA, 1976.

Clark, David. *Los Angeles: A City Apart.* Los Angeles: Windsor Publications, 1981.

Cleland, Robert. *The Cattle on a Thousand Hills: Southern California: 1850–1880.* San Marino: The Huntington Library, 1941.

Cultural Heritage Commission: Historic-Cultural Monuments. City of Los Angeles Cultural Affairs Dept., 1987.

Dakin, Susana Bryant. *A Scotch Paisano in Old Los Angeles: 1832–1852.* Berkeley: University of California Press, 1939.

Didion, Joan. *Slouching Toward Bethlehem.* New York: Dell Publishing, 1961.

Dumke, Glenn S. *The Boom of the Eighties in Southern California.* San Marino: The Huntington Library, 1944.

Fogelson, Robert M. *The Fragmented Metropolis: Los Angeles, 1850–1930.* Cambridge, MA, 1967.

Gebhard, David and Robert Winter. *A Guide to Architecture in Southern California.* Peregrine Smith, 1977.

Gleye, Paul. *The Architecture of Los Angeles,* in Collaboration with the Los Angeles Conservancy. Los Angeles: Rosebud Press, 1981.

Grenier, Judson A. *A Guide to Historic Places in Los Angeles County.* Prepared under the Historic team of the City of Los Angeles American Revolutionary Bicentennial Committee. Dubuque, IA, 1978.

Guinn, James M. *A History of California and an Extended History of Los Angeles and Environs.* 3 vols. Los Angeles Historic Record Co., 1915.

Hancock, Ralph. *Fabulous Boulevard.* (Wilshire Boulevard). New York, 1949.

McGroarty, John S. *California of the South: A History.* 4 vols., Chicago, 1933.

McWilliams, Carey. *Southern California Country: An Island on the Land.* 2nd ed., Salt Lake City: Peregrine Smith Books, 1983.

Nadeau, Remi. *City-Makers: The Men Who Transformed Los Angeles from a Village to a Metropolis, 1868–1876.* Garden City, NY, 1948.

Newmark, Harris. *Sixty Years in Southern California 1853–1913.* Maurice H. and Marco R. Newmark, eds. New York, 1916. 4th ed., 1970.

Pitt, Leonard. *The Decline of the Californios: A Social History of the Spanish-Speaking Californians, 1846–1890.* Berkeley: University of California Press, 1966.

Robinson, William W. *Ranchos Become Cities.* Pasadena, CA: San Pasqual Ranch, 1982.

Sherwood, Midge. *Days of Vintage, Years of Vision.* San Marino: San Marino Historical Society, 1982.

Smith, Sarah-Bixby. *Adobe Days.* Fresno: Valley Publishers, 1974. First edition, 1926.

Torrance, Bruce. *Hollywood, The First 100 Years.* Hollywood Chamber of Commerce and Fiske Enterprises, 1979.

200 Treasures of Metropolitan Los Angeles. Los Angeles: Travel Research and Publications Dept., Automobile Club of Southern California, 1980.

Vickery, Oliver. *Harbor Heritage.* Authors Book Co. publication, 1979.

Warner, Jonathan T., Benjamin Hayes and Joseph P. Widney. *An Historical Sketch of Los Angeles County, California.* Original ed. published by Louis Lewin and Co., 1886. Reprinted by O.W. Smith, 1936.

Weaver, John D. *El Pueblo Grande.* Los Angeles: Ward-Ritchie Press, 1973.

Workman, Boyle. *The City That Grew 1840–1936.* Los Angeles: Southland Publishing Co., 1936.

Wright, Doris. *Yankee in Mexican California.* Santa Barbara, 1977.

Note: *In addition to this bibliography, there is a short bibliography for each city in the* Directory *which lists materials and/or books available on local history.*

Index

D

E

F

G